DEFICITS, DEBT, AND AMERICAN POLITICS

"For most of the history of the United States, periods of growing indebtedness—a product of wars and economic crises—were followed by reductions in the debt-to-GDP ratio." But why have the last several decades failed to follow this pattern, leaving the national debt at its highest level since World War II? In this groundbreaking new book, author Marc Allen Eisner, who has devoted most of his scholarly career to studying the evolution of the US political economy, explores the significant changes in the fiscal conditions of the United States during the postwar period, embedding the discussion in a broader historical context. He demonstrates that the national debt is in part a product of reduced revenues and the growing costs of the largest entitlement programs, but it also reflects a long series of shocks, including two wars, the financial crisis and Great Recession, and the COVID-19 pandemic.

Deficits, Debt, and American Politics chronicles the history of the US debt in the postwar period, placed in the context of broader changes in the political economy and partisan politics. But it grounds this exploration in reader-friendly, chapter-length discussions of public finance, taxation, mandatory spending, and the budgetary process from a policy perspective. The volume concludes with a discussion of the challenges of comprehensive tax and program reforms in the current political climate.

Deficits, Debt, and American Politics assumes little prior knowledge on the part of the reader, making it an ideal book for courses on public policy and political economy taught at both the upper-level undergraduate and graduate level. The material on public finance, long-term trends in taxation and spending, and the budgetary process, often relegated to descriptive texts, will be invaluable in courses engaging the deficit and debt.

Marc Allen Eisner is the Henry Merritt Wriston Chair of Public Policy and Professor of Government at Wesleyan University. He is author of *Regulatory Politics in an Age of Polarization and Drift* (Routledge, 2017) and *The American Political Economy* (Routledge, 2014).

"This wonderful book is a rich intellectual exercise, full of information and insight about the fiscal and budgetary challenges the federal government has faced and often failed to meet. It is written with clarity and cogency that will appeal to students and public policy practitioners and commentators."

G. Calvin Mackenzie, *Goldfarb Family Distinguished Professor of Government Emeritus, Colby College, USA*

DEFICITS, DEBT, AND AMERICAN POLITICS

Paper Shackles

Marc Allen Eisner

Routledge
Taylor & Francis Group
NEW YORK AND LONDON

Designed cover image: Getty Images

First published 2023
by Routledge
605 Third Avenue, New York, NY 10158

and by Routledge
4 Park Square, Milton Park, Abingdon, Oxon, OX14 4RN

Routledge is an imprint of the Taylor & Francis Group, an informa business

Library of Congress Cataloging-in-Publication Data
Names: Eisner, Marc Allen, author.
Title: Deficits, debt, and American politics : paper shackles / Marc Allen Eisner.
Description: First Edition. | New York, NY : Routledge, 2023. |
Includes bibliographical references and index.
Identifiers: LCCN 2022057586 (print) | LCCN 2022057587 (ebook) |
ISBN 9781032497587 (hardback) | ISBN 9781032497549 (paperback) |
ISBN 9781003395331 (ebook)
Subjects: LCSH: Budget deficits–United States. | Debts, Public–United States. |
Fiscal policy–United States. | United States–Economic policy–21st century. |
United States–Politics and government–21st century.
Classification: LCC HJ2051 .E3657 2023 (print) |
LCC HJ2051 (ebook) | DDC 339.5/23/0973–dc23/eng/20230223
LC record available at https://lccn.loc.gov/2022057586
LC ebook record available at https://lccn.loc.gov/2022057587

ISBN: 9781032497587 (hbk)
ISBN: 9781032497549 (pbk)
ISBN: 9781003395331 (ebk)

DOI: 10.4324/9781003395331

Typeset in Bembo
by Newgen Publishing UK

For Dale F. Eisner (1934–2020)

CONTENTS

FIGURES

TABLES

PREFACE

Most of this book was written during a sabbatical that coincided with the first year of the COVID-19 pandemic. I had been interested in the debt for decades and witnessing the remarkable increase in deficits during the crisis was somewhat remarkable. During the postwar period, the debt-to-GDP ratio fell to a low of 23.2 percent in 1974, when I was in middle school. By the time I existed graduate school in 1989, the debt had increased to 39.4 percent of GDP. There was some real progress in managing the debt during the 1990s, but on the eve of the pandemic, the debt stood at 79.4 percent of GDP, and it is now projected to rise to historic levels in the next several years, a legacy that will be left to my adult children Jonathan and Benjamin, and my grandchildren, Parker and Molly. As I explored the history of the debt, I quickly concluded that the history of the past several decades is somewhat anomalous. For most of the nation's history, periods of growing indebtedness—a product of wars and economic crises—were followed by reductions in the debt-to-GDP ratio. Why were the last several decades a departure from this pattern? I hope that this volume helps answer this question.

During the pandemic, my wife Patricia was subjected to daily discussions—mostly uninvited—on subjects ranging from the growth of entitlement spending to the suspension of the debt ceiling. As always, I benefited from her wise counsel. Once the pandemic ended, I was pleased to share my discoveries with my students at Wesleyan University and several of my colleagues. I was given the rare opportunity to field test the larger argument of the book in a seminar dedicated to the subject. Given that I have devoted most of my scholarly career to studying the evolution of the US political economy, I embedded the discussion in a broader history of the changing environment of the postwar period, an approach I have adopted in this book.

I have dedicated this book to my father, Dale F. Eisner, who passed away in the spring of 2020, as the pandemic was manifesting itself in the United States. In one of our last discussions, I asked him to name his favorite president. As a traditional Republican and Korean War veteran, I had expected that he would name Dwight D. Eisenhower. Surprisingly, he responded that Bill Clinton was the best president in his lifetime. When I asked him why, he said: "He kept us out of wars, and he balanced the budget. Peace and fiscal responsibility."

Peace and fiscal responsibility.

Marc Allen Eisner

ABBREVIATIONS

ACRS	Accelerated Cost Recovery System
AFDC	Aid to Families with Dependent Children
AIME	Average indexed monthly earnings
AMT	Alternative minimum tax
AWI	Average wage index
BCA	Budget Control Act
BEA	Budget Enforcement Act
BTU	British Thermal Unit
CARES	Coronavirus Aid, Relief, and Economic Security Act
CBA	Congressional Budget Act
CBO	Congressional Budget Office
CEA	Council of Economic Advisors
CHIP	Children's Health Insurance Program
CMS	Centers for Medicare and Medicaid Services
COVID	Coronavirus disease
CPI	Consumer Price Index
CR	Continuing resolution
CUTGO	Cut-As-You-Go
DEFRA	Deficit Reduction Act
DI	Disability Insurance
EGTRRA	Economic Growth and Tax Relief Reconciliation Act
EITC	Earned Income Tax Credit
ERISA	Employee Retirement Income Security Act
ERTA	Economic Recovery Tax Act
FICA	Federal Insurance Contribution Act
FY	Fiscal Year

GAO	Government Accountability Office
GDP	Gross Domestic Product
GOP	Grand Old Party (Republican Party)
GRH	Gramm–Rudman–Hollings Balanced Budget and Emergency Deficit Control Act
GSE	Government-sponsored enterprise
HHS	Department of Health and Human Services
HI	Hospital Insurance
IRA	Individual Retirement Account
IRC	Internal Revenue Code
IRS	Internal Revenue Service
JGTRRA	Jobs and Growth Tax Relief Reconciliation Act
NPRM	Notice of proposed rulemaking
OASDI	Old Age, Survivors, and Disability Insurance
OBRA	Omnibus Budget Reconciliation Act
OECD	Organization for Economic Cooperation and Development
OMB	Office of Management and Budget
PAYGO	Pay-as-you-go
PIA	Primary insurance amount
SECA	Self-Employment Contribution Act
SMI	Supplementary Medical Insurance
TANF	Temporary Assistance for Needy Families
TEFRA	Tax Equity and Fiscal Responsibility Act
TRA	Tax Reform Act
VAT	Value-added tax

1

INTRODUCTION

As Far as the Eyes Can See

By any measure, the year 2000 is recent history, even if it feels as if it were part of another era. After the tumult of the 1970s and the early 1980s, inflation had finally been defeated. Alan Greenspan, who was appointed chairman of the Federal Reserve in 1987, had skillfully deployed monetary policy to support a period of remarkable economic stability in what would be described as the "Great Moderation." Productivity had been rising for a decade and the stock market was reaching record highs. Given the length of the expansionary period, many questioned whether the business cycle had been defeated. On the international stage, there were few signs of trouble. The collapse of the Soviet Union in 1991 and the end of the Cold War had allowed the United States to reduce defense discretionary spending from 5.2 to 2.9 percent of gross domestic product (GDP)—a postwar low—in less than a decade.[1] In response to the growth of the debt during the 1980s, Congress and presidents George H.W. Bush and Bill Clinton had imposed caps on discretionary spending—the outlays that are determined through the annual congressional appropriations process. They enacted a pay-as-you-go (PAYGO) process that required that changes in taxation and new mandatory spending—those programs that provide outlays automatically as a result of the underlying statutes—be deficit neutral. Simultaneously, increases in marginal income tax rates in 1990 and 1993, when combined with steady growth, had boosted federal revenues to 20 percent of GDP, a postwar record.[2] By 2000, the federal government was running a budget surplus for the fourth year in a row and the Congressional Budget Office (CBO) projected that surpluses would continue well into the future.

The movement to surpluses marked a sharp change from what had occurred in recent years. Following the economic chaos of the 1970s—a decade beset by high inflation, recessions, and low levels of productivity growth—Ronald

DOI: 10.4324/9781003395331-1

Reagan won the 1980 presidential election on the promise of significant tax cuts and a series of market-based reforms. As a result of successive tax cuts, top marginal income tax rates were slashed and revenues fell from 19.1 percent of GDP (1981) to 17.5 percent (1990) within a decade.[3] As a result of tax cuts, a deep recession, record peacetime defense spending, and the growth of entitlements, the national debt surged. Office of Management and Budget Director David Stockman warned President Reagan that the combination of tax cuts and spending would generate $200 billion deficits "as far as the eyes could see."[4] Between 1981 and 1990, the federal debt held by the public[5] grew from 25.2 to 40.9 percent of GDP, and would reach 47.9 percent of GDP by 1993.[6] Benjamin M. Friedman's contemporaneous critique, *Day of Reckoning*, captured the sense of dread that accompanied the growth in the debt. "No change of policy, economic or other, can now neatly restore the damage already done by this radical fiscal policy," Friedman declared. "Nations, like individuals, often have wished that they could return to whatever positions they occupied earlier, as if their mistakes had never been made. But history only runs in only one direction. The assets we have dissipated are gone. The debts we have incurred are real. The capital formation and productivity gains we have foregone are simply lost."[7]

President Clinton, inaugurated in 1993, faced this difficult fiscal environment. But by 2000, he hailed the new surpluses as "the long-term consequences of a long-term responsible budget policy."[8] Perhaps. But, as noted earlier, much could be attributed to fortuitous circumstances. In the 2000 presidential campaign, both major party candidates proposed tax cuts and new spending on the assumption that the factors that generated the surplus would continue over the next decade. As Louis Uchitelle warned in the *New York Times*, "in all the political debate about how to spend the rapidly emerging budget surplus, almost nothing is said about where it came from. It is a patchwork creation, hard to keep sewn together."[9] Clinton understood the political appeal of these proposals. Republicans yearned for a return to Reagan era tax rates. Democrats chided against the limited growth of domestic discretionary programs in the past decade. But he urged the nation to devote the surpluses to eliminating the debt: "if we continue, then we can honestly say for the first time since Andrew Jackson was president in 1835, the children of America will face the future unburdened by the mistakes of the past."[10]

Others viewed the projections of surpluses to be questionable given the budgetary implications of the aging of the population. As Allen Schick observed on the eve of the 2000 election, "the longer-term forecast is clear. Under current policy, the budget will incur large and growing deficits when the surge in the over-65 population forces the Social Security fund to draw down the trillions of dollars of accumulated surpluses." The "prospect of resurgent deficits," Schick warned, should lead Congress and the new president to pursue two priorities:

> do not spend the surplus before it is earned and do not repeat the policy mistakes of the early 1980s. Prudence in fiscal management cannot ensure that surpluses will persist, but it can guard against a return of runaway deficits.[11]

The best one might hope for in the 2000 elections, one might conclude, would be a divided government that could restrain Republicans from securing large tax cuts and temper the Democrats' desire to enact new social spending. In the end, the election would bring a Republican victory, with the election of George W. Bush and a narrow GOP majority in the House and Senate.

In his memoir, *The Age of Turbulence*, Alan Greenspan recounts the unusual dilemma that faced the federal government in the first year of the new millennium. As Greenspan recalls, suddenly the Federal Reserve's Federal Open Market Committee had to face a novel problem: the disappearance of the national debt. In an homage to Stockman, he noted: "Nearly a decade of rising productivity growth and budget discipline had put the U.S. government in a position to generate surpluses 'as far as the eyes could see.'"[12] The CBO's projections were nothing short of stunning.

> From 1969 through 1997, the Treasury sold ever-increasing amounts of debt to finance continuing deficits. As a result, debt held by the public climbed each year, peaking at $3.8 trillion in 1997. That trend has now reversed. At the end of fiscal year 2000, debt held by the public had dropped by $363 billion, to $3.4 trillion. The decline as a percentage of GDP has been even more dramatic. After reaching a plateau of about 50 percent of GDP from 1993 to 1995, that share fell to 35 percent in 2000 … if current policies remain in effect, debt will continue to fall.[13]

In 2000, the federal government ran a surplus of $236 billion, with a projected surplus of $281 billion for 2001. For the next ten-year period (2002–2011), the CBO projected surpluses of $5.61 trillion. Of this sum, off-budget surpluses—those accumulated in government trust funds to support programs like Social Security and Medicare—would account for almost $2.5 trillion. The remaining $3.1 trillion constituted the on-budget surplus. As the CBO noted: "Such surpluses would be sufficient by 2006 to pay off all debt held by the public that will be available for redemption."[14]

Chairman Greenspan considered various responses to these forecasts. He believed that eliminating the national debt was imperative. But what about the long term? As Greenspan explained:

> I came to a stark realization: chronic surpluses could be almost as destabilizing as chronic deficits. Paying off the debt was not enough. I decided

to propose a way for Uncle Sam to pay off his debts while leaving little or no additional surplus to invest once the debt reached zero.

Greenspan believed that surpluses would invite new spending, and "once spending is notched up, it is difficult to rein in."[15] He concluded that the best option would be to eliminate the debt, devote $1 trillion to cover obligations to Social Security beneficiaries as part of a larger Bush administration reform proposal to supplement the current system with one of private accounts, and then use a tax cut to bring revenues and expenditures into balance. But he urged caution, warning Congress that the "euphoria surrounding the surpluses" could lead to a dissipation of fiscal restraint. "We need to resist those policies that could readily resurrect the deficits of the past and the fiscal imbalances that followed in their wake."[16]

Greenspan's words of caution were ignored. The new Bush administration and Congress moved quickly to pass successive tax cuts. Congress allowed the discretionary spending caps and PAYGO requirements—components of what Clinton had described as "a long-term responsible budget policy"—to expire at the end of FY2002. Rather than reforming entitlements—for decades identified as a necessity by the Republican Party and conservative think tanks—Bush and Congress expanded them with a new prescription drug benefit under Medicare. And the projections of long-term surpluses could not take into account the terrorist attack of September 11, 2001, or the subsequent wars. In 2000, with a federal surplus of $236 billion (2.3 percent GDP), the CBO had projected a surplus of $505 billion by FY2006. As a result of the changes in policy and circumstances, the reality was a deficit of $248 billion (or 1.8 percent GDP) by that year. More importantly, the projections could not foresee the financial crisis and Great Recession, which drove the deficit from $161 billion (1.1 percent GDP) in 2007 to $1.4 trillion in 2009 (9.8 percent GDP).[17] Things improved slowly in the years after the recession, but with the extension of the Bush tax cuts and the passage of new tax cuts in 2017, trillion-dollar deficits were projected. And deficit projections were more than exceeded by the costs of responding to the COVID-19 pandemic. There was little reason to anticipate a return to halcyon days of 2000, when policymakers actively debated how to manage long-term surpluses.

In 2001, the CBO projected that the national debt could be largely erased in the foreseeable future, falling from 34.7 percent of GDP to 4.8 percent of GDP by FY2011 (some bonds have longer maturity and were thus unavailable for redemption by the end of the forecast period without paying a premium for early redemption).[18] In reality, spending grew from 17.7 percent of GDP (FY2001) to a peak of 24.3 percent of GDP (FY2009), before declining to levels above 20 percent of GDP.[19] Revenues declined, both as a result of tax cuts and the deepest recession since the Great Depression. As deficits mounted, the debt increased dramatically. By 2011, the debt had reached 65.5 percent of GDP and would only continue to grow. By 2019, as a result of increases in spending and additional tax cuts, the deficit had reached 4.7 percent of GDP and the debt had expanded to 79.4 percent of GDP, all under conditions of full employment.[20] All of this raised alarm. In its *Budget and Economic Outlook*, issued in January 2020, the CBO projected that under current laws, the publicly held debt would reach 98.3 percent of GDP by 2030, "the greatest since 1946 and more than twice the average over the past 50-years."[21] The Government Accountability Office concluded that to maintain the current level of publicly held debt relative to GDP over the 75-year projection period would require an immediate and permanent reduction of 13 percent in program spending, an immediate and permanent increase of revenue of 15 percent, or some combination of the two. To the extent that these measures were delayed, more drastic changes would have to be made in the future.[22] The next year, the global COVID-19 pandemic would force Congress to devote trillions of dollars to recovery and push the debt to 100.1 percent of GDP, with projections that the nation would quickly face the highest level of indebtedness in its history.[23] In two short decades, surpluses "as far as the eyes can see" would turn to unprecedented levels of national debt.

The Known and the Unknown

We have two sets of long-term projections separated in time by just over two decades. They could not be more divergent: a future of surpluses that could create the basis for the elimination of the national debt and a future of deficits that may render the debt unmanageable. If the first forecast proved so faulty, why would one place any faith in the second, or in any projections at all? The CBO is directed by law to make its forecasts using a baseline that assumes continuity. "In most cases," the CBO explains, "the laws governing revenues and direct spending [e.g., mandatory entitlement spending] are permanent, and the projections incorporate the effects of anticipated changes in the economy, demographics, and other relevant factors to which those laws are linked." For discretionary spending, it assumes that statutes governing appropriations will remain stable, extrapolating future spending from current levels on the basis of projected inflation.[24] In additional to the extended baseline forecasts, the CBO may consider alternative scenarios that make a set of reasonable assumptions regarding changes in public policy. The forecasts are valid to the extent that there is long-term stability in the laws and accuracy in the underlying assumptions regarding growth and demographics.

But the world is a messy place, and continuity in policy may be undermined by unforeseen events. As noted earlier, when the CBO made its projections in 2000, it could not anticipate the policy changes and exogenous shocks that would occur in the next two decades. There are knowns and unknowns, and many of the events of the period in question fell into the latter category and thus beyond the reach of baseline projections. But even if the CBO was wrong about future surpluses, it was correct about the growth of long-term entitlement liabilities and the constraints they would impose on discretionary spending. In 2001, the CBO warned that mandatory programs—primarily Social Security old-age pensions, Medicare, and Medicaid—would continue to claim a growing proportion of federal spending:

> As a share of total outlays, mandatory spending jumped from 32 percent in 1962 to 58 percent in 2000. If current policies remain unchanged, CBO estimates that mandatory spending will continue to grow faster than other spending, reaching…nearly twice the size of discretionary outlays, by 2005.[25]

The two largest non-means tested programs, Social Security and Medicare, were of particular importance. Combined, they accounted for more than a third of government spending. "CBO projects that the two programs combined will grow by more than $540 billion from 2001 to 2011—even before the surge in beneficiaries that is expected to begin shortly thereafter as increasing numbers of baby boomers retire."[26] In 2022, the CBO's *Long-Term Budget Outlook* projected that in three decades, mandatory spending would claim 56.3 percent of federal outlays, driven by Social Security (21.2 percent) and Medicare (19.5 percent). When mandatory spending was combined with net interest (23.8 percent of outlays), discretionary spending would dwindle to 19.9 percent of spending.[27] Of course, projections are contingent on the long-term fiscal effects of the COVID-19 pandemic, which remain unclear.

One can draw some good news from the opening vignette: policy matters. In the 1990s, Presidents and Congress arrived at a combination of policy and procedures that, when combined with a strong economy, allowed for a significant fiscal rebalancing. Tax rates were increased in 1990 and again in 1993, with top marginal rates increasing from 28 to 39.6 percent over the span of a few years. New constraints were placed on the budgetary process to control discretionary and mandatory spending. The results were evident by 2000, when policymakers were forced to contemplate the implications of projected surplus. Subsequent decisions by Congress and successive presidents made may have been politically attractive after a period of budgetary restraint, but they reversed the progress of the previous decade and placed the nation on an unsustainable fiscal path. Other decisions were possible. Undoubtedly, the future will offer opportunities to make needed reforms.

This good news, however, comes with significant caveats. The growth of mandatory spending is largely driven by demographics. For decades, analysts cautioned of the ramifications that the aging of the population would have for federal spending. As the nation ages and fertility rates drop, the implications for long-term fiscal sustainability are profound. Over the past several decades, the percentage of retirees in the population has increased steadily. Spending on the largest entitlement programs expanded accordingly. For decades, the payroll taxes were sufficient to assure that the trust funds that supported Social Security and Medicare Hospital Insurance would provide a cushion against this demographic wave. But the trust funds are being depleted and rapidly approaching insolvency. This will place ever greater pressures on federal outlays as the bonds that constitute the trust funds are redeemed from general revenues. Moreover, as the population ages, the demands placed on the revenues generated by a shrinking proportion of the population that is working age necessarily grow.[28] Thus, while policymakers will have some opportunities to change the trajectory of the debt, the opportunity set is constrained by the fiscal demands of an aging population.

Reforming entitlements is difficult under any circumstances, particularly when speaking of universal programs that provide support for a politically mobilized group like the elderly. But the difficulties are exacerbated by the fact that these programs serve an increasingly important role given the larger changes in the economy. The story of deficits and debts in the post-1970s era is embedded in a larger set of changes in the political economy, including the stagnation of incomes, a long-term decline in unionization, falling savings rates, and escalating household debt. During the decades since the passage of the Social Security Act of 1935, public and employment-based retirement benefits evolved in tandem. Many seniors could anticipate greater income security because Social Security would be supplemented by employment-based defined-benefit pensions that guaranteed support based on salary and years of service. Yet, in the post-1970s era, these pensions have been largely displaced by defined-contribution benefit pensions, which based retirement income on the contribution history and investment decisions of employees. Employment-based healthcare simultaneously became far less generous, forcing participants to bear an increasing share of costs. These changes both increased the insecurity of American households and increased their reliance on major social programs. Reform is greatly complicated by the unraveling of the employment-based safety net.[29]

The reform of major entitlement programs, the need for new revenues, and the difficult tradeoffs in discretionary spending are also frustrated by the dysfunction of Congress as an institution. Growing polarization—the widening ideological space between the two political parties—and narrow majorities in each chamber of Congress have significant consequences. Moderates of both parties that used to be central to forging bipartisan solutions have all but disappeared. When in the majority, parties seek to use parliamentary procedures to limit the voice of the minority, while the minority seeks to block the legislative process altogether. Gridlock ensues. Regular order has been replaced with a more combative form of politics and ongoing efforts on the part of the majority to turn to nontraditional or unorthodox forms of lawmaking to push through their legislative agendas.[30] While the effects of polarization and congressional dysfunction have found manifest expressions, in the fiscal arena, it has led to the repeated failure to execute even the basic functions that are central to the budgetary process. Budget resolutions fail to pass. Appropriations bills languish, forcing the federal government to rely on temporary funding through continuing resolutions while preparing for the possibility of funding lapses and shutdowns. At the extreme, brinksmanship over the debt ceiling raises the specter of defaulting on the existing debt thereby endangering the nation's credit.

Overview

This book explores the significant changes in the fiscal conditions of the United States during the postwar period. The anomalous features of the contemporary period are best seen when placed in historical context. This volume employs the terms "leveraging" and "deleveraging" as a shorthand way of describing the larger dynamic of public finance. Just as businesses may rely on the use of borrowed capital to finance their activities (leveraging), the federal government may place a greater reliance on debt relative to taxation to finance its activities. In both cases, leveraging involves the assumption of debt and the need to make interest payments. The federal government, like businesses, may also engage in deleveraging, reducing its levels of debt. For much of US history, growth in the debt was episodic, the product of economic or military crisis. Periods of growing indebtedness were followed by periods of deleveraging, reducing the debt as a share of GDP, as shown in Figure 1.1. In part, this was a product of policy (e.g., a combination of austerity and the imposition or retention of higher taxes) and economic growth. This pattern was evident in the 19th and early 20th centuries. Following the passage of the Funding Act of 1790, which authorized the federal government to assume the debt of the colonies and the bonded debt of the states, the national debt stood at 29.6 percent of GDP. By the eve of the War of 1812, it had fallen to 5.7 percent of GDP. The War of 1812 drove the debt up to 10.2 percent of GDP, in part reflecting the impact of the war on tariff revenues. But by 1834, the debt had been eliminated in its entirety. By 1860, the debt stood at 1.9 percent of GDP. But by the end of the Civil War, it had reached record levels of 31 percent of GDP. The federal government ran budget surpluses every year from 1866 to 1893, reducing the debt to 6.6 percent of GDP. Between 1900 and 1916, the nominal debt remained relatively stable. As a result of economic growth and inflation, however, the debt declined, from 6.6 percent of GDP to 2.7 percent of GDP, even though the federal government ran deficits in 1904–1905, 1908–1910, and 1913–1915, each time in the wake of recessions.

While the federal government imposed an income tax during the Civil War, it was allowed to expire in 1872. The Wilson–Gorman Revenue Act of 1894

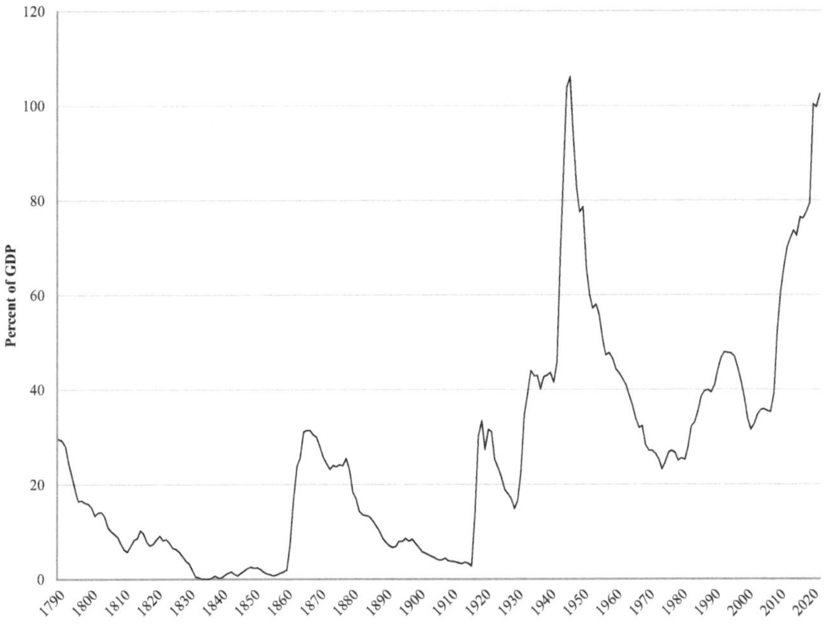

FIGURE 1.1 Federal Debt Held by the Public, 1790–2022

Source: Adapted from Congressional Budget Office (1790–1939) and OMB, *Budget of the United States, FY23, Historical Tables,* Table 7.1 (1940–2022).

lowered tariff rates and simultaneously imposed a new income tax of 2 percent on incomes over $4,000. But the income tax was ruled unconstitutional by the Supreme Court in 1895.[31] With the ratification of the Sixteenth Amendment to the Constitution (1913), the income tax became a permanent source of revenues. While the income tax was initially modest, its importance would be magnified as the US entered World War I.[32] Although the new income tax generated unprecedented revenues, they were greatly outpaced by the demands of the war, forcing the federal government to cover some three-quarters of the costs with debt. By 1919, the federal debt had reached 33.4 percent of GDP, slightly greater than the level of debt at the end of the Civil War. As in earlier episodes, the expansion of the national debt was followed by a period of deleveraging. While tax rates were partially reduced from their wartime highs, the federal government ran a surplus from 1920 to 1930. As a share of GDP, the national debt fell from 33.4 percent (1919) to 14.9 percent (1929), increasing to 16.5 percent the next year. By this point, however, the nation faced a new calamity: the Great Depression. Within the next decade, the debt grew to over 43 percent of GDP.

During World War II, an income tax that had previously focused on a narrow stratum of wealthy households was transformed into a highly progressive mass tax. Despite the growth in revenues, the federal government nonetheless placed a heavy reliance on debt financing and the publicly held debt reached an unprecedented 106.1 percent of GDP—more than three times the levels of debt incurred in World War I or the Civil War. In the immediate postwar decades, the retention of this tax system allowed for a return to the pattern of deleveraging witnessed in earlier episodes. As a result of steady revenues, inflation, and economic growth, the publicly held debt fell to a low of 23.2 percent of GDP by 1974. But by the early 1980s, the debt began to grow relative to GDP as a product of changes in tax policy that were incommensurate with levels of spending. The nation entered a new and extended period of growing indebtedness. By 2012, the debt (70.3 percent of GDP) was three times the level of 1974, and a decade later it approached the levels of World War II. Some of this growth was the product of crises. But unlike earlier episodes in the history of the debt, growing indebtedness became the default. Something significant had changed.[33]

The goal of this book is to explain the changes that began in the 1980s when the historical pattern of leveraging and deleveraging was broken. As in the past, debt was incurred as a product of crisis or choice. Apart from the 1990s—something of a brief respite in this saga—periods of growing indebtedness are no longer followed by prolonged periods of debt reduction. The explanation has programmatic and political dimensions. The decision in the 1980s to abandon the mass tax regime forged in World War II created an ongoing revenue constraint. The Republican Party embraced low taxes as a central unifying principle for its coalition. A majority of elected Republicans signed the Americans for Tax Reform's Taxpayer Protection Pledge, committing to oppose any tax increases. When in the majority, they used parliamentary procedures (most notably, the budget reconciliation process) to translate narrow majorities into significant tax cuts. As the revenue constraint was being locked into place, programmatic mandatory spending continued to grow as a share of federal outlays and GDP, placing increasing pressure on discretionary spending. Under conditions of growing political polarization, the two parties were locked in a zero-sum contest over a shrinking share of outlays. Congress became seemingly incapable of executing its basic fiscal duties. The only point of agreement between the two parties, if only by default, was the acceptance of growing debt.

The fiscal history of the postwar period will be developed in some detail in Part II of the book. As a foundation for this analysis, the chapters in Part I of the book provide a broad examination of spending, taxation, and debt. Chapter 2 begins with federal spending, placing it in cross-national and historical perspective. The most striking feature of the past several decades has been the inexorable growth of mandatory programs. As noted earlier, in the early 1960s, mandatory programmatic spending constituted less than a third of outlays, whereas discretionary spending—that portion of federal spending controlled by the budget process—accounted for roughly two thirds of outlays. As a result of demographics and the introduction of new programs (most notably, Medicare and Medicaid), mandatory spending increased steadily such that after 2015, it claimed some two-thirds of outlays.[34] The largest programs like Social Security and Medicare are broadly popular, raising the political costs of reform. Given their dominance in federal outlays, the chapter provides a brief overview of these programs. The growth of mandatory spending has had important implications for discretionary spending that relies on annual appropriations under the process outlined in the Congressional Budget Act of 1974. After discussing the budgetary process, the chapter explains how the process has broken down. Under conditions of growing political polarization, Congress increasingly fails to execute its core duties in budgeting. Procedures it has introduced to control spending and the magnitude of deficits have been circumvented routinely.

Chapter 3 turns to taxation. It is one of the core assertions of this book that the revenue constraint has been one of the central factors in generating deficits and debt. The chapter begins by placing taxation in cross-national and historical perspective. Taxation has always been a contentious issue in the United States, a nation born in tax revolt. As a broad generalization, significant increases in taxation have occurred only under conditions of crisis and these taxes were retained in subsequent years as a means of reducing the resulting levels of debt. But for much of the past several decades, there has been a strong commitment within the Republican Party to cut taxes and preserve a low-tax regime. As the income tax has lost much of its progressivity through deep cuts in top marginal tax rates, important changes in the composition of revenues have increased the reliance on payroll taxes—the most regressive form of taxation—while reducing the role of the corporate income tax. The chapter explores the system of tax expenditures—exemptions, exclusions, deferrals, and credits that are embedded in the Internal Revenue Code—that claim a larger proportion of GDP than is raised through the income tax. Tax expenditures have increased the porosity of the tax base, thereby contributing to the revenue constraint.

Chapter 4 examines deficits and the debt. Political opposition to the debt is as old as the Republic. Deficits and the debt have often been deployed as symbols of profligacy and excessive state expansion. They have been used to bolster the case for austerity in social spending. Although one should not understate the importance of symbolism in politics, the chapter explores important normative and practical concerns. After placing the debt in the larger context of government finances, it turns to some important normative questions. If public debt is deferred taxation, under what conditions is it permissible to defer taxes to future generations without violating norms of intergenerational equity? It also considers how a transition from tax financing to debt financing impacts on intragenerational equity. The chapter then turns to some of the more practical issues, including whether high levels of debt crowd out private investment, increase the probability of a fiscal crisis, or elevate the nation's vulnerability to foreign bondholders. From the perspective of the chapter, the greatest concern is the potential that projected growth in interest payments will place additional pressure on discretionary spending. To what extent will the costs of servicing the debt compromise the capacity of the federal government to spend money on national priorities?

Before we turn to the discussion of Part II of the book, a few comments are in order. The magnitude of the disjunction between revenues and outlays is best illustrated by considering some concrete figures. In 2019, the eve of the COVID-19 pandemic, federal revenues equaled 16.3 percent of GDP (this book will frequently refer to 2019 because revenues and spending during and in the immediate aftermath of the pandemic were anomalous).[35] In that same year, the combination of programmatic mandatory spending and net interest on the debt claimed 14.6 percent of GDP. Given the amount devoted to these two categories of spending, to keep within the revenue constraint—that is, to balance the budget—Congress would have to limit discretionary spending to 1.7 percent of GDP. But in 2019, discretionary spending claimed 6.3 percent of GDP (split more or less equally between defense and nondefense spending).[36]

The fact that Congress appropriates funds well in excess of what would be necessary to bring the budget into balance or even stabilize the debt-to-GDP ratio should come as no surprise. Both parties have long-standing commitments to certain policies that are consistent with their ideologies and important to their coalitions. The kinds of spending cuts necessary to work within the revenue constraints would undermine the integrity of these programs, in some cases, forcing their very elimination. Using 2019 figures, a discretionary spending cap of 1.7 percent of GDP—what would be necessary to balance the budget—would require a 73 percent reduction in discretionary outlays. Even if the decision were made to eliminate defense spending—an improbable event—nondefense discretionary spending would have to be cut by 45 percent (with comparable cuts in the defense budget if the decision were made to eliminate all nondefense discretionary spending). A decision to stabilize the debt-to-GDP ratio would require smaller cuts, but they would nonetheless undermine existing policy commitments. There is no clear path to fiscal stability without raising additional revenues. However, as mentioned earlier, members of the Republican Party have pledged to a low tax regime. Given this commitment, razor- thin majorities in a polarized Congress, and the multiple veto points that can be used to prevent tax increases (most notably, the Senate filibuster), the prospects for significant changes in revenues seem limited.

More important, there is a simple logic at play that ties into the incentive structure facing members of Congress. Most scholars of Congress cite re-election as the proximate goal for members of Congress.[37] While the current combination of tax and spending decisions carries long-term fiscal ramifications, it is also politically efficacious in the short term. It is not clear the extent to which constituents demand fiscal responsibility from their elected representatives. Some voters may be relatively indifferent to deficits; they may prefer them to the alternative of higher taxes and/or program cuts today. Younger voters may be indifferent to whether they pay higher taxes today or defer them to their future (and presumably wealthier) selves. At the extreme, however, older voters may prefer deficits. They benefit from the largest entitlement programs (Social Security and Medicare) and rather than facing program cuts, they would rather defer taxation to future generations of taxpayers.[38] If members of Congress place a high discount rate on the future, it may reflect both the electoral incentive and the preferences of their constituents.

Members of Congress could forge broad agreements to raise additional revenues and limit spending; they could create enforcement mechanisms (e.g., spending caps backed with mandatory sequestration). Indeed, Congress has arrived at such agreements on several occasions in the past three decades, albeit with mixed results. Presumably, members of Congress could lessen the political costs by acting as trustees rather than delegates. They could explain to their constituents that higher taxes and programmatic reform are necessary to control the growth in the debt and avoid foisting the costs on to future generations. But Republicans who violated their anti-tax pledge would face almost certain retribution in the form of a primary opponent backed by Americans for Tax Reform and the Club for Growth. Democrats who embraced entitlement reform would be charged with abandoning the social contract framed in the New Deal and would face a primary challenge from progressives. At the same time, they would fear that any GOP commitment to tax increases would prove ephemeral in an anti-tax environment. Regardless of party, members of Congress would need to risk their legislative careers in the name of long-term reform.[39] In short, fiscal responsibility is not incentive compatible.

Part II of the book turns to the fiscal record and the budgetary politics of the postwar period. Chapter 5 examines the immediate post-war period. During World War II, the income tax was transformed from an elite tax to a mass-based tax. The retention of high marginal tax rates for individuals and for corporations extended for the next several decades, allowing for higher levels of federal spending than in the interwar period and major new commitments (including an expanded military capacity, the creation of the interstate highway system, the expansion of Social Security, and the creation of Medicare and Medicaid). It also allowed for significant reduction in debt relative to the economy. The debt-to-GDP ratio fell to levels not witnessed since the 1920s. The period of postwar deleveraging was largely in keeping with earlier periods in US history.

The "Great Deleveraging" was interrupted by the stagflation of the 1970s (or the "Great Inflection"), which is the subject of Chapter 6. The coincidence of high inflation and high unemployment raised profound questions about the efficacy of Keynesian demand management. Stagflation also opened a window of opportunity for critics to contest active fiscal policy, taxation, means-tested social welfare policies, and regulation. The resulting debates elevated the status of supply-side arguments that tax cuts would generate higher levels of growth and revenues. Some critics on the Right found supply-side claims fantastical, but they welcomed tax cuts as a means of reducing the size of the federal government. By starving the government of revenues, it was argued, retrenchment would necessarily follow. Regardless, the advocacy of low taxes resonated with a nation beleaguered by stagflation and inflation-driven bracket creep, engaged in local tax revolt, experiencing higher levels of economic insecurity, and voicing plummeting levels of trust in the federal government in the wake of the Vietnam War and Watergate.

Chapter 7 turns to the 1980s and 1990s. Supply-side arguments and the larger critique of the welfare-regulatory state found an expression in public policy during the Reagan era. For present purposes, the most important impact was the deep tax cuts. Without proportionate reductions in spending, the trajectory of the immediate postwar decades was reversed. The growth in the debt forced a response in the 1990s, as noted in the opening vignette to this chapter. But the changes in tax policy did not entail a return to the progressive rate structure of the immediate postwar decades (indeed, top rates would never exceed one-half of what existed in the wake of the war). Given the powerful anti-tax sentiments, Democrats were limited in the extent to which they could raise taxes, even when briefly in unified control of the White House and Congress. But Congress and presidents imposed rules to govern their collective behavior and counter the electoral calculus described earlier in pursuit of deficit and debt reduction. In less than a decade, the process—when combined with tax increases, steady economic growth, and the end of the Cold War—generated surpluses and a reduction in the debt-to-GDP ratio, albeit temporarily.

Although the spending caps, PAYGO process, and tax increases of the 1990s were successful, it is doubtful that a similar policy mix could be imposed in the post-2000 period, as shown in Chapter 8. Unified Republican control of the White House and Congress following the 2000 elections brought successive tax cuts. Thereafter, the unified opposition to tax increases within the Republican caucus only worsened the revenue constraint. As mandatory spending continued to grow as a share of outlays, any meaningful spending caps would force members of Congress to cut discretionary spending, thus violating the electoral imperative. Finally, in sharp contrast to the 1990s experiment, polarization generated high levels of dysfunction. Congress lurched from one budgetary crisis to the next; stopgap funding measures became the norm. Congressional Republicans threatened to allow the nation to default on its debt to secure spending caps under the Budget Control Act of 2011. Thereafter, Congress repeatedly raised the caps to avoid their political consequences. It routinely suspended the debt ceiling and then reset it, forcing the Treasury to resort to extraordinary measures to meet its obligations. A core lesson of these episodes is clear: there are no rules that Congress can impose on itself that it cannot suspend at will. It is doubtful that layering another set of rules on top of the existing rules would generate different results. Matters were only made worse during this period by the series of crises, including the terrorist attack of September 11, 2001, dual wars in Afghanistan (2001–2021) and Iraq (2003–2011), the financial crisis (2007–2008) and Great Recession (2007–2009).

Chapter 9 concludes the historical narrative with the Trump presidency and the transition to the Biden presidency. During the Trump presidency, the Republican-controlled Congress made the decision, once again, to leverage narrow majorities to secure significant tax cuts via reconciliation, further reducing revenues as a share of GDP. In a replay of the 1980s and the 2000s, tax cuts were combined with a lack of spending restraint, driving the debt to higher levels despite a full-employment economy. In this context, the crisis of the COVID-19 pandemic proved particularly consequential, adding trillions of dollars of additional spending. With the election of Joe Biden, the government was once again under unified Democratic control and attention focused on proposals for new spending programs. Given the low costs of borrowing, the implications for the debt were largely dismissed. Between 2000 and 2020, the debt tripled, from 33.7 percent of GDP to over 100 percent of GDP and it is projected, in the next few years, to eclipse the record incurred following the Great Depression and World War II.[40]

Chapter 10 concludes the volume with some reflections on the factors shaping the contemporary history of the debt. Unfortunately, if the larger argument of the book is correct, there are no simple solutions to the current situation. A balanced budget amendment—a perennial response to deficits and the debt—is largely an exercise in symbolism. Given that its primary proponents are committed to blocking tax increases under any circumstances, one can surmise that balanced budget proposals are largely an effort to divert attention from taxation. Given the magnitude of the fiscal gap, as noted earlier, to achieve balanced budgets through the reduction of outlays would dramatically transform the role of the federal government in ways that would be unacceptable to supporters of either party. In the end, some combination of tax increases to raise the revenue constraint and systematic reform of the largest drivers of mandatory spending provide the only path to stabilizing the debt-to-GDP ratio. The core question is whether these changes are achievable given the polarization-driven gridlock that characterizes the contemporary Congress.

Notes

1 Office of Management and Budget (OMB), *Budget of the United States Government, Fiscal Year 2023* (Washington, DC: Government Publishing Office, 2022), Historical Tables, Table 8.4.
2 Ibid., Table 1.2.
3 Ibid.
4 Helen Dewar, "Stockman Issues Blunt Warning," *Washington Post,* April 19, 1983. Available at www.washingtonpost.com/archive/politics/1983/04/19/stockman-issues-blunt-warning/64b687b3-cb8a-4134-a215-81c4f697be3c/

5 All subsequent discussions of the debt in this chapter will refer to the debt held by the public unless otherwise noted.

6 OMB, *Budget of the United States Government, Fiscal Year 2023,* Historical Tables, Table 7.1.

7 Benjamin M. Friedman, *Day of Reckoning: The Consequences of American Economic Policy* (New York: Vintage Books, 1988), 87.

8 Quoted in Richard W. Stevenson, "10-Year Estimate of Budget Surplus Surges Once More." *New York Times,* December 29, 2000: A1. Available at www.nytimes.com/2000/12/29/us/10-year-estimate-of-budget-surplus-surges-once-more.html

9 Louis Uchitelle, "Taxes, the Market and Luck Underline the Budget Surplus." *New York Times*, October 20, 2000: A1. Available at www.nytimes.com/2000/10/20/us/taxes-the-market-and-luck-underlie-the-budget-surplus.html.

10 Quoted in Stevenson, "10-Year Estimate of Budget Surplus Surges Once More."

11 Allen Schick, " 'A Surplus, If We Can Keep It': How the Federal Budget Surplus Happened," *The Brookings Review* 18, 1 (2000): 39.

12 Alan Greenspan, *The Age of Turbulence: Adventures in a New World* (New York: Penguin Press, 2007), 213.

13 Congressional Budget Office (CBO), *The Budget and Economic Outlook: Fiscal Years 2002–2011* (Washington, DC: CBO, 2001), 14.

14 Ibid., xiv.

15 Greenspan, *The Age of Turbulence*, 218.

16 Ibid., 219.

17 OMB, *Budget of the United States Government, Fiscal Year 2023,* Historical Tables, Tables 1.1 and 1.2.

18 CBO, *The Budget and Economic Outlook: Fiscal Years 2002–2011,* 2.

19 OMB, *Budget of the United States Government, Fiscal Year 2023,* Historical Tables, Table 1.2.

20 Ibid., Tables 1.2 and 7.1.

21 CBO, *Budget and Economic Outlook: 2020–2030* (Washington, DC: CBO, 2020), 5, 7–8.

22 Government Accountability Office, *The Nation's Fiscal Health: Action is Needed to Address the Federal Government's Fiscal Future,* GAO-20-403SP (Washington, DC: Government Accountability Office, 2020), 31.

23 OMB, *Budget of the United States Government, Fiscal Year 2023*, Historical Tables, Table 7.1.

24 CBO, *The Budget and Economic Outlook: Fiscal Years 2002–2011,* 5–6.

25 Ibid, 78–79.

26 Ibid., 82.

27 CBO, *The 2022 Long-Term Budget Outlook* (Washington, DC: CBO, 2022). Calculations by author based on data supplement. Available at www.cbo.gov/system/files/2022-07/57971-Data.xlsx

28 "Older People Projected to Outnumber Children for First Time in U.S. History," Press Release CB18-41, March 13, 2018. U.S. Census Bureau. Available at www.census.gov/newsroom/press-releases/2018/cb18-41-population-projections.html

29 See Jacob S. Hacker, *The Great Risk Shift: The New Economic Insecurity and the Decline of the American Dream* (Oxford: Oxford University Press, 2006).

30 See Walter J. Oleszek, *The "Regular Order": A Perspective,* CRS Report R46597 (Washington, DC: Congressional Research Service, 2020).

31 See John F. Witte, *The Politics and Development of the Federal Income Tax* (Madison: University of Wisconsin Press, 1985), 70–76.

32 Ibid., 78.

33 OMB, *Budget of the United States Government, Fiscal Year 2023,* Historical Tables, Table 7.1.

34 Ibid., Table 8.3.

35 Ibid., Table 1.2.

36 Ibid., Table 8.4.

37 The classical statement of this assumption is David Mayhew, *Congress: The Electoral Connection* (New Haven: Yale University Press, 1974).

38 This argument is developed in James M. Buchanan and Richard E. Wagner, *Democracy in Deficit: The Political Legacy of Lord Keynes,* in *The Collected Works of James M. Buchanan,* vol. 8 (Indianapolis: Liberty Fund, 2000), 144–47.

39 Roy T. Meyers, "The Implosion of the Federal Budget Process: Triggers, Commissions, Cliffs, Sequesters, Debt Ceilings, and Shutdown," *Public Budgeting and Finance,* 34, 4 (2014): 16–17.

40 OMB, *Budget of the United States Government, Fiscal Year 2023,* Historical Tables, Table 7.1.

PART I

2

SPENDING

The Growing Dominance of Mandatory Programs

In a 2002 address, Under Secretary of the Treasury Peter R. Fisher likened the federal government to "a gigantic insurance company (with a sideline business in national defense and homeland security) which only does its accounting on a cash basis—only counting premiums and payouts as they go in and out the door." Given the long-term obligations, "it is not really an insurance company at all. It is an accident waiting to happen." The analogy was an obvious simplification: the side business is far more expansive than suggested. But the growing role of social insurance (most of which is classified as programmatic mandatory spending which occurs outside of the budget process) is the most striking features of federal outlays. Returning to the analogy, Fisher noted that an actual insurance company could "grow its way out by raising its premiums and its earnings on investments faster than its liabilities. The federal government, however, would have to raise taxes or borrow faster than it increases outlays."[1] We will reserve a discussion of taxation and the debt for Chapters 3 and 4, respectively. This chapter focuses on the spending size of the equation. As programmatic mandatory spending has come to dominate federal outlays and Congress has proven reluctant to restructure politically popular programs to alter the trajectory of growth, efforts to accommodate the revenue constraint have both squeezed the proportion of outlays devoted to discretionary spending and forced higher levels of borrowing.

This chapter starts by placing spending in a historical and cross-national perspective before turning to an examination of the long-term changes in the composition of outlays. The most important trend in the postwar period has been the inexorable growth of programmatic mandatory spending and the consequent declining share of outlays devoted to discretionary spending. Given the overwhelming role of mandatory spending, the chapter turns to a brief

DOI: 10.4324/9781003395331-3

discussion of the two largest programs: Social Security and Medicare. Both programs are growing steadily, driven by demographic forces beyond the control of Congress. The trust funds that support them are rapidly approaching insolvency; absent trust fund surpluses, the payroll taxes that finance the programs will be insufficient to cover the benefits. The chapter turns to an examination of discretionary spending, that portion of outlays that are controlled by annual congressional appropriations. The polarization-driven collapse of regular order in Congress has found a manifestation in the budget process, which has fallen into a perpetual state of crisis. While Congress has occasionally devised procedures that allowed it to exert some control over deficits, they have been of mixed success.

Federal Spending in Perspective

When viewed in historical context, expenditures are best expressed relative to gross domestic product (GDP). As one might expect, the data presented in Figure 2.1 show that federal spending almost tripled between 1930 and 1940, from 3.4 percent of GDP to 9.6 percent of GDP, largely reflecting the

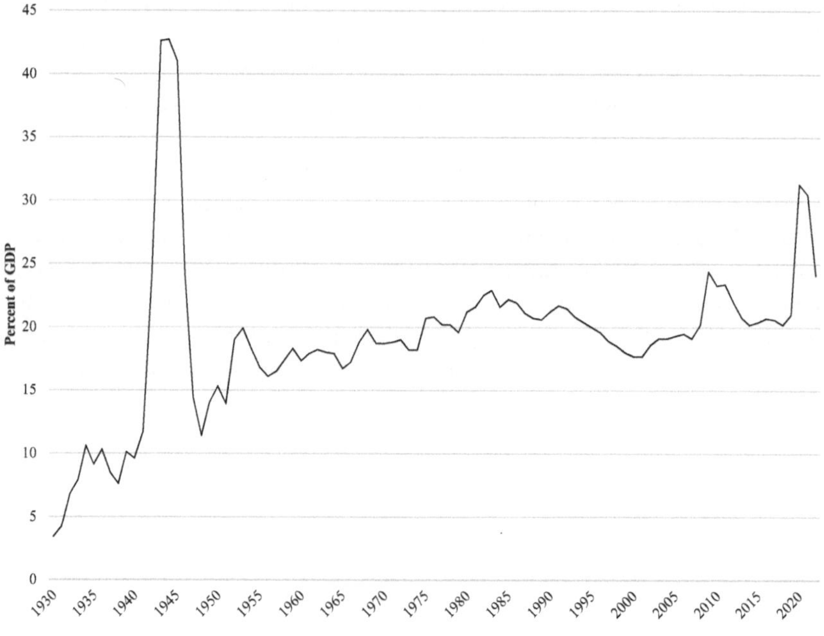

FIGURE 2.1 Federal Outlays, 1930–2022

Source: Adapted from OMB, *Budget of the United States, FY23*, Historical Tables, Table 1.2.

proliferation of policies introduced by the Roosevelt administration as part of the New Deal. This growth would seem trivial relative to the spike in spending during World War II, which exceeded 40 percent of GDP in 1943–1945. As the nation demobilized from the war, spending fell from 41 percent of GDP (1945) to a postwar low of 11.4 percent of GDP in 1948. Outlays would grow over the course of the next several decades, driven in part, by Cold War defense spending and, with the expansion of Social Security and the introduction of Medicare and Medicaid, the welfare state. Federal spending would exceed 22 percent of GDP by the early 1980s—roughly twice the level of 1948—largely as a product of the massive increase in defense spending during the Reagan presidency and the growth of social spending during the deep recession of the early 1980s. Spending would remain about 20 percent of GDP until the mid-1990s, when procedures imposed by Congress to control spending and reduce the deficit began to bear fruit. These controls, when combined with real GDP growth, allowed outlays to fall to 17.7 percent of GDP by 2000. Thereafter, a combination of growing entitlement spending, two protracted wars, and the government response to the financial crisis and the Great Recession reversed this trajectory. By 2008, spending once again exceeded 20 percent of GDP, moving within a range of 23.3 and 24.4 percent of GDP during the Great Recession and its aftermath, declining slightly in the next several years, before reaching a new peak of 31.3 percent of GDP as the federal government responded to the COVID-19 pandemic in 2020. While spending will fall in the wake of the pandemic, it is not projected to return to earlier levels.[2]

The growth in spending as a share of GDP is useful, but it can also obscure the magnitude of change. During periods of strong economic growth, the levels of government spending could increase in absolute terms but nonetheless decline relative to GDP. Similarly, during economic downturns, the reduction in GDP could magnify the increase in spending. For this reason, it is also useful to consider the level of federal spending per person, adjusted for inflation (all figures below are in 2012 dollars). In 1940, following seven years of New Deal recovery efforts, federal spending was $1,098 per capita. A decade later, spending had almost tripled, reaching $2,986 per capita, and increased to $3,871 by 1960. By 1970, following the growth of expenditures related to the Vietnam War and the expansion of social welfare, spending reached $5,392 per capita. In the 1970s, a decade that witnessed the difficulties of stagflation and growing concerns about levels of spending, per capita expenditures continued to grow, reaching $7,030 by 1980. The 1980s, a decade that was synonymous with the Reagan revolution and the aspirational goal of reducing the role of the federal government, per real capita spending increased to $8,568. The 1990s marked something of an anomaly. As a result of procedures enacted to control deficits, by 2000, spending had fallen slightly to $8,448 per capita. By 2010, per capita spending had increased to $11,689 and would continue to grow, reaching $12,289 by 2019, on the eve of the pandemic. To place things in perspective, federal outlays claimed approximately the same share of GDP in 1970 (21.2 percent) and 2019 (21 percent), but the inflation-adjusted per capita spending had more than doubled (from $5,392 to $12,289).[3]

Given the long tradition of anti-statism and the ideological embrace of market governance in the United States, one should not be surprised that public spending claims a smaller share of GDP than in other wealthy democracies. The most common comparisons are drawn between the United States and other members of the Organization for Economic Cooperation and Development (OECD). Reflecting cross-national differences in governmental structures, OECD figures include all levels of government (e.g., federal, state, and local). Unsurprisingly, the United States, at 37.7 percent of GDP (2015), fell well below the OECD average of 40.9 percent and European nations with strong statist and corporatist traditions, including France (57 percent), Finland (57 percent), Denmark (54.8 percent), Sweden (50.2 percent), and Germany (44 percent). In terms of overall spending relative to GDP, the United States had far more in common with other liberal market-based economies, including Great Britain (42.9 percent), New Zealand (39.5 percent), and Australia (37.2 percent).[4] Data at this level of aggregation do not reveal cross-national differences in spending priorities. Once again, using 2015 figures, the US government spent more on healthcare (24.2 percent GDP) than any other OECD country, and well above OECD averages (18.7 percent); unsurprisingly, its defense spending (8.8 percent GDP) was above the OECD average (5.1 percent) and second only to Israel (14.9 percent). At the same time, the US spent considerably less on "social protection"—a broad category that includes non-healthcare related social welfare policies—than the OECD average (20.8 percent GDP versus 32.6 percent GDP, respectively).[5]

A cross-national comparison may be less revelatory for another reason. It focuses exclusively on spending rather than a more comprehensive array of policy instruments that may be used to achieve policy goals. The US relies less on social insurance than many European welfare states. But it deploys more indirect policy tools, including tax expenditures, loan guarantees, and regulations. The US may lack comprehensive healthcare, provide less generous public pensions for the elderly, and invest less in public housing. But it incentivizes employment-based health insurance and pensions by exempting contributions from income taxation and subsidizes homeownership through the deductibility of home mortgage interest and real estate taxes.[6] We will discuss tax expenditures, the provisions in the Internal Revenue Code that subsidize various forms of activity, in Chapter 3.

The Changing Composition of Spending

Examinations of the growth in aggregate government spending may obscure an important issue. Ideally, we would be interested in understanding how the combination of governmental responsibilities changes over time. A growth in overall government spending might reflect uniform incremental growth in spending across all programmatic areas. Alternatively, it may obscure the fact that some responsibilities are claiming an ever-greater share of resources whereas others are declining as a share of government outlays and GDP.[7] The past several decades have witnessed profound changes in the composition of outlays, a point that will be developed with some concrete data below. As a generalization, during the past half century, the portion of outlays and GDP devoted to the largest social welfare programs have greatly outpaced other components of government spending. At the same time, defense has declined in importance.

Let us examine the changing composition of spending in greater detail. At the broadest level, spending can be divided into three categories: (1) discretionary spending, (2) mandatory or direct spending, and (3) net interest payments on the debt. According to the Government Accountability Office, discretionary spending "refers to outlays from budget authority that is provided in and controlled by appropriation acts."[8] This category is divided into defense and non-defense discretionary spending. Discretionary spending includes many of the things that citizens consider to be central to what the government does (e.g., national defense, education, federal law enforcement, infrastructural investments, transportation, and regulations). Annual discretionary spending is determined through the federal budget process. In contrast, direct or mandatory spending, the terms are used synonymously,

> refers to budget authority that is provided in laws other than appropriation acts and the outlays that result from such budget authority....By defining eligibility and setting the benefit or payment rules, Congress controls spending for these programs indirectly rather than directly through appropriations acts.[9]

Programmatic mandatory spending includes the largest fiscal commitments of the federal government (e.g., Social Security, Medicare, Medicaid, veterans pensions). In these programs, the federal government is legally obliged to make payments to parties that fulfill the requirements established by the authorizing statutes. Social Security and Medicare hospital insurance, currently the largest components of programmatic mandatory spending, are funded through a dedicated payroll tax. Other programmatic mandatory programs like Medicaid and the noncompulsory components of Medicare, are classified as "appropriated entitlements." Spending is mandated by statute and recipients have a legal claim on benefits, but annual appropriation acts nonetheless serve as the source of funding. The levels of programmatic mandatory spending can be changed through revisions in the authorizing legislation. Finally, there is interest payments on the debt. Congress periodically passes legislation raising the debt

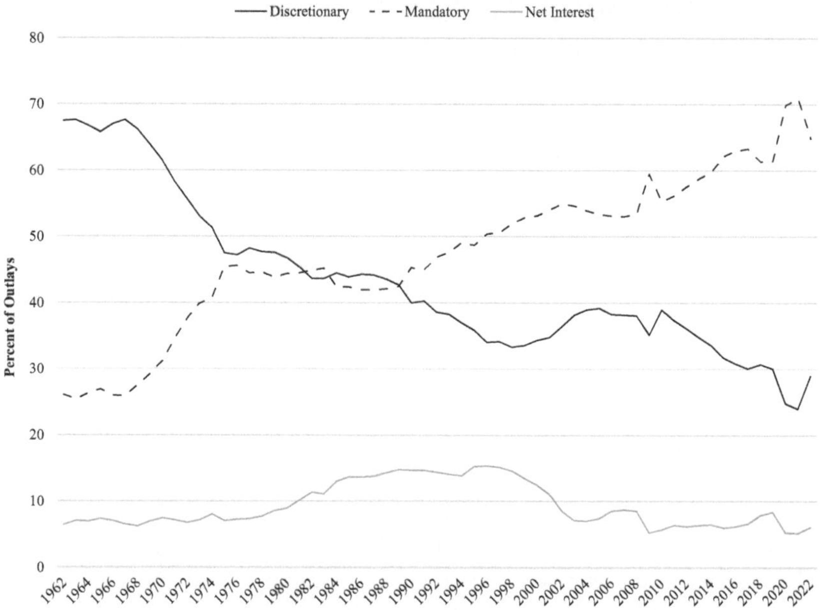

FIGURE 2.2 Composition of Outlays, 1962–2022

Source: Adapted from OMB, *Budget of the United States, FY23*, Historical Tables, Table 8.3.

limit, thereby authorizing the Treasury to issue debt and incur interest liabilities. The changing composition of the budget, using these broad categories, is presented in Figure 2.2.

One of the more striking features of the period in question is the dramatic reduction of defense spending as a percentage of federal spending. In 1962, defense spending claimed 49.2 percent of federal outlays (9 percent GDP). The defense budget would decline relative to the remainder of federal outlays in the 1970s, falling to a low of 22.8 percent (4.8 percent GDP) in 1980. During the Reagan administration's unprecedented peacetime expansion of the military, the defense budget increased to 28.1 percent of outlays (5.9 percent GDP) by 1987. Thereafter, the end of the Cold War and new budgetary rules brought steady reductions in defense spending as a share of federal outlays, which fell to a low of 16.2 percent of outlays (2.9 percent GDP) in 1999. The next decade would bring growth in defense spending, reflecting the heightened concern with terrorism and the dual wars in Afghanistan and Iraq. But defense spending would increase to a peak of 20.5 percent of outlays (4.1 percent GDP) in 2008 before once again entering a period of decline, well below historical levels. By 2019, national defense would constitute 15.2 percent of outlays or 3.2 percent of GDP, a remarkable change.[10]

During this same period, non-defense discretionary spending expanded as a share of federal outlays before entering a period of decline. It constituted 18.3 percent of the budget in 1962 (3.3 percent GDP), increasing to a peak of 24.9 percent of outlays (5 percent GDP) in 1978. Thereafter, non-defense discretionary spending would steadily fall as a share of federal spending and GDP. As a result of budgetary rules, the levels of non-defense discretionary spending would fall to levels comparable to defense discretionary spending by the late 1990s. By 2019, when defense spending fell to 15.2 percent of outlays, non-defense spending claimed 14.9 percent of outlays (3.1 percent GDP).[11]

The falling share of defense and non-defense discretionary spending is largely a reflection of the most significant trend over the period: the growth in programmatic mandatory spending. In 1962, programmatic mandatory spending comprised 26.1 percent of the budget (4.8 percent GDP), one-half of which was claimed by Social Security. Over the course of the next several decades, the introduction of new programs—most notably, Medicare and Medicaid—the expansion of Social Security, and the aging of the population drove higher levels of spending. By 1993, programmatic mandatory spending had risen to constitute a majority (50.3 percent) of federal outlays (10.5 percent GDP). In 2009, as the nation was reeling from the Great Recession, programmatic mandatory spending—some of which, like Medicaid and supplemental nutrition, is means tested—spiked to 62.1 percent of outlays (15.1 percent GDP), before falling back to recent levels. But since 2015, it has remained above 60 percent of outlays, exceeding 65 percent of outlays in several years. Interest payments increased in the 1970s—a reflection of the high-inflation environment—but declined significantly in subsequent decades, falling more precipitously in the post 2000 period (1.8 percent GDP and 8.4 percent of outlays in 2019), despite the growing debt-to-GDP ratio. When programmatic mandatory spending is combined with interest payments, the vast majority of federal outlays fall outside of the budgetary process.[12]

The changing composition of spending has important consequences. First and foremost, absent reform, a growing share of federal spending will be driven by factors outside of the direct control of Congress. The escalating costs of Social Security, Medicare, and to a lesser extent Medicaid are a function of the aging of the population (and in the case of health policies, the medical inflation rate). Certainly, Congress can make statutory changes to control the growth of key mandatory programs; given the impending insolvency of the trust funds supporting Social Security and Medicare, reform is unavoidable. But entitlement reform is difficult, given the political mobilization of the elderly in response to benefit cuts and the impediments to building broad bipartisan coalitions in an era of heightened polarization.

A second consequence of the changing composition of spending is that Congress has relinquished much of its power over the executive branch. The Constitution assigned primary responsibility for fiscal policy to Congress.

Under Article I, Section 9, "No money shall be drawn from the Treasury, but in Consequence of Appropriations made by Law." The power to spend—the "power of the purse"—is a legislative power. By vesting Congress with the power of the purse, the Constitution provided it with an important advantage vis-à-vis the other branches of government. Following Zachary Price, some executive powers are resource-independent (e.g., the power to veto legislation or grant clemency). In these cases, the president could exercise the powers even if Congress provided little more than the presidential salary. But other powers are resource-dependent, and in these cases, Congress possesses "near-complete discretion to impose whatever limits and conditions it chooses."[13] For this category of presidential action, there is little practical presidential power absent congressional appropriations. This provides Congress with a remarkable source of power: the ability to force presidents to negotiate over national priorities and to do so on an annual basis. But as Josh Chafetz has argued, as mandatory spending has grown to dominate federal spending, "Congress has ceded the institutional advantage of annual appropriations."[14]

A third consequence: the congressional budget process which focuses on discretionary spending has been transformed into a battle over a shrinking proportion of federal spending. Writing in 1992, Aaron Wildavsky noted that as entitlements expand,

> the budgetary system becomes loaded with many constants and few variables. Put plainly, the prevalence of entitlements means that but a minority of programs and agencies remain to absorb the vast majority of cuts. Resource allocation becomes a lot harder when you have to take three-fifths of total spending (entitlement plus interest) off the table.[15]

As budgetary politics increasingly assumes the form of a zero-sum game such that increases (or even stability) in the funding of one program can be secured only through budget cuts for another, the potential for conflict escalates. When placed in the contemporary context of a polarized Congress, each party is increasingly tempted to use parliamentary procedures to thwart the opposition with the result that the budgetary process is in a permanent state of disarray. Appropriations bills languish, the threat and reality of government shutdowns loom, and minorities are willing to engage in brinksmanship to extract victories.

Mandatory Spending and the Growth of Social Insurance

Social Security and Medicare provide income and healthcare security to the elderly population. Their claim on federal spending cannot be overstated. In 2019, Social Security accounted for 23.4 percent of outlays (4.9 percent GDP) while Medicare accounted for 14.5 percent of outlays (3.0 percent GDP). Social Security is projected to grow to claim 23.6 percent of outlays (5.3 percent GDP) by 2027. That same year, Medicare is projected to claim 16.5 percent of outlays (3.8 percent of GDP). The nation's program to provide retirement income and health insurance to the elderly will claim a combined 9.1 percent of GDP. By way of comparison, the entirety of defense and non-defense discretionary spending is projected to be 6.2 percent of GDP.[16] The CBO projects that by 2052, Social Security and Medicare will claim a combined 12.4 percent of GDP, whereas discretionary spending will fall to 6 percent of GDP.[17]

Traditionally, financial security in retirement was understood as resting on a "three-legged stool."[18] The three legs were private savings, private pensions, and Social Security. The role of Social Security and Medicare in supporting security in retirement and the potential difficulties in introducing reform efforts will be, in part, a product of the adequacy of savings and private pensions. Recent decades have witnessed a collapse of savings rates and a growth in household debt. As for private pensions, they have become far less generous as employers have shifted from providing defined-benefit plans (which guaranteed a lifetime retirement income based on years of employment and salary) to defined-contribution plans (which made pension savings a function of individual contributions and investment decisions). With two of the legs on the "three-legged stool" weakened, the role of government programs has never been greater. Unfortunately, the policies have never faced greater fiscal challenges. Let us turn briefly to the two key programs and the problem of insolvency.

Social Security

The Social Security Act of 1935, the statutory foundation of the US welfare state, authorized old-age pensions. Pensions were to be funded through a payroll tax split evenly by employer and employee up to a maximum taxable earnings cap. Benefits would be paid to individuals once they attained the age of 65, the age of eligibility commonly adopted in private pension plans. Rather than creating a traditional welfare program with general revenues supporting citizens on a means-tested basis, old-age insurance was framed as a form of forced savings facilitated by the government. As Theda Skocpol and G. John Ikenberry observe, it was presented as a program in which

> individual prospective "beneficiaries" put away "contributions" for their own eventual retirements....The system supposedly established a kind of contractual bond or promise to repay with interest between the government and each individual contributor, thereby giving each person a sacred right eventually to collect the benefits he or she had earned.[19]

Even if this framing was far from accurate, it has contributed to the ongoing support for Social Security. While the original program exempted large occupational categories, during the postwar period it was successively expanded to cover the vast majority of workers. And with the Social Security Act Amendments of 1956, a new Disability Insurance program was created, providing cash benefits to workers aged 50-64.[20]

Social Security currently provides support for over 65 million people, roughly one-in-six Americans. Of this sum, 54 million receive their benefits through Old Age and Survivors Insurance (45 million retirees, 3.1 million dependents, and 6 million survivors). Another 10 million receive support through Disability Insurance. Reflecting, in part, the growth of the elderly population and longer life expectancies of retirees, the number of beneficiaries has doubled since 1975.[21] At present, some 93 percent of workers (including self-employed) are covered, with earning subject to the payroll tax. In 2020, Social Security provided $1.1 trillion in benefits, 86.4 percent of which went to Old Age and Survivors Insurance recipients, with the remainder supporting those on Disability Insurance.[22]

Social Security benefits are determined through the application of a formula that focuses on the 35 years with the highest earnings subject to the payroll tax. Taxable earnings that occur before age 60 are adjusted using the average wage index whereas earning that occur at age 60 or later are counted in nominal dollars. In this step of the process, the goal is a simple one: to adjust earnings for wage growth. The second step adds a measure of progressivity. The sum for the 35-year period is divided by the number of months (420) to determine the average indexed monthly earnings (or AIME). The Primary Insurance Amount (or PIA) is determined by applying different factors (90, 32, and 15 percent) to successive increments of income. In 2020, for example, benefits were the sum of 90 percent of the first $960 of AIME, 32 percent of earnings between $961 and $5,785, and 15 percent of earnings above $5,785, up to a maximum monthly benefit ($3,011 per month at full retirement age).[23] While there is an element of progressivity in the calculation of benefits, it is partially offset by the fact that lifetime earnings and longevity are correlated. The real value of the benefits is protected over time through a cost-of-living allowance or COLA. As of 1975, benefits were indexed for inflation, using the Consumer Price Index for Urban Wage Earners and Clerical Workers.[24]

Financing Social Security and the Trust Fund

The mechanism for financing the Social Security system is relatively straightforward. There are two trust funds: the Federal Old-Age and Survivors Insurance (OASI) Trust Fund and the Federal Disability Insurance (DI) Trust Fund. The primary source of revenues is the payroll taxes (or FICA taxes, authorized under the Federal Insurance Contribution Act) which are paid by employee and employer and remitted to the Treasury; self-employed workers pay the combined components under the Self-Employment Contribution Act.

The current FICA tax is 7.65 percent for employer and employee (6.2 percent for Social Security and 1.45 percent for Medicare). Of the 12.4 percent FICA tax earmarked for Social Security, 10.03 percent is credited to the OASI Trust Fund and the remainder to the DI Trust Fund. In addition to these taxes, higher earning recipients pay income tax on a portion of their benefits, which is remitted primarily to the Social Security trust funds (with the remainder going to the Medicare Hospital Insurance Trust Fund). A third major source of income is interest from the Treasury on special issue bonds that are retained in the Social Security system's two trust funds.[25]

The taxes earmarked for Social Security are received by the general fund of the Treasury and are used to cover the costs of benefits and the administrative costs, in what is described as a pay-as-you-go system.[26] When the funds entering the system exceed the benefit payments and administrative costs, the surplus revenues in the general fund are credited to the appropriate trust fund accounts in the form of special-issue, nonmarketable, Treasury securities. Interest is credited in the form of additional securities. The assets in the trust funds are counted as liabilities against the Treasury's general fund. When revenues are insufficient to cover the benefits and administrative costs, the trust funds redeem the securities from the general fund of the Treasury. Deferring a discussion of public finances for Chapter 4, the securities held in trust funds are counted as part of the gross debt, but not as part of the debt held by the public since they represent internal debt that one part of the government (the Treasury) owes to another part of the government (the relevant trust fund). Nonetheless, when they are redeemed, they must be repaid through the general fund (and ultimately through the taxes that feed the general fund or additional borrowing).

Medicare

The Social Security Act Amendments of 1965 established compulsory hospital insurance for the elderly (Medicare Part A) and voluntary subsidized insurance for outpatient services (Medicare Part B). The act also created Medicaid to provide federal grants-in-aid to the states to finance means-tested healthcare. State participation in Medicaid was voluntary, but participating states had to cover citizens in key categorical programs (Aid to the Blind, Aid to Families with Dependent Children, and Aid to the Permanently and Totally Disabled).[27]

Any discussion of Medicare must be premised on the understanding that the program has undergone significant changes since its inception. Given the space limitations, this discussion can only provide a broad overview of the key components.[28] Medicare Part A was created to provide hospital insurance to the elderly. Coverage was subsequently extended to individuals under age 65 receiving Social Security DI (after a two-year waiting period), and individuals with end-stage renal disease and amyotrophic lateral sclerosis (with no waiting period). Part A provides coverage for the first 60 days of inpatient hospital, with the patient responsible for a deductible. Coverage for days 61–90 is available with a daily coinsurance paid by the patient, and an additional 60 days over the life of the recipient with a daily copayment. It also provides for up to 100 days in a skilled nursing facility subject, once again, to a daily coinsurance payment for stays that exceed 20 days, some home healthcare visits, and hospice care.[29] Medicare Part A is funded by the payroll tax. Medicare Part B provides supplemental medical insurance for physician visits and other outpatient services and is fully voluntary. It covers 80 percent of the costs after the patient meets an annual deductible. Each participant is responsible for a standard monthly premium. Since 2007, higher income beneficiaries have been required to pay "income-related adjustment amounts." Part B is funded through a combination of premiums and general revenues.[30]

Medicare, as originally designed, operated on a fee-for-service basis. Intermediaries (in the case of Part A) or carriers (in the case of Part B) under contract with the Centers for Medicare and Medicaid Services in the Department of Health and Human Services (HHS) processed claims and made payments. Concerns that this model created incentives for cost escalation stimulated reform efforts.[31] The Tax Equity and Fiscal Responsibility Act of 1982 authorized Medicare to contract with private health plans, which would provide benefits that were at least as comprehensive as under traditional Medicare. Following demonstration projects and intensive debates, Congress created a new Medicare Part C (Medicare+Choice) under the Balanced Budget Act of 1997. Under Part C, beneficiaries could choose to receive their Part A and Part B benefits through Medicare-approved private companies, usually health maintenance organizations or preferred-provider organizations. These companies would receive a capitation fee from Medicare. Beneficiaries, in turn, often paid additional premiums to plans, which differed along various dimensions including coverage (e.g., hearing, vision, dental services), restrictions on providers, and out-of-pocket expenses. It was hoped that Part C would contain costs. But as Congress constrained reimbursement rates to reduce deficits, the number of plans declined, leaving some seniors involuntarily disenrolled. In 2003, Congress responded by raising payments, partially obviating the goal of cost containment, and rebranded Part C as Medicare Advantage.[32]

Finally, Medicare Part D provides a voluntary insurance program for prescription drugs. Although Congress and several administrations had struggled for four decades to provide a drug benefit, it was finally enacted with the Medicare Prescription Drug, Improvement, and Modernization Act of 2003. Under the original Bush administration proposal, the program was introduced as a cost-savings measure to incentivize migration from fee-for-service to Part C plans. Ultimately, congressional concerns that this proposal was a thinly veiled privatization effort, combined with the lack of Part C programs in rural areas, led Congress to make the benefit universal.[33] Plans differ significantly on levels of coverage and premiums. As with Part B, higher income households pay income-related premiums. After beneficiaries pay a deductible, they pay a copayment or coinsurance, both of which vary by plan. Medicare Part D is financed through a combination of premiums and general revenues.[34]

Reform debates commonly treat Medicare and Medicaid as separable. Medicare provides healthcare for the elderly whereas Medicaid is provided on a means-tested basis. But the two programs are tightly intertwined for beneficiaries who qualify for both programs. The dual eligible population usually attains this status through one of two pathways. First, Medicaid recipients become eligible for Medicare at age 65, but given their incomes, Medicaid covers some or all of enrollees' premiums, deductibles, and copayments. The other major pathway involves those who are enrolled in Medicare through age or disability and then become eligible for Medicaid as their resources are depleted by high medical costs or the need for institutional care. Medicaid has been of particular importance for those requiring long-term care. Medicare A and B will cover some medical costs, but Medicaid is responsible for long-term residential care beyond the 100-day limit provided by Medicare. As a result, Medicaid is the primary payer for nursing home care, covering 62 percent of residents.[35] The levels of support provided to dual-eligible beneficiaries is something of an uneven patchwork. While Medicare has uniform standards and benefit packages, there is a good deal of variation in Medicaid eligibility rules and benefits on a state-by-state basis.[36]

Financing Medicare and the Trust Funds

The financial structure of Medicare is more complicated than Social Security. Medicare Part A is funded primarily through the payroll tax and operates on a pay-as-you go basis, much like Social Security, with surpluses credited to the Hospital Insurance (HI) Trust Fund as special-issue securities. The Supplementary Medical Insurance (or SMI) Trust Fund consists of two accounts for Part B and Part D, both of which rely on premiums and transfers from the general fund. Between fiscal years 1967 and 1973, the costs of Part B were split equally between premiums and general revenues. Subsequent changes in the matching formula have increased the reliance on general revenues (e.g., in 2020, premiums covered 25.5 percent of Part B costs for enrollees aged 65 and older, and 21.5 percent for those who were disabled and under the age of 65, with the remainder drawn from general revenues).[37] The Part B account does not rely heavily on income from the assets in the SMI Trust Fund. On an annual basis, the Secretary of HHS sets the premiums for Part B and the general revenue contributions to cover the benefit costs. Thus, while the costs of Part B have increased steadily over time and are projected to increase well into the future, the program remains relatively stable. For the Part D account, premiums cover a minority of the costs (28.9 percent) with the remainder coming from general revenues.[38] Like the Part B account, the Part D account will maintain its balance for an indefinite period. Part C plans draw from the HI and the SMI trust funds to cover expenses.

The Problem of Cost and Long-Term Insolvency

For Social Security and Medicare, concerns have focused on the long-term adequacy of the trust funds. The difficulty faced by the trust funds is relatively straightforward, given demographic trends. There are some 73 million baby boomers, born between 1946 and 1964, and all will have crossed the age threshold for Social Security and Medicare by 2031. While the population has aged, the fertility rate has fallen below 1.7 children per woman, well under the replacement rate of 2.1 children per woman. As a result, by 2034, the over 65 population will be larger than the under 18 population.[39] These trends are commonly expressed as the age dependency ratio (i.e., the number of people aged 65 and above, divided by the number of people aged 20 to 65). Between 1945 and 2015, the age dependency ratio essentially doubled from 0.124 to 0.247. That is, by 2015, there were 24.7 elderly individuals for every 100 working-age Americans. The Social Security Trustees project that the age dependency ratio will continue to increase until it peaks in 2080, at which point there will be 43.6 elderly individuals for every 100 working-age Americans.[40] A larger population of beneficiaries translates into higher levels of outlays while a relatively smaller population of payroll taxpayers translates into reduced revenues.

The Social Security Trustees are required by law to report annually to Congress on the status of the trust funds and calculate the 75-year actuarial deficit. While the trust funds accumulated significant surpluses over the course of the past several decades, costs surpassed revenues in 2021. The combined OASDI trust fund is projected to be insolvent by 2034.[41] The Trustees urged Congress to

> address the projected trust fund shortfalls in a timely way in order to phase in necessary changes gradually and give workers and beneficiaries time to adjust to them. Implementing changes sooner rather than later would allow more generations to share in the needed revenue increases or reductions in scheduled benefits.[42]

What will happen if the trust funds became insolvent? The Social Security Act provides little guidance in answering this question. It establishes that individuals who meet the program's eligibility requirements are entitled to benefits and requires that they be paid only from the trust funds. Should the trust funds be insufficient to cover the costs of the benefits, however, the Treasury would not have the legal authority to issue full benefits under the Antideficiency Act, thereby forcing benefit cuts.[43] Congress could amend the Social Security Act to authorize a draw on general revenues. But without such a change, according to the Trustees, the payroll tax will be sufficient to cover a projected 78 percent of benefits.[44]

In Medicare, concerns have focused on the adequacy of the trust funds and the escalating costs. Between 1990 and 2019, Medicare outlays grew from $95.8 billion to $643.9 billion; in inflation-adjusted dollars, this has been an increase of more than 400 percent. As a share of spending, Medicare expanded from 7.6 to 14.5 percent of federal outlays.[45] The Congressional Budget Office (CBO) projects that Medicare spending would grow from 3.5 percent of GDP (2020) to an average of 4.1 percent of GDP (2026–2030), increasing to 5.9 percent of GDP by 2052.[46] However, the long-term healthcare costs of the COVID-19 pandemic increase the uncertainty connected with any projections of the future.

Cost escalation is important because, unlike Social Security, Medicare draws on the general fund to support the non-compulsory parts of the program. When Congress passed the Medicare Modernization Act of 2003, it required the Trustees to issue a warning letter if the reliance on general revenues became excessive. Under the provisions of the statute, the president would be required to submit legislation responding to the warning within 15 days of submitting a budget, which would then be considered by Congress under expedited procedures. The Trustees issued warning letters annually between 2006 and 2013, and annually since 2018. President George W. Bush submitted a legislative proposal in 2008, but Congress failed to act on it. Since that time, the funding warning has failed to generate either legislative proposals or legislative action.[47]

The Medicare Board of Trustees also compiles an annual report on the financial operations and actuarial status of the trust funds. The HI trust fund supporting Medicare Part A never attained the kinds of surpluses that were available to Social Security. On July 1, 1966, some 19 million individuals automatically became beneficiaries; unlike Social Security, they had not spent their working lives to prefund future healthcare costs. "Medicare's structure precluded it from experiencing a 'grace period' in which its trust funds could build up some measure of reserves from previous surpluses," Rick Mayes notes. As a result, it "began operation as a genuine 'pay as you go' system."[48] The Medicare Trustees project annual deficits until the HI trust fund is depleted in 2026. As with Social Security, there is no statutory authority to draw on the general fund. Absent legislative action, revenues would cover 90 percent of expenditures, a figure which would fall to 78 percent by 2044.[49] Unlike the HI trust fund, the SMI trust fund cannot become insolvent. Premiums and the transfers from the general fund of the Treasury are set on an annual basis. The primary concern is the long-term escalation of costs. The Trustees project that Part B expenditures will increase from 1.81 percent of GDP (2020) to

3.5 percent of GDP by 2094, the end of the 75-year period; Part D expenditures are projected simultaneously to increase from 0.47 percent of GDP to 0.95 percent of GDP.[50]

Taken as a whole, Social Security and Medicare raise three profound challenges for policymakers. First, as trust fund surpluses are depleted, redemptions will require transfers from the general fund of the Treasury. These transfers will need to be covered through higher tax rates, reductions in discretionary spending, or additional borrowing. Second, given the ongoing cost escalation in Medicare Part B and D, the pressure on the general fund will increase significantly over time, once again forcing a reliance on tax increases, greater constraints on discretionary spending, or forays into debt markets. Finally, absent statutory change that would permit financing via the general fund, both programs will be forced to reduce the level of support provided to beneficiaries, thereby increasing the level of insecurity for the elderly. Assuming that deep cuts would be politically difficult to impose, one can anticipate that the gap between the payroll tax and program expenditures would fall on the general fund, which could further add to the draw on debt markets.

The Budget Process and Discretionary Spending

Discretionary spending, that portion of expenditures determined by annual congressional appropriations, includes some 30 percent of federal outlays. The institutional framework for discretionary spending was established with the Congressional Budget Act or CBA (Titles I–IX of the Congressional Budget and Impoundment Act of 1974). On the institutional side, the CBA established budget committees in the House and Senate to coordinate the budget process and to develop spending targets. Prior to the passage of the Act, Congress had been dependent on the economic projections provided by the OMB, the Council of Economic Advisors, and the Treasury, all of which were under the control of the president. The CBA remedied this situation by creating a new CBO, staffed with professional economists and analysts. The CBO informs deliberations by providing Congress, on an ongoing basis, with estimates of the budgetary implications of bills approved by House or Senate committees. It also is required to produce, on an annual basis, baseline budget and economic projections for the next ten years in its *Budget and Economic Outlook*, based on current laws and reasonable assumptions about future economic conditions. It also produces, once again on an annual basis, the *Long-Term Budget Outlook* covering the next thirty years, to place exiting policies in the context of long-term trends and discuss policy alternatives.[51] As Philip G. Joyce observes, the CBO's "highest profile situations" have occurred "when the executive has proposed a change in policy and CBO has been asked to analyze it. This is the strongest indication that the main goal of creating CBO—that is, to support Congress in asserting its independence from the president in the budget process—has been effectively achieved."[52]

The Budget Cycle

The CBA strengthened the role of Congress in the budget process. But the president retained a central role in shaping the budget, both as a result of the president's control of the executive branch and its vast analytical resources, and the primacy of the president's budget in the overall budget process. The development of the president's budget, as the OMB explains,

> involves the simultaneous consideration of the resource needs of individual programs, the allocation of resources among the agencies and functions of the Federal Government, and the total outlays and receipts that are appropriate in light of current and prospective economic conditions.

The budget estimates are heavily impacted by the underlying economic and technical assumptions (e.g., projected economic growth rates, inflation, interest rates, unemployment, and the number of people eligible to participate in major programs). The executive budget formulation process is a protracted affair, which begins roughly 18 months before the start of the relevant budget year. As one might expect, the extended timetable forces ongoing revisions of underlying assumptions, small changes which can change estimates by billions of dollars.[53]

In the late spring of the year preceding transmission to Congress, the OMB and other actors in the Executive Office of the President work with department and agency heads to develop priorities and evaluate the adequacy of existing budgets; economic projections developed by the OMB, the CEA, and the Treasury are incorporated into the development of budgetary aggregates and planning totals. These are used as guidance by agencies as they prepare their budget requests, which are submitted for review to the OMB in the early fall. Given that appropriations for the next fiscal year have not occurred at this point, the agency actions are made in an environment of uncertainty about congressional actions. *The Budget of the United States Government* contains a statement of the president's policy goals ("the budget message"), a multi-volume appendix with detailed requests for the "budget year" (the relevant fiscal year) and supporting materials. The president is required by law to submit the budget no later than the first Monday in February, although there is some flexibility during presidential transitions. The president also submits a Mid-Session Review by July 15, to update requests in light of changes in economic conditions and law.[54]

While the president's budget remains important as a statement of the administration's policies, its status has fluctuated over time. In the immediate postwar decades, Congress showed deference to the president's budget as a statement of national policy. Changes, where they occurred, were relatively marginal. The primacy of the president's budget declined following the passage of the CBA. In the past several decades, Allen Schick explains,

> the president's recommendations have been little more than opening bids in a bargaining process. Rather than revealing his true preferences at the outset, the president often submits unrealistic proposals that have no chance of adoption and whose main function is to position him for the tough negotiations at the end of the process.[55]

The change has reflected several factors, including the growth of mandatory spending that necessarily constrains presidential aspirations, the growing institutional capacity of Congress in the post reform era, the role of the CBO in providing baseline projections that are independent of those reflected in the president's budget, and the heightened role of interest groups and media that actively monitor the budget process and provide critiques of, and alternatives to, the president's proposals.

The Congressional Budget Process

Following the submission of the president's budget, the congressional stage of the budget process commences. The relative centralization of the executive budget process can be contrasted with Congress, which has remained highly fragmented. With competing political parties, a decentralized structure with multiple access points for a diversity of mobilized interests, and the electoral goals of individual actors, the outcome of the congressional budget process remains highly uncertain. While the CBA sought to impose order by creating a timetable for executing various functions before the start of the new fiscal year, Congress has failed to meet its obligations on a regular basis, forcing a reliance on continuing resolutions as a means of temporarily funding government to prevent a funding gap that could force a government shutdown.

The Budget Committees integrate several factors in evaluating the president's proposal. The CBO provides its projections on the budget and economic outcomes (the *Budget and Economic Outlook*). Standing committees submit their "views and estimates" reports, which inform the Budget Committees about potential new spending legislation and the budgetary demands of ongoing programs in their jurisdictions. Following hearings, the Budget Committees report a budget resolution and, by April 15, a concurrent budget resolution. Under the CBA, there was a series of two budget resolutions: a first resolution passed in May and a second, binding resolution, which was to be passed by September 15. By 1980, when it was clear that this calendar was unworkable, the first resolution was considered binding and the second resolution was abandoned, for reasons that will be discussed below.

The budget resolution reports budget aggregates and provides Section 302 (a) allocations of spending authority (named after the relevant section of the CBA) to the House and Senate Appropriations Committees, with allocations by budgetary function and subfunction. It also reports the total revenue, the resulting deficit/surplus, and implications for the debt. Social Security receipts and outlays are not included in the resolution. The Appropriations Committees, subsequently, provide Section 302 (b) allocations to their subcommittees to set limits on the spending authority in their appropriation bills for substantive issue areas (e.g., "Agriculture, Rural Development, Food and Drug Administration, and Related Agencies; Interior, Environment, and Related Agencies").[56] By design, the budgetary process should culminate in the passage of the appropriations bills prior to the beginning of the new fiscal year.[57] Even though the CBA changed the beginning of the fiscal year from July 1 to October 1 to provide Congress with more time to complete its work, as will be noted below, this deadline has proven elusive.

Direct or mandatory spending is not formally subject to the appropriations process. Most entitlement spending is provided automatically via permanent appropriations in the authorizing legislation. For "appropriated" entitlements like Medicaid, Congress must provide funding through the appropriation process but does not have the discretionary authority to allocate less than is required to meet its obligations. Nonetheless, the budget process can have significant implications for these programs through the reconciliation process.[58] Budget resolutions may include reconciliation instructions that direct specific committees to propose revisions in revenue or mandatory spending laws to meet budgetary targets. While reconciliation was originally conceived "as a comparatively minor fallback mechanism for reconciling one year's tax and spending policy with budget targets," George Hager explains, by the 1990s it "mushroomed into Congress' most powerful deficit reduction tool."[59] Under the CBA, reconciliation was one of the final stages in the budget process, occurring in late September. But as concerns with the deficit grew, reconciliation was applied to the first resolution, thereby making the figures in that resolution binding if no second resolution was passed and rendering the second resolution moot.[60] By the 2000s, deficit control had been largely abandoned and reconciliation had evolved to be the vehicle of choice in passing tax cuts, as will be explained in Chapter 3.

When there are reconciliation instructions, the committees of jurisdiction submit the resulting legislation to the Budget Committees, which are barred from making any substantive changes. If reconciliation instructions were sent to multiple committees, the resulting legislation may be combined to create a single omnibus reconciliation bill, thereby facilitating subsequent consideration on the floor of the two chambers. There has been great variation in reconciliation instructions since the passage of the CBA. Some have been relatively modest, reinforcing the policy status quo. But the scope of reconciliation instructions can be remarkably broad, involving multiple committees, seeking significant changes in spending and revenue, and using the expedited process to pursue a policy agenda that would flounder under the normal legislative process.[61] The first clear sign that reconciliation could be used to make broad and substantial policy changes came with the Omnibus Budget Reconciliation Act (OBRA) of 1981, which cut federal expenditures by more than $130 billion over three years and targeted key social welfare programs, including food stamps, Aid to Families with Dependent Children (AFDC), Medicaid, school lunches, and public housing. As Lance T. LeLoup wrote, "the events of 1981 demonstrated that the new congressional budget process, designed to strengthen Congress vis-à-vis the president, could in fact be a powerful tool for presidential leadership given disciplined, supportive majorities in both houses."[62]

The temptation to use reconciliation as a means of achieving significant changes in mandatory programs is a product of the simple fact that the consideration of reconciliation bills is fast-tracked. In the House, the Rules Committee will issue a special rule limiting the time for debate and the number and scope of the amendments. In the Senate, more importantly, debate is limited to 20 hours, thereby forestalling the use of the filibuster and the need for a supermajority of 60 votes to bring the bill to a vote. In 1985 and 1986, the Senate adopted the so-called Byrd rule, named after Senator Robert C. Byrd (D-WV), the architect of the CBA, as a means of limiting the consideration of non-budgetary matters during reconciliation. It was Byrd's contention that the reconciliation process, if used improperly, could short-circuit Senate norms and undermine careful consideration of important substantive policy issues. As Byrd noted in 1985, the budget process had become "a Pandora's box which has been opened to the abuse of the reconciliation process….if we are going to preserve the deliberative process," which was "the outstanding, unique element" of the Senate, "action must be taken now to stop this abuse of the budget process."[63] The Byrd rule was made permanent with the Budget Enforcement Act, Title XIII of OBRA 1990.

Under the Byrd rule, a senator can raise a point of order against extraneous matters in reconciliation bills. After consultation with the Senate Parliamentarian, the presiding officer can strike extraneous provisions unless the Byrd rule is waived by three-fifths of the Senate. A provision can be considered extraneous under several criteria. Obviously, provisions that do not result in changes in revenues or expenditures (or the conditions under which revenues are generated or outlays are made) would be considered extraneous. Related, changes in revenues and outlays cannot be merely incidental to the non-budgetary components. Provisions are also considered extraneous if they result in changes that are not in compliance with the reconciliation instructions. Provisions must be in the jurisdiction of the relevant committees. Provisions are also considered extraneous if they recommend changes in Social Security (although not Medicare). Provisions are also extraneous if they increase the deficit for fiscal years that are outside the "budget window" specified by the budget resolution.[64]

Budget resolutions may also include provisions for so-called deficit-neutral reserve funds. The use of the term "reserve fund" is something of a term of art, since the budget resolution does not actually provide any funds. Under the provisions of the CBA, committees receive allocations based on spending levels that are established in the budget resolution. But the resolution is based on existing law. Reserve funds are designated to adjust overall budget aggregates for specific matters, thereby providing committees with the flexibility to report new legislation without facing a point-of-order for exceeding committee allocations. Practice changed over time, as fiscal conditions changed. In the 1990s, for example, reserves had to be deficit neutral. But as the budget turned to surplus, Congress used reserves to set aside projected future surpluses for tax cuts or increased spending.[65] As Molly E, Reynolds explains, while these reserve funds occasionally serve a purpose, "they have largely come to be seen as symbolic measures," a means for members of Congress "to signal that action in a particular policy area is important to them."[66] While reserve funds were initially used sparingly, by the FY2016 budget resolution, the Senate approved no fewer than 183 reserve funds. As Alice M. Rivlin and Pete Domenici note, "Reserve funds are effectively 'Sense of the Congress' resolutions that … allow members of Congress to be for a politically popular program or activity without addressing how to fund the activity."[67]

Congressional Budgeting versus the Deficit

During the 1980s, growing partisan conflict and record peacetime deficits forced Congress to develop new procedures for budgeting. As Paul L. Posner explains: "Members needed more formal institutions to enable them to make the hard choices and trade-offs that once were embedded in folkways, centrist coalitions, and other informal institutional arrangements."[68] These rules, layered on top of those established under the CBA, made the process of budgeting more complex. The first significant attempt to alter the process came with the Balanced Budget and Emergency Deficit Control Act or Gramm-Rudman-Hollings Act (GRH) of 1985. GRH established declining deficit limits, with the goal of achieving a balanced budget in 1991. The Act created a rather complex enforcement mechanism. In the event that a joint report by the CBO and OMB concluded that the deficit limit had been breached, the Comptroller General of the General Accounting Office would issue a report to the president that would result in an order for mandatory across-the-board sequestration. When the role assigned to the Comptroller General (formally part of the legislative branch) was declared unconstitutional, Congress amended GRH so that the OMB would trigger sequestration.[69] It also provided new set of deficit targets, with the goal of achieving a balanced budget by 1993.[70]

GRH had its origins in the Republican-controlled Senate and was fast-tracked without extended debate. When the proposal moved to the Democratic House, there were concerns that sequestration would cut most deeply in social spending, which had been targeted for reductions by the Reagan administration, placing these programs and their constituencies at a strategic disadvantage. As Darrell M. West explains: "The combination of automatic, across-the-board cuts and the disproportionate amount of social welfare dollars in the federal budget meant that either Reagan or Republicans in general could employ the strategy of delay and deadlock to their own partisan advantage." They could "fall back on a procedural device that would reduce social welfare spending more than military expenditures."[71] In response, Democrats exempted key social programs from sequestration (e.g., Social Security, Medicaid, AFDC, Supplemental Security Income, food stamps, various nutrition programs) and subjected others to limited sequestration (e.g., Medicare, veterans' medical care). It required that sequestration would fall equally between defense and non-defense discretionary spending.

The extent to which GRH could yield significant deficit reduction was severely compromised from the beginning. The fixed deficit reduction targets proved overly rigid and created incentives to engage in various forms of budget gimmickry while the decision to exempt the largest mandatory programs necessarily limited GRH's impact. As CBO Direct Robert D. Reischauer notes,

> sequestration turned out to be something of a toothless tiger, defanged by optimistic economic and technical assumptions, accounting gimmicks and changes in the deficit targets....GRH may have taken taxes and entitlements off the table, thereby increasing the chances that discretionary programs would absorb most of whatever adjustment occurred.[72]

Ultimately, dissatisfaction with the process and the repeated failure to meet deficit targets led to its abandonment.

Following a budget summit, President Bush and congressional leaders agreed on a new mechanism for deficit reduction. The resulting legislation—the Budget Enforcement Act (BEA) of 1990—was passed as part of OBRA 1990. It imposed spending caps on domestic, defense, and international discretionary spending for the next three years, FY 1991–1993. If the caps were breached in one of the categories, sequestration would occur only within that category, thereby limiting the ability of Congress to shift cuts to the defense budget. For FY 1994–1995, the final two years covered by the BEA, Congress would work with a single cap for all of discretionary spending. The spending limits could be adjusted to reflect changes in budget concepts and definitions, inflation, and emergencies. As for mandatory spending and taxation, the BEA introduced "pay-as-you-go" or PAYGO procedures. On an annual basis, new legislation that increased mandatory spending or reduced revenues would have to be accompanied by provisions that rendered the effects deficit neutral. The OMB would record the budgetary effects of changes in revenue and direct spending program on a PAYGO scorecard. Where a debit existed at the end of the session, the OMB would force sequestration in non-exempt mandatory programs. The system established under the BEA was extended, with some modifications and new discretionary spending caps, by OBRA 1993 and the Budget Enforcement Act of 1997. With this latter Act, PAYGO was extended to 2002.[73]

While the new discretionary caps were preferable to the GRH deficit targets, the new process had some clear limitations. With respect to discretionary spending, the caps were grounded in a presumption that spending would be reduced in real terms, insofar as they were increased at a rate below inflation. Moreover, there was no mechanism by which increases in discretionary spending could be offset by increases in revenues.[74] As for PAYGO, it only applied to new mandatory spending rather than to the growth in spending authorized by earlier statutes. Thus, the process would not provide a means of addressing the growth in the programs that were claiming an increasing share of federal outlays. The same rule existed for revenues that fell as a result of previously enacted legislation. As with GRH, key programs were exempt from sequestration or given partial exemptions.

Finally, the BEA's provisions—like those of GRH before it—proved to be subject to various forms of strategic avoidance. The timing of changes in tax and spending programs could be manipulated to veil their budgetary implications; normal expenditures could be moved off budget (as supplemental or emergency appropriations). Scoring—the process of estimating the budgetary effects of new legislation—became "a valued political art."[75] Indeed, as deficits turned to surpluses, Congress waived some of the strictures of the BEA, on several occasions mandating via statute that the balances on the PAYGO scorecards be set to zero. To be a bit more charitable, one might argue that the BEA embodied conflicting notions of budgeting. If deficits are all that matter, then the imposition of caps to control budgetary aggregates made great sense. But as Joseph White notes, any budgetary rule "that ignores programmatic consequences essentially removes the reason to budget (or govern) at all."[76] By the late 1990s, under conditions of growing surpluses, Congress could no longer subordinate the impact that the caps were having on the integrity of government programs. The provisions of the BEA were allowed to expire in 2002 and the balances for the PAYGO scorecard were statutorily set to zero, thereby bringing an end to sequestration. Congress and President Obama would resurrect PAYGO with the Statutory Pay-As-You-Go Act of 2010, but once again, its impacts have been limited by Congress requiring that some new spending not be recorded in the PAYGO scorecard. For example, the series of statutes passed in 2020 in response to the COVID-19 pandemic explicitly stated that the trillions of dollars in new spending would not be entered on the PAYGO scorecards (or in the case of the American Rescue Plan Act of 2021, that they would be deferred).

A third approach to controlling deficits and reducing the debt was introduced in the Budget Control Act of 2011. The circumstances leading up to the passage of the Act were somewhat complicated and will be discussed in some detail in Chapter 8. For present purposes, the Act empowered a Joint Committee on Deficit Reduction to propose \$1.2–\$1.5 trillion cuts in spending in exchange for increases in the debt ceiling. Under the Act, if the Committee failed in this task (which it did), the debt ceiling would be raised, but this would trigger multi-year caps on discretionary spending (divided equally between defense and non-defense spending) backed by sequestration over the period 2013–2021, to achieve the \$1.2 trillion spending reductions. As with earlier efforts, the Budget Control Act exempted key social programs from sequestration.[77] Sequestration, as envisioned under the Act, failed to have the intended impact on congressional spending decisions. While members of the House and Senate could rarely find sufficient agreement to pass annual appropriations bills in a timely fashion—if at all—they could agree that the targets set by the Budget Control Act were unachievable. As a result, Congress simply raised the spending caps repeatedly and extended sequestration into the future.

The record of deficit controls attempted through procedural mechanisms illustrates a fundamental problem. Congress will abide by the rules it designs for itself to the extent that they are compatible with the underlying incentive structure. In the words of Roy T. Meyers, "rules fail because they are endogenous to the political institutions that wrote them, meaning that they can be changed whenever the institutions want. Rules that would produce politically uncomfortable results are more likely to be changed."[78] In the 1980s, GRH could be avoided through budgetary gimmicks, customized assumptions, and rosy economic scenarios. While the BEA was more successful, it was jettisoned as budget deficits turned to surpluses and within a decade, the gains of the 1990s had been vanquished. The Budget Control Act aspired to reverse the trajectory and reduce the debt, but Congress repeatedly raised spending caps to avoid the constraints it imposed on itself. In 1985, when Congress enacted GRH, federal outlays were 22.2 percent of GDP. While this figure would fall in the 1990s, by 2019, outlays had grown to 21 percent of GDP.[79] The history of the debt during this period does not reveal a comparable level of stability. In 1985, the debt held by the public was equal to 35.3 percent of GDP. When Congress passed the Budget Control Act, the debt stood at 65 percent of GDP, and by 2019, the eve of the COVID-19 pandemic, it had grown to 79.4 percent of GDP.[80] This suggests that the driver of the debt may be less a story of expenditures than it is a story of taxation, the subject of Chapter 3.

The Budgetary Process in Disarray

The budget process provided a means of disaggregating the task of budgeting for discretionary spending so that discrete decisions could be subjected to debate, oversight, and democratic accountability. However, "regular order," wherein a budget resolution is followed by the consideration and passage of individual appropriations bills by the House and Senate before the start of the fiscal year, has been largely abandoned and replaced with a disorderly process (if the term *process* can be applied at all). The evidence is overwhelming. Although the CBA set a target of April 15 for the passage of a budget resolution, this date has rarely been met. Of greater concern, since 1998 Congress has frequently failed to adopt a formal budget resolution at all (see Table 2.1).[81] Under the CBA, the appropriations bills are to be passed before the start of the fiscal year on

TABLE 2.1 Budget Resolutions and Appropriations, FY 1990–2022

Fiscal Year	*Budget resolution (date of passage)*	*Appropriations bills enacted before FY*	*Continuing resolutions*	*Supplemental appropriations*
1990	05-18-1989	1	3	2
1991	10-09-1990	0	5	3
1992	05-22-1991	3	4	3
1993	05-21-1992	1	1	4
1994	04-01-1993	2	3	7
1995	05-12-1994	13	0	0
1996	06-29-1995	0	13	4
1997	06-13-1996	8	0	1
1998	06-05-1997	1	6	1
1999	None	1	6	2
2000	04-15-1999	4	7	2
2001	04-13-2000	2	21	2
2002	05-10-2001	0	8	2
2003	None	0	8	3
2004	04-11-2003	3	5	3
2005	None	1	3	6
2006	04-28-2005	2	3	3
2007	None	1	4	1
2008	05-17-2007	0	4	2
2009	06-05-2008	0	2	2
2010	04-29-2009	1	2	3
2011	None	0	8	0
2012	None	0	5	0
2013	None	0	2	1
2014	None	0	4	1
2015	None	0	5	0
2016	05-05-2015	0	3	1

(continued)

TABLE 2.1 Cont.

Fiscal Year	*Budget resolution (date of passage)*	*Appropriations bills enacted before FY*	*Continuing resolutions*	*Supplemental appropriations*
2017	01-13-2017*	0	3	1
2018	10-26-2017	0	5	2
2019	None	5	3	2
2020	None	0	2	5
2021	02-05-2021	0	5	2
2022	08-24-2021	0	4	9

*Congress passed a "shell" budget resolution for 2017 without totals to initiate reconciliation process.

Source: Vital Statistics on Congress (Brookings Institution, 2021), Tables 7.2, 7.5, and 7.6. Congressional Budget Office, *Supplemental Appropriations Enacted Since Fiscal Year 2000.* Congressional Research Service, Appropriations Status Table, various years.

October 1. But the full set of appropriations bills was last enacted by the start of the fiscal year in 1995. Performance was particularly dismal in subsequent decades. Four appropriations bills were enacted on time for FY2000. Since that time, most years have witnessed no appropriations bills passed before the start of the fiscal year.[82] Absent appropriations bills, Congress must rely on continuing resolutions to extend temporary funding or risk a government shutdown. In the 1980s, government shutdowns occurred on four occasions, each lasting a single day. During the 1990s, shutdowns were more protracted. Of the four shutdowns, the most significant occurred in 1995–1996, extending 21 days, as President Clinton and the GOP majority battled over spending priorities. The government shutdown of 2013 lasted 16 days. Five years later during the Trump administration, two shutdowns (2018 and again in 2018–2019) lasted a combined 38 days.[83]

The repeated failure of Congress to meet the deadlines established in the CBA reflects several factors. The budget process is primarily concerned with discretionary spending—a declining share of federal outlays. As discretionary spending shrank as a share of outlays and as a share of GDP, the budget process became increasingly conflictive. The decision to fund one set of programs had consequences for the resources available for other programs. The conflicts, unsurprisingly, transformed the passage of budget resolutions and the enactment of appropriations bills into protracted struggles. The routine failure of Congress to meet the deadlines established in the CBA was undoubtedly a product, at least in part, of this dynamic. A second factor involves the various procedural remedies described above to control the deficit and debt. Under the CBA, Congress expanded its capacity to engage in fiscal policymaking, thereby reducing its deference to the executive branch. The budget resolution was the primary vehicle for coordinating Congress's fiscal policymaking activities.

The changes enacted in GRH and, to a greater extent, the BEA of 1990, had important ramifications for the balance of power. The changes in process shifted power from Congress to the president by elevating the role of the president and the OMB in monitoring spending and imposing sequestration. Within a decade, Congress had reclaimed the power of the purse and ceded ground to the executive. On the intra-institutional dimension, the Budget Committees' power was compromised by the agreement to impose multi-year discretionary spending caps negotiated between the leadership of the two chambers and the president.[84] As a result of the procedural changes, their role was diminished, and the locus of decision-making moved to the Appropriations Committees. As *Congressional Quarterly* noted in 2018, "The Budget Committees have so visibly lost clout in recent years that the suggestion is now being made that the panels should be abolished."[85]

Conclusion

In an ideal world, decisions about spending would reflect a larger normative judgment about the government's role in society, one that reflects democratic deliberation and the constraints imposed by revenues. In an ideal world, decisions would be made under conditions of transparency and accountability such that the tradeoffs they entail would be evident to all. This ideal world, alas, does not exist. As the largest of the mandatory programs have matured, expanded, and become more important in providing protections against the risks of the life and business cycle, they have placed significant pressure on discretionary spending. Congress could respond by reforming mandatory programs, a decision that would carry high political costs even under the best of circumstances. As the zero-sum nature of discretionary spending and growing polarization have eroded regular order, there is little evidence that Congress can execute the basic function established under Article I Section 8 of the Constitution: "to provide for the common defense and general welfare of the United States," not to mention the more difficult tasks of reform. Alternatively, it could turn to the revenue side of the ledger and raise new taxes. Chapter 3 explores the issue of taxation.

Notes

1 Peter R. Fisher, "Beyond Borrowing: Meeting the Government's Financial Challenges in the 21st Century," Remarks of Under Secretary of the Treasury Peter R. Fisher to the Columbus Council on World Affairs, Columbus, Ohio." Available at www.treasury.gov/press-center/press-releases/Pages/po3622.aspx

2 Office of Management and Budget (OMB), *Budget of the U.S. Government, Fiscal Year 2023* (Washington, DC: Government Publishing Office, 2022), Historical Tables, Table 1.2.

3 Ibid., Table 1.3 and U.S. Census Bureau, Decennial Census of Population and Housing. Available at www.census.gov/programs-surveys/decennial-census/decade.html. Calculations by author.
4 OECD, Government at a Glance 2017 (Paris: OECD Publishing, 2017), 74. Data available at http://dx.doi.org/10.1787/888933531820
5 Ibid., 77. Data available at http://dx.doi.org/10.1787/888933534784
6 See Christopher Howard, *The Welfare State Nobody Knows: Debunking Myths About U.S. Social Policy* (Princeton: Princeton University Press, 2007).
7 See Kenneth N. Bickers, "The Programmatic Expansion of the U.S. Government," *Western Political Quarterly,* 44,4 (1991): 891–914.
8 Government Accountability Office, *A Glossary of Terms Used in the Federal Budget Process,* GAO-05-734SP (Washington, DC: Government Accountability Office, 2005), 46.
9 Ibid., 66.
10 OMB, *Budget of the U.S. Government, Fiscal Year 2023,* Historical Tables, Tables 8.3 and 8.4.
11 Ibid.
12 Ibid.
13 Zachary S. Price, "Funding Restrictions and the Separation of Powers," *Vanderbilt Law Review,* 71, 2 (2018): 361.
14 Josh Chafetz, "Congress's Constitution," *University of Pennsylvania Law Review,* 160, 3 (2012): 728, 729.
15 Aaron Wildavsky, *The New Politics of the Budgetary Process,* 2nd ed. (New York: HarperCollins, 1992), 274.
16 OMB, *Budget of the U.S. Government for Fiscal Year 2023,* Historical Tables, Tables 8.3 and 8.4.
17 Data from the CBO's Long-Term Budget Outlook (2022) available at www.cbo.gov/system/files/2022-07/57971-Data.xlsx
18 See Larry DeWitt, "Origins of the Three-Legged Stool Metaphor for Social Security." Research Notes & Special Studies by the Historian's Office, Research Note Number 1. Available at www.ssa.gov/history/stool.html
19 Theda Skocpol and G. John Ikenberry, "The Road to Social Security" in Theda Skocpol, *Social Policy in the United States: Future Possibilities in Historical Perspective* (Princeton: Princeton University Press, 1995), 162.
20 Tamar Breslauer and William R. Morton, *Social Security: Major Decisions in the House and Senate Since 1935,* CRS Report RL30920 (Washington, DC: Congressional Research Service, 2021), 14.
21 Social Security Administration, "Social Security Beneficiary Statistics," available at www.ssa.gov/OACT/STATS/OASDIbenies.html, and Social Security Administration, "Fact Sheet," available at www.ssa.gov/news/press/factsheets/basicfact-alt.pdf
22 Social Security Administration, FY 2021 President's Budget, Tables i.4 and i.5. Available at www.ssa.gov/budget/FY21Files/2021BST.pdf
23 This discussion draws on Barry F. Huston, *Social Security: The Trust Funds,* CRS Report for Congress, RL33028 (Washington, DC: Congressional Research Service, 2019), 8–9, CBO, *Social Security Policy Options, 2015* (Washington, DC: Congressional Budget Office, 2015), 13–15, and Social Security Administration, "Primary Insurance Amount," available at www.ssa.gov/oact/cola/piaformula.html

24 See Julie M. Whittaker, *Social Security: Cost-of-Living Adjustments*, CRS Report for Congress, 94–803 (Washington, DC: Congressional Research Service, 2017).
25 This discussion draws on Huston, *Social Security.*
26 Federal spending draws on two groups of funds: federal funds and trust funds. The federal funds group is dominated by the general fund, which is financed largely by the individual and corporate income tax. In contrast, the trust funds are financed through taxes that are legally dedicated to a specific purpose (e.g., the payroll tax is dedicated to the Old-Age Survivors and Disability Insurance or OASDI trust funds). By law, the revenues that are assigned to trust funds cannot be comingled with the general fund. See Chapter 4.
27 See Rosemary Stevens and Robert Stevens, "Medicaid: Anatomy of a Dilemma," *Law and Contemporary Problems*, 35, 2 (1970): 359–63.
28 This discussion draws on "An Overview of Medicare," *Issue Brief, November 2017* (Washington, DC: The Henry J. Kaiser Family Foundation, 2017) and B. Guy Peters, *American Public Policy: Promise and Performance*, 10th ed. (Los Angeles: Congressional Quarterly, 2016), 281–84.
29 "2020 Medicare Parts A and B Premiums and Deductibles." (Washington, DC: Centers for Medicare & Medicaid Services, 2020). Available at www.cms.gov/newsroom/fact-sheets/2020-medicare-parts-b-premiums-and-deductibles
30 Ibid.
31 Timothy Stoltzfus Jost, "Governing Medicare," *Administrative Law Review*, 51, 1 (1999): 44–45.
32 See Thomas G. McGuire, Joseph P. Newhouse, and Anna D. Sinaiko, "An Economic History of Medicare Part C," *The Milbank Quarterly*, 89, 2 (2011): 293–332.
33 See Thomas R. Oliver, Philip R. Lee, and Helen Lipton, "A Political History of Medicare and Prescription Drug Coverage," *The Milbank Review*, 82, 2 (2004): 283–54.
34 "An Overview of Medicare." Information on premiums, costs and coverage from Drug Coverage (Part D). Available at www.medicare.gov/part-d/index.html
35 "Medicaid's Role in Nursing Home Care," KFF June 20, 2017. Available at www.kff.org/infographic/medicaids-role-in-nursing-home-care/
36 Medicare Payment Advisory Commission and the Medicaid and CHIP Payment and Access Commission (MACPAC), *Beneficiaries Dually Eligible for Medicare and Medicaid Data Book* (Washington, DC: MACPAC, 2018), 4.
37 Board of Trustees for the Federal Hospital Insurance and Federal Supplementary Medical Insurance Trust Funds, *The 2020 Annual Report of the Board of Trustees for the Federal Hospital Insurance and Federal Supplementary Medical Insurance Trust Funds* (Washington, DC: Government Publishing Office, 2020), 79.
38 Ibid., 103.
39 "By 2030, All Baby Boomers Will Be Age 65 or Older: 2020 Census Will Help Policymakers Prepare for the Incoming Wave of Aging Boomers," U.S. Census Bureau, December 10, 2019. Available at www.census.gov/library/stories/2019/12/by-2030-all-baby-boomers-will-be-age-65-or-older.html
40 Board of Trustees, Federal Old-Age and Survivors Insurance and Federal Disability Insurance Trust Funds, *The 2020 Annual Report of the Board of Trustees of the Federal Old-Age and Survivors Insurance and Federal Disability Insurance Trust Funds* (Washington, DC: Government Publishing Office, 2020), 95.
41 Board of Trustees of the Federal Old-Age and Survivors Insurance and Disability Insurance Trust Funds, *2021 Annual Report, Federal Old-Age and Survivors Insurance*

and Disability Insurance Trust Fund (Washington, DC: Government Publishing Office, 2021), 4–6.

42 Ibid., 1–4, 5.

43 Barry F. Huston and William R. Morton, *Social Security: What Would Happen If the Trust Funds Ran Out?* CRS Report RL33514 (Washington, DC: Congressional Research Service, 2019), 10.

44 Board of Trustees (Social Security), *The 2021 Annual Report,* 4.

45 OMB, *Budget of the United States Government, Fiscal Year 2023,* Historical Tables, Tables 8.1, 8.2, and 8.3. Data from the CBO's Long-Term Budget Outlook (2022) available at www.cbo.gov/system/files/2022-07/57971-Data.xlsx

46 CBO, *An Update to the Budget Outlook: 2020 to 2030* (Washington, DC: CBO, 2020), 20.

47 See Patricia A. Davis, Christopher M. Davis, and Todd Garvey, *Medicare Trigger,* CRS Report RS22796 (Washington, DC: Congressional Research Service, 2020).

48 Rick Mayes, "The Origins, Development, and Passage of Medicare's Revolutionary Prospective Payment System," *Journal of the History of Medicine and Allied Sciences* 62, 1 (2007), 25–26.

49 The Board of Trustees, Federal Hospital Insurance and Federal Supplementary Medical Insurance Trust Funds, *2020 Annual Report of the Board of Trustees of the Federal Hospital Insurance and Federal Supplementary Medical Insurance Trust Funds* (Washington, DC: Government Publishing Office, 2020), 10, 40–44. Patricia A. Davis, *Medicare: Insolvency Projections,* CRS Report RS20946 (Washington DC: Congressional Research Service, 2020), 8.

50 Ibid., 95, 118.

51 CBO, "Products." Available at www.cbo.gov/about/products. See Robert D. Reischauer, "Getting, Using, and Misusing Economic Information," in *Making Economic Policy in Congress*, ed. Allen Schick (Washington, DC: American Enterprise Institute, 1983), 38–65.

52 Philip G. Joyce, *The Congressional Budget Office: Honest Numbers, Power, and Policymaking* (Washington, DC: Georgetown University Press, 2011), 209.

53 OMB, *Budget of the U.S. Government, Fiscal Year 2021* (Washington, DC: U.S. Government Publishing Office, 2020), Analytical Perspectives, 80.

54 See discussion of the formulation of the president's budget in James V. Saturno, Bill Heniff, Jr., Megan S. Lynch, and Jessica Tollestrup, *Introduction to the Federal Budget Process,* CRS Report 98-721 (Washington, DC: Congressional Research Service, 2012), 9–10, and Office of Management and Budget, *Budget of the U.S. Government, Fiscal Year 2021,* Analytical Perspectives, 79–80.

55 Schick, *The Federal Budget,* 90–91.

56 Ibid., 122–23.

57 This discussion is based on Heniff, et al., *Introduction to the Federal Budget Process.*

58 Mindy R. Levit, D. Andrew Austin, and Jeffrey M. Stupak, *Mandatory Spending Since 1962,* CRS Report RL33074 (Washington, DC: Congressional Research Service, 2015), 1–2, and Schick, *The Federal Budget,* 57–58.

59 George Hager, "The Budget: Reconciliation Now a Major Tool," *CQ Magazine,* October 28, 1995: 3286.

60 Lance T. LeLoup, *Parties, Rules, and the Evolution of Congressional Budgeting* (Columbia: The Ohio State University Press, 2005), 44, 78.

61 Schick, *The Federal Budget,* 122.

62 LeLoup, *Parties, Rules, and the Evolution of Congressional Budgeting,* 70. See Robert W. Hartman, "Congress and Budget-Making," *Political Science Quarterly,* 97, 3 (1982): 381–402, and Molly E. Reynolds, *Exceptions to the Rule: The Politics of Filibuster Limitations in the U.S. Senate* (Washington, DC: Brookings Institution Press, 2017), 79–146.

63 Quoted in Bill Heniff, Jr., *The Budget Reconciliation Process: The Senate's "Byrd Rule,"* CRS Report RL30862 (Washington, DC: Congressional Research Service, 2016), 2.

64 Heniff, *The Budget Reconciliation Process,* 3, 5.

65 See "Informed Budgeteer: Are Reserve Funds Used as Intended? S. 1: A Case Study," *Budget Bulletin,* Senate Budget Committee Republican Staff, 108th Congress, 1st Session, No. 14, 15 July 2003. Available at www.budget.senate.gov/imo/media/doc/bb14-2003.pdf.

66 Molly E. Reynolds, "Considering the Budget Resolution in the Senate: Challenges and Consequences of Reform" (Washington, DC: Center for Effective Public Management, Brookings Institution, 2017). Available at www.brookings.edu/wp-content/uploads/2017/05/gs_20170511_budget-resolutions_paper.pdf.

67 Alice M. Rivlin and Pete Domenici, *Proposal for Improving the Congressional Budget Process* (Washington, DC: Bipartisan Policy Center, 2015), 20.

68 Paul L. Posner, "Budget Process Reform: Waiting for Godot," *Public Administration Review,* 69, 2 (2009): 240.

69 *Bowsher v. Synar,* 478 U.S. (1986) 714. See Molly E. Reynolds, "The Office of Management and Budget and the Congressional Budget Process: The View from Capitol Hill," in *Executive Policymaking: The Role of the OMB in the Presidency,* ed. Meena Bose and Andrew Rudalevige (Washington, DC: Brookings Institution Press, 2020), 50.

70 This discussion draws on Megan Suzanne Lynch, *Statutory Budget Controls in Effect Between 1985 and 2002,* CRS Report R41901 (Washington, DC: Congressional Research Service, 2011), 1–8, and LeLoup, *Parties, Rules, and the Evolution of Congressional Budgeting,* 93–106.

71 Darrell M. West, "Gramm-Rudman-Hollings and the Politics of Deficit Reduction," *The Annals of the American Academy of Political and Social Science,* 499 (1988): 97.

72 Robert D. Reischauer, "Taxes and Spending under Gramm-Rudman-Hollings," *National Tax Journal,* 43, 3 (1990): 229.

73 Lynch, *Statutory Budget Controls in Effect Between 1985 and 2002,* 8–11.

74 Philip G. Joyce, "Congressional Budget Reform: The Unanticipated Implications for Federal Policy Making," *Public Administration Review,* 56, 4 (1996): 320.

75 Allen Schick, "A Surplus, If We Can Keep It: How the Federal Budget Surplus Happened," *The Brookings Review,* 18, 1 (2000): 38.

76 Joseph White, "What Not to Ask of Budget Processes," 227.

77 See Bill Heniff Jr., Elizabeth Rybicki, and Shannon M. Mahan, *The Budget Control Act of 2011,* CRS Report R41965 (Washington, DC: Congressional Research Service, 2011).

78 Roy T. Meyers, "The 'Ball of Confusion' in Federal Budgeting: A Shadow Agenda for Deliberative Reform of the Budget Process," *Public Administration Review,* 69, 2 (2009): 214.

79 OMB, *Budget of the United States Government, Fiscal Year 2023,* Historical Tables, Table 8.4.

80 Ibid., Table 7.1.

81 The Brookings Institution, *Vital Statistics on Congress* (2019), Table 7.3. Available at www.brookings.edu/wp-content/uploads/2019/03/Chpt-7.xlsx

82 Ibid., Table 7.6. Drew DeSilver, "Congress has Long Struggled to Pass Spending Bills on Time." Pew Research Center, January 16, 2018. Available at www.pewresearch.org/fact-tank/2018/01/16/congress-has-long-struggled-to-pass-spending-bills-on-time/

83 Clinton T. Brass, Ida A. Brudnick, Natalie Keegan, Barry J. McMillion, John W. Rollins, Brian T. Yeh, *Shutdown of the Federal Government: Causes, Processes, and Effects,* CRS Report RL34680 (Washington, DC: Congressional Research Service, 2018).

84 Jasmine Farrier, *Passing the Buck: Congress, the Budget, and Deficits* (Lexington: University of Kentucky Press, 2004), 153.

85 "The Budget Committees Are Not What They Used to Be," *CQ Magazine* (June 11, 2018). Available at http://library.cqpress.com/cqmagazine/weeklyreport115-000005334011

3

TAXATION

Building the Revenue Constraint

Although there has been great variation both historically and cross-nationally in what nations aspire to do, there is also a great commonality. Every exercise of governmental power, from the creation and maintenance of armed forces—the most fundamental function of a state—to the management of risks associated with the business cycle, the lifecycle, or the environment, is contingent on the extraction of revenues. It follows that the ability to generate sufficient revenues sets distinct limits on the quality and success of core public policies.[1] Yet, taxation remains highly contentious, particularly in the United States. For much of US history, taxation was complicated by constitutional constraints and an anti-statist culture. While the constitutional constraints were partially eliminated with the ratification of the Sixteenth Amendment which authorized the income tax, the cultural features have proved quite resilient. In the contemporary period, the capacity to secure adequate revenues has been frustrated by intense partisan battles. While the demand for social provision appears to be boundless, the difficulties of providing adequate funding have found a clear manifestation in the deficit and the debt.

This chapter begins with a broad overview of taxation from a theoretical, historical, and comparative perspective. It turns to consider the long-term changes in the composition of revenues. During the postwar period, there has been a declining reliance on the corporate income tax; the individual income tax has been stripped of much of its progressivity and there has been a greater reliance on payroll taxes, the most regressive form of taxation. The chapter proceeds to a brief exploration of tax expenditures, the provisions in the tax code that provide exemptions, deductions, deferrals, and credits that have the effect of reducing tax liability and further compromise the ability to raise revenues. Finally, it

DOI: 10.4324/9781003395331-4

concludes with a discussion of tax policymaking and the growing importance of the reconciliation process in Congress.

Taxation in Perspective

Taxation is unique among public policies. Most government programs have distinct beneficiaries, and in most cases, participation is voluntary. Senior citizens are not required to accept Social Security; low-income citizens are not forced to accept housing vouchers. In sharp contrast, the requirement to pay taxes is universal and backed by the coercive power of the state. Some wage earners may have incomes that fall below the threshold for the individual income tax. But they are nonetheless subject to the payroll tax, excise taxes, and state and local sales taxes. Citizens are required by law to finance government programs regardless of whether they are simultaneously the beneficiaries of, or politically sympathetic to, these programs. Given the universal and coercive nature of taxation, one should not be surprised that tax resistance has been widespread. Taxation is "perhaps the only state policy that can be counted on to generate frequent resistance through history and all over the world."[2] This has been particularly the case in the United States, where anti-statism has found its clearest expression in antitax sentiments. Policymakers may seek to make the nature of this relationship appear opaque and less politically salient, by relying on less visible sources of taxation (e.g., sales taxes, excise taxes, tariffs) rather than more visible forms of taxation (e.g., income taxes) or by earmarking taxes to draw a connection between the tax and the promise of future benefits (e.g., the payroll tax and Social Security). But the popular resistance to taxation has placed constraints on the scope and generosity of government programs and created incentives to find other means of providing services, for example, by creating tax incentives for businesses to provide employment-based health insurance and pensions.

The debates over taxation have raised important questions regarding the relationship between the citizen and the state, particularly in the late 19th and early 20th centuries. Edwin R.A. Seligman, the primary authority on taxation during this period, provided some insights into one of the core areas of disagreement. Writing in 1910, he explained that the benefit theory of taxation, which prevailed among critics of the income tax, assumed that "individuals should contribute to the support of government in accordance with the benefits or advantages which they derived from government action." In this view, taxes were akin to "an insurance premium, or a periodic payment made by the individual in order to guarantee the continuance of his profits in this joint-stock enterprise." The thin understanding of citizenship and the state which provided a foundation for the benefit theory could be contrasted with "the more organic conception of the relation of the individual to the state." Seligman argued that the correct metaphor was the family. "The citizens are not stockholders but brethren" and "the essence of taxation is a moral as well as a legal obligation." As the benefit theory receded, it was replaced by the faculty or ability theory, which "taught that the measure of general obligation to the support of government is, in the state as in the family, the capacity on the part of the individual to contribute to that support."[3] As Ajay K. Mehrotra observes in his fine study, *Making the Modern American Fiscal State*, the tax reform which culminated in the income tax "was used to reconfigure the relationship between the citizen and the state. It was used to renegotiate a new social contract, to reinvigorate the imagined community of the modern American polity."[4] Following this insight, one might well view contemporary changes in taxation to constitute efforts to renegotiate the social contract, and to resurrect benefit theory and the concept of citizenship it represented.

A long history of American anti-statism has shaped the politics of taxation. In the words of Aaron L. Friedberg: "at the moment of its conception, the new nation had a strong anti-statist strain encoded into its political DNA; one that would reproduce itself and continue to fulfill its protective function in subsequent generations."[5] This anti-statism found one clear expression in the original constitutional design which fragmented power and created a government of limited, enumerated, and delegated powers. It found a second expression in the orientation toward taxation. As Julian E. Zelizer notes, opposition to taxation has been "the most concrete manifestation of anti-statism. Hostility toward federal taxation has remained extremely strong in all income brackets, ranging from blue-collar workers who were central beneficiaries of New Deal programs to elite financial investors."[6] While there has been a general antitax sentiment, there has been an asymmetry in the larger partisan contests and debates. Tax cuts have been a core goal of the Republican Party for much of its existence. However, as will be argued in Chapters 6 and 7, the opposition to taxation attained a heightened importance since the 1970s and has become a unifying principle for the conservative coalition. Reflecting the larger antitax features of the culture, Republican claims regarding the negative consequences of taxation have rarely been countered by the Democratic Party or other pro-tax groups, despite the constraints that revenues place on their aspirations. When tax increases are advocated, they have been narrowly focused on top-income earners and often packaged with guarantees that middle-class households will be protected. "Over time," Fred Block explains, "this asymmetry can be expected to have an impact on public opinion. When conservative arguments for tax cuts are not publicly answered and rebutted, then these ideas gradually become common sense."[7] The antitax claims are familiar: taxation undermines the incentives for entrepreneurship and limits growth. It provides the resources for boundless government expansion and social engineering. Because these claims are largely met with silence, antitax sentiments are reinforced, thereby limiting the scope of policy proposals that can be presented in public debates.

Taxation in Historical and Comparative Perspective

Revenues are best expressed relative to GDP. As the data presented in Figure 3.1 reveal, revenues grew dramatically during the New Deal, from a low of 3.5 percent of GDP (1933) to a high of 7.7 percent of GDP (1938). With the US entry into World War II, revenues expanded from 6.7 percent of GDP to a record high of 19.8 percent (1945). In hopes of limiting the reliance on debt financing, Congress and the Roosevelt administration raised the corporate income tax. More importantly, with respect to the individual income tax, Congress raised marginal tax rates and cut exemptions to broaden the tax base, thereby creating a system of mass income taxation for the first time in the nation's history. Over the course of the postwar decades, revenues moved within a relatively narrow range, often tracking the business cycle and significant changes in the tax code. During the early 1980s, for example, as a result of the Economic Recovery Tax Act of 1981 and a deep and protracted recession, revenues fell from 19.1 (1981) to 17 percent of GDP (1983). Concerns with the mounting deficits led Congress to raise rates in 1991 and again in 1993. When combined with buoyant growth in the 1990s, revenues rose from 17 percent of GDP (1992) to a postwar record of 20 percent (2000). Thereafter, sequential tax cuts secured by President Bush and Congress took a toll, with

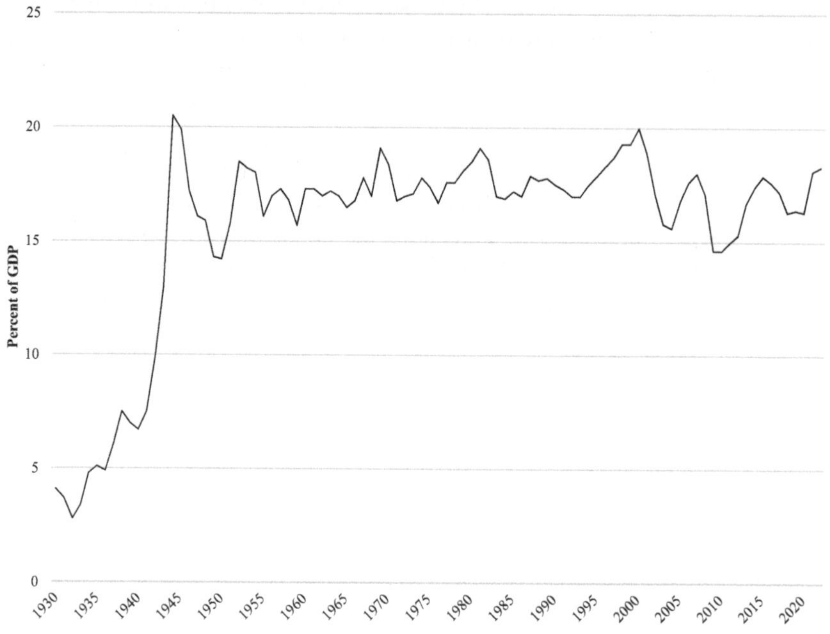

FIGURE 3.1 Federal Receipts, 1930–2022

Source: Adapted from OMB, *Budget of the United States, FY23*, Historical Tables, Table 1.2.

revenues falling to 15.8 percent of GDP by 2003. The financial crisis and Great Recession brought a sharp decline in revenues, to a post-recession low of 14.5 percent of GDP (2010–2011). Although revenues increased with the economic recovery, a new round of tax cuts during the Trump presidency brought revenues to 16.4 percent of GDP (2019), despite a growing economy and low levels of unemployment.[8]

The balance of federal, state, and local revenues has changed in important ways over time. At the beginning of the 20th century, the majority of revenues were generated by local governments.[9] In 1902, for example, local revenues constituted 53 percent of total revenues, followed by federal taxes (38 percent) and state taxes (9 percent). The introduction of the income tax following the ratification of the Sixteenth Amendment (1913) had important consequences. Yet, by 1938, the federal government was responsible for only 41 percent of total receipts. State governments had almost tripled their share of receipts (26 percent) from the turn of the century, whereas the local share had fallen to 32 percent.[10] The growth in state taxation was, in part, a product of the proliferation of grant-and-aid programs following the passage of the Social Security Act of 1935 that relied on a combination of federal and state revenues.[11] Taken as a whole, in the 1937–1938 fiscal year, grants-in-aid to the states totaled $633 million, requiring state matches of approximately 20 percent of state revenues (exclusive of payroll taxes).[12] Fiscal centralization would continue during the postwar period. In 1948, for example, state and local government revenues equaled 25 percent of total government receipts, whereas the federal government claimed three-quarters of total receipts. By 1980, state and local taxes had grown to 32.2 percent of total revenues, reflecting once again, the expansion of grants-in-aid. By 2019, on the eve of the COVID-19 pandemic, total government receipts were equal to 26.2 percent of GDP. Federal taxation accounted for 62.6 percent of the total (16.4 percent GDP), with state and local governments responsible for the remainder (9.8 percent GDP).[13]

The levels of taxation in the United States are low relative to other wealthy nations. The OECD compiles revenue statistics for member nations; given the different governmental structures, it reports aggregate revenues (e.g., combining federal, state, and local revenues for the United States). For 2016, US revenues at all levels were equal to 25.9 percent of GDP, well below the OECD average of 34.3 percent of GDP and even further below high-tax nations like Denmark and France that collected, respectively, revenues of 46.2 and 45.4 percent of GDP. Another interesting comparison that seems counterintuitive to many observers: whereas the average OECD country taxes personal income at 8.2 percent of GDP, the personal income tax in the United States is 10.4 percent of GDP. A related comparison worth making involves the taxation of consumption. Most OECD countries rely heavily on the Value-Added Tax (VAT), as reflected in the fact that the OECD average is 11 percent of GDP. In the United States, in contrast, the taxes on goods and services equal 4.4 percent of GDP, the lowest of any OECD country.[14]

The US reliance on the income tax reflected the Progressives' belief in the importance of taxation as an instrument of income redistribution, an emphasis that carried forward for several decades.[15] While the redistribution of income via the tax system made implicit sense, high marginal rates rendered the revenue system highly vulnerable to political challenges, which both limited the extent to which it could serve as an instrument of redistribution and constrained resources available for social expenditures. The contemporary story of taxation is one of successive rate reductions which have stripped the income tax of much of its progressivity. The VAT, in contrast, is less visible and, with some exceptions, universally applied. As a result, it has proven far more stable as a source of revenue, free from the class-based politics that have shaped debates over the income tax in the United States. This stable source of revenue has allowed for a higher level of redistribution via social programs. In the words of Harold Wilensky:

> Among the myths embraced by the American left, the most misleading is that the road to equality runs through progressive income taxes and taxes on business and property....the main mistake is to believe that by riveting one's attention on the tax side of the taxing/spending equation, one can achieve much of anything on the center-left agenda.

As Wilensky observes, the combination of a more regressive tax system and progressive spending programs has proven far more stable than one that relies heavily on the income tax.[16]

Another problem with the income tax is that it has become a major vehicle for delivering benefits via the system of tax preferences or expenditures. That is, a large portion of revenue has been exempted from taxation as a matter of policy. As will be developed later in this chapter, tax expenditures have been used to subsidize employment-based healthcare and retirement and home ownership, among other things, essentially enlisting the revenue system as a surrogate for spending. While this has had the effect of expanding the public investment in social welfare—albeit somewhat invisibly—the benefits have been concentrated among the top quintile of the income distribution. Ironically, the prevalence of tax expenditures has simultaneously limited the utility of the tax as an instrument of revenue generation and undermined the income tax as a tool of redistribution. Moreover, the heavy reliance on tax expenditures has created the misperception that the federal government bears no credit for employment-based benefits like pensions and healthcare.[17]

The Changing Composition of Revenues

While the overall level of revenues relative to GDP has moved within a relatively narrow band during the postwar period, there have been important shifts

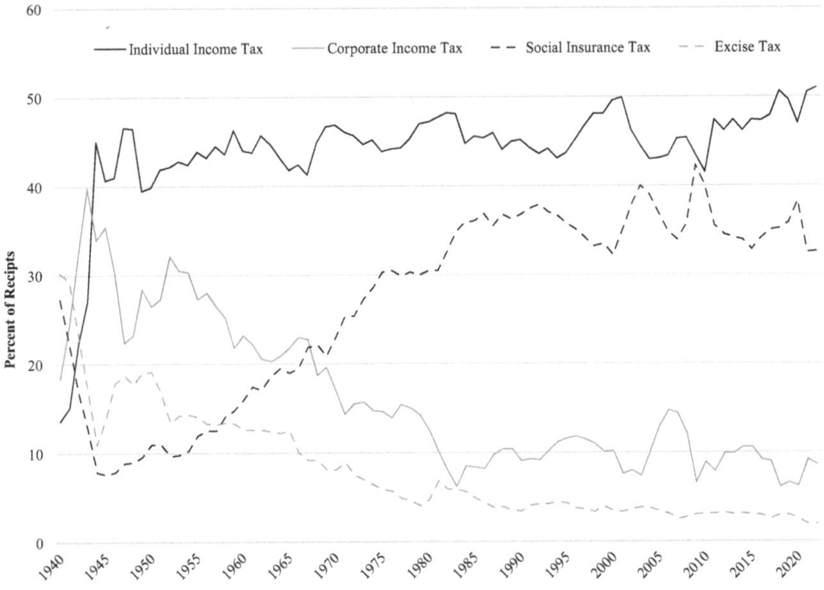

FIGURE 3.2 Composition of Receipts, 1940–2020

Source: Adapted from OMB, *Budget of the United States*, FY2023, Historical Tables, Table 3.2.

in the composition of revenues, as shown in the data graphically represented in Figure 3.2. In 1946, the individual income tax which had expanded dramatically as a result of World War II, was the single largest source of revenues (41 percent of the total). The corporate income tax, also expanded during the war, accounted for 30.2 percent of the total. Social insurance and retirement receipts (hereafter, payroll taxes) provided 7.9 percent. By 1968, as a product of a series of amendments to the Social Security Act, the payroll tax had displaced the corporate tax as the second largest source of revenue (22.2 and 18.7 percent, respectively). Over the course of the next several decades, the corporate tax would continue to decline in importance. In 2019, it accounted for 6.6 percent of revenues, whereas the individual income tax provided 48.9 percent and the payroll tax another 35.4 percent of revenues respectively. Let us place the changing composition of revenues in historical context.

For much of the nation's history, federal revenues were largely generated by customs from the tariff, excise taxes on goods and services, and land sales. Congress first introduced an income tax during the Civil War. Under the Civil War taxes, corporations were not taxed separately as entities, rather, their profits were treated as liabilities for owners and investors subject to the individual income tax. The income tax was allowed to expire in 1872, leaving the tariff as the primary source of revenues. The tariff served as an important tool in

Republican coalition building, providing protection for industries and funding internal improvements. In 1894, Congress passed the Wilson–Gorman Tariff Act which offset modest tariff reductions with an individual and corporate income tax (corporations, under this system, were taxed as separate entities, a distinction that would carry on subsequently). This time, the income tax ran afoul of the Supreme Court, which struck it down in *Pollock v. Farmers Loan & Trust* (1895), concluding that it constituted a violation of the Article I requirement that direct taxes be levied among the states based on population.[18] The corporate tax would be reintroduced in 1909—once again, connected to the larger issue of tariff reduction. But this time, it was framed as an excise tax on the privilege of doing business under the corporate form or organization. The income tax was finally added to the mix with the ratification of the Sixteenth Amendment (1913), which authorized Congress "to lay and collect taxes on incomes," thereby placing the individual and corporate income tax on firm constitutional foundations.

When the income tax was enacted in 1913, the top marginal tax rate was a relatively modest 7 percent and was concentrated among top income earners. With United States entry into World War I, the top rate ratcheted up with the passage of successive revenue bills and with the Revenue Act of 1918, the top rate would reach 77 percent, a combination of the income tax and a surtax. As Edwin R.A. Seligman noted in 1918, the wartime taxes were "the highwater mark thus far reached in the history of taxation. Never before, in the annals of civilization, has an attempt been made to take as much as two-thirds of a man's income by taxation," a decision that reflected the great "appreciation of the democratic principles of fiscal justice."[19] The significance of the changes in the revenue structure cannot be overstated. As W. Elliot Brownlee explains, at the beginning of Woodrow Wilson's presidency, the income tax was in its infancy; the tariff, while weakened, remained a primary source of revenues. The expansion of the income tax constituted a "progressive shift" that was "without equal in the history of American taxation." It effectively "broke the dominance of the tariff over the federal revenue system."[20] By the 1920s, rates were reduced, albeit to 25 percent, a marginal rate that would have been unimaginable before the war.

To stem growing budget deficits, the top rate was driven up to 63 percent in 1932. But by 1934, the federal government still relied heavily on excise taxes (45.8 percent of revenues) relative to the individual income tax and the corporate income tax, which accounted for 14.2 and 12.3 percent of revenues respectively.[21] Following the passage of the Social Security Act of 1935, however, these sources of revenue were supplemented with payroll taxes, which were first collected in 1937, to fund old age pensions. Despite the rhetoric surrounding the income tax, it provided a declining source of revenue during the turbulent 1930s. Moreover, when the income tax was combined with the excise taxes on consumer goods (e.g., alcohol and tobacco) and the new payroll taxes, the revenue system exhibited little progressivity. As Truman C. Bigham noted in 1937,

> an unusually large portion of the tax revenue has been derived from indirect taxes. The base of the income tax has not been enlarged sufficiently to offset this. Taken as a whole, these imposts increase the regressivity in the tax system and tend to defeat the efforts to redistribute wealth downward—an unfortunate result in the light of the numerous state taxes of like nature.

In Bigham's judgment, there was "no such thing as a New Deal tax policy."[22] Some of the more progressive taxes—including an undistributed profit tax enacted in 1936—were lowered and/or repealed in the wake of the 1937–1938 recession, which businesses framed as inimical to recovery. By 1940, the income tax provided less than one-third of revenues, while the more regressive excise and payroll taxes accounted for some 60 percent of revenues.[23]

A coherent tax policy would emerge as the nation faced the costs of World War II. The wartime increase in the corporate tax was substantial when placed in context. During the 1930s, top corporate tax rates increased from 13.75 percent (1932–1935) to 19 percent (1938–1939). But by 1942–1945, taxable income over $50,000 faced a rate of 40 percent. With the introduction of an excess profits tax, corporations faced additional tax liabilities.[24] The changes in the individual income tax were far more momentous. In 1935, 8.6 percent of adults filed returns. By 1945, largely as a result of reductions in the value of the personal exemption, this figure would stand at 84.6 percent.[25] Moreover, Congress passed the Current Tax Payment Act of 1943 to authorize tax withholding, a change that simplified collections (even if it was achieved by providing a partial forgiveness of existing tax liabilities). As more households were drawn into the income tax system, Congress raised rates significantly. Between 1935 and 1945, the lowest marginal rate increased from 4 to 23 percent, whereas the top rate grew from 63 to 94 percent.[26] In the words of one observer, during the war, "the income tax spread from the country club group district down to the railroad tracks and then over to the other side of the tracks."[27] As John F. Witte notes, the difference between the two world wars could not be more pronounced: "Although the top rates during World War I rose to almost confiscatory levels, the tax never reached the vast majority of citizens. That situation changes with the much larger revenue needs of World War II, and, most important, the mass wartime income tax remained."[28]

The approach to corporate taxation is somewhat unique in the United States. Corporate profits are taxed first at the level of the enterprise and, second, at the level of individual investors. Corporate tax reform efforts in the immediate postwar decades were shaped both by debates over the integration of the provisions of the corporate and individual income tax (ending so called "double taxation") and the relative burden that should be placed on corporate income versus household income as sources of revenues, particularly if reform was considered in the context of revenue neutrality.[29] Efforts to cut top rates were largely stymied. Top marginal rates remained at high levels, such that by the election of Ronald Reagan in 1980, the top corporate rate was 46 percent (on taxable income over $100,000).[30] The individual income tax remained at historically high levels as well. The highest and lowest rates for the individual income tax were 94 and 23 percent, respectively, in 1945. By 1963, they stood at 91 and 20 percent. Even if there were significant rate cuts as a result of the Revenue Act of 1964, by 1980, the top marginal rate was 70 percent whereas the bottom rate was 14 percent, evidence of the long-term legacy of the wartime mass tax system.[31] Individual and corporate rates would fall significantly in the 1980s as a result of the Economic Recovery Tax Act (1981) and the Tax Reform Act (1986), as will be explored in Chapter 7. By lowering individual rates below corporate rates, the 1986 act created incentives for corporations to reorganize to become so-called pass-through entities (e.g., partnerships) to avoid taxation at the level of the corporation. Profits were allocated to individual shareholders or partners and then they were taxed at lower rates.[32]

The growing role of the payroll tax, which has accounted for more than one-third of revenues since 1983, is important for several reasons. First, payroll taxes are among the most regressive forms of taxation. Consider the tax for Social Security Old Age, Survivors and Disability Insurance. Employees and employers pay a rate of 6.2 percent each (a combined total of 12.4 percent), subject to a maximum taxable earnings cap which is adjusted annually.[33] While low-income earners may fall below the personal exemption for the income tax, they remain subject to the payroll tax. The significance of the growth of the payroll tax is magnified by the broad changes in income taxation in the post-1980 period. During this period, the income tax was stripped of much of its progressivity, with top rates falling to less than one-half of what they had been in the immediate postwar decades. As the income tax became far flatter and less important as a means of redistributing income, the nation was relying more heavily on the most regressive form of taxation.

Second, the growing importance of payroll taxes would be consequential for the general fund of the Treasury. The general fund is the destination for income taxes, corporate taxes, and some excise taxes and is used to fund much of the federal government's commitments. Trust funds, in contrast, contain resources that are legally segregated from the general fund, pre-committed for specific programs and thus are unavailable to cover the daily activities of government. The rate reductions of the post-1980 period occurred in a political environment that was fueled by a powerful anti-tax sentiment. Revenue increases, where they occurred, were often earmarked for the trust funds, reflecting the difficulties of raising taxes in this political environment. The changing composition of revenues depleted the general fund, forcing efforts to control deficits on discretionary spending that relies on general revenues.[34] As noted earlier, Wilensky argued that more regressive forms of taxation can provide a stable revenue base, allowing for a more comprehensive set of welfare state policies that can carry the weight of income redistribution. In the US case, however, the growing importance of payroll taxes failed to generate the needed resources because revenues were channeled into trust funds rather than the general fund. Universal entitlement programs like Social Security and, to a lesser extent, Medicare (which relies on a combination of payroll tax, premiums, and general revenue) are islands of stability in a turbulent fiscal sea. While they draw on a steady stream of payroll taxes, other programs explicitly designed to redistribute income depend on income taxes and the general fund.

Third, we can return to the insight of Edwin R.A. Seligman at the beginning of this chapter. The benefit theory of taxation, as Seligman noted, was grounded in a thin vision of citizenship, wherein citizens were engaged in a relationship of reciprocal exchange with the state and taxes were analogous to insurance premiums. The normative arguments that provided a foundation for the income tax, in contrast, embodied a more organic view of the nation and citizenship. The metaphor of the family replaced the metaphor of the joint stock company. The growing reliance on payroll taxes explicitly earmarked to fund benefits that would be received by taxpayers was a product, in part, of an anti-statist ideology that was skeptical of the government's capacity to exercise fiscal stewardship. The reliance on payroll taxes marked a return to a benefit-theory-based conception of taxation. In Mehrotra's words, "the anti-tax sentiments of the late 20th century" reflected "an ideology that reinforced the dissolution of society as a national community...appeals to taxing citizens based on their 'ability to pay' became increasingly rare. When they were articulated, they generally fell on deaf ears."[35]

The Problem of Tax Expenditures

The concept of "tax expenditure" was developed, in large part, by Stanley S. Surrey, Assistant Secretary of the Treasury for Tax Policy (1961–1969). Surrey, and other tax analysts, had long observed that much of government spending occurs through the tax system rather than the budget, and yet these tax provisions are rarely subjected to inquiry. They are "buried in the intricacies of the tax law; compared with direct programs which undergo more systematic scrutiny, they are rarely examined."[36] Following Surrey, Section 3(3) of the Congressional Budget and Impoundment Control Act of 1974 defined tax expenditures as "revenue losses attributable to provisions of the Federal tax laws which allow a special exclusion, exemption, or deduction from gross income or which provide a special credit, a preferential rate of tax, or a deferral of tax liability." The term was adopted for a simple reason. Government may pursue its policy goals through the budget, appropriating funds for specified purposes.

Alternatively, it could seek to achieve the same objectives through the tax system. Whether the federal government promotes healthcare through spending or through the special tax treatment of employer-provided health insurance, the decision carries fiscal implications, even if they appear on different sides of the ledger.[37]

While tax expenditures and spending may have some comparable fiscal implications, there are nonetheless important differences. As the CBO explains:

> Unlike many spending programs, tax expenditures are not subject to annual appropriations. Because of that budgetary treatment, tax expenditures are less transparent than discretionary spending or spending on benefit programs. In fact, most tax expenditures are not explicitly recorded in the federal budget.[38]

Because tax expenditures are not subject to the budgetary process, they bear a striking resemblance to mandatory spending. That is, once they are placed into the Internal Revenue Code, their impacts are automatic and not subject to annual appropriations decisions. Absent affirmative decisions to eliminate them, their fiscal impacts and their influence on key decisions about work, savings, investment, and retirement can continue indefinitely.

Tax expenditures raise a host of concerns for policy analysts. For example, is the provision of tax incentives the most efficient way to achieve policy goals? To what extent are tax expenditures integrated with spending programs? To what extent do they work at cross purposes? While important issues, they are beyond the scope of this chapter. Let us focus on two issues: their fiscal impact and the implications for equity.

The Fiscal Impact of Tax Expenditures

From the perspective of long-term fiscal policy, we are particularly concerned with the impact that tax expenditures have on revenue generation. To what extent have they increased the porosity of the tax base, requiring higher marginal rates to generate revenues? The OMB publishes an annual assessment of the fiscal consequences of tax expenditures, projecting the revenue effects over a ten-year horizon. Although there are 165 tax expenditures as of this writing, a few of the largest tax expenditures are illustrative of their focus and magnitude. The figures below are for 2019, the eve of the COVID-19 pandemic. Given the uncertain environment created by the pandemic, the projections should be read with caution. The largest tax expenditure supports the provision of healthcare. In 2019, the exclusion of employer contributions for medical insurance premiums cost \$202.3 billion, with a ten-year projected impact of \$3.1 trillion. Tax expenditures also supported retirement security by excluding from taxation contributions to defined-contribution pensions (\$75.7 billion;

$1.3 trillion 2020–2029), defined-benefit pension plans ($71.7 billion; $808.8 billion, 2020–2029) and individual retirement accounts ($20.5 billion; $303.4 billion, 2020–2029). The tax code also supports housing through the exclusion of net imputed rental income ($121.3 billion; $1.6 trillion, 2020–2029), deductibility of mortgage interest on owner-occupied homes ($25.1 billion; $644.7 billion, 2020–2029), capital gains exclusion on home sales ($43.6 billion; $593.7 billion, 2020–2029), and deductibility of property taxes on owner-occupied homes ($6 billion; $268.1 billion, 2020–2029).[39]

When taken in aggregate, the CBO estimated that tax expenditures totaled some $1.8 trillion in 2020, some 8.1 percent of GDP. To place things in perspective, tax expenditures were equivalent to the total revenue generated from the individual income tax and greater than the revenues collected through the payroll tax (5.9 percent of GDP). Since tax expenditures are an alternative to budgetary outlays, another comparison is worth noting. For 2020, mandatory spending claimed some 12.9 percent of GDP. Discretionary spending and net interest on the debt constituted 6.4 and 1.7 percent of GDP, respectively, a combined 8.1 percent or the equivalent of tax expenditures.[40]

Tax Expenditures and Equity

When viewed in comparative perspective, the United States is commonly presented as a welfare state laggard. As explained in the last chapter, expenditures as a proportion of GDP are relatively low when compared with other wealthy nations. The assessment of Fred Block and Margaret R. Somers is quite representative:

> The combination of lower taxes and much higher military and national security spending means that the United States allocates a far smaller share of GDP for domestic programs than most other developed nations, which are far more generous in assisting the elderly, the unemployed, and especially the poor.

Apart from the New Deal and the Great Society—the two "big bangs" in the history of the American welfare state—the United States "has been a laggard in public social provision since the last decades of the nineteenth century, and the pattern persists today."[41] While one can acknowledge the above-mentioned patterns of spending, some scholars correctly note that expenditures constitute only one means of implementing welfare policy. Christopher Howard, most notably, has directed scholarly attention to the "hidden welfare state," that exists in the United States. It employs a more diverse mix of policy instruments to achieve social welfare goals. The United States, Howard observes, places less emphasis on social spending (the visible welfare state) than other affluent nations, but simultaneously deploys other indirect forms of assistance, including tax expenditures, loan guarantees, and regulations. Indeed, when these forms of assistance are considered, the US welfare state does not seem exceptionally small. The interesting question, as a result, is not the traditional question of why the United States does less in terms of social spending than European states. "Rather, the question is why governments of similar size devote comparable resources to pursuing similar policy objectives through such a diverse mix of policy tools."[42]

The prevalence of tax expenditures serving welfare functions, Howard argues, is in part a product of some of the factors that have been identified as impediments to the visible welfare state. One can contrast, for example, direct social provision with the use of tax expenditures. The former necessarily involves bureaucratic expansion and the explicit growth in government's claim over GDP. The latter, in contrast, creates market incentives and takes the form of tax cuts, thereby heightening their appeal to conservatives and centrists. Some members of Congress who voted to eliminate Aid to Families with Dependent Children in 1996—the largest income support program for nonelderly citizens—simultaneously advocated the expansion of the Earned Income Tax Credit (EITC), which rewarded work effort with tax-based incentives. Moreover, tax expenditures, as suggested above, fit the incentive structure faced by reelection-minded legislators in a fragmented Congress. Members of Congress can provide tax expenditures without bearing responsibility for a political backlash or an expansion of expenditures that overtly expand the deficit.[43]

There is little question that the hidden welfare state supplements the visible welfare state. One might conclude that the mix of tax-based incentives and spending is simply another expression of American exceptionalism. And yet, to the extent that the hidden welfare state provides "upside down" assistance, to use Stanley S. Surrey's phrase, the results are not benign in terms of equity. In a progressive tax system with graduated marginal rates, vertical equity demands that those with higher incomes should face higher tax liabilities than those with lower incomes. Horizontal equity, in contrast, demands that those with similar economic circumstances be treated alike. The system of tax expenditures undermines equity along both dimensions. With a few notable exceptions (the EITC, the Child Tax Credit) those with higher marginal rates receive greater benefits from the largest tax expenditures. On the horizontal dimension, one's tax liability should not be a function of whether one can take advantage of the idiosyncrasies of the tax code or secure the services of skilled accountants or tax attorneys. Let us focus on the problem of vertical equity.

The CBO analyzed the distribution of benefits from ten of the largest tax expenditures for 2013. While there have been changes in the tax code since this analysis, it is illustrative of the extent to which tax expenditures violate norms of equity. The expenditures in question included four exclusions from taxable income (employer-sponsored health insurance, net pension contributions and earnings, capital gains on assets transferred at death, and a portion of Social Security and Railroad Retirement benefits), three itemized deductions (certain taxes paid to state and local governments, mortgage interest payments, and charitable contributions), two tax credits (the EITC and the Child Tax Credit), and preferential tax rates on capital gains and dividends. Although they constituted a small subset of the tax expenditures in the Internal Revenue Code at the time of the study, they accounted for some two-thirds of the total costs, claiming more than 5.7 percent of GDP. The CBO analyzed the distribution by quintile based on before-tax income, both in dollar terms and as a share of after-tax, after-transfer income.[44]

When these ten tax expenditures are taken as a whole, the CBO found that 51 percent of the cash benefits accrued to the top quintile with the highest pre-tax incomes. The CBO also looked at the cash benefits received by percentiles within the highest quintile and estimated that 30 percent of the benefits went to the top 5 percent of income earners, with 17 percent going to the top 1 percent. In sharp contrast, the middle quintile received 13 percent of the cash benefits whereas the poorest quintile received 8 percent. The distribution of expenditures as a share of after-tax, after-transfer income was more U-shaped, as one might expect given the lower income base in the first and second quintile. Tax expenditures constituted 11.7 percent of after-tax, after-transfer income for the lowest quintile, 7.3 percent for the middle quintile, and 9.4 percent for the top quintile. When looking at the percentiles within the top quintile, the CBO estimated that households in the 96th to 99th percentiles received benefits equal to 9.9 percent of their after-tax income, whereas the top 1 percent fared the best, with benefits of 13.1 percent of after-tax income.[45]

Tax Policymaking

Under the Constitution (Article I, Section 8), Congress, is granted "the Power to lay and collect Taxes, Duties, Imposts and Excises, to pay the Debts and provide for the common Defense and general Welfare of the United States." There were a few restrictions placed on the raising of revenues. Under the Origination Clause (Article I, Section 7), all tax bills must "originate in the House of Representatives," although the Senate may propose amendments. Under the Uniformity Clause (Article I, Section 8), federal taxes must be "uniform throughout the United States." Article I, Section 9 required that all direct taxes had to be apportioned on the basis of population, a requirement that formed the basis for declaring the income tax unconstitutional (a position that was remedied by the Sixteenth Amendment). Article I, Section 9, also prohibited taxes or duties to be laid on articles exported by any state.

Tax policy is developed and implemented in a system characterized by a significant degree of institutional fragmentation, a legacy of the system of checks and balances that diffused responsibility. Primary jurisdiction for tax policy rests with two committees: the House Ways and Means Committee and the Senate Finance Committee. Given the Origination Clause, Ways and Means has been preeminent. Reflecting the complexity of tax policy, members of the two committees place a heavy reliance on staff members in the formation and evaluation of policy. They are also assisted by the staff of the Joint Committee on Taxation, which conducts ongoing analyses of tax policy and provides estimates of revenues for Congress, serving a role on the revenue side that is analogous to that played by the CBO on issues of spending. While revenue bills must originate in Congress, it has delegated a great deal of authority to the president, the Treasury, and the Internal Revenue Service (IRS). Although the relevant committees play a central role in making tax policy, comprehensive change has usually originated in proposals from the executive branch.[46] Indeed, the most momentous changes in tax policy over the course of the postwar period—the Revenue Act of 1964, the Reagan and Bush Era tax cuts—have usually required presidential advocacy. We will have an opportunity to discuss these tax cuts in the chapters in Part II of the volume.

Making Tax Policy in Congress

Several significant changes in the postwar period had important implications for the politics of taxation. First, the congressional reforms of the 1970s created even more fragmentation in an already highly decentralized institution. Over the course of the immediate postwar decades, the House Ways and Means Committee tightly controlled tax policy, particularly under Wilbur Mills (D-AR), who chaired the committee from 1958 to 1974. Mills selected centrist members largely from safe districts and eschewed open hearings, thereby lessening the influence of localism and clientele groups. When he assumed the chairmanship, Mills abolished subcommittees, thereby consolidating his control. On important tax bills, Mills was able to build a consensus on Ways and Means, achieve bipartisan support before moving bills to the floor, and secure closed rules to prevent floor amendments.[47] While the Ways and Means Committee tightly controlled the basic features of tax policy, things were different when the venue changed to the upper chamber. As Catherine E. Rudder explains, the Senate Finance Committee "was much less restrained … and saw itself as a court of appeals for those who felt their interests had been damaged or neglected in the House."[48] In the words of Randall Strahan: "Policy outcomes in the House tended to be more oriented toward maintaining federal revenues; those in the Senate tended to bear the imprint of clientele interests seeking reduced tax burdens."[49]

During the 1970s, a wave of reforms democratized processes in the House, fundamentally depleting the power that had been concentrated in Ways and Means and decentralizing power over tax policy. Committee membership and staff were expanded, and subcommittees were reintroduced, thereby creating power centers to contest the dominance of the chair. Since 1911, Democratic members of the Ways and Means Committee had served as the Democratic Party's Committee on Committees, controlling assignments to standing committees in the chamber. It was stripped of this power; henceforth committee assignments would be subject to nomination by the Democratic Party Steering and Policy Committee and caucus approval. Committee markup sessions were opened to the public unless the majority of the committee voted otherwise, creating new access points for lobbyists and opportunities for position-taking and entrepreneurship on the part of individual members. And closed rules, once used to insulate the policy process, were no longer certain.[50] As Sven Steinmo remarks:

> Unfortunately for the coherence of the American tax code, the legislature's answer to the cronyism of revenue politics was to distribute responsibility for taxation ever more widely. This made … an already porous system even more loophole-ridden. In the context of the continuing institutional conflict between the legislative and executive branches of government, especially in the Watergate era, Congress had no incentive to yield tax-writing power to the executive branch.[51]

As the political insulation of the Ways and Means Committee fell victim to the reforms of the period, legislators faced a new environment in which they were forced to write tax bills in the open and use roll call votes on most tax expenditures. As R. Douglas Arnold notes, one ironic lesson of the reforms was that "tax preferences thrive in the sunshine."[52]

As a result of the institutional fragmentation and high levels of interest group access, the formation and passage of tax legislation occurs in a highly politicized environment, rife with interest group lobbying and flush with contributions from political action committees. The charged political environment is, in part, a product of the complexity and redistributive features of most tax bills. Even those that are ostensibly designed to raise revenue frequently include a combination of tax increases and tax breaks.[53] The fragmentation has been combined with a second complication: the growing partisan polarization of Congress. The impact of polarization is most distinctive when partisan contests involve economic issues, including social welfare programs, regulation, and taxation.[54] In these contests, there is little question where the Republican Party will fall. The conservative coalition may be plagued by internecine battles. But as will be developed in Chapter 7, there is broad support for lower levels of taxation.[55] This creates something of a downward ratchet in taxation. Taxes can be cut under Republican majorities, but the GOP has been strongly opposed to any tax increases. The downward ratchet in taxation, when combined with a lack of comparable moves on the spending side, has had predictable ramifications for the deficit and debt.

Reconciliation and Tax Policy

Polarization and procedural complexity have come, increasingly, to define the congressional politics of taxation. Even if bills can be passed by the House with relative ease given the power vested in the Speaker, they face a far more complicated procedural environment as they enter the Senate. The growing reliance on the filibuster and the need to secure supermajorities has had a major impact on levels of legislative productivity. Under these conditions, the kinds of extensive bipartisan debates and votes over comprehensive changes in the tax code comparable to what occurred with the Tax Reform Act of 1986 are no longer possible. Instead, significant changes in tax policy have occurred through the reconciliation process. This process has allowed even slim majorities to maximize their influence over tax policy. At the same time, the peculiar features of reconciliation have shaped the form that tax bills have taken. Most important from the perspective of taxation, under the Byrd rule (see Chapter 2) the most important criterion is that provisions cannot increase the deficit for fiscal years that are outside the "budget window" specified by the budget resolution, forcing changes in the tax code to sunset.[56]

We shall return to reconciliation and its role in tax policy in Chapters 8 and 9. For now, a few points are worth emphasizing. First, one cannot avoid the conclusion that reconciliation, introduced in the CBA as a minor provision and a means of deficit reduction, has both grown in importance and has become the favored vehicle for revenue measures that have the opposite effect. As the experience of the two-term presidency of George W. Bush reveal, tax bills that could not have survived the supermajority rules in the Senate were passed via reconciliation. The 2001 and 2003 tax cuts were scored by the CBO to have a ten-year impact of $1.35 trillion and $349.7 billion, respectively.[57] They played a significant role in reversing the efforts of the past decade that had successfully turned deficits into surpluses and placed the nation on the course of long-term debt reduction, even if they were passed by slim majorities and with minimal deliberation.

Second and related, there remains a great deal of uncertainty as to the fiscal effects of changes in tax policy that are moved rapidly through the reconciliation process. As with the efforts to control spending, much will depend on the underlying assumptions. Unsurprisingly, there may be strong incentives to tailor assumptions to shape the scoring of revenue bills. When scoring the revenue impacts of a reconciliation bill, there may be strategic efforts to select or comingle baselines to produce the desired results. A current law baseline assumes that sunsetting tax provisions will expire on schedule. The decision to pass "tax extenders" would be scored as having an impact on revenues. In contrast, a current policy baseline assumes a continuation of tax cuts even if they are scheduled to expire. Under this baseline, an extension of provisions scheduled to sunset would have no effect on revenues. Toggling between baselines can veil the magnitude of proposed cuts. For example, if one scores cuts as temporary under current law and then, when the time comes to extend the sunset, shifts to the current policy baseline, the fiscal effects of the extension are already factored into the new budget window, thereby obscuring the implications for revenue.[58] Similarly, further complexity has arisen through the adoption of dynamic scoring, which projects the changes in revenues that would stem from the proposed tax legislation, often concluding that the reductions in revenues would be less significant given their role in stimulating growth. Critics raise obvious concerns that the results of dynamic scoring are sensitive to the underlying assumptions about long-run responses to policy change, future budgetary effects, and monetary and fiscal policy reactions.[59]

Third, the use of budget windows and sunset clauses may be necessary given the requirements of the reconciliation process, but they may only obscure the significance and longevity of the changes in question. They may assuage concerns over the impact on revenues by allowing legislators to present even controversial policy changes as temporary, thereby allowing them to preserve claims to fiscal responsibility. Opponents may rationally prefer sunsets to permanent tax changes, on the theory that today's partisan majorities may be fleeting. The process can be easily manipulated, however, in ways that obscure the fiscal ramifications of change. This is true in two senses. First, what constitutes a budget window has changed over time. Over the course of the past several decades, the budget window has expanded from one year in the 1980s to ten years in 1999. "In theory, there is nothing standing in the way of a budget window lasting twenty or thirty years, or even longer," Ellen P. Aprill and Daniel J. Hemel explain. "The rule against out-year deficit effects accomplishes little if the budget window lasts an entire generation."[60] Regardless of the window, in many cases, sunsets are often little more than an inconvenience insofar as Congress subsequently extends sunset dates, allowing one to conclude that there may be few things as permanent as temporary tax provisions. Many of the Bush tax cuts that were scheduled to expire were extended as the economy was reeling from the Great Recession, only to become entrenched in the tax code. By 2012, fully 82 percent of the tax provisions that were scheduled to expire as required under the Byrd rule, had become permanent.[61]

Fourth, the vagaries of the Byrd rule and the reconciliation process may create impediments to reform. The decision to fast-track complicated tax legislation may compromise the ability to identify and correct errors prior to passage (the 2017 tax act, for example, contained some 70 errors that needed technical corrections by Congress or the IRS, many of which failed to occur).[62] The truncated timeline for congressional action makes it impossible for Congress to consider the kinds of far-reaching reforms that could be used to broaden the tax base or eliminate special interest provisions embedded in the system of tax expenditures. Efforts to enact significant reform may fall outside of the budget window, however construed. At the same time, efforts to simplify provisions of the IRC may be considered "incidental" and thus extraneous to the reconciliation process, whereas the kinds of provisions that are deemed acceptable may simply result in added complexity. In the words of Aprill and Hemel, the Byrd rule "causes Congress to add complexity to the Internal Revenue Code," creating

> a tangle of provisions with looming expiration dates as well as others that will not come into effect again for another eight years. Uncertainty as to whether temporary provisions will be extended makes it harder for taxpayers to develop long-term plans.[63]

In short, the reconciliation process—never intended as a primary vehicle for tax policy—cannot bear the weight that it has been assigned.

Finally, reconciliation may import higher levels of conflict into a policy area that is already prone to sharp partisan and interbranch disputes. Reconciliation is explicitly used to circumvent the need for a supermajority in the Senate. Absent reconciliation, the need to build larger coalitions to avoid the threat of filibuster may necessitate extended debate, but debate can have a moderating effect, increasing both the quality and stability of the policy change. If reconciliation is used to limit the voice of the minority, as has become the norm, the results can be problematic. In practice, it has allowed the majority to impose tax provisions without the need for a single vote from the opposition. Free from the need to secure support from Democrats, for example, Republican majorities may impose changes that are more extreme in their distributional effects, providing deeper rate cuts for corporations and high-income earners while providing fewer benefits to lower income households. All of this may be reversed subsequent years, when the balance of partisan forces shifts. Similarly, the expedited nature of the reconciliation process may generate conflicts between the president and Congress insofar as it does not contain a mechanism for careful interbranch consultation about policy priorities.[64]

Conclusion

Debate over the deficits and the debt are accompanied by a common refrain: "Washington has a spending problem." While not discounting the claim that there are programs that demand greater budgetary scrutiny and reform, the problems are not restricted to one side of the ledger. Washington also has a revenue problem. In the immediate postwar period, the mass-tax regime that was established during World War II provided a steady stream of revenues, allowing for an expansion of public investment and social provision while reducing the debt-to-GDP ratio. But changes in the tax code that commenced in the 1980s lowered marginal income tax rates, reduced the role of the corporate tax, and shifted a larger share of the tax burden to payroll taxes. Tax expenditures, in turn, rendered the tax base quite porous while providing most of the benefits to the same households that had been the recipients of lower marginal tax rates. To the extent that this low-tax regime and the preservation of tax expenditures have become a core commitment of one of the two political parties, the obstacles to reform are considerable. In an age of political polarization, the kinds of broad coalitions that are necessary for significant reform are unavailable, and the reconciliation process provides a convenient vehicle for securing and extending tax cuts with the slimmest of majorities.

Notes

1 See Sheldon D. Pollock, *War, Revenue, and State Building: Financing the Development of the American State* (Ithaca, NY: Cornell University Press, 2009), 1–20.
2 Isaac William Martin, Ajay K. Mehrotra, and Monica Prasad, "The Thunder of History: The Origins and Development of the New Fiscal Sociology," in *The New Fiscal Sociology: Taxation in Comparative and Historical Perspective,* ed. Isaac William Martin, Ajay K. Mehrotra, and Monica Prasad (Cambridge: Cambridge University Press, 2009), 4.
3 Edwin R. A. Seligman, "The Progress of Taxation during the Past Twenty-Five Years and Current Tendencies," *American Economic Association Quarterly*, 11, 1 (1910), 338–39, 341, 342. For a much more detailed discussion, see E. R. A. Seligman, "Progressive Taxation in Theory and Practice," *American Economic Association Quarterly*, 9, 4 (1908): 1–334.
4 Ajay K. Mehrotra, *Making the Modern American Fiscal State: Law, Politics, and the Rise of Progressive Taxation, 1877–1929* (New York: Cambridge University Press, 2013), 13.
5 Aaron L. Friedberg, *In the Shadow of the Garrison State: America's Anti-Statism and Its Cold War Grand Strategy* (Princeton: Princeton University Press, 2000), 9.
6 Julian E. Zelizer, *Governing America: The Revival of Political History* (Princeton: Princeton University Press, 2012), 107.
7 Fred Block, "Read Their Lips: Taxation and the Right-Wing Agenda," in *The New Fiscal Sociology,* 69.
8 Office of Management and Budget (OMB), *Budget of the U.S. Government, Fiscal Year 2023* (Washington DC: Government Publishing Office, 2022), Historical Tables, Table 1.2.
9 See Randall G. Holcombe and Donald J. Lacombe, "The Growth of Local Government in the United States from 1820 to 1870," *The Journal of Economic History*, 61, 1 (2001): 184–89.
10 Ballard C. Campbell, *The Growth of American Government: Governance from the Cleveland Era to Present* (Bloomington: Indiana University Press, 2015), 215.
11 See Robert Jay Digler and Michael H. Cecire, *Federal Grants to State and Local Governments: A Historical Perspective on Contemporary Issues*, CRS Report R40638 (Washington, DC: Congressional Research Service, 2019), 18–19.
12 Daniel S. Gerig, Jr., "The Financial Participation of the Federal Government in State Welfare Programs," *Social Security Bulletin,* January 1940: 21.
13 OMB, *Budget of the U.S. Government, Fiscal Year 2023*, Historical Tables, Table 14.1.

14 OECD (2019) Tax Revenue (indicator). Available at https://data.oecd.org/tax/tax-revenue.htm#indicator-chart
15 See Monica Prasad, *The Land of Too Much: American Abundance and the Paradox of Poverty* (Cambridge: Harvard University Press, 2012), 125–29.
16 Harold L. Wilensky, *Rich Democracies: Political Economy, Public Policy, and Performance* (Berkeley: University of California Press, 2002), 715. See Monica Prasad and Yingying Deng, "Taxation and the Worlds of Welfare," *Socio-Economic Review,* 7 (2009): 431–57.
17 See Christopher Howard, *The Hidden Welfare State: Tax Expenditures and Social Policy in the United States* (Princeton: Princeton University Press, 1997). On the misperceptions associated with tax-based benefits, see Suzanne Mettler, *The Submerged State: How Invisible Government Policies Undermine American Democracy* (Chicago: University of Chicago Press, 2011).
18 *Pollock v. Farmers Loan & Trust Company,* 157 US 429 (1895).
19 Edwin R. A. Seligman, "The War Revenue Act," *Political Science Quarterly,* 33, 1 (1918): 18–19.
20 W. Elliot Brownlee, "Wilson and Financing the Modern State: The Revenue Act of 1916," *Proceedings of the American Philosophical Society,* 129, 2 (1985): 173.
21 OMB, *Budget of the U.S. Government, Fiscal Year 2023,* Historical Tables, Table 2.2.
22 Truman C. Bigham, "Economic Effects of the New Deal Tax Policy," *Southern Economic Journal,* 3, 3 (1937): 273–74, 270. See Zelizer, *Governing America,* 113.
23 Dennis S. Ippolito, *Why Budgets Matter: Budget Policy and American Politics* (University Park: Penn State University Press, 2015), 138–39.
24 Department of the Treasury, Internal Revenue Service, "Corporate Income Tax Brackets and Rates, 1909–2002," Data Release, 288. Available at www.irs.gov/pub/irs-soi/02corate.pdf.
25 Thomas Piketty and Emmanuel Saez, "Income Inequality in the United States, 1913–2002," November 2004, Table A0. Available at https://eml.berkeley.edu/~saez/piketty-saezOUP04US.pdf.
26 Department of the Treasury, Internal Revenue Service, U.S Individual Income Tax: Tax Rates for Regular Tax: Lowest Bracket [IITTRLB], available at https://fred.stlouisfed.org/series/IITTRLB, and Department of the Treasury, Internal Revenue Service, U.S Individual Income Tax: Tax Rates for Regular Tax: Highest Bracket [IITTRHB], available at https://fred.stlouisfed.org/series/IITTRHB.
27 Randolph E. Paul, "History of Taxation in the United States," *William & Mary Annual Tax Conference,* 646 (1955): 11.
28 John F. Witte, *The Politics and Development of the Federal Income Tax* (Madison: University of Wisconsin Press, 1985), 110.
29 Steven A. Bank, "The Rise and Fall of Post-World War II Corporate Tax Reform," *Law and Contemporary Problems* 73, 1 (2010): 208.
30 Department of the Treasury, Internal Revenue Service, "Corporate Income Tax Brackets and Rates," 288.
31 Department of the Treasury, Internal Revenue Service, U.S Individual Income Tax: Tax Rates for Regular Tax: Lowest Bracket [IITTRLB] and Department of the Treasury. Internal Revenue Service, U.S Individual Income Tax: Tax Rates for Regular Tax: Highest Bracket [IITTRHB].
32 Mark P. Keightley and Molly F. Sherlock, *The Corporate Income Tax System: Overview and Options for Reform*, CRS Report R42726 (Washington, DC: Congressional Research Service, 2014), 1.

33 Social Security Administration, OASDI and SSI Program Rates & Limits, 2020. Available at www.ssa.gov/policy/docs/quickfacts/prog_highlights/RatesLimits2020.html
34 See Eric M. Patashnik, *Putting Trust in the US Budget: Federal Trust Funds and the Politics of Commitment* (Cambridge: Cambridge University Press, 2000), 40–62, and Allen Schick, *The Federal Budget: Politics, Policy, Process* (Washington, DC: Brookings Institution Press, 2007), 184–85.
35 Mehrotra, *Making the Modern American Fiscal State,* 414–15.
36 Stanley S. Surrey, "Tax Expenditures," *Challenge* 18, 6 (1976): 54.
37 US Congress, Joint Committee on Taxation, *Estimates of Federal Tax Expenditures for Fiscal Years 2019–2023,* JCS-55-19, 2.
38 Congressional Budget Office (CBO), *The Budget and Economic Outlook: 2020–2030* (Washington, DC, CBO, 2020), 27.
39 OMB, *Budget of the U.S. Government, Fiscal Year 2021* (Washington, DC: Government Publishing Office, 2020), Analytical Perspectives, 162–65.
40 CBO, *The Budget and Economic Outlook: 2020–2030,* 27. Data available at www.cbo.gov/system/files/2020-01/56020-data-underlying-figures.xlsx
41 Fred Block and Margaret R. Somers, *The Power of Market Fundamentalism: Karl Polanyi's Critique* (Cambridge: Harvard University Press, 2014), 194.
42 Christopher Howard, *The Welfare State Nobody Knows: Debunking Myths about U.S. Social Policy* (Princeton: Princeton University Press, 2007), 24.
43 See Howard, *The Hidden Welfare State,* 10–11.
44 CBO, *The Distribution of Major Tax Expenditures in the Individual Income Tax System* (Washington, DC: CBO, 20013), 2.
45 Ibid., 15.
46 Eric Solomon, "The Process for Making Tax Policy in the United States: A System Full of Friction," *The Tax Lawyer,* 67, 3 (2014): 547–58.
47 See Robert V. Remini, *The House: The History of the House of Representatives* (New York: Harper Collins, 2006), 406–07, and Allen Schick, "The Ways and Means of Leading Ways and Means," *The Brookings Review,* 7, 4 (1989): 16–23.
48 Catherine E. Rudder, "Tax Policy: Structure and Choice," in *Making Economic Policy in Congress,* ed. Allen Schick (Washington, DC: American Enterprise Institute for Public Policy Research, 1983), 200.
49 Randall Strahan, "Agenda Change and Committee Politics in the Postreform House," *Legislative Studies Quarterly,* 13, 2 (1988): 179.
50 Eric Schickler, *Disjointed Pluralism: Institutional Innovation and the Development of the U.S. Congress* (Princeton: Princeton University Press, 2001), 211–12.
51 Sven Steinmo, *Taxation and Democracy: Swedish, British and American Approaches to Financing the Modern State* (New Haven: Yale University Press, 1993), 141.
52 R. Douglas Arnold, *The Logic of Congressional Action* (New Haven: Yale University Press, 1990), 202.
53 Schick, *The Federal Budget,* 163.
54 See Frances E. Lee, "Agreeing to Disagree: Agenda Content and Senate Partisanship, 1981–2004," *Legislative Studies Quarterly,* 33, 2 (2008): 199–222.
55 See Jacob S. Hacker and Paul Pierson, "Tax Politics and the Struggle over Activist Government," in *The Transformation of American Politics: Activist Government and the Rise of Conservatism,* ed. Paul Pierson and Theda Skocpol (Princeton: Princeton University Press, 2007), 256–80.
56 Heniff, *The Budget Reconciliation Process,* 3, 5.

57 See CBO, "H.R. 1836 Economic Growth and Tax Relief Reconciliation Act of 2003," Congressional Budget Office Cost Estimate, May 26, 2001, available at www.cbo.gov/sites/default/files/107th-congress-2001-2002/costestimate/hr1836omb0.pdf, and CBO, "H.R. 2 Jobs and Growth Tax Relief Reconciliation Act of 2003," Congressional Budget Office Cost Estimate, May 23, 2003, available at www.cbo.gov/sites/default/files/108th-congress-2003-2004/costestimate/hr250.pdf

58 See David Kamin and Rebecca Kysar, "Temporary Tax Laws and the Budget Baseline," *Tax Notes*, (October 2, 2017): 125–32.

59 See Alan J. Auerbach, "Dynamic Scoring: An Introduction to the Issues," *American Economic Review*, 95, 2 (2005): 421–25.

60 Ellen P. Aprill and Daniel J. Hemel, "The Tax Legislative Process: A Byrd's Eye View," *Law and Contemporary Problems,* 81 (2018): 131.

61 Ali Sutherland, "Ghosting in Tax Law: Sunset Provisions and Their Unfaithfulness," *Hastings Constitutional Law Quarterly,* 46 (2019): 492.

62 Brian Faler, "Democrats Put Tax Hikes on Fast Track—After Knocking GOP's Haste on Tax Cuts," *Politico,* Sept. 13, 2021. Available at www.politico.com/news/2021/09/13/democrats-tax-hikes-511664

63 Aprill and Hemel, "The Tax Legislative Process," 133.

64 Rebecca M. Kysar, "Tax Law and the Eroding Budget Process," *Law and Contemporary Problems,* 81, 2 (2018): 93–94, and Rebecca M. Kysar, "Reconciling Congress to Tax Reform," *Notre Dame Law Review,* 88, 5 (2013): 2146.

4

THE FISCAL GAP

Why Deficits and the Debt Matter

This book is premised on a simple assertion: the size of the deficit and debt matters. As with most simple assertions, this one needs some explication and qualifications. Let us preface the discussion with a few key points. First, claims about the deficit and debt are often ideologically charged because they are viewed, by many, as emblematic of state intervention in markets and society. In 2011, for example, Tea Party Republicans in the House of Representatives used the need to raise the debt limit as an opportunity to extract deep spending cuts and consideration of a balanced budget amendment. They were willing to risk defaulting on the debt—an act that would have had catastrophic ramifications for international financial markets—because they viewed themselves as fighting the activist state more broadly. While there may be some reasonable arguments for a balanced budget amendment, one suspects that many advocates are really seeking to bind the hands of those who would seek to employ policy to counter market outcomes or limit the influence of democratic politics. We will have an opportunity to discuss the symbolic politics of the deficit below. For current purposes, it is sufficient to state that the deficit and debt will be treated not as symbols of some political pathology—real or imagined—but as fiscal imbalances.

Second, concern over deficits and the debt is contingent on a fundamental question: Why were deficits incurred in the first instance? This is not an easy question to answer. Unlike businesses and state and local governments, the federal government does not treat capital expenditures and operating outlays differently. Businesses maintain capital accounts and charge depreciation against their current accounts. As Robert Eisner notes: "Most of the large corporations in the United States would find themselves in deficit if they had to include capital expenditures rather than depreciation charges in their profit

DOI: 10.4324/9781003395331-5

and loss statements."[1] Similarly, state governments, functioning under balanced budget requirements, finance capital outlays (e.g., for infrastructure) separately, essentially moving them off budget. To fail to distinguish between capital expenditures and outlays, is akin to treating investments in new infrastructure that would increase long-term economic productivity the same as one might treat current outlays that appease one's local constituents or fund current consumption.

Why are deficits generated in the first place? Sometimes, they may be counter-cyclical. During economic downturns, taxable income falls, driving down revenues while increased demand for transfer programs like unemployment compensation, Medicaid, and the Supplemental Nutrition Assistance Program drives up expenditures. These automatic stabilizers minimize the duration and severity of a recession, and their impact necessarily declines as an economy enters recovery. During upturns in the business cycle, they have the opposite effect. To account for the cyclical fluctuations in the economy, one might ask whether the budget is in balance across the business cycle rather than focusing on a single year. In other cases, deficits may be episodic and connected to national emergencies. During significant wars, for example, deficits may prove unavoidable. During World War II, the deficit peaked at almost 30 percent of GDP (1943). But with the defeat of Germany and Japan, the budget was in surplus by 1947.[2] Attention would turn to managing the debt. The same could be said of expenditures in the wake of natural disasters and most recently, the COVID-19 pandemic, although none has required spending as a share of GDP comparable to the level of World War II.

One can contrast the impact of automatic stabilizers with structural deficits, and the structural component of the deficit and its implications for the debt are the chief concern in this volume. If one filters out the impact of automatic stabilizers, the structural deficit is the gap between revenues and spending when the economy is functioning at its potential. It reflects a fundamental imbalance between levels of spending and levels of taxation that extends over time. There are some convincing arguments that a long-term structural deficit is sustainable, if the debt does not grow faster than the economy. But if the debt grows faster than GDP, the resulting costs of financing the debt may crowd out other forms of spending. This is the path the United States is currently on, and we will turn to the implications later in this chapter.[3]

This chapter explores the core question of why the debt matters. The discussion is prefaced with a brief primer on the deficit and debt, placing them in the larger context of government finance. The chapter turns to an examination of the political symbolism of deficits and the debt. To what extent are objections to deficits really objections to activist government or departures from market governance? The chapter then considers some normative dimensions of the debt. If the debt is deferred taxation, under what conditions is it permissible to impose obligations on future generations? What are the normative implications of making a transition from government financing via taxation to a heavier reliance on debt? The chapter concludes with some practical questions. For example, is there some level of national indebtedness that compromises economic growth? Another question made salient by the recent memories of the financial crisis and Great Recession: How does debt raise the probability of fiscal crises? To what extent does reliance on foreign holdings of the debt alleviate or exacerbate these problems? To what extent do the demands of debt financing foreclose the options open to elected officials?

Placing the Debt in Context

It is useful to preface the larger discussion of the debt with a brief consideration of the debt and its relationship to federal finances. Federal spending, when taken as a whole, draws on two groups of funds: federal funds and trust funds. The federal funds group is dominated by the general fund, which is used to finance the daily and long-term operations of the federal government (it also includes several special and revolving funds that are not directly relevant to the current discussion).[4] The general fund is financed primarily through tax receipts from the individual and corporate income tax. When these revenues are insufficient to cover the expenditures, the resulting deficit is met through borrowing. As represented in Figure 4.1, deficits have been the norm in the postwar period. As the Treasury sells government securities, it converts deficits into debt. At the most basic level, the federal debt represents the accumulation of past deficits in the federal funds group, money that has been borrowed but not repaid. In contrast, the trust funds are financed through taxes that are legally dedicated to a specific purpose (e.g., the payroll tax is dedicated to Social Security Old Age and Disability Insurance and Medicare Hospital Insurance). By law, the taxes that are assigned to trust funds cannot be comingled with the general fund. Unlike the federal funds, trust funds can become depleted and ultimately insolvent, but they cannot incur deficits.

An important distinction can be drawn between debt that is held by the public and the intragovernmental debt, which closely tracks the distinction between federal funds and trust funds. Let us address them in turn. The debt held by the public includes all the borrowing from individuals and entities outside of the federal government (i.e., financial institutions, state and local governments, foreign governments, the Federal Reserve, foreign central banks) to cover deficits in the general fund. The Treasury issues several marketable debt instruments. It issues Treasury bills—with a maturity of up to one year—and a variety of securities with longer maturities (i.e., Treasury notes, bonds, inflation-protected securities, and floating rate notes).[5] The demand for securities of various maturities is, in part, a product of economic conditions (e.g., during periods of higher inflation, longer-term securities become less attractive to investors). The mix of short-, medium-, and long-term securities determines

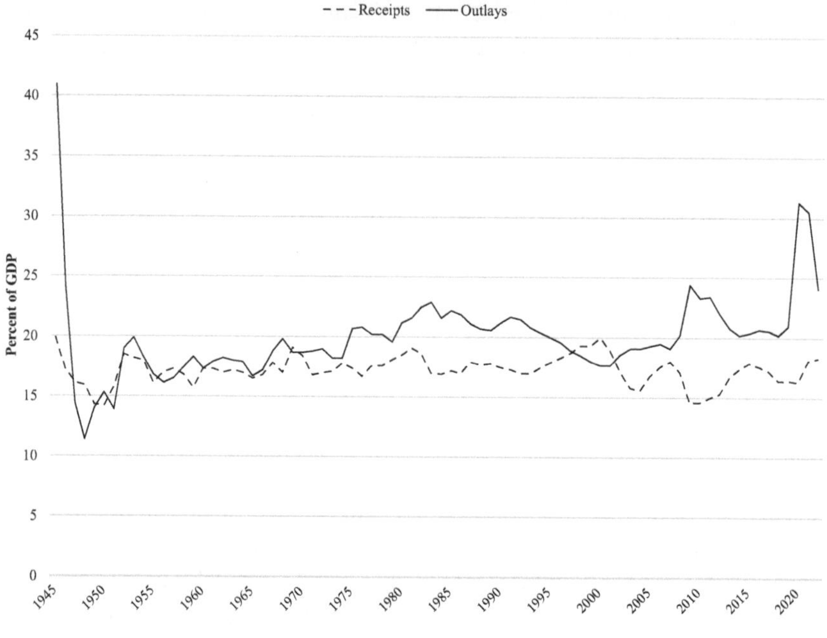

FIGURE 4.1 Receipts and Outlays, 1945–2022

Source: Adapted from OMB, *Budget of the United States, FY 23*, Historical Tables, Table 1.2.

the maturity structure of the debt. The central objective of the Treasury's debt management is simultaneously to meet the financial needs of the government and to do so at the lowest cost over time. Short-term securities can reduce the cost of financing compared with long-term securities that carry a higher premium. Refinancing short-term securities carries a higher rollover risk, however. That is, when the security matures, debt may have to be refinanced at a higher interest rate due to factors outside of the Treasury's control (e.g., stronger than expected economic growth, changes in the Federal Reserve's monetary policy, or higher inflation). Thus, the Treasury must find an optimal balance between the costs of longer-term debt and the rollover risks of short-term debt, while maintaining a reputation for regular and predictable issuance of debt.[6]

The significance of these decisions is obvious when one considers the annual costs of paying interest on the debt, which have varied over the last several decades from a high of 3.4 percent of GDP (16.2 percent of outlays) in 1990 to a much more manageable range of 1.4 to 2 percent of GDP (7.1 to 9.5 percent of outlays) in the period 2015–2019. Note that while the debt was far smaller as a share of GDP in 1990, the much larger debt of the post-2015 period has occurred in an environment of low inflation and low interest rates.[7] But changes in interest can have an immediate impact on interest payments, given that trillions of dollars of debt mature on an annual basis. At the end of the 2019 fiscal year, for example, 61 percent of the debt held by the public—some $9.9 trillion—would be maturing in the next four years, forcing the Treasury to issue new debt at prevailing rates.[8]

The second component of the debt is the federal intragovernmental debt that is held by the Treasury in trust funds or accounts. This debt is not part of the Treasury's support of financing the deficit but consists of funds that are held on behalf of specific programs. The largest of these trust funds support entitlement programs for the elderly, Social Security (the Old Age and Survivors Trust Fund and the Federal Disability Insurance Trust Fund) and Medicare (the Hospital Insurance Trust Fund). In case of Social Security, revenues from a portion of the payroll tax and taxes paid on benefits by higher earning households are retained in the general fund, but they are credited to the relevant trust fund as special issue, interest-bearing, government securities that can be redeemed when program expenditures exceed revenues. The largest trust funds have built up significant surpluses over time. But as a result of demographic change, Social Security and Medicare are forced to rely, increasingly, on the redemption of securities in their trust funds and, in both cases, the trust funds face impending insolvency, as noted in Chapter 2. Although the intragovernmental debt is not a product of deficits incurred through the congressional budget process, it nonetheless part of the federal debt and is subject to the federal debt limit.[9]

Setting Limits on the Debt

Congress delegates authority over the issuance of debt to the Treasury, but this delegation has not been complete. Over the nation's history, Congress has retained the responsibility to authorize the issuance of new debt and restrict the size of the federal debt. The nature of these restrictions has changed form, however. Prior to World War I, Congress exerted detailed control over the issuance of debt. It authorized the Treasury to borrow funds for specific purposes (e.g., to fund the Louisiana Purchase, to build the Panama Canal), required the Treasury to use specific debt instruments and controlled the interest rates, maturities, and the redemption schedules. Because Congress placed strict controls on the Treasury's authorized bond sales, after securities were redeemed, they could not be reissued. As a result, the debt incurred even during significant events like the War of 1812 and the Civil War only had a short-term impact on aggregate levels of debt.[10] One might argue that the pattern of leveraging and deleveraging discussed in Chapter 1 was partially an artifact of the way in which Congress authorized the issuance of debt. Things changed significantly in the 20th century. When Congress passed the Second Liberty Bond Act in 1917, it provided the Treasury with greater flexibility over the maturity and redemption of bonds, thereafter allowing it to refinance existing World War I debt with lower interest bonds. By 1939, Congress had dramatically increased the Treasury's authority by authorizing an aggregate debt limit; Congress finally set a single overall debt limit with the Public Debt Act of 1941, granting the Treasury the freedom to make decisions about appropriate debt instruments and maturities.[11]

The statutory debt limit, which is the total amount of money that the federal government is authorized to borrow to meet its legal obligations, includes both debt that is held by the public and the intragovernmental debt.[12] While the creation of a statutory debt limit provided the Treasury with greater flexibility in managing the finances of the federal government, it necessitated that Congress routinely and explicitly authorize increases in the debt. The existence of a debt ceiling is somewhat redundant. As the Government Accountability Office (GAO) notes, the debt limit

> only restricts Treasury's authority to borrow and finance the decisions already enacted by Congress and the President. It does not restrict Congress's ability to pass spending and revenue legislation that affects the level of debt, nor does it otherwise constrain fiscal policy.[13]

Indeed, the United States is an anomaly in this regard (e.g., the only other nation with a debt ceiling is Denmark, where it is set sufficiently high to prevent the need for statutory action).

Since 1939, Congress has raised the debt ceiling some 100 times—in some years, on multiple occasions. At times, the need to raise the debt ceiling has created an opportunity for extended debate, as members of Congress have sought to focus attention on the long-term trajectory of the debt, the fiscal imprudence of the majority or the current presidential administration, or to make the case for changes in policies and practices that could limit the need for future increases. In 1979, following some temporary lapses in the debt ceiling that forced the Federal Reserve to make emergency loans to the Treasury, the House enacted the Gephardt rule—named after Representative Richard Gephardt (D-MO), its author. Under the Gephardt rule, once the House passed the budget resolution, it would automatically generate an engrossed joint resolution raising the debt limit to a level deemed appropriate. The Senate has not adopted a similar rule and the House version has been modified or repealed as control of the chamber has shifted between parties and the majority sought to use votes on the debt ceiling for messaging purposes.[14] While the debates over the debt limit have been frequently contentious, Congress has never failed to increase the debt limit given the potentially catastrophic consequences. The federal government would be forced to delay or cancel many of its obligations, including payments under Social Security, Medicare and Medicaid, grants to the states, tax refunds, and salaries for government employees. Perhaps most consequential would be the impact on credit markets. As the Office of Budget and Management (OMB) explains: "If Treasury were unable to make timely interest payments or redeem securities, investors would cease to view US

Treasury securities as free of credit risk and Treasury's interest costs would increase." Given that interest rates are benchmarked to Treasury rates, interest rates across the economy would rise. "Foreign investors would likely shift out of dollar-denominated assets, driving down the value of the dollar and further increasing interest rates on non-Federal, as well as Treasury debt."[15]

The Size of the Debt

How large is the US debt? The answer rests on definitional issues. The broadest measure of the debt is the gross debt, which combines the publicly held debt and intragovernmetnal holdings. Although there are some 100 trust funds in the federal government, the most consequential are connected to Social Security and Medicare. Historically, when revenues from the payroll tax exceeded expenditures, the Treasury borrowed the surplus to fund other government activities and credited bonds to the trust funds that would be available for redemption when program expenditures exceeded revenues. As the OMB explains, "issuing debt to Government accounts … is an internal transaction of the Government, made between two accounts that are both within the Government itself." Nonetheless, intragovernmental debt is debt: these transactions create "a binding claim against the Treasury" which will have to pay the claims "by the collection of revenues or by borrowing."[16] Given the special status of intragovernmental debt, analysts usually present the debt held by the public as the most relevant measure of the debt. While the current dollar value of the debt may attract great attention in contemporary political debates, its magnitude is difficult to evaluate in historical or cross-national perspective. As a result, it is common to express the debt relative to GDP. In 2020, gross federal debt was 128.4 percent of GDP whereas the publicly held debt was a more modest 100.3 percent of GDP.[17] As Figure 4.2 suggests, the debt has grown significantly in the postwar period.

An alternative measure of the debt that gained some currency in the United States is debt held by the public net of financial assets. There is an argument that borrowing only accounts for one side of many government transactions. Often the borrowing is used to acquire assets that offset some or all of the underlying costs. As the OMB explains, the federal government "holds significant financial assets, which can be offset against the debt held by the public and other financial liabilities to achieve a more complete understanding of the Government's financial condition." The federal government's financial assets include cash balances in Treasury accounts, federal loans and the future payments of interest and principal they represent, preferred stock in government-sponsored enterprises (GSEs) like the Federal National Mortgage Association (Fannie Mae) and the Federal Home Loan Mortgage Corporation (Freddie Mac), and non-federal securities that were acquired as part of the response to the financial crisis of 2007–2008 or held in the National Railroad Retirement Investment

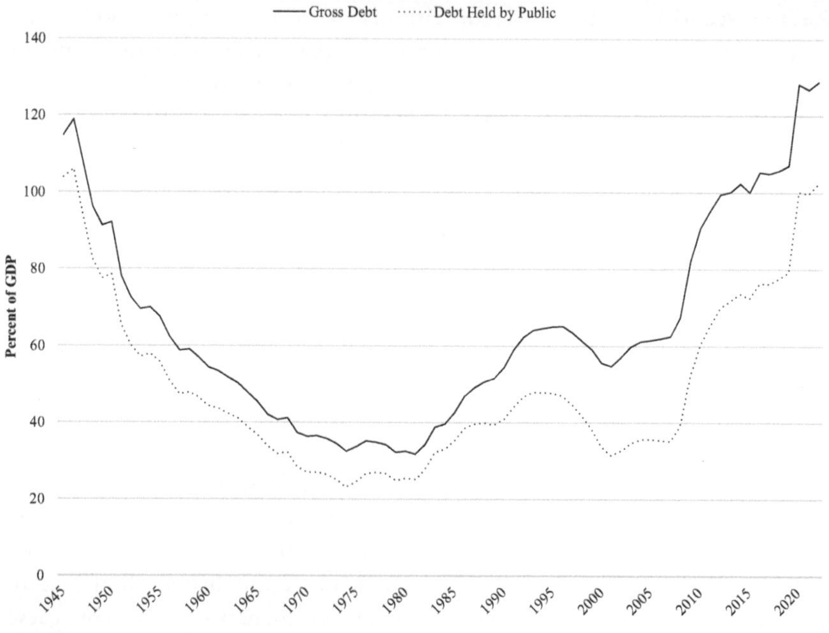

FIGURE 4.2 National Debt, 1945–2022

Source: Adapted from OMB, *Budget of the United States, FY23*, Historical Tables, Table 7.1.

Trust. The difference between the debt held by the public and the debt held by the public net of financial assets and liabilities is significant. For example, in 2020, the first measure of the debt constituted 100.1 percent of GDP. When adjusted for financial assets and liabilities, it fell to 85.8 percent of GDP.[18]

Which measure of the debt is the most informative? Economists tend to be more interested in the publicly-held debt as the most useful measure insofar as it has important implications for understanding the level of economic stimulus and changes in interest rates. Moreover, given that private businesses must compete with the federal government in capital markets, it may provide insights into the extent to which public debt is crowding out private investment activities. In 2020, for example, the debt held by the public accounted for 36.2 percent of total credit market debt.[19] The debt held by the public is, as a result, the most cited measure. At the same time, one can argue that gross debt is an important measure of the debt for two reasons. First, as noted earlier, the statutory debt limit sets a ceiling on the combination of publicly-held and intragovernmental debt and, as a result, the latter measure can provide information on whether Congress will be forced to engage in deliberations over the debt limit which have become increasingly combative.[20] Second, while there are important reasons to distinguish between different components of the gross debt, in the end, intragovernmental debt is debt owed by the federal government to the trust funds. When the expenditures for key programs like Social Security and Medicare exceed revenues, the Treasury needs to redeem the bonds it issued. It can fund the redemptions through tax increases, reduced spending on other programs, or the issuance of debt to the public.[21] Given the strong opposition to tax increases and the ongoing growth of mandatory spending—issues that were addressed in previous chapters—public borrowing is the default response to trust fund redemptions. intragovernmental debt, in short, is converted into publicly held debt. To some extent, the debt held by the public is a backward-looking measure, representing the cumulative effects of past borrowing. The gross debt, insofar as it represents future liabilities, provides a sense of what the future holds.

The Balanced Budget as Symbol

The symbolic importance of deficits and debt in the United States reflects, in part, the enduring force of the anti-statist features of American political culture discussed in the last chapter. The animosity toward centralized governmental power has been combined with a strong preference for the market over the state, and communities and civil organizations (and to some extent, local and state governments) over the national government.[22] In the words of James D. Savage,

> balanced and unbalanced federal budgets have served as powerful and politically evocative symbols of competing visions of government and society....A balanced national budget signified a popular willingness and ability to limit the purpose and size of the federal government, to restrain its influence in the economy, to protect states' rights, to maintain the Constitution's balance of powers, and to promote republican virtues.[23]

Policymakers have needed to make overtures to the symbol of balanced budgets, even when policy has moved decisively in the opposite direction. During the crisis of the Great Depression, for example, when President Roosevelt expanded social provision and created the foundations of the modern welfare state, he made rhetorical appeals to balanced budgets and segregated spending into the "general budget" which was balanced (or soon to be balanced) and the "recovery and relief" budget which was in deficit.

While the appeal of balanced budgets and the objection to debt resonate with the anti-statist features of American political culture, one of the core concerns is the perceived excesses of democratic politics and the implications for the expansion of public provision. One of the best examples can be found in the book *Democracy in Deficit*, by James M. Buchanan and Richard E. Wagner. They claim that democratic politics will invariably produce deficits and debt unless restrained by a constitutional rule. If we assume that deficits and debt are simply deferred taxation, they argued, life-cycle considerations loom large in shaping preferences toward alternative means of financing government. Younger citizens may be indifferent insofar as the present value of taxes paid today is the actuarial equivalent to the stream of future payments required to service the debt. Older citizens, in contrast, have a shorter time horizon, and "will regard debt finance as lowering the price" of "public services, thereby desiring a larger public budget under debt finance than under tax finance." The resulting stream of tax liabilities will be inherited by the young and by the unborn. Deficit financing, in essence, would reduce the price for government services, thereby incentivizing higher levels of consumption (in essence, government services would be "on sale"). Given that younger constituents are neutral and older constituents rationally prefer debt financing, the political calculus is evident: "The net pressures on the politicians clearly tend toward expanded spending, with the 'unrepresented' being those yet-unfranchised future taxpayers who must bear the liabilities chosen by their ancestors." They conclude:

> Budgets cannot be left adrift in the sea of democratic politics....The elected politicians, who must be responsive to their constituents, the governmental bureaucracy as well as the electorate, need something in the way of an external and "superior" rule that will allow them to forestall the persistent demands for an increased flow of public-spending benefits along with reduced levels of taxation.

Buchanan and Wagner defend a balanced budget rule as a means of forcing discipline and, they argue, tying the hands of those who would seek to use discretionary fiscal policy to manage the economy. "Precisely because we have allowed the Keynesian teachings to destroy the constraining influence of...our fiscal constitution, restoration must now involve something more formal, more specific, more explicitly confining than that which fell victim to the Keynesian onslaught."[24]

Arguments for balanced budget rules, like that present above, often obscure the larger normative questions about the government and the role it should play in the economy and society more generally. They provide a means of deploying the symbolic importance of balanced budgets to limit the size and scope of government and to frame an agenda that could not receive sufficient support through democratic processes. As Brian Barry observes, these arguments are thinly veiled claims that the market, rather than the state, "should determine what gets produced and who receives what income." Barry continues that the "political problem" solved by a balanced budget amendment "is how to get democratic approval for tying the hands of elected governments in perpetuity."[25] We will have the opportunity to discuss a few examples of proposed balanced-budget rules in subsequent chapters. As a generalization, they have focused on domestic spending and have been advocated by actors who reject tax increases as a means—even a partial means—of balancing the budget. In some cases, they have incorporated the goal of reducing spending to a level compatible with historical levels of revenues as a share of GDP, something that would prove impossible without retrenchment in key social policies. The debates, as Mark Blyth explains, often "take the form of a morality play between 'good austerity' and 'bad spending' that may lead us into a period of self-defeating budget cuts."[26]

Debt and Equity

The symbolic power of balanced budgets has been part of the political rhetoric in the United States since the early days of the Republic. But there are normative and practical claims about why the debt matters that go beyond the symbolic. Let us begin with the normative claims. When the debt is deployed for its symbolic value, proponents of balanced budgets often use the debate over fiscal policy to support a particular vision of the proper size and scope of government. Although there are normative claims, they are often left implicit. Yet, there are normative arguments about the debt that need serious consideration. Arguably, the most important normative issues involve equity. With respect to intergenerational equity, the core question is simple: What responsibilities do current generations have to future generations? Under what conditions do current period actors have the right to impose the costs of financing current expenditures on to future period actors, in effect forcing a transfer of wealth from tomorrow's generations to today's generation? A somewhat different issue involves intragenerational equity, and here there are two core concerns: the impact of efforts to control the size of the debt and the ramifications of debt-financing on levels of wealth inequality.

We must begin this discussion with a simple premise. Ultimately, all government spending decisions must be covered by revenues. The decision to run a deficit in a given year and thus contribute to the debt is simply a decision to defer taxation to some point in the future, where the costs are borne by future citizens (or our future selves). The decision of today's population to enjoy benefits while deferring the costs to future generations without their consent raises important intergenerational equity concerns. Obviously, the current generation has asymmetrical power relative to those who have yet to be born. Its decisions along multiple dimensions (e.g., natural resource use, climate stability, investments in capital, infrastructure, and labor training) can significantly impact the quality of life and the options available to future generations.[27] In the area of fiscal policy, one influential approach to the issue of intergenerational equity has been generational accounting. Under one prominent version of generational accounting, one determines a generation's lifetime net tax rate (that is, taxes paid minus transfer payments). The existence of a fiscal gap—transfers in excess of receipts—will force future generations to bear a larger lifetime net tax rate, thereby violating norms of intergenerational equity.[28] Under generational accounting, today's policymakers would be encouraged to adopt tax and spending rules to equalize the lifetime net tax rates across generations or, at the very least, reduce the magnitude of the intergenerational transfers.

The generational accounting approach, while intuitively attractive, has some clear limitations. Most notably, it depends heavily on our assumptions about future generations. The record of the past century has been one of remarkable growth in inflation-adjusted per capita GDP. Leaving aside questions of income distribution, today's population is far more affluent than past generations. Even the more pessimistic projections of growth conclude that future generations will be far wealthier than today's generation. How does this bear on intergenerational equity? Neil H. Buchanan cautions that we may not want to over-emphasize the interests of future generations, particularly if they are going to enjoy a higher level of prosperity.

> Simple utilitarianism...would appear to argue unambiguously in favor of redistributing from future generations to current generations.... If a future generation is going to have higher incomes than a current generation, redistribution across time from the future to the present will increase total utility.[29]

Moreover, efforts to address intergenerational equity could have unanticipated consequences. Much will depend on the use of resources that are effectively borrowed from future generations. Investments made today could have the effect of increasing economic productivity, thus raising the real income of future generations. To forestall these investments in the name of equity would compromise the wealth of future generations. The same case cannot be made as easily for the decision to borrow from the future to fund higher levels of current consumption. The imposition of higher taxes today, moreover, could impede the growth that would lead to higher levels of prosperity for future generations. Ironically, a concern for future generations could be used to justify policies that would impoverish those very generations.

Should we sacrifice consumption and pay higher taxes today in the hope of helping future generations—or as it is commonly phrased, to reduce the burdens placed on our grandchildren? One might be skeptical, given the uncertainty one would face about the kinds of decisions that future generations of voters and policymakers might make. One might accept higher taxes or reduced spending today, only to discover that collective decision-making at some future point results in policies that provided few or no benefits to one's heirs. In this context, a more rational response to the concern over the impact of long-term deficits on one's grandchildren might take the form of personal savings rather than changes in fiscal policy. That is, one might advocate a low tax regime and build private estates that could be bequeathed to future generations.[30] The largest intergenerational transfers are not government programs imposing today's costs on future generations, but the product of gifts and bequests that convey benefits on future generations, albeit lightly touched by the tax system. These transfers exacerbate and perpetuate income inequality and thus inequity across time.

In sharp contrast, the largest *intra*generational transfers are a result of government policies. Social welfare policies are centrally important in furthering intragenerational redistribution. One can argue that any reforms that would be proposed in the name of intergenerational equity should be evaluated in light of the impact on intragenerational equity.[31] For example, if current expenditures on core social policies, particularly mean's tested programs (e.g., Medicaid, Temporary Assistance for Needy Families, or nutritional assistance), were reduced in hopes of alleviating future generations of the responsibilities of repaying the debt, it could contribute to higher levels of intragenerational inequity today. We would be trading one form of inequity for another. If policymakers sought to address fiscal imbalances by raising the payroll tax, the same results would be forthcoming. These taxes are highly regressive: some 60 percent of taxpayers—and virtually all taxpayers in the bottom two quintiles of the income distribution—pay more in payroll taxes than in the income tax.[32] One might argue that it would be preferable in terms of equity to accept fiscal imbalances today and rely on future financing from general revenues raised through a progressive income tax, an inheritance tax, or a wealth tax, then to pursue a policy of austerity or saddle today's low- and moderate-income households with higher tax liabilities.

From the Tax State to the Debt State

The concerns with intragenerational equity are relevant to the larger fiscal story of the past several decades. Wolfgang Streeck has argued that the post-1970s decades witnessed the decline of the "tax state" and the rise of the "debt state" not just in the United States but in other OECD countries. During the immediate postwar decades, as noted in Chapter 1, growing public expenditures were financed by tax revenues; when combined with economic growth, this combination facilitated a steady reduction in the debt-to-GDP ratio. But as a result of changes in tax policy, revenues largely stagnated while expenditures continued to grow. The result, inevitably, was a reversal of the deleveraging of the immediate postwar decades as the United States (and other nations) incurred increasing levels of public debt. As Streeck notes: "Overall, growing public debt was a part of a general rise of indebtedness in capitalist countries, which coincided with low growth and indeed may have been the result of attempts to sustain and restore economic performance."[33] As the US government incurred ever-greater debt, so did households. With the encouragement of public policies that enhanced access to credit (particularly in the housing market), households compensated for stagnant wages and the limited support provided by government transfers by accepting higher levels of indebtedness. During the 1980s, the federal government increasingly relied on debt financing rather than taxation to meet its obligations. As Streeck observes, this was a decision ripe with ethical implications: "by replacing tax revenue with debt, governments contributed further to inequality, in that they offered secure investment opportunities to those whose money they would or could no longer confiscate and had to borrow instead. Unlike taxpayers, buyers of government bonds continue to own what they pay to the state, and in fact collect interest on it, typically paid out of ever less progressive taxation; they can also pass it on to their children."[34]

Debt financing results in intragenerational transfers of wealth insofar as the holders of the debt are wealthier than those whose income taxes fund the interest payments. Since the early 1980s, there has been a growing concentration of ownership of the public debt among the wealthiest households which perfectly tracks the change in federal finances. Almost two-thirds of the increase in the financial assets held by the top 1 percent of the wealth distribution took the form of government bonds and GSE debt—the mortgage-backed securities that pooled the household debt mentioned earlier. While there was a "savings glut" among the wealthiest, it was fed largely by "dissaving" by the federal government (i.e., the issuance of debt) and households that were incurring higher levels of mortgage debt. Treasuries are backed by the full faith and credit of the federal government; GSE debt carries the same guarantee, albeit implicitly. While the demand for dollar-denominated safe assets was great among foreign investors, the demand by the wealthiest households in the United States was almost as great.[35] "The distribution of the public debt is tightly correlated with the distribution of wealth more generally," observes Sandy Brian Hager. "When the share of wealth owned by wealthy households and large corporations increases or decreases, so, too, does their share of the public debt. Thus, there is an intimate relationship between growing inequality, on the one hand, and a rising public debt, on the other." Following Streeck, he notes that the governments "rely on borrowing from elites instead of taxing them. And in choosing to furnish elites with risk free assets rather than to levy taxes on their incomes, the debt state comes to reinforce existing patterns of social inequality."[36] Even if the policies that are funded via debt were intended to reduce overall inequality—a questionable assumption in the past several decades—the wealth transfers that accompany public debt may contribute to higher levels of inequality.[37]

The Practical Consequences of the Debt

The growth in the debt has received a greater deal of attention because of its practical consequences. First, there is the concern that public debt can constrain economic growth as private firms are forced to compete with the government in capital markets (the so-called crowding out effect). A second important claim is that there is some level of indebtedness that can trigger a fiscal crisis that would have devastating ramifications for the United States and the global economy. Third, there have been concerns regarding the growth of foreign bondholders both with respect to the resulting cross-national transfers of wealth and the threat that major bondholders could liquidate their positions, destabilizing the US economy. Some of these claims have been deployed to bolster calls for austerity, even if the empirical support is somewhat tenuous. Yet, there is a fourth practical concern: if the debt continues to grow as projected, the costs of servicing the debt could displace other national priorities, a political "crowding out," if you will. While some of these practical concerns seem overstated—in part, a product of the unique status of US debt—others should be taken seriously.

Debt versus Growth and the Problem of "Crowding Out"

One of the more enduring claims about the debt is that it can depress economic growth through the "crowding out" effect. Government and corporations actively compete for funds in capital markets. The growing demands of the public sector—when combined with the virtually risk-free nature of government bonds—may force corporations to pay a higher rate to secure funds. To the extent that such investments no longer make economic sense to profit-seeking firms, growth rates will be reduced. Lower capital investment will deplete future productivity and future incomes (once again, an outcome that would have implications for intergenerational equity). This is important because there are two paths to reducing the debt-to-GDP ratio and they are not mutually exclusive. One path is to reduce the debt through austerity, cutting spending and/or raising taxes to reduce deficits and potentially generate surpluses that can be used to retire existing debt. A second and more attractive path is through economic growth. If the rate of economic growth exceeds the rate at which new debt is incurred, the debt-to-GDP ratio will fall. As noted in Chapter 1, this second path was adopted in the immediate postwar decades. If the crowding out effect is significant, the growth in public debt may inhibit the kinds of investments that could produce higher rates of economic growth. If there is a negative correlation between the size of the public debt and rates of growth, it should inform decisions about fiscal policy.

The CBO's *Long-Term Budget Outlook* engages the crowding out argument on a regular basis when discussing the impact of the growth of the federal debt: "When the government borrows in financial markets, it does so from people and businesses whose saving would otherwise finance private investment, such as factories and computers." As capital investment declines, "workers would, on average, have less capital to use in their jobs…they would be less productive, they would receive lower compensation, and they would thus be less inclined to work."[38] Prior to the COVID-19 pandemic, the CBO projected that reducing the debt over the next 30 years to achieve a level of 42 percent of GDP (the average for the postwar period) would raise the growth rate by 0.1 percent per year, such that by the end of the period, GDP would be 4.3 percent higher, and GDP per capita would be some $4,200 greater (in 2019 dollars) than if the debt had continued on its current trajectory.[39]

A few caveats are important at this point. Historically, the "crowding out" argument has been deployed as part of a critique of Keynesianism. During the Great Recession, critics argued that rather than using expansionary fiscal policy to raise levels of demand, the superior strategy would be one of "expansionary austerity." John Quiggin, a critic of this position, describes the core contention as follows:

> whenever government budgets are in deficit and public debt is excessive, austerity is the appropriate response. By reducing public demands on capital markets, it is claimed, austerity will make it easier to fund private investment. Thus, austerity is presented as an expansionary policy that will promote economic growth.[40]

Quiggin recognizes that Keynes supported generating surpluses when the economy was booming; his critique focuses on the claim that nations could essentially "cut their way to growth" following the financial crisis. From a historical and cross-national perspective, the empirical support for expansionary austerity is quite thin, particularly when applied to economies that are functioning below potential output.[41] The "crowding out" argument, as developed earlier, is not a critique of Keynesianism or debt, per se. Rather, there is the question of whether there is some level of indebtedness—a threshold—beyond which the rate of growth is depressed. Indeed, some studies have reported that there is a positive correlation between debt and growth up to a particular threshold and perhaps no correlation at moderate levels of indebtedness. But once a particular threshold is reached, the growth rate is reduced. There is no consensus, however, on what the threshold is: estimates range from relatively low levels (e.g., 60 percent of GDP) to relatively high levels (e.g., 95–120 percent of GDP).[42]

Another caveat: the relationship between debt and growth is not uniform across countries or across time, and the United States may be less prone to this relationship given the global demand for US securities in the current environment and the role of the dollar as the world's reserve currency. There was a steady decline in real interest rates after the 1990s which reflected two factors. First, there was a global savings glut, with a surplus of savings in Asia and the oil-producing states of the Middle East and North Africa. Second, much of this savings flowed into the United States, as investors looked for safe liquid assets like Treasuries. The flight to safety only accelerated in the period following the global financial crisis. While the persistent low interest rates have created challenges for monetary policy, they have significantly reduced the costs of managing the federal debt. To the extent that the global savings glut reflects demographics and a long-term mismatch between savings and investment, the United States may not have to confront issues of crowding out for some time, if at all.[43]

Indeed, advocates of Modern Monetary Theory—a heterodox school of thought that attracted some attention in the wake of the financial crisis—claim that the argument about crowding out, and many of the concerns addressed later in this chapter, fail to take note of the United States's exceptional position. The dollar has been a fiat currency since the collapse of Bretton Woods in 1971. The government does not have to worry about claims being placed on its gold reserves or a basket of foreign currency reserves and thus, has the freedom to create money. A government that creates its own money does not need to raise revenues in order to spend; the national debt simply is not debt as conventionally understood. A nation that spends and borrows money that it creates has the freedom to use fiscal policy to pursue desired levels of employment without concerns about the size of the debt. Indeed, persistent deficits may be necessary if the private sector fails to generate a level of demand necessary to achieve employment targets. The resulting deficits can be financed through the issuance of Treasuries (indeed, Treasuries may serve an important function for investors). But Treasuries can also be purchased by the Federal Reserve, which can create new currency reserves for this purpose. Indeed, these new reserves could be used to pay off debt, essentially purchasing Treasuries as they mature. Of course, politicians who fail to understand the nature of debt may make poor decisions regarding fiscal policy or the debt limit. But the main concern for Modern Monetary Theory is the inflation that could result from expanding the economy beyond its potential capacity.[44] Modern Monetary Theory has not been embraced by most economists (in the words of one critic, it is "a policy polemic for depressed times…that promises full employment and price stability at little cost").[45] Yet, its insights into the unique position of the United States should be kept in mind as we consider other practical concerns about the debt.

The Vulnerability to Fiscal Crisis

Does debt increase the vulnerability to fiscal crisis? The CBO's annual report, *Long-Term Budget Outlook,* identifies some of the risks associated with the current trajectory of the debt. In addition to the concerns over growth, the CBO also routinely warns that fiscal crisis is one of the most significant risks the nation faces as debt levels increase. It notes:

> High and rising federal debt increases the likelihood of a fiscal crisis because it erodes investors' confidence in the government's fiscal position

> and could result in a sharp reduction in their valuation of Treasury securities, which would drive up interest rates on federal debt because investors would demand higher yields to purchase Treasury securities. For example, concerns about the U.S. government's fiscal position could lead to a sudden increase in inflation expectations, fear of a large decrease in the value of the U.S. dollar, or a loss of confidence in the federal government's ability or commitment to repay its debt in full. [46]

What if US debt loses its risk-free status? If investors question whether a government is willing or able to repay outstanding debt, they may demand a higher risk premium. This risk premium raises the budgetary costs of managing interest on the debt, thereby worsening a government's fiscal position. As Treasury yields rise, so do the interest rates that banks charge to consumers and businesses, neither of which are good for the economy. Certainly, governments can manage the level of debt and seek to restore confidence. But the means of accomplishing this feat—raising taxes and cutting public services—have significant economic and political ramifications, which only become larger if the government delays its response to growing debt-to-GDP ratios. In the worst-case scenario, the crisis of confidence may lead investors to retreat from a US debt market. The collapse in the value of government debt could cascade into the financial system more generally because banks, mutual funds, and pension funds hold government securities in their portfolios.[47]

As noted earlier, there has been a good deal of research seeking to determine whether levels of public debt can reach a level that compromises growth via the crowding out effect. There is related research on whether there is some tipping point at which the probability of fiscal crisis increases. While there is no consensus on either point, attention has returned to the issue in the wake of the unprecedented levels of fiscal stimulus during the COVID-19 pandemic, which raised the debt-to-GDP ratio to the highest level since World War II, and projections that without changes in tax and spending policies, levels of debt may grow rapidly in the next several decades. Recent research from the Federal Reserve Bank of Kansas City concludes that at current levels of debt (approximately 100 percent of GDP), the probability of default is "virtually zero." But the risks "rise quickly as debt continues to grow beyond certain thresholds." As debt approaches 200 percent of GDP (the CBO's long-term projection), the risk of default reaches 10 percent. "At debt levels above 200 percent of GDP, the probability of default increases dramatically."[48]

The good news is clear. The CBO baseline projections assume that current laws governing taxation and spending remain unchanged. Even if the probability of default increases with the debt-to-GDP ratio, there is nothing that mandates that the United States remain on the current fiscal trajectory. As the CBO notes: "financial markets show little indication of a fiscal crisis in the near future."[49] Interest rates remain low, suggesting little pressure in the paper market. But the good news comes with a significant caveat. As Carlo Cottarelli, former director of the International Monetary Fund, cautions "low interest rates can lead to a false sense of security" that could lull policymakers into deferring the kinds of politically unpopular policy changes that would stabilize debt levels at a sustainable level.[50] Moreover, unexpected events could rapidly change the fiscal situation. In an era of political polarization and gridlock, the greatest source of insecurity regarding the future may take the form of a failure to raise the debt ceiling to extract political concessions, a decision that could carry significant ramifications for the perception of the risk-free nature of US debt. In 2011, for example, efforts to use the debt ceiling to force budgetary concessions brought the nation to the brink of default, resulting in a downgrade in the US credit rating (see Chapter 8).

Foreign Bondholders, Interest, and the "Nuclear Option"

A frequently raised warning is that, to the extent that debt is held by foreign entities, it can compromise national autonomy. Since the late 1970s, the United States has relied heavily on foreign parties to fund the debt. Between 1980 and 2000, foreign holding of federal debt increased from 17.8 to 30.5 percent. In the wake of the financial crisis, it peaked at 48.5 percent (2011–2012), before receding to 33–40 percent by 2020–2021.[51] At the end of 2020, foreign holders of Treasury securities held $7.1 trillion, approximately one-third of the publicly held debt. The top holders of the debt included Japan ($1.3 trillion, or 17.7 percent of the total), China ($1.1 trillion, or 15.2 percent of the total), and the United Kingdom ($441 billion, or 6.2 percent of the total). Of the $7.1 trillion in foreign-held debt, some 60 percent was held by governments.[52] Treasuries are in great demand among foreign governments and private investors for several reasons. Because of the lower default risk and greater liquidity, US debt may be viewed as superior to competing investments. Indeed, in the tumultuous conditions following the financial crisis and during the COVID-19 pandemic, the demand for US debt grew as foreign investors perceived it as a safe haven and a store of value. Moreover, given that the dollar serves as the world's reserve currency, Treasury securities are in high demand for use as collateral in international transactions. To what extent should the foreign holdings of US debt raise concerns for policymakers?

Interest payments to domestic holders of debt are transfers between groups of citizens (i.e., taxpayers and bondholders). While these transfers carry consequences for the distribution of wealth as suggested earlier, they impose no net cost on the United States. In contrast, interest payments to foreign bondholders constitute a transfer of wealth across borders. As the CBO notes, this is of particular concern as interest payments become a larger share of the budget: "because foreign investors hold a significant portion of Treasury securities, the increase in outlays represents an increase in payments to foreign investors and thus a reduction in domestic income relative to total U.S. economic output."[53] While this is true, it may be useful to view the role of foreign purchases of debt in a different context, one which bears on the earlier discussion of the crowding out effect. Domestic savings can be disaggregated into household savings, business savings, and government savings. Absent any borrowing from abroad, government deficits (in essence, negative government savings) could deplete private savings, necessarily placing constraints on investment (which can be disaggregated into public and private investment). Under these conditions, deficit financing could crowd out private investment; interest rates could rise, rendering some private investments unprofitable. The depletion of US capital stock, and the technology it embodies, could have long-term ramifications for growth and productivity. In this context, foreign purchase of US Treasuries may allow for higher levels of private investment and a growth in GDP. In the words of Marc Labonte and Jared C. Nagel: "The ability to borrow from foreigners avoids the deleterious effects on U.S. interest rates, private investment, and GDP, to an extent, even if it means that the returns on some of this investment now flow to foreigners instead of Americans. In other words, all else equal, foreign purchases of Treasury securities reduce the federal government's borrowing costs and reduce the costs the deficit imposes on the broader economy."[54]

But does the reliance on foreign holders of debt raise other vulnerabilities? If the debt increases to unsustainable levels, could foreign bondholders lose their confidence in US Treasuries? Is there reason to believe that they would be more sensitive to the risk of default than their domestic counterparts? For example, foreign bondholders may suspect that the probability of default is higher to the extent that the debt is externally held, and the costs of default would fall most highly outside of national borders. They may demand higher risk premiums, or they may liquidate their holdings at an earlier point than might otherwise be the case.[55] What had been traditionally viewed as a safe haven could be seen as imposing a level of risk requiring higher levels of returns. Perhaps. But the decision of whether to divest from Treasury securities (or taper the level of investment) does not occur in a vacuum. Foreign investors do not purchase Treasuries to accommodate the financing needs of the United States, nor do they focus solely on rates of return. They acquire holdings to reinvest the proceeds of trade surpluses. They may see Treasuries, once again, as a stable store of value for foreign reserves and as a means of insuring against speculation on their exchange rates. Foreign investors would have to decide to substitute even more risky alternatives for US debt, none of which would carry comparable benefits.

Nonetheless, the reliance on foreign bondholders does create some vulnerability, albeit limited, to changes in the economic strategies of foreign bondholders and US policymakers. Take the case of China. Persistent trade surpluses with the United States combined with a domestic demand deficiency to create the need to export capital. China's holdings of US debt made strategic sense insofar as the demand for dollar-denominated Treasuries raised the value of the dollar relative to the yuan, which was undervalued and pegged to the dollar, thereby reducing the cost of Chinese goods sold in US markets (and simultaneously raising the costs of US exports). While the US trade deficit helped propel China's economic growth, the US simultaneously benefited from lower consumer prices and lower interest rates. But as China sought to elevate the yuan in the international economy, it shed some of its holding of US debt. Fortunately, given the depth of the market for US debt, the Chinese taper did not have significant ramifications.[56]

In the end, there is little question that the United States has benefitted from the global market for Treasury securities. It has provided a critical source of funding that has minimized concerns over the potential role of debt finance in crowding out private sector investment. The demand for US debt has proven robust, even during trying economic times, as foreign governments and private investors have sought a safe haven for their funds. The low levels of default risk, the liquidity of debt markets, and the use of Treasury securities as collateral in international transactions have combined to reduce the borrowing costs of the federal government. While growth in the size of the debt over the next several decades could raise questions about sustainability and increase the costs of debt financing, these concerns are largely independent of the source of funding.

The Debt as Paper Shackles

In *The Economic Consequences of the Peace*, John Maynard Keynes devoted a great deal of attention to World War I debt, "the vast paper entanglements which are our legacy from war finance both at home and abroad." He proclaimed: "We shall never be able to move again, unless we can free our limbs from these paper shackles."[57] This evocative term describes one of the great practical consequences of the debt. Even if the United States faces few obstacles in attracting domestic and foreign entities to purchase its debt, the resulting interest payments can limit its ability to pursue objectives that are selected as the result of democratic deliberation. Resources that are devoted to debt repayment cannot be used for other purposes, regardless of their justification or their level of political support. If revenue constraints remain in place and debt grows faster than GDP, interest payments will continue to deplete what is available for other forms of spending. While concerns over the role of debt in crowding out private investments may be overstated given the role of global debt markets, the potential for a political crowding out may be the most significant consequence of the debt.

To make sense of this claim, let us place interest payments in the larger budgetary context. The composition of federal spending has changed significantly over the course of the last several decades. Although spending was addressed in some detail in Chapter 2, a few comments are important at this juncture. Since 1970, programmatic mandatory spending—a category dominated by Social Security, Medicare, and Medicaid—has grown from some 31 percent of outlays to 61.4 percent (or from 5.8 to 12.9 percent GDP). During that same period, discretionary spending has shrunk from 61.5 to 30 percent of outlays (or from 11.5 to 6.3 percent GDP). The remainder of government spending is interest on the debt, which has grown from 7.5 to 8.6 percent of total government outlays (or from 1.4 percent of GDP to 1.8 percent of GDP). In 2019, the year before the COVID-19 pandemic, net interest payments equaled $375.6 billion.[58]

The OMB classifies outlays by function. To place interest payments in the larger context, in 2019 they exceeded the combined outlays for natural resources and environment ($37.8 billion), education, training employment and social services ($136.7 billion), transportation ($97.1 billion), general science, space, and technology ($32.4 billion), energy ($5 billion), and the total expenditures on federal administration of justice, including federal corrections ($57.9 billion). Another comparison: the costs of servicing the debt exceeded the combined outlays for the Environmental Protection Agency, the Department of Energy, the National Aeronautics and Space Administration, the National Science Foundation, the Department of Transportation, the Department of the Interior, the Department of Education, the Commerce Department, the civilian construction of the Army Corps of Engineers, and the combined international assistance programs.[59] Although one cannot predict where the president and Congress would devote the resources currently used to finance the debt, it is clear that the debt can constrain levels of spending in areas that could prove critical in pursuing national goals.

Interest on the debt is highly variable. In 1995–1998, interest payments claimed more than 15 percent of outlays (roughly 3 percent of GDP). Since that time, the importance of net interest payments declined as a share of outlays and GDP, reflecting the global savings glut and the flight to safety in a particularly chaotic period. But the CBO and the GAO project that net interest payments will only grow over time, absent a policy intervention, placing significant constraints on policymakers. According to the CBO's long-term extended baseline projections, federal spending will grow from a pre-pandemic level of 21 percent of GDP (2019) to 30 percent of GDP (2052), whereas revenues will increase at a much slower pace, from 16.4 percent of GDP to 19.1 percent of GDP. As a result of the fiscal gap, the federal debt held by the public is projected to reach 185 percent of GDP. While programmatic mandatory spending would continue its unrelenting growth as a share of outlays, the most striking changes come in net interest. While interest payments constituted 1.8 percent of GDP in 2019 (8.4 percent of outlays), by 2046 they are projected to grow to 5.7 percent of GDP (20.1 percent of spending), surpassing total Medicare spending (5.6 percent of GDP). By 2049, net interest is projected to grow to 6.5 percent of GDP (22.2 percent of outlays), surpassing Social Security as the largest commitment of the federal government. By 2052, net interest is projected to constitute 7.2 percent of GDP or 23.9 percent of federal outlays. Another point of comparison: in 2019, net interest and mandatory spending comprised 14.7 percent of GDP (70 percent of outlays). By 2052, they are projected to claim over 24.2 percent of GDP (80 percent of outlays).[60] The GAO's long-term fiscal projections and simulations arrive at comparable results.[61]

The constraints on spending may become most acute during periods of crisis. Economic recessions, natural disasters, pandemics, and national security emergencies are, in many cases, unpredictable events. But higher levels of indebtedness can limit the extent to which policymakers can prepare for their occurrence and mount an adequate response to mitigate their effects. In the area of fiscal policy, the debt may make policymakers unwilling to place too great a reliance on deficit financing as part of a recovery efforts, particularly when the debt is the focus of partisan politics. For example, the American Recovery and Reinvestment Act of 2009, the key fiscal stimulus package passed in response to the Great Recession, was limited in size, in part, over fears of the political backlash over rapidly growing deficits. In the Spring of 2020, the nation faced the emergency of COVID-19. The government's initial response was hampered by the National Strategic Stockpile which had been depleted and never replenished, in part, as a result of the debt-induced sequestration resulting from the Budget Control Act of 2011 and ongoing partisan battles over the funding of the Department of Health and Human Services.[62] While Congress passed much larger emergency measures in response to the pandemic than it had during the financial crisis, proposals for ongoing relief during the summer of 2020 ran afoul of concerns over the size of the publicly held debt which by then was approaching a level not seen since the immediate aftermath of World War II. By 2021, the aspirations of the new Biden administration were moderated significantly by the demands that the Build Back Better Plan have minimal impact on the debt, that it not require a reversal of earlier tax cuts, and that it not contribute to inflation which had spiked to levels not seen since the early 1980s.

Conclusion

This chapter has explored some of the normative and practical ramifications of the debt, particularly as the debt-to-GDP ratio grows. While there are arguments that excessive levels of debt can have a "crowding out effect," raise the risk of a fiscal crisis, and subject debt financing to the uncertainties of the international arena, most of these claims come with significant qualifications. Treasury securities have some unique features. The perception of their virtual risk-free nature, the liquidity of the debt market, and the dollar's status as the world's reserve currency, combine to ensure high levels of demand. Even if projections of a growing debt-to-GDP ratio are troubling, there are few concerns, at present, of the nation's ability to finance its debt. But the projected growth of interest as a share of government outlays carries an important consequence: it places serious constraints on what government can aspire to accomplish. Aaron Wildavsky once described the budget as "the life-blood of the government, the financial reflection of what government does or intends to do." The debate over "what ought to be in the budget is nothing less than a theory stating what the government ought to do."[63] Absent changes on the revenue or expenditure side, the budget will cease to serve this function. Discretionary spending is caught between two pincers: programmatic mandatory spending and interest on the debt, both of which are projected to increase. Presidents and members of Congress will be placed in the unenviable position of seeking to preserve what they can, while watching the gap between collective aspirations and public policy widen.

Notes

1 Robert Eisner, "Budget Deficits: Rhetoric and Reality," *The Journal of Economic Perspectives,* 3, 2 (1989): 75.
2 Office of Management and Budget (OMB), *Budget of the U.S. Government, Fiscal Year 2023* (Washington, DC: Government Publishing Office, 2022), Historical Tables, Table 1.2.
3 See the discussion in Congressional Budget Office (CBO), *Automatic Stabilizers in the Federal Budget: 2020–2030* (Washington, DC: CBO, 2020).
4 For an overview of the federal funds and trust funds, see OMB, *Budget of the U.S. Government, Fiscal Year 2021* (Washington, DC: Government Publishing Office, 2020), Analytical Perspectives, 287–93.
5 See Grant A. Driessen, *How Treasury Issues Debt,* CRS Report R40767 (Washington, DC: Congressional Research Service, 2016).
6 Kenneth D. Garbade, *Treasury Debt Management under the Rubric of Regular and Predictable Issuance: 1982–2012* (New York: Federal Reserve Bank of New York, 2015), 6, 163.
7 OMB, *Budget of the U.S. Government, Fiscal Year 2021, Analytical Perspectives,* 30.
8 Government Accountability Office (GAO), *The Nation's Fiscal Health: Action is Needed to Address the Federal Government's Fiscal Future,* GAO-20-403SP (Washington, DC: GAO, 2020), 27.
9 Ibid., 8.
10 See George J. Hall and Thomas J. Sargent, "A History of U.S. Debt Limits," NBER Working Paper 21799 (December 2015), 5, 30.
11 D. Andrew Austin, *The Debt Limit: History and Recent Increases,* CRS Report RL31967 (Washington, DC: Congressional Research Service, 2015), 7. This discussion draws on the report more generally.
12 GAO, *Debt Limit: Market Response to Recent Impasses Underscores Need to Consider Alternative Approaches,* GAO-15-476 (Washington, DC: GAO, 2015), 7.
13 GAO, *The Nation's Fiscal Health,* 40.
14 See D. Andrew Austin and Seam M. Still, *Cleaning the Air on the Debt Limit,* CRS Report R45011 (Washington, DC: Congressional Research Service, 2021), 3–12.

15 OMB, *Budget of the U.S. Government, Fiscal Year 2021,* Analytical Perspectives, 42.
16 Ibid., 31.
17 OMB, *Budget of the U.S. Government, Fiscal Year 2023,* Historical Tables, Table 7.1.
18 OMB, *Budget of the U.S. Government, Fiscal Year 2022,* Analytical Perspectives, 29. See Austin, *Overview of the Federal Debt*, 23.
19 OMB, *Budget of the U.S. Government, Fiscal Year 2022,* Analytical Perspectives, 24.
20 Committee for a Responsible Federal Government, "Q&A: Gross Debt versus Debt Held by the Public, September 11, 2017." Available atwww.crfb.org/sites/default/files/QAGrossvsNominalDebt.pdf.
21 Eric M. Patashnik, *Putting Trust in the US Budget: Federal Trust Funds and the Politics of Commitment* (Cambridge: Cambridge University Press, 2000), 6.
22 See Aaron L. Friedberg, *In the Shadow of the Garrison State: America's Anti-Statism and Its Cold War Grand Strategy* (Princeton: Princeton University Press, 2000), 1–13.
23 James D. Savage, *Balanced Budgets and American Politics* (Ithaca, NY: Cornell University Press, 1988), 5.
24 James M Buchanan and Richard E. Wagner, *Democracy in Deficit: The Political Legacy of Lord Keynes,* in *The Collected Works of James M. Buchanan* (Indianapolis, IN: Liberty Fund, 2000), vol. 8, 145–46, 182–83.
25 Brian Barry, "Does Democracy Cause Inflation? Political Ideas of Some Economists," in *The Politics of Inflation and Economic Stagnation,* ed. Leon N. Lindberg and Charles S. Maier (Washington, DC: The Brookings Institution, 1985), 317.
26 Mark Blyth, *Austerity: The History of a Dangerous Idea* (Oxford: Oxford University Press, 2013), 12.
27 See Lukas Meyer, "Intergenerational Justice," *The Stanford Encyclopedia of Philosophy* (Summer 2016 Edition), ed. Edward N. Zalta. Available at https://plato.stanford.edu/archives/sum2016/entries/justice-intergenerational/.
28 See Alan J. Auerbach, Jagadeesh Gokhale, and Laurence J. Kotlikoff, "Generational Accounts: A Meaningful Alternative to Deficit Accounting," NBER Working Paper No. 3589 (1991). Cambridge, MA: National Bureau of Economic Research.
29 Neil H. Buchanan, "What Do We Owe Future Generations?" *George Washington Law Review,* 77, 5/6 (2009): 1280.
30 Joseph White, "Making 'Common Sense' of Federal Budgeting," *Public Administration Review,* 58, 2 (1998), 104–05.
31 See Michael Doran, "Intergenerational Equity in Fiscal Policy Reform," *Tax Law Review,* 61 (2008): 260–62.
32 Linda Sugin, "Payroll Taxes, Mythology, and Fairness," *Harvard Journal on Legislation,* 51 (2014): 119.
33 Wolfgang Streeck, "The Politics of Public Debt: Neoliberalism, Capitalist Development and the Restructuring of the State." *German Economic Review,* 15, 1 (2014): 153. For the larger argument about the debt state, see Wolfgang Streeck, *Buying Time: Delayed Crisis of Democratic Capitalism* (London: Verso, 2014).
34 Wolfgang Streeck, *How Will Capitalism End? Essays on a Failing System* (London: Verso, 2016), 53.
35 Atif Mian, Ludwig Straub, and Amir Sufi, "The Saving Glut of the Rich," NBER Working Paper 26941 (2021). Available at www.nber.org/papers/w26941
36 Sandy Brian Hager, *Public Debt, Inequality, and Power: The Making of a Modern Debt State* (Berkeley: University of California Press, 2016), 11–12, 6, 64.
37 See Kirill Borissov and Adrei Kalk, "Public Debt, Positional Concerns, and Wealth Inequality," *Journal of Economic Behavior and Organization,* 170 (2020): 96–111.

38 CBO, *The 2021 Long-Term Budget Outlook* (Washington DC: CBO, 2021), 11.
39 CBO, *The 2019 Long-Term Budget Outlook* (Washington DC: CBO, 2019),11–12.
40 John Quiggin, *Zombie Economics: How Dead Ideas Still Walk among Us* (Princeton, NJ: Princeton University Press, 2010), 213.
41 See Mark Blyth, "The Austerity Delusion: Why a Bad Idea Won Over the West," *Foreign Affairs,* 92.3 (2013): 41–56, and Jane G. Gravelle and Thomas L. Hungerford, *Can Contractionary Fiscal Policy Be Expansionary?* CRS Report R41849 (Washington, DC: Congressional Research Service, 2013).
42 See Carlo Cottarelli, *What We Owe: Truths, Myths, and Lies about Public Debt* (Washington, DC: Brookings Institution Press, 2017), 47–53; Carmen M. Reinhart and Kenneth S. Rogoff, "Growth in a Time of Debt," *American Economic Review, 100,* 2 (2010):573–578; Christina Checherita-Westphal and Phillip Rother, "The Impact of High Government Debt on Economic Growth and its Channels: An Empirical Investigation for the Euro Area," *European Economic Review, 56,* 7 (2012): 1392–1405; and Balázs gert, " Public Debt, Economic Growth and Nonlinear Effects: Myth or Reality?" *Journal of Macroeconomics, 43* (2015): 226–38.
43 Robert Barsky and Matthew Easton, "The Global Savings Glut and the Fall in U.S. Real Interest Rates: A 15-Year Retrospective," *Federal Reserve Bank of Chicago, Economic Perspectives,* 1 (March 2020). Available at www.chicagofed.org/publications/economic-perspectives/2021/1
44 See James W. Douglas and Ringa Raudla, "Who is Afraid of the Big Bad Debt? A Modern Money Theory Perspective on Federal Deficits and Debt," *Public Budgeting & Finance,* 40, 3 (2020):6–25.
45 See Thomas I. Palley, "Modern Monetary Theory (MMT): The Emperor Still Has No Clothes," February 2014, Available at www.thomaspalley.com/docs/articles/macro_theory/mmt_response_to_wray.pdf
46 CBO, *The 2019 Long-Term Budget Outlook*, 13.
47 Cottarelli, *What We Owe,* 32.
48 Huixin Bi, Wenyi Shen, and Shu-Chun S. Yang, "U.S. Federal Debt Has Increased, but Appears Sustainable for Now," *KcFED Economic Bulletin,* Federal Reserve Bank of Kansas City, November 16,2020, 2. Available at www.kansascityfed.org/documents/7088/US_FederalDebtIncreasedAppearsSustainableForNow_EB.pdf
49 CBO, *The 2019 Long-Term Budget Outlook*, 13.
50 Cottarelli, *What We Owe,* 40.
51 OMB, *Budget of the U.S. Government, Fiscal Year 2023,* Analytical Perspectives, 55.
52 US Treasury, Major Foreign Holdings of Treasury Securities. Available at https://ticdata.treasury.gov/Publish/mfh.txt.
53 CBO, *The 2019 Long-Term Budget Outlook*, 13.
54 Marc Labonte and Jared C. Nagel, *Foreign Holdings of Federal Debt,* CRS Report RS22331 (Washington, DC: Congressional Research Service, 2021), 4. This paragraph draws on their discussion, 3–5.
55 Cottarelli, *What We Owe,* 40.
56 Wayne M. Morris, "China's Currency Policy," *In Focus* (IF10139) (Washington, DC: Congressional Research Service, 2019), and Kimberly Amadeo, "US Debt to China, How Much, Reasons Why, and What if China Sells," *The Balance,* April 19, 2020, available at www.thebalance.com/u-s-debt-to-china-how-much-does-it-own-3306355

57 John Maynard Keynes, *The Economic Consequences of the Peace* (London: MacMillan and Co., 1920), 262.

58 Data from CBO, Historical Budget Data. Available at www.cbo.gov/system/files/2020-01/51134-2020-01-historicalbudgetdata.xlsx

59 *Budget of the U.S. Government, Fiscal Year 2023*, Historical Tables, Tables 3.2 and 5.3.

60 Data supplement to CBO, *2022 Long-Term Budget Outlook*, available at www.cbo.gov/system/files/2022-07/57971-Data.xlsx

61 GAO, *The Nation's Fiscal Health*, 22–28.

62 Yeganeh Torbati and Isaac Arnsdorf, "How Tea Party Budget Battles Left the National Emergency Medical Stockpile Unprepared for Coronavirus," *ProPublica*, April 3, 2020. Available at www.propublica.org/article/us-emergency-medical-stockpile-funding-unprepared-coronavirus

63 Aaron Wildavsky, "Political Implications of Budgetary Reform," *Public Administration Review*, 21, 4 (1961): 184.

PART II

5

THE GREAT DELEVERAGING

Growth and Debt in the Wake of the War

For much of US history, the debt exhibited a distinct dynamic. Episodes of crisis-driven leveraging were followed by periods of deleveraging. Part of this was simply a product of the way the debt was authorized by Congress, which controlled the purposes for borrowing, interest rates, and maturity. Debt, once issued, could not be refinanced. In part, it was a product of post-crisis austerity. For example, in the wake of the Civil War and World War I, the federal government ran persistent budget surpluses, reducing the size of the debt-to-GDP ratio. Calls for austerity—a reduction in government spending, the scaling back of social provision—have been common in response to growing indebtedness, often supplemented with the assertion that a reduction in government's claim on GDP would have beneficial implications for the debt while preventing the public sector from crowding out the private investment that could propel economic growth. The case for "expansionary austerity" is difficult to reconcile with the experience of the immediate postwar period (1946–1980), the subject of this chapter.

World War II would raise the debt-to-GDP ratio to the highest levels in the nation's history, approximately three times what existed in the aftermath of these earlier conflicts. But in the decades following World War II, there were steady reductions in the debt-to-GDP ratio comparable to the longer historical pattern. By 1974, it had fallen by more than 78 percent. But there was a fundamental difference. The reduction in indebtedness was combined with a dramatic expansion in federal outlays relative to GDP, from the postwar low of 11.4 percent of GDP (1948) to 21.2 percent of GDP (1980). Even more striking, given the growth in the economy during this period, inflation-adjusted federal outlays increased by 593.6 percent.[1] The growth in federal spending was initially driven by Cold War defense budgets. But the maturation of the social

DOI: 10.4324/9781003395331-7

welfare state introduced in the New Deal, the introduction of new programs like Medicare and Medicaid, and the expansion of social provision would force a significant rebalancing by the late 1960s. Budgets were rarely in balance, and surpluses were rare. But it is one of the arguments of this chapter that steady economic growth and the retention of the mass-based income tax forged during the war provided the fiscal means of reconciling greater government provision and debt reduction.

While the configuration of policies carried a number of benefits ranging from historical reductions in poverty and inequality to greater security across the life cycle and the business cycle, it would also prove fragile. By the late 1960s, growing inflation stimulated by the Vietnam War and expanded social spending raised concerns for policymakers. Things would become more dire by the 1970s, when stagflation gave rise to robust debates about the efficacy of Keynesian demand management and set the stage for dramatic changes in the tax system in the 1980s that would initiate a new period of growing indebtedness. The problem of stagflation—both the challenges it posed for policymakers and the opportunities it created for those intent on contesting the set of policies put in place in the previous decades—will be the subject of Chapter 6. The goal of this chapter is to offer a brief overview of the combination of policies that were enacted in the immediate postwar decades, in part, because some of these policies would become important drivers of federal spending whereas others would become targeted for reform or elimination. The period covered in this chapter also provides something of a corrective to the claim that austerity provides the best (or only) path to the reduction of the debt.

Postwar Prosperity and Debt Reduction

Although there was great trepidation that, absent the stimulus of wartime spending, the nation would return to slow growth and high unemployment, the immediate postwar period was one of great prosperity and stability. While Congress had failed to pass a bill guaranteeing full employment, it passed the Employment Act of 1946, which provided the blueprint for a new institutional infrastructure for macroeconomic management and assigned the president the responsibility of promoting maximum employment, production, and purchasing power. Even if the first decade and a half after the passage of the Employment Act witnessed a relatively conservative fiscal policy mix, the Council of Economic Advisors—a product of the 1946 Act—would increasingly draw on Keynesian theory to manage the business cycle, supplemented in 1958 with the Phillips curve, which purported to represent a stable tradeoff between unemployment and inflation. Recessions, which occurred in 1949, 1953, 1957, and 1960, were relatively mild, with peak unemployment rates ranging from 5.9 to 7.9 percent.[2] Despite the growing confidence in discretionary fiscal policy during this period, most of the credit for reducing the magnitude of the fluctuations in the business cycle should be assigned to automatic stabilizers—a sharply graduated income tax and means tested social transfer payments like unemployment insurance—that had a countercyclical effect, stimulating the economy during downturns and restraining demand during the peaks of the business cycle.[3] The next decade, in contrast would witness recessions in 1970, 1974–1975, and 1980. The 1974–1975 recession was particularly protracted, with a peak unemployment rate of 9 percent.[4] As will be detailed in Chapter 6, the combination of high inflation and unemployment during the 1970s vanquished much of the faith in Keynesian demand management and the Phillips curve.

Manufacturing employment, as one might expect, was driven to new heights during World War II, claiming some 16 million workers (38.5 percent of the workforce) at its 1944 peak. The share of the workforce engaged in manufacturing would go into decline, thereafter, falling to 20.4 percent by 1980.[5] While manufacturing employment would recede, there was remarkable stability in manufacturing's share of real GDP, suggesting that productivity gains were an important part of the story.[6] Much of the manufacturing workforce was unionized, largely a product of new legal protections enacted during the New Deal and preserved during World War II. While the unionization rate would peak at 35.5 percent of the nonagricultural workforce in 1945, a combination of public policy (most notably the passage of the Taft Hartley Act in 1947, which among other things authorized "right-to-work" states) and the shift of employment from manufacturing to services would place unionization levels on a path of long-term decline. By 1970, private sector unionization would stand at 27.4 percent of the workforce, falling to a quarter of the private sector workforce in the next decade.[7]

Unions were important, in part, because they created an institutional mechanism to translate economic growth into the burgeoning affluence of the middle class. The 1948 multi-year agreement between General Motors and the United Auto Workers served as a model for postwar contracts. It provided cost-of-living adjustments and, more importantly, an annual "Improvement Factor" that would range between 2 and 4 percent to reward productivity gains, thereby assuring that the growth of the period would find an expression in higher wages. The contract also provided a host of benefits, including employment-based healthcare and defined-benefit pensions, both of which would be subsidized through the system of tax expenditures. These contracts constituted a core element of what has been described as a growth coalition.[8] As Barry Bluestone and Bennett Harrison explain, during this "heyday of American economic power…industrialists were able to reap healthy profits while affording these concessions to organized labor. The so-called social contract between labor and management even proved advantageous to the corporate sector, for it assured some semblance of labor peace needed for continued economic expansion."[9]

One expression of the efficacy of the growth coalition was the increase in labor's share of GDP. Between 1950 and 1970, labor's share increased from 63.6 percent to a record 65.9 percent of GDP, before entering a period of decline.[10] Related, household wealth became far more equally dispersed. Consider changes in the Gini coefficient, a widely adopted statistical measure of dispersion, that ranges between 0 (perfect equality) and 1 (perfect inequality). As a result of the Great Depression and World War II, the Gini coefficient fell from 0.489 (1929) to 0.369 (1945). By 1968, the United States had achieved the greatest level of equality in the postwar period, with a Gini coefficient of 0.351. Other indicators reinforce this conclusion. Once again, as a result of the great levelers—depression and war—the top 1 percent's share of national income fell from 18.4 (1929) to 11.1 percent (1945). By 1973, however, the top 1 percent's share of income dipped to a record low of 7.7 percent. On the other end of the spectrum, the percentage of households with pre-tax incomes below the official poverty line receded, declining from 32.8 percent in the immediate postwar period (1948) to a record low of 11.1 percent by 1973.[11] Performance along each of these dimensions would erode in subsequent years, most notably in the post-1980 period.

None of this occurred simply as the unintended consequence of growth. Rather, falling levels of income inequality and the reductions in poverty were also a product of policy decisions, which will be reviewed later in the chapter. Obviously, taxation played an important role. Much of the progressivity introduced into the tax code during World War II was retained in the subsequent decades. In addition to high marginal income tax rates, the federal government channeled the fiscal fruits of growth into social provision through the creation and expansion of welfare and healthcare policies. By the early 1970s, then, it appeared that the United States had arrived at a relatively successful model. Economic growth had been robust over the course of the past two decades. Policymakers had not defeated the business cycle, but automatic stabilizers and interventions informed by Keynesian theory had proven sufficient to limit the magnitude of its fluctuations. Policymakers would have to make decisions about the optimal combinations of inflation and unemployment, but the Phillips curve had proven to be a relatively reliable guide to the tradeoffs. As the economy grew, labor gained a growing share of GDP and could expect real, inflation-adjusted, growth in incomes and consumption opportunities.

What is somewhat striking in this context is that the period also brought steady reductions in the level of debt relative to the economy. The federal government ran a relatively conservative policy mix in the late 1940s, generating surpluses in 1947–1949, allowing for what one analyst referred to as "the Great Debt Redemption."[12] Both President Truman and President Eisenhower advocated balanced budgets even if they rarely achieved them. Subsequent presidents would continue to acknowledge the importance of balanced budgets, at least during periods of economic prosperity, as emblematic of responsible government. But the empirical record is clear. While there were occasional budget surpluses—in FY1947–1949, 1951, 1956–1957, 1960 and 1969—deficits were the norm. In the decade of the 1950s, the annual average deficit was −0.04 percent of GDP, increasing to −0.8 percent in the 1960s, and 2 percent in the 1970s.[13]

The primary source of deleveraging came from different sources: inflation in the immediate aftermath of the war and economic growth. The role of inflation was particularly important in reducing the debt-to-GDP ratio in the immediate postwar decade. Between 1946 and 1955, the ratio was cut by some 40 percent. During that decade, inflation was an average of 4.2 percent, including the peak inflation of 14.4 percent that followed demobilization in 1947. The long maturity of the debt at the time—9 years in 1945–1948 and declining slightly to 8.17 years in 1950—allowed inflation to erode the real value of the debt. The role of inflation was of somewhat lesser importance subsequently. Following the end of the Korean War, Eisenhower's conservative fiscal policy mix contributed to a lower inflation rate. And while inflation would rise in the late 1960s and the 1970s, its impact was moderated by a dramatic shortening in the maturity of the debt (2.67 years by 1975), which allowed investors to demand an inflation risk premium.[14] More important: the role of economic growth. While the commitment to a full-employment economy was sporadic at best before the 1960s, the thirty-five years following World War II was a period of growing national prosperity, even if the economy began to exhibit significant problems in the 1970s. Between 1947 and 1980, GDP grew from $250 billion to $2.86 trillion, an inflation-adjusted increase of 340.6 percent.[15] Expressed in 2012 dollars, the real GDP per capita increased from $14,128 in 1948 to $29,701 during this period, creating a level of affluence and consumer choices that would have been unimaginable a generation earlier.[16] Even if the nominal debt grew over much of the period, it was outpaced by the growth in GDP.

Table 5.1 presents a summary of some key indicators. For present purposes, note that over the post 1945 period, outlays increased from 15.3 percent of GDP (1950) to 21.2 percent of GDP (1980). Federal receipts increased over the period as well, from 14.2 to 18.5 percent of GDP. Despite the small but relatively persistent budget deficits, there were substantial reductions in the debt, relative to GDP. The debt in 1945 reached a staggering 103.9 percent of GDP and would reach a record level of 106.1 percent the next year. But the debt-to-GDP ratio would decline steadily over the next few decades, falling to a low of 23.2 percent of GDP by 1974. A growing economy, when combined with steady revenues and a measure of budgetary restraint, was sufficient to move the nation to a level of debt comparable to what had existed in 1931.[17] Let us examine the tax and spending decisions in greater detail.

TABLE 5.1 Summary of Outlays, Receipts, Deficits/Surpluses, and Debt, 1945–1980 (Percentage of GDP)

Fiscal Year	*Outlays*	*Receipts*	*Surplus or Deficit (–)*	*Publicly Held Debt*
1945	41.0%	19.9%	–21.0%	103.9%
1950	15.3	14.2	–1.1	78.6
1955	16.8	16.1	–0.7	55.8
1960	17.3	17.3	0.1	44.3
1965	16.7	16.5	–0.2	36.8
1970	18.7	18.4	–0.3	27.1
1975	20.7	17.4	–3.3	24.6
1980	21.2	18.5	–2.6	25.5

Source: Office of Management and Budget, *Budget of the United States Government, Fiscal Year 2023* (Washington, DC: Government Publishing Office, 2022), Historical Tables, Tables 1.2, 7.1.

Taxation and the Preservation of the Wartime Tax Regime

As noted in Chapter 3, World War II marked the transformation of the income tax from an elite tax that touched a narrow stratum of households to a mass tax that drew revenues from a majority of Americans. "This transformation of the income tax during the war," Sheldon D. Pollack explains,

> gave the American state a powerful tool for revenue extraction that it has never relinquished. Whereas the partisan politics of the New Deal had failed to significantly alter the structure of the income tax regime, the crisis of total war brought about a radical restructuring of the entire fiscal system of the American state.[18]

Indeed, the individual income tax, which accounted for 15.1 of receipts in 1941, would expand to become the single largest source of revenue, reaching a wartime high of 45 percent by 1944. Relative to the economy, the individual income tax would increase from 1.1 to 9.2 percent of GDP during this same period. It would remain the most important source of revenues after World War II.[19]

The success in transforming the revenue system was striking, particularly given the strong anti-tax sentiments that have been one of the few constants in US history. Under the dire conditions of World War II, the population was far more receptive to calls for sacrifices at home, particularly if they could be linked to supporting those who were fighting and dying overseas. Far more interesting was the preservation of much of the World War II tax regime in subsequent decades. In the wake of the war, Congress passed the Revenue Act of 1945, which repealed the excess profits tax and reduced corporate tax rates while simultaneously cutting individual income tax rates from their wartime highs (the top bracket fell from 94 to 86.45 percent, whereas the bottom rate fell from 23 to 19 percent). Republicans, who had gained control of Congress in the 1946 midterms, pressed for additional cuts. With the Revenue Act of 1948, passed over Truman's veto, Congress secured further cuts to the individual tax rates (the top bracket fell to 82.13 percent whereas the bottom bracket fell to 16.6 percent), an increase in the individual exemption and a new exemption for taxpayers over age 65.[20] Truman used the spike in inflation at the onset of the Korean War to justify reversing these tax cuts, arguing that war finance should be grounded in direct taxation.[21] In a 1950 address to Congress, he stated: "We must make every effort to finance the greatest possible amount of needed expenditures by taxation." Taxes would provide a "basic weapon in offsetting the inflationary pressures exerted by enlarged government expenditures" and would "maintain the fiscal position of the Nation in the soundest possible condition."[22] The Revenue Act of 1951 raised the top marginal income tax rate to 91 percent (the bottom bracket was raised to 20 percent).[23] When combined with the excess profits tax, revenues increased from 14.2 percent of GDP (1950) to 18.5 (1952) and 18.3 percent of GDP (1953). The surplus of 1.9 percent GDP (1950) turned to deficit for the remainder of the war, but the wartime deficits were relatively small, peaking at 1.7 percent of GDP in 1953.[24] Remarkably, between 1950 and 1953, the debt held by the public declined from 78.6 to 57.2 percent of GDP.[25]

Following the election of Dwight D. Eisenhower, the Korean War drew to a close, with an armistice signed in July 1953 and the withdrawal of troops in the fall. With the reduction of expenditures, Eisenhower announced in his 1954 State of the Union address, that it was time to "thoroughly revise our whole tax system" to "remove the more glaring tax inequities, particularly on small taxpayers; reduce restraints on the growth of small business; and make other changes that will encourage initiative, enterprise and production."[26] In his budget message, he presented 25 recommendations "directed toward removing the most serious tax hardships and tax complications, and reducing the tax barriers to continued economic growth." At the same time, he warned that "we must choose our path carefully between inadequate revenues on the one hand and repressive taxation on the other. I am anxious to have taxes reduced as fast as that can be done without building up inflationary deficits."[27] In the end, the Internal Revenue Code of 1954 retained high marginal tax rates for individuals, with a top rate of 91 percent and a bottom rate of 20 percent. Scheduled cuts in wartime corporate tax rates and excise taxes were deferred, pending further reductions in the deficit. But the tax code provided a host of tax exemptions and exclusions that lowered tax liabilities, including liberalized deductions for dependents, medical expenses, and charitable contributions, a new deduction for childcare expenses, and the codification of the exemption of employer contributions to health insurance from taxable income. Businesses did not receive a rate cut, but they benefited from several provisions, including an increase in depreciation allowances and an extension of the period that losses could offset profits.[28]

After the codification of tax changes in 1954, the remainder of the Eisenhower administration was characterized by restraint in taxation. While the president would advocate tax cuts in principle, they were always tied to the question of the deficit and debt. As Dennis S. Ippolito explains, "Eisenhower's conception of 'fiscal integrity' went beyond short-term calculations." His initial position that tax cuts would need to be financed via surpluses evolved such that "when these surpluses occurred, he opted instead for debt reduction."[29] Eisenhower abjured tax reductions even during the recession of 1957–1958. While they could have been justified on economic grounds, the growth of the deficit—a product of the countercyclical growth in recession-related transfers like unemployment compensation—proved incompatible, at least for Eisenhower, with rate reductions. During 1959 and 1960, high levels of taxation were cited by Keynesian economists as contributing to a sluggish recovery, albeit to no avail. The lack of stimulus exerted a "fiscal drag" that impeded the transition to a full employment economy. Despite these arguments, which would become more influential in the 1960s, the mass-based tax regime inherited from World War II was preserved, even after a two-term Republican presidency.

The efforts to retain the high rate structure gave way to significant tax cuts during the early 1960s. The economy, which had fallen into a recession in April 1960, was entering recovery but there were ongoing concerns over fiscal drag and mounting evidence of slowing productivity. In this context, President Kennedy advocated an immediate tax bill to stimulate the economy followed by more comprehensive tax reform. The Revenue Act of 1962 was focused on corporations, granting a new 7 percent investment tax credit and increased depreciation allowances. Comprehensive tax reform, as originally envisioned, would have provided corporation and individual income tax rate reductions, partially offset by the reduction or elimination of key tax expenditures that would simplify the tax code and broaden the tax base. When Congress passed the Revenue Act of 1964 in the wake of Kennedy's assassination, many of the reform elements had disappeared or been partially offset by new provisions or the expansion of existing provisions. Nonetheless, the rate reductions were significant, and only achieved by President Johnson's willingness to moderate his FY1965 budget proposal. Individual tax rates were cut across the board. The top rate dropped from 91 to 70 percent. The lowest tax rate fell from 20 to 14 percent and, with the creation of the minimum standard deduction, the overall effects were somewhat progressive. The top corporate rate was cut as well, from 52 to 48 percent.[30]

The Revenue Act of 1964, the largest tax cut thus far in US history, was justified, in part, on supply-side grounds. Rate reductions could increase the after-tax returns, thereby creating incentives to work, produce, and invest.

One impact could be increased revenues, a product of economic growth. But its primary justification fell on the demand side, as households with higher after-tax incomes would engage in higher levels of consumption. What of the budgetary implications? "By the time the tax cut of 1964 was enacted," Herbert Stein notes, "budget-balancing had ceased to have an important influence on fiscal decisions and compensatory finance had taken its place." Discussions of balanced budgets were largely perfunctory and ritualistic. Where balanced budgets were engaged, it was in the context of the "more elastic concepts," including "the idea that the hypothetical full-employment budget should be balanced" or the notion that the "actual budget should come into balance when high employment was reached."[31] The focus, in the end, was economic growth. Between 1961 and 1966, when the 1964 tax cut was fully implemented, the annual growth rate of inflation-adjusted GDP averaged 5.7 percent, peaking at 8.5 percent in 1965.[32] The unemployment rate simultaneously fell from 6.7 to 3.8 percent.[33] Revenues fell from 17.3 to 16.8 percent of GDP. Individual income taxes dropped from 7.6 to 7.1 percent of GDP, whereas corporate income taxes increased from 3.8 to 3.9 percent of GDP.[34] But given the robust growth, the budgetary implications were minimal: the deficit, which stood at 0.6 percent of GDP in 1961 doubled to 1.2 percent in 1962, before declining to 0.2 percent in 1965 and 0.05 percent in 1966.[35]

Following the passage of the 1964 tax cuts, high rates of growth when combined with the escalation of domestic and Vietnam War spending raised concerns about inflation and the growing budget deficit. By 1967, the Johnson administration had proposed that Congress enact a temporary tax surcharge. The next year, Congress provided a 10 percent surcharge on individual and corporate income taxes, after heated exchanges with Ways and Means Committee Chairman Wilbur Mills (D-AR) that forced the administration to accept $6 billion in reduced spending. As a result of the Revenue Expenditure and Control Act of 1968, revenues increased from 17 to 19.1 percent of GDP, the highest level since 1945. The budget, which had been in deficit since 1960 briefly returned to a modest surplus of 0.3 percent of GDP in 1969.[36] While the 1968 statute was a temporary expedient, the Tax Reform Act of 1969 was far more substantial. Among other things, it raised additional revenue by temporarily extending the surcharge at 5 percent, repealing the investment tax credit, increasing the capital gains tax, and enacting the individual and corporate minimum taxes. The minimum tax, introduced to limit the extent to which individuals and corporations could shelter their income from taxation through the use of various tax shelters, would become formalized as the Alternative Minimum Tax in 1978. The provisions to raise revenue were partially offset by increases in the exemptions and minimum standard deduction, which lent the reforms greater progressivity.[37] With the exception of temporary surcharges, the rate reductions from the Revenue Act would prove quite durable. Indeed, they would remain largely in effect until 1980.[38]

TABLE 5.2 Percentage Composition of Federal Revenues by Source, 1945–1980

Fiscal Year	*Individual Income Tax*	*Corporate Income Tax*	*Social Insurance Tax*	*Excise Tax*	*Other*
1945	40.7%	35.4%	7.6%	13.9%	2.4%
1950	39.9	26.5	11.0	19.1	3.4
1955	43.9	27.3	12.0	14.0	2.8
1960	44.0	23.2	15.9	12.6	4.2
1965	41.8	21.8	19.0	12.5	4.9
1970	46.9	17.0	23.0	8.1	4.9
1975	43.9	14.6	30.3	5.9	5.4
1980	47.2	12.5	30.5	4.7	5.1

Source: Office of Management and Budget, *Budget of the United States Government, Fiscal Year 2023* (Washington, DC: Government Publishing Office, 2022), Historical Tables, Table 2.2.

When viewed as a whole, the period separating the war and the 1980s was one of rather remarkable stability in tax policy, even if tax policy was hotly contested in the turbulent economy of the 1970s (see Chapter 6). Taken as a whole, receipts were 17.2 percent of GDP in 1946, rising to 18.4 percent by 1970 and 18.5 percent by 1980. But there were significant changes in the composition of revenues (see Tables 5.2 and 5.3). The individual income tax, which was responsible for 41 percent of revenues in 1946 (7.1 percent GDP), would only grow in importance, yielding 47.2 percent of receipts (8.7 percent GDP) by 1980, despite the rate cuts enacted after the Revenue Act of 1964. Much of this was a product of bracket creep. As R. Douglas Arnold explains, Congress "escaped electoral retribution for expanding the tax burden…by allowing the hidden hand of inflation to increase real taxes." As inflation raised nominal incomes, it pushed individuals into higher tax brackets, increasing their tax burdens. "Citizens were unable to hold their representatives accountable for the increased taxes they were paying because there were no identifiable governmental actions on which to lay the blame and for which legislators had been forced to choose sides."[39] The corporate income tax, which was responsible for 30.2 percent of revenues in 1946 (5.2 percent GDP), would decline in importance, however. By 1970, it accounted for 14.3 percent of receipts (3.1 percent GDP) and 12.5 percent of receipts (2.3 percent GDP) by 1980. The real area of change came in the area of social insurance taxes, which, as a result of successive increases in the Social Security payroll tax and the introduction of Medicare, grew from 7.9 percent of revenues in 1946 (1.4 percent GDP) to 23 percent of revenues (4.2 percent GDP) in 1970, more than double the receipts from the corporate tax. By 1980, social insurance taxes would generate 30.5 percent of receipts (5.7 percent GDP).[40]

TABLE 5.3 Composition of Federal Revenues by Source, 1945–1980 (Percentage of GDP)

Fiscal Year	*Individual Income Tax*	*Corporate Income Tax*	*Social Insurance Tax*	*Excise Tax*	*Other*
1945	8.1%	7.1%	1.5%	2.8%	0.5%
1950	5.7	3.7	1.6	2.7	0.5
1955	7.1	4.4	1.9	2.2	0.5
1960	7.6	4.0	2.7	2.2	0.7
1965	6.9	3.6	3.1	2.1	0.8
1970	8.6	3.1	4.2	1.5	0.9
1975	7.6	2.5	5.3	1.0	0.9
1980	8.7	2.3	5.7	0.9	0.9

Source: Office of Management and Budget, *Budget of the United States Government, Fiscal Year 2023* (Washington, DC: Government Publishing Office, 2022), Historical Tables, Table 2.3.

Spending: Guns or Butter?

The decades separating World War II and 1980 exhibited three broad trends. At the broadest level, spending grew relative to GDP. With demobilization from the war, outlays fell to a postwar low of 11.4 percent of GDP, a level below 1941. But spending increased steadily thereafter, to an annual average of 17.2 percent of GDP in the 1950s, 18.1 percent of GDP in the 1960s, and 19.4 percent of GDP in the 1970s. In constant dollars (FY2012), outlays which were at an annual average of $634 billion in the 1950s, more than doubled by the decade of the 1970s, reaching $1.274 trillion.[41] But there were significant shifts in the composition of spending during this period. Initially, spending was driven by Cold War defense expenditures, which constituted a majority of outlays in the 1950s. But subsequently, defense spending would decline as a share of outlays and GDP as a result of expanded domestic spending, particularly with respect to programmatic mandatory spending. Let us examine defense and domestic spending in turn.

The Rise of the National Security State

As the nation demobilized from World War II, defense spending fell from 89.5 percent of outlays (36.6 percent GDP) in 1945 to 30.6 percent of outlays (3.5 percent GDP) in 1948. But defense policy would quickly undergo a transformation, both in terms of its institutional infrastructure and the larger strategic orientation. Frustration over the lack of coordination between the War Department (which included the Army and the Army Air Corps) and the Navy during World War II had led to intense deliberation over the unification of the military services. Senator Truman, who chaired the Special Senate Committee to Investigate the National Defense Program, had been central to these discussions before being elected to the vice presidency and, ultimately, ascending to the presidency. While the National Security Act of 1947 didn't achieve unification, it created a new organizational framework, which included a new Secretary of Defense, the creation of the National Security Council to advise the president and a new Central Intelligence Agency. The Act also created an independent Department of the Air Force and merged the Department of War and the Navy to create a new National Military Establishment, which would be renamed the Department of Defense, as a result of 1949 amendments to the National Security Act. On the strategic side, the National Security Council's 1950 policy paper, NSC 68, argued that the containment of communist expansion would be the primary challenge of the postwar period. The Soviet Union had detonated its first atomic bomb in 1949, and NSC 68 concluded that by the mid-1950s, it would have the capacity to deploy atomic weapons. The implication was clear: the threat of Soviet communism could be contained only if the US invested heavily in its military capacities, potentially doubling the defense budget from 1948 to 1949 levels.[42]

Any reluctance that President Truman had to NSC 68 dissipated in June 1950, when North Korea attacked South Korea and the US authorized the deployment of air and ground forces. The fiscal demands of the Korean War were significant. Between 1950 and 1953, national defense spending increased from 32.2 to 69.4 percent of total outlays (4.9 to 13.1 percent GDP).[43] Before the war ended, Eisenhower had been elected president and the White House and Congress were under unified Republican control for the first time since the 1920s. While Eisenhower accepted the findings of NSC 68, he also questioned whether the proposed levels of defense spending were compatible with the long-term achievement of balanced budgets. In his estimation, the only path to meeting the strategic goal of deterring the Soviets would involve a reliance on airpower and an expanded nuclear arsenal, a cheaper option than turning the United States into a garrison state.[44] By 1955, defense spending had fallen to 10.5 percent GDP, some 62.4 percent of outlays. For the remainder of the Eisenhower presidency, spending would move within the range of 9.0–9.9 percent of GDP, while steadily declining from 60.2 to 50.2 percent of outlays between 1956 and 1960.[45]

Levels of defense spending would remain high in the 1960s, in part as a product of the war in Vietnam, which demanded a level of inflation-adjusted spending comparable to what the US spent in World War I.[46] Although US engagement in Vietnam dated back to early 1961, hostilities escalated following the passage of the Gulf of Tonkin Resolution in 1964, which authorized President Johnson "to take all necessary measures to repel any armed attack against the forces of the United States and prevent any further aggression."[47] The decline in defense spending relative to the economy, which began under Eisenhower, was briefly reversed in 1967, and it would peak at 9.2 percent of GDP by 1968. But from that point forward, the decline continued such that by the formal Agreement Ending the War and Restoring Peace in Viet-Nam, which entered into force in 1973, it had fallen to 5.7 percent of GDP, and would fall to 4.8 percent of GDP by 1980. As will be discussed in Chapter 6, Congress was increasingly looking to the "peace dividend" to fund domestic commitments. The decline in defense as a share of outlays was even more striking (see Table 5.5). Defense claimed a majority (50.2 percent) of outlays in 1960. Despite the costs of the war, by 1968, it had fallen to 46.1 percent of outlays and by 1980, it stood at just 22.8 percent, approximately one-half of the level of 1968.[48]

Domestic Spending

In 1968, at the height of the Vietnam War, Congress had agreed to President Johnson's request for a tax surcharge but only if paired with domestic spending cuts, which would compromise the welfare programs that had been introduced as part of the Great Society. After leaving the White House, Johnson recalled that he could not have "the woman I really loved—the Great Society" and "that bitch of a war on the other side of the world."[49] Congress had forced the President to make the classic tradeoff between guns and butter—warfare and welfare—and in his judgment, the guns had prevailed. Yet, one of the most striking features of the immediate postwar decades is the expansion of domestic spending as a share both of GDP and outlays. By 1977, less than a decade after the Johnson presidency ended, domestic discretionary spending had grown to claim a greater share of outlays than national defense. More striking, programmatic mandatory spending had grown to claim more than twice what was being spent on defense. From every indication, the welfare state was increasingly eclipsing the warfare state. Guns would never disappear as part of the mix, but they would never again claim a share of GDP or outlays comparable to the butter.

While the Johnson presidency is rightly associated with a historic expansion in domestic spending, it was in some ways an acceleration of trends exhibited in previous presidential administrations. There were important new domestic policies introduced in the final days of World War II and in the immediate postwar period. While they would create enduring fiscal commitments on the part of the federal government, they were also able to draw on a steady flow of revenues, as noted earlier. The Servicemen's Readjustment Act of 1944 (or GI Bill) was passed out of concern that veterans would enter an environment of high unemployment comparable to what had existed at the end of World War I. The GI Bill provided returning veterans with extended unemployment compensation (up to one year), educational assistance, and low-interest mortgages with zero down payments—a boon to the home construction economy and postwar suburbanization. The original GI Bill would set a precedent for future conflicts. Comparable benefits were extended to Korean War veterans under the Veterans' Readjustment Assistance Act of 1952. With the War Orphans' Educational Assistance Act of 1956, benefits were extended to the children of service members who had died from injuries incurred in the line of duty. Similarly, the Post-Korean Conflict and Vietnam Era GI Bill was enacted under the Veterans Readjustment Benefits Act of 1966, once again extending the social provision initiated by the GI Bill. Veterans' benefits took the form of an appropriated entitlement. That is, while classified as mandatory spending, funding was drawn directly from the general fund. The costs were significant. For example, the original GI Bill provided benefits to 7.8 million veterans, at a cost of some $139.6 billion and its Korean War counterpart covered an additional 2.4 million veterans at a cost of $37.2 billion (all costs expressed in 2020 dollars).[50]

One of the largest domestic commitments of the period came in the construction of the interstate highway system. In 1944, Congress provided for the designation of a 40,000 mile National System of Interstate Highways, albeit without funding for construction. In 1952, Congress passed the Federal-Aid Highway Act, authorizing a 50–50 federal state match and authorizing $25 million for construction. The support for the system grew under the Eisenhower presidency, as the President emphasized the defense-related rationale. The Federal-Aid Highway Act authorized $350 million (1956–1957), with the federal government assuming 60 percent of the costs. The Federal Aid Highway and Highway Revenue Acts of 1956 dramatically expanded funding, authorizing an additional $1 billion for FY1957, $1.7 billion for 1958, and $2 billion for 1959. Up to this point, expenditures on the Interstate were drawn from the general fund of the Treasury. But with the passage of the 1956 act, a new Highway Trust Fund was created to finance construction through excise taxes on fuel and other motor vehicle-related user taxes.[51] This was a product of Eisenhower's commitment to complete the system without contributing to the budget deficit.

In the mid to late 1940s, Congress turned to key areas of social policy: healthcare, nutritional assistance, and public housing. Congress passed the Hospital Survey and Construction Act of 1946 to address a pressing shortage of hospital facilities, particularly in rural communities, that was a product of the dearth of new investment during the depression and World War II. With the Act, Congress provided funds for states to develop inventories of their hospitals and clinics. States with shortages were provided with funding to cover a portion of the costs of construction.[52] Concerns over food security came to the forefront during the war, when many conscripts exhibited signs of malnutrition. With the National School Lunch Act of 1946, Congress created the National School Lunch Program, which adopted a grant formula to provide states with matching funds based on the number of school-aged children and state per capita income.[53] In 1949, Congress passed the Housing Act, which was one of the statutes promoted by President Truman as part of his "Fair Deal."

The Act provided federal loans to local redevelopment agencies to acquire and clear slums for redevelopment, reactivated a federal low-income public housing program that had been suspended during the war, authorized federal funds to subsidize the construction of 810,000 public housing units over the next six years, and promoted homeownership through an expansion of the Federal Housing Administration's mortgage insurance program.[54] In each case, the new commitments would be extended into the future. For example, the National School Lunch Program would be expanded with the Special Milk Program (1954) and the Child Nutrition Act (1966), which created the School Breakfast Program. A series of public housing statutes would be passed in the late 1950s and early 1960s, culminating in the creation of the Department of Housing and Urban Development in 1965.

Arguably, the most significant expansion of social welfare in the immediate postwar period came in Social Security. By 1950, the value of Social Security benefits had been eroded by inflation and the program covered only about one-half of the nation's workers. The Social Security Act Amendments of 1950 addressed these two problems by granting a 77 percent average increase in benefits and providing coverage to some 10 million additional workers by extending Social Security to self-employed, agricultural, and domestic workers (provisions were also passed to cover the employees of state and local government and nonprofit entities, albeit voluntarily). Amendments in 1952 and 1954 would provide additional benefit increases, of 12.5 and 13 percent, respectively, while folding new occupational categories into the program. The Social Security Amendments of 1956 created a new Disability Insurance program, providing cash payments to disabled workers aged 50–64. The program was liberalized in 1958 to provide support to the dependents of disabled workers and, again, in 1960, when disability coverage was extended regardless of age. Within a decade, Social Security had rapidly evolved toward the goal of providing universal coverage.[55] As a result of population growth and the programmatic expansion, the number of workers covered by Social Security increased from 48.3 million in 1950 to 72.5 million in 1960; the number of beneficiaries grew from 2.9 to 14.3 million during this same period. The growth would continue thereafter, such that between 1970 and 1980, the number of covered workers increased from 93.1 to 113.7 million; the number of beneficiaries expanded from 25.2 to 35.1 million.[56]

The Second Big Bang

The Johnson administration is often referred to as the second big bang in the history of the US welfare state, building on the initiatives of the first big bang of the New Deal. The Revenue Act of 1964, as noted earlier, was designed explicitly to stimulate the economy and achieve full employment, which President Johnson understood as being essential to support his larger social policy goals.

In the 1964 State of the Union message, Johnson announced his intention of waging a War on Poverty. In his letter of transmittal for the 1964 Economic Report of the President, he informed Congress: "We cannot and need not wait for the gradual growth of the economy to lift this forgotten fifth of our Nation above the poverty line." Johnson explained: "Today, as in the past, higher employment and speedier economic growth are the cornerstones of a concerted attack on poverty," and hence the need for the proposed tax cut.[57]

Economic stimulus was a critical component of Johnson's program, but taken by itself, it was insufficient. Over the course of 1964 and 1965, new legislation proliferated, contributing to the growth of domestic discretionary and mandatory spending. The Economic Opportunity Act of 1964 established the Office of Economic Opportunity and several new programs, including the Community Action Program, Job Corps, and the Volunteers in Service to America. More significantly, Congress passed the Food Stamp Act of 1964 to authorize an expansion of supplemental nutritional assistance for low-income households. In 1965, Congress passed the Elementary and Secondary Education Act, which authorized an expansion of federal funding of education. While educational funding would remain heavily dependent on state and local taxes, the new Act provided a means of using additional federal resources to improve education in school districts characterized by higher levels of poverty and lower levels of academic achievement. That same year, the Office of Economic Opportunity created Head Start, to provide preschool education for disadvantaged children. The Johnson administration also liberalized eligibility requirements for Aid to Families with Dependent Children or AFDC, a program created under the Social Security Act of 1935, initially, to provide grants-in-aid to states to provide income support to poor families where fathers were deceased, disabled, or absent. As the program was expanded to provide support for families with unemployed fathers and the federal government responded to lawsuits challenging state-level eligibility requirements, AFDC evolved into the largest income support entitlement program for the non-elderly population. Between 1960 and 1970, the number of AFDC recipients increased from 3 to 8.5 million, reaching 10.8 million by 1980. The expansion would continue after Johnson. The Social Security Act Amendments of 1972 created Supplemental Security Income, funded through general revenues, to provide means-tested assistance to the needy aged, blind, and permanently disabled, consolidating and strengthening federal control over categorical aid programs first authorized under the Social Security Act 1935. By 1980, 4.1 million Americans were receiving Supplemental Security Income.[58]

But from a fiscal perspective, the most significant changes came in the area of healthcare. The greatest gap in the Social Security Act of 1935 was the failure to include national health insurance, something Roosevelt had hoped would be remedied in the near future. Successive efforts to extend coverage to health insurance, most notably under Truman, floundered in the immediate postwar decades. Arguably, the most important contribution to health insurance came with the Internal Revenue Code of 1954, which codified the deductibility of medical expenses and the exemption of employer contributions to health insurance from employee's personal income and payroll taxes.[59] Although a system of national health insurance was out of reach, Johnson made healthcare a cornerstone of the Great Society and the first matter on the legislative calendar in 1965. As noted in Chapter 2, the resulting Social Security Act Amendments of 1965 established Medicare, which provided compulsory hospital insurance for the elderly (Medicare Part A) funded through the payroll tax and voluntary subsidized insurance for outpatient services (Medicare Part B) financed through a combination of premiums and general revenues. It also created Medicaid to provide federal grants-in-aid funded from general revenues to the states to finance means-tested health care. State participation in Medicaid was voluntary and required significant state expenditures, but participating states were required to extend coverage to citizens in key categorical programs (Aid to the Blind, AFDC, and Aid to the Permanently and Totally Disabled).[60] Between 1966 and 1980, the total number of Medicare beneficiaries would increase from 19 to 28 million, whereas Medicaid would grow from 4 to 19.6 million.[61]

When taken together, the immediate postwar decades witnessed important changes in the priorities expressed through federal spending, as reflected in Tables 5.4 and 5.5. Nondefense discretionary spending would grow to exceed defense spending by the last years of the 1970s. Programmatic mandatory

TABLE 5.4 Composition of Outlays, Budget Enforcement Act Categories, 1962–1980 (Percentage of GDP)

Fiscal Year	*Total Outlays*	*Discretionary*		*Mandatory*	
		Defense	*Nondefense*	*Programmatic**	*Net Interest*
1962	18.2%	9.0%	3.3%	5.7%	1.2%
1963	18.0	8.7	3.5	5.5	1.3
1964	17.9	8.3	3.6	5.6	1.2
1965	16.7	7.2	3.8	5.3	1.2
1966	17.2	7.6	4.0	5.3	1.2
1967	18.8	8.6	4.1	5.7	1.2
1968	19.8	9.2	4.0	6.4	1.2
1969	18.7	8.4	3.5	6.3	1.3
1970	18.7	7.8	3.7	6.7	1.4
1971	18.8	7.1	3.9	7.4	1.3
1972	19.0	6.5	4.0	7.9	1.3
1973	18.2	5.7	3.9	8.2	1.3
1974	18.2	5.4	3.9	8.5	1.4
1975	20.7	5.5	4.4	10.3	1.4

(continued)

TABLE 5.4 Cont.

Fiscal Year	*Total Outlays*	*Discretionary*		*Mandatory*	
		Defense	*Nondefense*	*Programmatic**	*Net Interest*
1976	20.8	5.0	4.8	10.3	1.5
1977	20.2	4.8	4.9	9.7	1.5
1978	20.2	4.6	5.0	9.7	1.6
1979	19.6	4.6	4.8	9.3	1.7
1980	21.2	4.8	5.1	10.1	1.9

* Does not include undistributed offsetting receipts.

Source: Office of Management and Budget, *Budget of the United States Government, Fiscal Year 2023* (Washington, DC: Government Publishing Office, 2022), Historical Tables, Table 8.4.

TABLE 5.5 Composition of Outlays, Budget Enforcement Act Categories 1962–1980 (Percentage of Outlays)

Fiscal Year	*Discretionary*		*Mandatory*	
	Defense	*Nondefense*	*Programmatic**	*Net Interest*
1962	49.2%	18.3%	31.0%	6.4%
1963	48.3	19.4	30.6	7.0
1964	46.4	20.3	31.1	6.9
1965	43.2	22.6	31.9	7.3
1966	43.9	23.2	30.9	7.0
1967	45.7	21.9	30.5	6.5
1968	46.1	20.1	32.1	6.2
1969	45.0	18.8	33.5	6.9
1970	41.9	19.6	35.6	7.4
1971	37.6	20.7	39.4	7.1
1972	34.4	21.3	41.7	6.7
1973	31.4	21.7	45.3	7.1
1974	30.0	21.3	46.9	8.0
1975	26.4	21.2	49.6	7.0
1976	24.2	23.1	49.5	7.2
1977	23.8	24.3	48.2	7.3
1978	22.8	24.9	48.0	7.7
1979	23.2	24.4	47.4	8.5
1980	22.8	24.0	47.7	8.9

* Does not include undistributed offsetting receipts.

Source: Office of Management and Budget, *Budget of the United States Government, Fiscal Year 2023* (Washington, DC: Government Publishing Office, 2022), Historical Tables, Table 8.3.

spending—a category that includes Social Security, Medicare, and Medicaid and other entitlement programs like AFDC and unemployment compensation—would grow even more rapidly. Between 1962 and 1980, programmatic mandatory spending would expand from 5.7 percent of GDP to 10.1 percent of GDP; during that same period, it would grow from 31 to 47.7 percent of outlays. Social Security would be the largest among the mandatory programs, expanding from 2.4 percent of GDP in 1962 (13.2 percent of outlays) to 4.2 percent of GDP (19.8 percent of outlays) by 1980. Medicare, which began providing benefits in 1966 would grow rapidly from 0.3 percent of GDP to 1.1 percent of GDP by 1980 whereas Medicaid would grow from 0.1 percent of GDP to 0.5 percent of GDP. Combined, they would claim 7.6 percent of outlays by the end of the period. The growth of mandatory spending would become the dominant trend in subsequent decades, such that by 2019, on the eve of the COVID-19 pandemic, it would account for almost two-thirds of outlays, roughly twice defense and nondefense discretionary spending combined.[62]

Conclusion

From the perspective of the 1980, much had changed since US demobilization from World War II. The institutional infrastructure for national defense was completely reconfigured, with the creation of a new Department of Defense, National Security Council, and the Central Intelligence Agency. Macroeconomic management—which was, at best, inchoate, for much of the 1930s—went through a similar institutional transformation following the passage of the Employment Act of 1946. Congress and a series of presidents made new and enduring policy commitments, guaranteeing education for veterans, funding the Interstate Highway System, and building on the precedents set in the 1930s to provide a far more extensive welfare state. The expansion of Social Security and the creation of significant new entitlement programs, most importantly Medicare and Medicaid, would have long-term fiscal consequences. This chapter focused on policies with the greatest budgetary importance. But the period also witnessed a transformation of the federal government's role in education, civil rights, and regulation. Federal outlays almost doubled relative to the economy by 1980, a trend that was made far more impressive given the strong record of growth.[63]

But what of the debt? The reduction of the debt relative to GDP can occur as a result of inflation, austerity, and/or economic growth. Inflation was certainly an important part of the story in the immediate postwar years, but its effects were quickly (if temporarily) moderated. Congress can tailor its tax and spending decisions to generate surpluses that can be used to redeem existing debt. But the relative infrequency of surpluses during the postwar period suggests that austerity did not contribute to debt reduction, even if deficits, where they occurred were relatively small. In fact, the gap between revenues and outlays over the period forced Congress to raise the statutory limit on the federal debt 42 times. We turn then to our third factor. Sustained economic growth increases the GDP and, as long as the growth rate exceeds the rate at which new debt is issued, the debt-to-GDP ratio will decline. Between 1946 and 1974, real GDP increased by some 243 percent.[64] This period of growth coincided with the great deleveraging of the postwar period, as debt fell from a record 106.1 percent of GDP (1946) to a low of 23.2 percent (1974).[65]

The ability of the federal government to simultaneously expand its responsibilities and engage in long-term deleveraging was also a product of the tax regime forged during the war and largely maintained in the immediate postwar period. But beneath this stability, there were subtle indicators of change. During the 1940s and 1950s, the institutional linkages between taxes and expenditures were central to fiscal decision making, as exhibited by Eisenhower's unwillingness to cut tax rates. But by the early 1960s, a commitment to active Keynesian management had resulted in the "growing acceptance of tax policy as a tool to regulate the economy," as Dennis S. Ippolito has argued. As tax policy was viewed increasingly as an instrument of economic management, "the tax side of the budget was detached from balanced-budget principles."[66] Yet, much of the World War II mass tax system remained in place.

By the 1970s, as the US economy encountered a combination of high inflation and high unemployment, policymakers encountered a crisis of economic theory and the policy mix that characterized the past few decades proved fragile. Keynesian economists, who had come to dominate fiscal policymaking, had assumed a stable Phillips curve tradeoff between inflation and unemployment. The coincidence of rising inflation and high unemployment undermined the theoretical consensus that had guided economic policymaking and opened a window of opportunity for policy change. Opponents of the policies that characterized the immediate postwar decades argued that deep tax cuts would offer a solution to the chaotic economic environment. The budgetary implications of tax cuts were of secondary importance and would not be fully recognized until the 1980s, when the nation entered a period of rapidly growing indebtedness. The period of deleveraging would come to an abrupt close. We turn to this period in Chapter 6.

Notes

1 Office of Management and Budget (OMB), *Budget of the United States Government, Fiscal Year 2023* (Washington, DC: Government Publishing Office, 2022), Historical Tables, Tables 1.2, 7.1; US Bureau of Economic Analysis, Real Gross Domestic Product [GDPC1], available at https://fred.stlouisfed.org/series/GDPC1

2 Federal Reserve Bank of St. Louis, NBER based Recession Indicators for the United States from the Period following the Peak through the Trough [USREC], available https://fred.stlouisfed.org/series/USREC, and US Bureau of Labor Statistics, Civilian Unemployment Rate [UNRATE], available at https://fred.stlouisfed.org/series/UNRATE

3 J. Bradford De Long, "Keynesianism, Pennsylvania Avenue Style: Some Economic Consequences of the Employment Act of 1946," *The Journal of Economic Perspectives,* 10, 3 (1996): 47.

4 Federal Reserve Bank of St. Louis, NBER based Recession Indicators for the United States from the Period following the Peak through the Trough [USREC].

5 "The Decline of Manufacturing." The FRED Blog, April 21, 2014. Available at https://fredblog.stlouisfed.org/2014/04/the-decline-of-manufacturing/?utm_source=series_page&utm_medium=related_content&utm_term=related_resources&utm_campaign=fredblog

6 See YiLi Chien, "Is U.S. Manufacturing Really Declining?" On the Economy Blog, Federal Reserve Bank of St. Louis, April 11, 2017. Available at www.stlouisfed.org/on-the-economy/2017/april/us-manufacturing-really-declining

7 US Department of Commerce, *Historical Statistics of the United States from Colonial Times to 1970* (Washington, DC: Government Printing Office, 1976), Series D 951.

8 See Nelson Lichtenstein, *State of the Union: A Century of American Labor* (Princeton: Princeton University Press, 2002), 125–32, and Marc Allen Eisner, *The American Political Economy: Institutional Evolution of Market and State*, 2nd ed. (New York: Routledge, 2014), 100–03.

9 Barry Bluestone and Bennett Harrison, *The Deindustrialization of America: Plant Closings, Community Abandonment, and the Dismantling of Basic Industry* (New York Basic Books, 1982), 17.

10 Share of Labor Compensation in GDP at Current National Prices for United States [LABSHPUSA156NRUG]. Available at https://fred.stlouisfed.org/series/LABSHPUSA156NRUG

11 US Census Bureau, Current Population Survey, 1968 to 2021 Annual Social and Economic Supplements (CPS ASEC), Table A5, B4, available at www.census.gov/data/tables/2021/demo/income-poverty/p60-273.html, and Anthony B. Atkinson, Joe Hasell, Salvatore Morelli, and Max Roser, "The Chartbook of Economic Inequality," 2017, available at http://chartbookofeconomicinequality.com/wp-content/uploads/DataForDownload/AllData_ChartbookOfEconomicInequality.xlsx

12 See Hedwig Reinhardt, "The Great Debt Redemption 1946–1947," *Social Research,* 15, 2 (1948): 170–93.

13 OMB, *Budget of the United States, Fiscal Year 2023,* Historical Tables, Tables 1.3 and 7.1, calculations by author.

14 Joshua Aizenman and Nancy Marion, "Using Inflation to Erode the U.S. Public Debt," NBER Working Paper 15562 (Cambridge, MA: National Bureau of Economic Research, 2009), 4, 8–9.

15 US Bureau of Economic Analysis, Gross Domestic Product [GDPA], available at https://fred.stlouisfed.org/series/GDPA, and US Bureau of Economic Analysis, Real Gross Domestic Product [GDPC1]. Available at https://fred.stlouisfed.org/series/GDPC1

16 US Bureau of Economic Analysis, Real gross domestic product per capita [A939RX0Q048SBEA]. Available at https://fred.stlouisfed.org/series/A939RX0Q048SBEA

17 OMB, *Budget of the United States, Fiscal Year 2023,* Historical Tables, Table 7.1.

18 Sheldon D. Pollack, *War, Revenue, and State Building: Financing the Development of the American State* (Ithaca: Cornell University Press, 2009), 263.

19 OMB, *Budget of the United States, Historical Tables,* Tables 2.2 and 2.3.

20 US Department of the Treasury, Internal Revenue Service, US Individual Income Tax: Tax Rates for Regular Tax: Highest Bracket [IITTRHB], available at https://fred.stlouisfed.org/series/IITTRHB, and US Department of the Treasury, Internal Revenue Service, US Individual Income Tax: Tax Rates for Regular Tax: Lowest Bracket [IITTRLB], available at https://fred.stlouisfed.org/series/IITTRLB, August 25, 2022.

21 On Korean War financing, see Rosella Cappella Zielinski, *How States Pay for Wars* (Ithaca, NY: Cornell University Press, 2016), 29–46.

22 Harry S. Truman, "Special Message to the Congress Reporting on the Situation in Korea," July 19, 1950. Available at www.presidency.ucsb.edu/node/230983

23 US Department of the Treasury, Internal Revenue Service, US Individual Income Tax: Tax Rates for Regular Tax: Highest Bracket [IITTRHB], and US Department of the Treasury, Internal Revenue Service, US Individual Income Tax: Tax Rates for Regular Tax: Lowest Bracket [IITTRLB].

24 OMB, *Budget of the United States, Fiscal Year 2023,* Historical Tables, Table 1.2.

25 Ibid., Table 7.1.

26 Dwight D. Eisenhower, "Annual Message to the Congress on the State of the Union," January 7, 1954. Available at www.presidency.ucsb.edu/node/232936

27 Budget of the Budget, *The Budget of the United States Government for the Fiscal Year Ending June 30, 1955* (Washington, DC: Government Printing Office, 1954), 14.

28 See John F. Witte, *The Politics and Development of the Federal Income Tax* (Madison: University of Wisconsin Press, 1985), 146–50.

29 Dennis S. Ippolito, *Why Budgets Matter: Budget Policy and American Politics* (University Park: Penn State University Press, 2015), 165.

30 For a discussion of the legislative history of the Revenue Act, see Witte, *The Politics and Development of the Federal Income Tax*, 155–65, and Herbert Stein, *The Fiscal Revolution in America,* rev. ed. (Washington DC: American Enterprise Institute, 1990), 422–53.

31 Stein, *Fiscal Revolution in America,* 454.

32 US Bureau of Economic Analysis, Real Gross Domestic Product [A191RL1Q225SBEA]. Available at https://fred.stlouisfed.org/series/A191RL1Q225SBEA

33 US Bureau of Labor Statistics, Unemployment Rate [UNRATE]. Available at https://fred.stlouisfed.org/series/UNRATE

34 OMB, *Budget of the United States, Fiscal Year 2023,* Historical Tables, Table 2.3.

35 Ibid., Table 1.3.

36 Ibid.

37 See Witte, *The Politics and Development of the Federal Income Tax*, 165–75.

38 US Department of the Treasury, Internal Revenue Service, US Individual Income Tax: Tax Rates for Regular Tax: Highest Bracket [IITTRHB], available at https://fred.stlouisfed.org/series/IITTRHB, and US Department of the Treasury, Internal Revenue Service, US Individual Income Tax: Tax Rates for Regular Tax: Lowest Bracket [IITTRLB], available at https://fred.stlouisfed.org/series/IITTRLB, November 24, 2020.

39 R. Douglas Arnold, *The Logic of Congressional Action* (New Haven: Yale University Press, 1990), 196–97.

40 OMB, *Budget of the United States, Fiscal Year 2023,* Historical Tables, Tables 2.2, 2.3.

41 Ibid., Table 1.3.

42 Jack A. LeCuyer, *A National Security Staff for the 21st Century* (Carlisle Barracks, PA: Strategic Studies Institute, US Army War College, 2012), 1–7, and Grant Madsen, *Sovereign Soldiers: How the U.S. Military Transformed the Global Economy After World War II* (Philadelphia: University of Pennsylvania Press, 2018), 195.
43 OMB, *Budget of the United States, Fiscal Year 2023,* Historical Tables, Table 6.1.
44 Madsen, *Sovereign Soldiers,* 220, 229.
45 OMB, *Budget of the United States, Fiscal Year 2023,* Historical Tables, Table 6.1.
46 Stephen Daggett and Nina M. Serafino, *Costs of Major U.S. Wars and Recent U.S. Overseas Military Operations,* CRS Report RS21013 (Washington, DC: Congressional Research Service, 2001), 2.
47 Nina M. Serafino, *Military Interventions by U.S. Forces from Vietnam to Bosnia: Background, Outcomes, and "Lessons Learned" for Kosovo,* CRS Report RL30184 (Washington, DC: Congressional Research Service, 1999), 11–12.
48 OMB, *Budget of the United States, Fiscal Year 2023,* Historical Tables, Tables 8.3 and 8.4.
49 Quoted in Mark Atwood Lawrence, "How Vietnam Killed the Great Society," *New York Times,* September 22, 2017. Available at www.nytimes.com/2017/09/22/opinion/vietnam-war-great-society.html
50 Cassandria Dortch, *Veterans' Educational Assistance Programs and Benefits: A Primer,* CRS Report R42785 (Washington, DC: Congressional Research Service, 2020), 24–27, 30.
51 John Williamson, *Federal Aid to Roads and Highways Since the 18*th *Century: A Legislative History,* CRS Report R42140 (Washington DC: Congressional Research Service, 2012), 7–8.
52 See V.M. Hoge, "The Hospital Survey and Construction Act," *The Social Security Bulletin*, 9, 4 (1946): 15–17, and Barbara English, *The Hill-Burton Uncompensated Services Program,* CRS Report 98-968 (Washington, DC: Congressional Research Service, 2006).
53 Gordon W. Gunderson, *The National School Lunch Program: Background and Development,* US Department of Agriculture Food and Nutrition Service, FNS-3 (Washington, DC: Government Printing Office, 1971), 14–20.
54 Maggie McCarty, Libby Perl, and Katie Jones, *Overview of Federal Housing Assistance Programs and Policy,* CRS Report RL34591 (Washington, DC: Congressional Research Service, 2019), 3. For a discussion of Truman's Fair Deal, see William E. Leuchtenburg, *In the Shadow of FDR: From Harry Truman to Barack Obama* (Ithaca, NY: Cornell University Press, 2009), 33–36.
55 Larry DeWitt, "The Development of Social Security in America," *Social Security Bulletin*, 70, 3 (2010): 10–14.
56 Social Security Administration, "Ratio of Social Security Workers to Beneficiaries, Calendar Years 1940–2013." Available at www.ssa.gov/history/ratios.html
57 Council of Economic Advisors, *Economic Report of the President* (Washington, DC: Government Printing Office, 1964), 12.
58 US Department of Health and Human Services, Administration for Children and Families, "AFDC Caseload Data 1960–1995." Available at www.acf.hhs.gov/ofa/resource/tanf-and-afdc-historical-case-data-pre-2012. Data on Supplemental Security Income from Lenna D. Kennedy, "SSI at Its 25th Year," *Social Security Bulletin*, 62,2 (1999): 54–56.
59 See James W. Henderson and Beck A. Taylor, "Employer-Sponsored Health Insurance: Past, Present and Future," *Journal of Forensic Economics*, 15, 2 (2002): 181–94.

60 See Rosemary Stevens and Robert Stevens, "Medicaid: Anatomy of a Dilemma," *Law and Contemporary Problems*, 35, 2 (1970): 359–63.

61 US Census Bureau, "Medicare Enrollment—National Trends 1966–2013." Available at www.census.gov/history/pdf/medicare1966-2013.pdf

62 OMB, *Budget of the United States, Fiscal Year 2023,* Historical Tables, Tables 8.3 and 8.4.

63 Ibid., Table 1.2, and US Bureau of Economic Analysis, Real Gross Domestic Product [GDPCA], available at https://fred.stlouisfed.org/series/GDPCA

64 US Bureau of Economic Analysis, Real Gross Domestic Product.

65 OMB, *Budget of the United States, Fiscal Year 2023,* Historical Tables, Table 7.1.

66 Dennis S. Ippolito, *Deficits, Debt, and the New Politics of Tax Policy* (Cambridge: Cambridge University Press, 2012), 76–77.

6

THE GREAT INFLECTION

Stagflation and the Death of a Consensus

In 1964, James Tobin, a former member of Kennedy's Council of Economic Advisors (CEA), observed that "economic growth has come to occupy an exalted position in the hierarchy of goals of government policy, both in the United States and abroad."[1] There was a new confidence that policymakers could use the tools of Keynesian economics to fine-tune the economy and secure broad abundance. But during the 1970s, stagflation—a combination of high inflation and high unemployment that seemed incompatible with the expectations of the Phillips curve—created great uncertainty for policymakers. Frank E. Morris, a veteran of the Kennedy Treasury Department and later President of the Federal Reserve Bank of Boston, gave voice to the frustration in 1978: "If Keynesianism is not bankrupt, it is at least in disarray." Economic policy was "being made in at least a partial vacuum of economic theory" and the confidence that policymakers once felt "in our ability to use the Keynesian system to generate outcomes for the economy which were highly predictable has been shaken."[2]

This chapter explores the great inflection of the 1970s, an episode that is embedded in the larger historical narrative presented in Chapter 5. The core argument is straightforward. Following the positive economic performance of the previous decades and the expectations it engendered, stagflation created an enormous challenge. It generated fascinating debates over economic theory that contested the Keynesian consensus. At the same time, stagflation opened a window of opportunity for critics to relitigate the efficacy of the welfare state and regulatory policies that had been introduced in the past few decades. Their efforts were reinforced by the successful advocacy of policy think tanks on the Right, which popularized arguments to a broader public that was rapidly losing faith in the federal government and antagonistic

DOI: 10.4324/9781003395331-8

to the demands of taxation. Ultimately, supply-side arguments prevailed, providing the intellectual justification for a departure in the 1980s from the mass-based tax regime inherited from World War II. The resulting fiscal gap would turn the deleveraging of the immediate postwar period into a period of growing indebtedness.

From Growth to Stagflation

During the 1950s, Keynesian economists added the Phillips curve to their theoretical arsenal. The curve, which captured the inverse relationship between the price level and the unemployment rate, offered some guidance in managing the economy. As Arthur M. Okun, former CEA Chair, noted: "Empirically, the Phillips curve looked like a winner for the United States. Annual increases in prices (and wages) relative to the unemployment rates for 1954 to 1968 fit a hyperbola like a glove," thereby providing economic policymakers with a greater ability to understand the ramifications of fiscal policy decisions.[3] The Phillips curve also served an important political function. As Sidney Weintraub observed: "Phillips-curve Keynesianism" embodied "the conviction that the inflation ill could be mitigated only by the unemployment ailment. With Phillips curves being hailed as reflecting 'natural laws,' a new prison fence was erected to deter public policy. Full employment wore a high price tag. A flat price trend might cost intolerable unemployment."[4]

In 1970–1971, inflation proved particularly resistant to policy interventions and in short course, the nation would experience an "inflationary recession" or what would be known, subsequently, as stagflation, a toxic combination of inflation and high unemployment rates (see Figure 6.1). For reasons that would be the source of prolonged debate, the stable trade-off assumed under the Phillips curve no longer held. As Okun observed at the time, inflation and unemployment "have become intertwined and combined in a way that is historically unprecedented and, by the verdict of many economic textbooks, theoretically impossible."[5] With respect to inflation, it was clear that several factors were relevant, including the stimulus of Vietnam War and social spending and the popular expectations of rising incomes, all of which were inherited from the 1960s. The exogenous shock of failed world harvests (1972 and 1973) and an oil embargo (1973) had a significant impact when introduced into an economy that was already prone to inflation.[6] Stagnation was somewhat more complicated, tied to a host of factors including the aging capital stock and the technology it embodied (one of the negative consequences of not having suffered the devastation faced by other nations in World War II) and, with the maturation of the postwar trade system created under the General Agreement on Tariffs and Trade that subjected US firms to growing competition from foreign imports. Productivity lagged significantly behind that of key competitors, contributing to inflation and economic stagnation.

FIGURE 6.1 Inflation and Unemployment, 1960–1990

Source: Adapted from World Bank, Inflation, consumer prices for the United States [FPCPITOTLZGUSA] and US Bureau of Labor Statistics, Unemployment Rate [UNRATE].

From the perspective of the mid-1970s, Richard N. Goodwin, a presidential advisor to Kennedy and Johnson, recalled that "only a decade ago, our principal problem seemed to be how to arrive at the fairest distribution and wisest use of mounting national wealth." But now, there were "important signs that our present economic deterioration is different from the past setbacks—more profound" and this perception was "reinforced by the newly apparent inability of traditional economic policies to cope with the difficulties."[7] Indeed, by 1976 the signs of decline were ubiquitous. Deindustrialization was gaining attention, as companies—particularly in the Rust Belt—moved production to "right-to-work" states in the South and West and then, in many cases, began to offshore or outsource production. Between 1950 and 1976, the US share of global GDP had fallen from 34.3 to 24.6 percent. In the years following World War II, the United States was responsible for 50 percent of the world's oil and steel, which now stood at 15 and 20 percent, respectively. The US share of world exports fell from 32 to 11 percent during this same period. Trade surpluses, once relatively common, would become elusive and then unimaginable.[8] This pattern of decline and the unemployment and dislocations it generated were combined with high rates of inflation. Clearly, the economy was no longer capable of supporting the expectations of price stability and growth that had prevailed in the recent past.

The poor economic performance found salient symbols in gas lines and shuttered factories. High inflation raised nominal incomes, pushing households into higher tax brackets. "Bracket creep" provoked popular tax revolts and a proliferation of state-level anti-tax ballot measures. As Michael McGrath explains, "The combination of wage stagnation, high unemployment rates, and inflation during the 1970s...brought into question the idea that economists and policy experts could think their way out of difficult problems." They "underscored a growing fear that America's best days were in the past."[9] A contemporaneous analyst, Edward Foster, feared that the economy "apparently beyond the reach of government attempts to control it, may destroy confidence" and inspire "fear that the social contract under which we have operated in the past is no longer operative."[10] Elmer B. Staats, Comptroller General and veteran of the Bureau of the Budget, likened inflation to a "cancer on the body politic," a "disease that destroy and spreads—and if not cured can be fatal to our way of life."[11] The economic malaise was reinforced by the chaos of conflictive politics and failed public policies: the "credibility gap" of the Johnson administration's foreign policy pronouncements, the revelations of the Watergate break ins, the resignations of Vice President Agnew and then President Nixon, and the humbling termination of the Vietnam War, combined to lower popular faith in public institutions. In 1964—the birth of Johnson's Great Society—faith in government peaked at 77 percent. But between 1970 and 1980, this figure had fallen from 54 percent to a low of 27 percent.[12]

Muddling through an Uncertain Environment

As policymakers of both parties sought to manage the economic problems, they moved through a series of responses.[13] When Nixon entered office, he faced an inflation rate of 5.46 percent, which had accelerated from 4.2 percent in 1968. While a contractionary policy might have stopped inflation in its tracks, Nixon was convinced that the high unemployment rates in the recession that marked the final year of the Eisenhower presidency had ensured his 1960 loss to Kennedy. His policy of "gradualism," which combined spending cuts and a restrictive monetary policy, nonetheless pushed the economy into a mild recession that lasted from late 1969 into late 1970. While the unemployment rate peaked at 6.1 percent, inflation remained surprisingly immovable. As Paul W. McCracken, Nixon's first CEA Chair, recalls:

> What stubbornly refused to appear on stage was conclusive improvements of the price level. By the second quarter of 1970, with production declining and unemployment rising, consumer prices were still moving upward at a rate of over 6 percent per year.[14]

Congress responded by passing the Economic Stabilization Act of 1970, which authorized the president to control prices, wages, rents, salaries, interest rates, and corporate dividends.

Although Nixon had not requested the authority granted in the Economic Stabilization Act, in August of 1971, he announced his New Economic Policy. Nixon's policy ended the convertibility of dollars into gold thereby abandoning the Bretton Woods system, enacted a 10 percent surcharge on imports to force a realignment of exchange rates, and imposed a 90-day wage/price freeze via executive order. By the end of the 90-day period, Nixon moved forward with a series of mandatory and voluntary wage/price controls supervised by a Cost of Living Council. In August, Nixon also proposed tax cuts to stimulate the economy and reduce unemployment. Nixon described the Revenue Act of 1971 as "historic tax-cut legislation," noting "the most important thing this act means is jobs."[15] The Act repealed the excise tax on automobiles and lowered the individual income tax by increasing the minimum standard deduction and accelerating increases in the personal exemption. But the greatest benefits accrued to business. The Act reinstated the investment tax credit which had been repealed in 1969, codified provision that accelerated depreciation allowances, and created "Domestic International Sales Corporations (or DISCs) to provide special tax treatments for export sales of US manufacturers.[16]

While inflation was negligible and the price controls found support in public opinion, unemployment remained elevated. As the 1972 elections approached, Nixon promoted an expansion of deficit spending, promising a return to balanced budgets in 1973, once the unemployment rate had fallen to an acceptable level. The Federal Reserve supported Nixon's policy by increasing the money supply, arguing that the combination of low inflation and high unemployment signaled room for expansionary policy. Nixon was reelected in a landslide and moved to a more restrictive fiscal policy as promised. A new 60-day price freeze was imposed in June of 1973, followed by a lifting of the freeze on a sector-by-sector basis during the summer. But the Watergate revelations, resistance from business and organized labor to a continuation of wage/price controls, and skepticism regarding the efficacy of Nixon's policy mix took their toll. In 1974, when the authority granted under the Economic Stabilization Act expired, Congress declined to reauthorize the statute.[17]

In 1971, when Nixon announced his New Economic Policy, inflation stood at 4.3 percent. While the inflation rate would fall over the course of the next year, failed world harvests and an oil embargo limited the efficacy of the controls. By October of 1973, the nation had fallen into a recession and, remarkably, by 1974, an annual inflation rate of 11.1 percent was combined with an unemployment rate of 5.6 percent. Nixon had adopted his policy of gradualism five years earlier, in hopes of fighting inflation without inducing a recession. By the last year of his presidency, he was forced to fight inflation rates that were more than twice as high but to do so in the midst of a recession.

Gerald Ford inherited this "inflationary recession" upon Nixon's resignation, and he returned to standard economic policy instruments. Mandatory controls were no longer in the opportunity set, so Ford was forced to rely on voluntary price-wage policy, exhorting government, consumers, labor, and businesses to exercise restraint and "Whip Inflation Now." He combined this with deregulation efforts designed to reduce prices and barriers to new investment. As the recession continued and the unemployment rate exceeded 8 percent, Ford shifted emphasis from inflation to jobs and called on Congress to pass a $16 billion tax cut. The resulting Tax Reduction Act of 1975, largely a stopgap measure as more comprehensive revenue legislation was working its way through Congress, provided temporary tax cuts for individuals and businesses. Its greatest legacy was the creation of the Earned Income Tax Credit (EITC) for the working poor.[18]

The Tax Reform Act of 1976 was a testament both to the changing institutional context in Congress and the growing uncertainty about policy. As noted in Chapter 3, under the chairmanship of Wilbur Mills (D-AK), tax policy was formulated in a highly insulated environment. Mills' departure and reforms in Congress created a far more porous environment. Liberal Democrats sought reforms that would close corporate loopholes and provide broader tax relief, whereas Republicans sought to tie tax reductions to spending ceilings, thereby limiting the budgetary consequences. In the end, neither side prevailed. The Tax Reform Act provided some relief to individual taxpayers through an increase in the standard deduction and the extension of the tax credit created the year before. For higher income households, it expanded the individual minimum tax while creating a unified rate schedule for estate and gift taxes (with a $175,000 exemption). When combined with the extension of the EITC, the effects were largely progressive. On the corporate side, the Act delayed a scheduled decrease in the investment tax credit, temporarily cut small business tax rates and increased the long-term capital gains holding period. As John F. Witte notes, the Tax Reform Act failed in two important ways. "Other than the investment credit, the bill did little for capital formation and investment." Moreover, "the bill seemed to do little for the middle class, which was suffering from inflation and the rapid escalation of state and local taxes. …This momentary loss of sensitivity to the middle class and the growing perception of a capital crisis set the tone for the next five years of tax politics."[19]

While inflation gradually fell to 5.7 percent under Ford, by 1976, when he faced Jimmy Carter in the presidential election, it was combined with an unemployment rate of 7.7 percent.[20] In the campaign, Carter ran as an outsider, drawing on populist sentiments and standing in opposition to the federal bureaucracy and the Great Society programs that were increasingly being targeted by conservative think tanks, a point to be developed in greater detail below. The economic chaos provided an opportunity to popularize the "misery index," the combination of the inflation rate and the unemployment rate, to illustrate Ford's failed economic policies. Carter promised that he would not use unemployment to fight inflation. Under Ford, the misery index for 1976 was 13.4, and this, combined with the pardon of Richard Nixon, virtually assured his defeat.[21]

By the Carter presidency, Congress sought to legislate statutory targets for unemployment and inflation with the Humphrey–Hawkins Full Employment and Balanced Growth Act of 1978, only to discover that the economy does not comply with legislative directives. Carter moved between voluntary price controls, a continuation of deregulation, and deficit reduction to combat inflation. Policymakers debated the merits and demerits of industrial policy, citing the performance of foreign competitors—most notably, Japan and West Germany—and the accomplishments of US mobilization during the two world wars. But by the end of the decade, nothing had worked to return the economy to the favorable performance of a decade earlier and a new oil embargo pushed inflation to new peacetime highs. As Okun suggested, stagflation was a "new problem. Yet, we are dealing with it with old policies that are unlikely to solve it."[22]

With respect to taxation, Carter had promoted reforms to eliminate many of the tax expenditures that had proliferated in the past several years to reduce the tax liabilities of corporations, potentially using the new revenues to provide broader tax relief. But the goal of reform was stymied by significant divisions within the administration. With the growing sense that standard Keynesian policies offered few solutions to stagflation, many turned to the tax code as a means of promoting capital formation, resulting in successive iterations of Carter's proposal. In the end, Congress passed the Revenue Act of 1978 that provided some tax relief for individuals, largely through increases in the standard deduction and personal exemption. Top and bottom tax marginal rates remained stable, but the complex system of tax brackets was reduced from 25 to 15. The EITC was made permanent.[23] But with inflation-induced bracket creep and the imposition of scheduled increases in the Social Security tax, the changes for many taxpayers were imperceptible. With respect to corporations, tax expenditure reform was jettisoned, and business received a reduction in corporate tax rates (from 48 to 46 percent) and maximum capital gains rates (from 39 to 28 percent).[24] It was never clear whether the changes in the revenue code were intended to stem inflation or promote growth. As Judith Stein notes: "The story of Carter's tax reform is the tale of a reasonable bill, thoughtfully calibrated and recalibrated in the White House, that was first ignored in the Congress and then replaced by a bill that not only eliminated Carter's reforms but discarded historic principles of interclass equity and methods of promoting business investment."[25]

In 1979, as the unemployment rate and the inflation rate were rising in tandem, Carter famously delivered what would be known as his "malaise" speech. The President lamented that "the true problems of our Nation are much deeper—deeper than gasoline lines or energy shortages, deeper even than inflation or recession." He described "a crisis that strikes at the very heart and soul and spirit of our national will" and creates "growing doubt about the meaning of our own lives and in the loss of a unity of purpose for our nation."[26] Carter turned to a policy of budgetary austerity to fight inflation with the aspiration to balance the budget during a second term, the former goal reinforced by the tight monetary policy of his newly appointed head of the Federal Reserve, Paul Volcker. The next year, as Carter stood for reelection, the nation was in recession, with double-digit inflation. His earlier critique of the Ford administration's economic policies came back to haunt him. With a misery index approaching 20 percent—well in excess of the misery index of 1976—there was little evidence that Carter had discovered the policy mix to fight stagflation.

In Search of a Solution

While the economic challenges of the 1970s were important, from the perspective of this chapter, we are primarily interested in how they set the stage for changes in tax policy. The combination of inflation and stagnation led to fascinating policy debates. Mainstream Keynesians (or neo-Keynesians) who defined the dominant paradigm in the immediate postwar decades focused on how changes in aggregate demand would impact on the Phillips curve trade-off. But much of the difficulty of the period came from unforeseen supply-side shocks (e.g., crop failures, the oil embargo) and a sharp decline in productivity that exacerbated inflationary forces. As economist Richard X. Chase declared in 1976, "the American economy entered a non-Keynesian world." Keynesians, whose models seemed ill-suited to the new environment, "were by and large, unaware of what was happening *even while it was happening*." He continues: "Like generals who attempt to win a current war by waging the last one, mainstream economists had their weapons and their strategies tied to past conditions no longer completely relevant."[27]

Post-Keynesians and institutionalists argued that traditional fiscal and monetary policies should be supplemented with wage/price or incomes policy. Some looked to the northern European model, where governments were managing inflation through neo-corporatist interest intermediation, in essence negotiating wage and price agreements via tripartite bargaining with labor and business peak associations. But in the United States, low levels of union density and weak business associations limited the applicability of the model.[28] Post-Keynesians argued that, despite the institutional differences, an incomes policy might be enacted through the tax system, freeing fiscal and monetary policy to promote reductions in unemployment. Sidney Weintraub and Henry C. Wallich, for example, argued that the federal government should levy a surcharge on the corporate profits tax for businesses that granted wage increases in excess of some inflationary guidepost. "The added tax burden may be expected to stiffen the company's back in wage negotiations" leading to a "lower rate of wage increases, and a slowing of the rate of inflation."[29] Others argued that corporations could be allowed to enjoy accelerated depreciation schedules—thereby increasing productivity—in exchange for their compliance with wage and price guidelines.[30]

Others focused on the slump in productivity, the growing trade deficit and persistent unemployment. Drawing on the examples of Europe, Japan, and economic mobilization during World War II, institutional economists argued that the United States should develop an industrial policy to propel growth in industries that could deliver high wages and international competitiveness. A national planning board, working with organized labor and business, could be used to set medium- and long-term priorities, coordinate economic policies, and finance industrial change. While proposals proliferated in the mid- to late 1970s, they raised concerns on several grounds. First, the same institutional factors that limited the availability of neo-corporatist solutions created a barrier to national planning, as did the fragmented institutional structure of the US government. Second, the proposals would elevate the role of the state in the economy at a time when there was growing skepticism about government intervention and calls for deregulation and enhanced market governance. The opposition on the Right was grounded in support for free markets. But even the New Left was hesitant to support Carter's calls for an Economic Revitalization Board out of concerns that it would be subject to capture by corporate interests.[31] Third, there was skepticism that an effective industrial policy could be funded effectively. In Japan and Western Europe, industrial policy relied on credit-based systems of industrial finance. In some cases (e.g., Japan), government set interest rates on a sectoral basis, to channel capital to strategic industries. In others (e.g., West Germany), banks provided patient capital for long-term industrial goals. The United States, in sharp contrast, relied on a capital market-based system of corporate finance where investments in the stock market were disaggregated and responsive to short-term profitability.[32] The industrial policy debates failed to yield a solution.

The Conservative Critique

While neo-Keynesians, post-Keynesians, and institutionalists offered their proposals, on the other end of the spectrum, a competing set of arguments rejected the Keynesian consensus and called for a reduction in the role of the state in the economy. The proposed remedy was to cut taxes and expenditures, reform welfare and regulations to allow market forces to prevail, and use monetary policy to facilitate rather than drive economic growth. From the perspective of long-term debt, the arguments regarding tax policy would prove to be the most consequential. But they were part of a much larger critique of the policies that had emerged out of the New Deal and the immediate postwar decades.

The critique exhibited growing skepticism about the Phillips curve tradeoff and, more broadly, the efficacy of discretionary policy interventions. Economist Milton Friedman argued that the inflation of the era was the inevitable result of politically driven attempts to stimulate the economy. Friedman and Edmund Phelps (writing separately) challenged the Phillips curve tradeoff in the late 1960s. Friedman's formulation was particularly influential, given that he presented it in his 1967 presidential address to the American Economic Association. His basic argument was that at the "natural" rate of unemployment, there was no difference between the actual inflation rate and the expected inflation rate. Efforts to stimulate the economy to achieve unemployment rates below the natural rate would raise the actual inflation rate, much as Keynesians suggested. But then the expected inflation rate would rise to match the actual rate. The Phillips curve would shift upward, in essence, providing a less favorable combination of inflation and unemployment. Successive interventions aimed at reducing the unemployment rate below the natural rate would reduce the lag between actual and expectational inflation, as people more rapidly responded to price increases. In Friedman's words: "there is always a temporary trade-off between inflation and unemployment; there is no permanent trade-off. The temporary trade-off comes not from inflation per se, but from unanticipated inflation, which generally means, from a rising rate of inflation."[33] While the short-term Phillips curve may well behave as Keynesians suggested, in the long term the Phillips curve was a vertical line. Thus, in the long run, policymakers did not have the latitude to select an unemployment rate other than the natural rate.[34] Rather than using policy in a discretionary fashion to achieve a particular level of inflation or unemployment, Friedman argued that the Federal Reserve should publicly announce a goal of providing for a steady rate of monetary growth compatible with stability in the price of final products. While Friedman's critique of the Phillips curve did not appear to fit the experiences of the late 1960s, with the onset of stagflation in the 1970s, it appeared to many to be prescient.

Friedman's critique of the Phillips curve was reinforced by the contributions of rational expectations economists, most notably, Robert E. Lucas Jr. and Thomas J. Sargent. The core assumption was that private economic actors understand government policy actions, revise their expectations about the future accordingly, and adapt strategically to policy interventions (Sargent would open the first chapter of a subsequent volume on rational expectations and inflation with a Chinese proverb: "The government has strategies. The people have counterstrategies").[35] The implications of rational expectations were important. The core assumption raised concerns about the capacity of policymakers to model behavior and accurately anticipate the effects of policy interventions. More importantly, macroeconomic policies would prove ineffective (the "policy ineffectiveness" proposition)[36] precisely because they would be incorporated into the decisions of consumers, workers, and firms. Rational expectations, as Bennett T. McCallum explained, "provides theoretical support for the view that the monetary and fiscal policy-makers should not attempt to engage in activist countercyclical policies of the type associated with the term 'fine tuning'." Rather, they "should strive to eliminate unsystematic fluctuations in variables under their control, such as the money stock and the level of government spending."[37]

The critique of discretionary fiscal and monetary policy was accompanied by a growing interest in supply-side economics, a term that was embraced to distinguish it from the demand-side focus of standard Keynesianism. The core arguments drew on classical economics and the historical precedents of tax cuts in the 1920s and 1964. Arthur D. Laffer argued that supply-side economics was grounded in "the essential tenet of classical economics," namely, "that *people alter their behavior when economic incentives change.* If the incentives for doing an activity increase relative to alternative activities, more of the attractive activities will be done."[38] Impediments to these activities will have the opposite effect. Under current levels of taxation, he argued, businesses employ fewer workers and either acquire less capital or use existing capital less intensively; employees with lower after-tax wages face disincentives to work; investors who are forced to accept lower after-tax yields have fewer incentive to save. Tax reductions on wages and salaries, it follows, would increase incentives for individuals to enter the workforce, increase their working hours, and defer retirement. All of this would expand the supply of labor and the output of goods and services. Corporate income tax cuts, particularly if combined with investment tax credits and accelerated depreciation, could stimulate higher levels of capital formation, whereas the reduction of taxes on investment could incentivize the higher levels of private savings necessary to fund the expansion.

In sum, tax cuts provided the means of unleashing supply-side forces that would have important implications for inflation, productivity, and unemployment. But what were the consequences for revenues? This was an important question given that Republicans had repeatedly cited deficits as emblematic of irresponsible Democratic governance. According to Laffer, although it was true that tax cuts would "lessen the amount of revenue collected per unit," it would "increase the employment of the lower taxed factor" and "increase the employment of other factors, hence increase their tax payments." It would have the additional benefit of reducing government spending "as the number of unemployed and the number of welfare recipients declines." While these factors would partially mitigate the effects of tax cuts on deficits and debt, Laffer admitted that the full impact of tax cuts on fiscal solvency remained "an empirical question."[39] Laffer's argument was popularized by Jude Wanniski as the "Laffer curve" in the editorial pages of the *Wall Street Journal,* the *Public Interest,* and subsequently in the pages of his popular 1978 book *How the World*

Works.[40] Soon, the Laffer curve was enthusiastically deployed in policy debates to suggest that tax cuts would provide rapid growth and a painless victory over stagflation while generating an increase in revenues. Tax cuts would pay for themselves.

Some critics on the Right found the argument underlying the Laffer curve to be unpersuasive. Martin Feldstein, President of the National Bureau of Economic Research, subsequently identified some of the more "extravagant" claims made by the new supply-siders. He noted that the Laffer curve proposition that a tax cut "would actually increase tax revenue because it would unleash an enormously depressed supply of effort" to be "the height of supply-side hyperbole." Even if tax cuts would increase the budget deficit, supply-siders claimed that it "would not reduce the funds available for investment in plant and equipment because tax changes would raise the saving rate by enough to finance the increased deficit," a position he described as "remarkable."[41] Nonetheless, the extravagant claims would prove politically useful in the 1980s as the Reagan administration and Republicans in Congress sought to frame the justification for the largest tax cuts in US history while making the claim that they were committed to the achievement of balanced budgets (see Chapter 7).

The Politics and War of Ideas

In the immediate postwar decades, Keynesianism had become the consensus position, and a generation of scholars had been trained in Keynesian economics. By the 1960s, the CEA became an advocate of Keynesian demand management; it was approaching its duties with a confidence that was reflected in the aspiration to engage in macroeconomic "fine-tuning." This confidence was badly shaken by stagflation. While crisis created the opportunity for scholars of different theoretical stripes to join the debate over economic management, how can one explain the triumph of supply-side economics and the proposals it justified? Let us consider three parts of an explanation. First, the success can be ascribed to the intrinsic simplicity of supply-side arguments and their effective advocacy by policy think tanks and key congressional staffers. Second, some conservatives may have doubted the promise of supply-side economics, particularly with respect to the effects on revenues. But they supported tax cuts in the belief that the resulting deficits could be used to leverage reductions in the size and scope of the federal government, a strategy that would be referred to as "starve the beast." Third, the debates over fiscal policy were occurring in the midst of growing anti-tax sentiment in several of the states. Politicians understood that voters battered by bracket creep, increases in the Social Security tax, and rising property taxes would reward elected officials and candidates who advocated deep tax cuts.

The Corporate Countermobilization and the War of Ideas

Part of the explanation for the success of supply-side economics stemmed from the simplicity of the core argument, which facilitated its dissemination within the larger policy community. As John L. Campbell explains, this simplicity allowed the Laffer curve to serve as "a powerful pedagogical symbol" that "generated tremendous publicity in newspapers and magazines and helped put supply-side economics at the center of the burgeoning policy debate."[42] Wanninski's *How the World Works*, popularized supply-side economics to a broad audience (a review in *Commentary* assured potential readers "permanently frightened by early mishaps in analytical geometry" that the Laffer curve "is no more technical than an aphorism").[43] The same could not be said of competing proposals for incomes policy, corporatist intermediation, or industrial policy that were difficult to popularize, in part, because of their complexity. And the general argument of supply-side economics fit well with a broader critique of government. James Tobin, veteran of the Kennedy CEA, decried the position as a combination of "simplistic diagnoses and remedies," summarizing the core argument in stark terms: "The government did it all—by spending too much, taxing too much, borrowing too much, and printing too much money. Let the government turn off all those spigots and there will be no more inflation."[44]

The success in the war of ideas was also a product of the growing number and sophistication of business and conservative think tanks. During the early 1970s, the passage of new environmental and occupational safety and health regulatory statutes imposed unprecedented costs on the corporate economy. And as Nixon imposed mandatory controls in 1971, Herbert Stein, Nixon's second CEA Chair, explained, "the competitive struggle for wage and income shares was not suspended. The mere fact that the government assumed the leadership in determining wages and prices just transferred the struggle to the political arena of Washington, an arena in which power is less limited than in the markets."[45] Corporations and trade associations responded by expanding their lobbying efforts, forming political action committees to finance business-friendly candidates, and investing in think tanks that could more effectively shape the policy debates. Between 1973 and 1975, several new think tanks were founded, including the Heritage Foundation, the Cato Institute, the Institute for Contemporary Studies, and the International Institute for Economic Research. The Heritage Foundation was the first to break with the model of established think tanks like the Brookings Institution, which had broader scholarly pretentions, to engage in explicit policy advocacy. The focus on advocacy was shared by the new breed of think tanks and, increasingly, by some of the older think tanks, including the Hoover Institution and the American Enterprise Institute.[46]

As Campbell explained, the think tanks excelled at translating academic research into forms that were easily understood by non-specialists. They effectively disseminated them to policymakers through policy papers, conferences, and testimony before congressional committees. They popularized them to a broader audience through newspaper editorials, appearances in the mass media, popular books distributed through the Book-of-the Month Club or excerpts in the *Readers' Digest*. As noted earlier, Milton Friedman had done much to shape the academic debates over macroeconomic policy and the limitations of the Phillips curve. He had been making this argument for the past several decades as a professor at the University of Chicago. Friedman received the Nobel in economics in 1976, in recognition of his contributions. But in 1977 he had retired to become a visiting scholar at the Federal Reserve Bank of San Francisco and the Hoover Institution. Since 1966, Friedman had popularized his arguments through a regular column in *Newsweek* magazine. In 1980, he expanded his national audience through a television series and a best-selling book, *Free to Choose,* that would sell over 1 million copies.[47]

As supply-side theory was being popularized by think tanks, it was simultaneously gaining adherents on Capitol Hill. Economists who served important roles as congressional staffers helped members refine their arguments and consider the broader policy implications. Norman B. Ture, for example, was a Chicago School economist with a long pedigree in government service as a veteran of the Treasury and a staff member of the Joint Economic Committee of Congress. In that latter capacity, he had assisted Ways and Means Committee Chair Wilbur Mills (D-AR) frame the Kennedy–Johnson tax cut. In 1977, he founded the Institute for Research on the Economics of Taxation, a free market think tank devoted to promoting supply-side tax cuts. Paul Craig Roberts, an economist with a Virginia PhD, served as economic counsel to Representative Jack Kemp (R-NY), who had become interested in supply-side economics through his interactions with Wanniski and Laffer. With the counsel of Ture and Roberts, Kemp would work with Senator William Roth (R-DE) in crafting a legislative proposal in 1977 that would cut individual income tax rates by one-third over a three-year period, drawing parallels with the 1964 tax cut. While federal receipts would fall initially, Kemp and Roth argued that resulting incentives would spur growth and allow the federal government to recoup the lost revenues. The Republican National Committee endorsed the Kemp–Roth tax in 1978, as did Republican candidates seeking congressional office. Kemp–Roth was introduced on multiple occasions and promoted through three days of events where former president Gerald Ford and presidential aspirant Ronald Reagan crossed the country on a Boeing 727 jet nicknamed the "Republican Tax Clipper." Indeed, Senator Sam Nunn (D-GA) almost succeeded in securing an amendment to the Revenue Act of 1978 that would have included a version of Kemp–Roth (albeit with 5 percent annual rate reductions tied to spending limits) only to be rebuffed by the threat of a presidential veto.[48]

As Kemp and Roth were focusing on deep cuts in the individual income tax, support was growing within the Senate Finance Committee for changes in the business tax that could propel growth along the lines suggested by supply-side economics. The discussions revolved around changes in the rules for business that would allow companies to depreciate investments on an accelerated schedule. Under existing law, companies were allowed to depreciate assets over their expected useful life. High inflation, it was argued, eroded the value of depreciated assets and created disincentives for investment in new capital. The proposed changes would create a new "10-5-3" formula that would allow businesses to write off buildings in ten years, other equipment in five years, and light vehicles in three years. The impetus for liberalized depreciation came from the "Carleton group," a collection of business lobbyists that met for strategy and information-sharing breakfasts at Washington's Carlton Hotel. The Carlton group combined influential experts in tax policy, most notably Charles Walker, Deputy Secretary of the Treasury under Nixon, Ernst Christian, tax lawyer and veteran of the Ford Treasury, and Richard Rahn, the chief economist for the US Chamber of Commerce and former executive director of the Council for Capital Formation. Regular participants included representatives of corporations and trade associations that could deploy their own lobbyists and campaign contributions to promote policy change. While the group was influential in shaping the debates over corporate taxation and building support in Congress, the proposal for accelerated depreciation, like the Kemp–Roth tax cut, would have to be deferred until after the 1980 elections.[49]

Starve the Beast, Embrace the Deficits

The contention that deep tax cuts would generate new revenues—perhaps even sufficient to balance the budget—was viewed as somewhat extravagant, even if it would become popularized among some advocates of the Laffer curve. In the 1980s and beyond, critics of the tax cuts, which were framed with supply-side arguments, would cite the growing deficits and debt as evidence of a bad economic theory that had been translated into bad public policy with predictable results. Yet, for some critics of supply-side arguments in the 1970s, the generation of deficits was not problematic. It was precisely the point. Even if advocates of tax cuts might prefer balanced budgets, deficits could create pressures to reduce the overall size and scope of the federal government. In the long run, the budget could be balanced but only after the postwar expansion of the federal government had been reversed. Deficits could be used to justify austerity rather than as a means of making the case for higher levels of taxation.

In 1978, Friedman made precisely this case in the Heritage Foundation's *Policy Review*. He argued that fiscal conservatives who had focused on the deficit rather than overall levels of public expenditures had been the "unwitting hand-maidens of the big spenders." In Friedman's account, history revealed a clear pattern: laws are passed to increase federal spending and, in response to the resulting deficits, fiscal conservatives consent to tax increases. "As soon as the new taxes are imposed and passed, the big spenders are off again, and then there is another burst in government spending and another deficit." The growth in the size of government, he argued, was only facilitated by concerns over the budget. Tax cuts, in contrast, could create the deficits that would be instrumentally important in making the case for spending cuts. "We assign you a budget. Now it's your job to spend that in the most effective way."[50] The observation that tax cuts and the resulting deficits and the debt could force changes in expenditures would evolve into an argument commonly referred to as "starve the beast."

For decades, Republicans had gained a reputation for their fidelity to balanced budgets. But as Herbert Stein explained, even if Republicans claimed to be "the champions of the balanced budget they never allowed that to stand in the way of their effort to get taxes—especially their own—reduced." The balanced budget was really "an argument against government spending and for tax reduction, not against deficits that result from tax reduction."[51] By the late 1970s, Bruce Bartlett observes: "Instead of being viewed as the height of fiscal irresponsibility, cutting taxes without any corresponding effort to cut spending was now seen as the epitome of conservative fiscal policy." Efforts to change the course of government spending by raising the salience of budget deficits were now viewed as counterproductive, because they frequently resulted in higher taxes without changing the underlying political dynamic. "The only way off the treadmill of higher spending leading to higher taxes leading to still more spending was to refuse to play the game. Just cut taxes, the conservative intelligentsia now argued, and concern about deficits will be channeled into lower spending."[52]

Would "starve the beast" work as a strategy for reducing the size of government? While the rhetoric of "starve the beast" would find an expression in the 1980s and beyond—a point that will be illustrated in Chapter 7—there is little evidence that deficits had the intended effect on the size and scope of government. As William Niskanen, a member of Reagan's CEA explained, in retrospect "starve the beast" was not only implausible under theory, but it was also inconsistent with the empirical record. More important, it "led too many conservatives and libertarians to be casual about the sustained discipline necessary to control federal spending directly." Under deficit financing, citizens would rationally demand more of government services that appeared less expensive than they actually were (the so-called fiscal illusion). The challenge was not to leverage deficits to impose fiscal constraint, but the more difficult task, "to try to convince voters to reduce their demand for the services financed by federal deficits. Until that time, some increase in federal taxes appears to be a necessary part of a fiscal policy to balance the budget."[53]

Mobilizing Anti-Tax Sentiment

While debates over competing economic and political theories raged in Washington, a populist movement spread across much of the nation. Inflation had accelerated each year since 1976, breaking into the double digits (11.3 percent) by 1979. As inflation pushed households into higher tax brackets, the payroll tax was increased from 9.6 percent (split between employee and employer) in 1970 to 12.26 percent by 1979. While there was modest tax relief in the Revenue Act of 1978, its impact was largely invisible, overwhelmed by growing household tax burdens. In 1978 and 1979, 37 states passed new statutes cutting property taxes, whereas 28 states reduced income taxes. The greatest attention focused on California's Proposition 13 (1978), which required that property assessments be rolled back to 1975 levels, a 1 percent cap be placed on the tax rate, and that annual increases in assessed value be limited to 2 percent. Proposition 13 also placed new constraints on the taxing authority of the state legislature, requiring a two-thirds majority to pass tax increases. Some participants in the tax revolt of the late 1970s, as Simon Hall argues, drew on the tactics and aspirations of the New Left and the civil rights movement. Limitations on the property tax, they argued, could provide relief to low-income households and force states to place a greater reliance on the income tax, thereby increasing the overall progressivity of the state revenue system. Others represented the New Right and saw rising property taxes as an attack on the American dream of homeownership and the means by which states would fund programs that were anathema to the New Right's agenda. As Hall notes, tax reform efforts like Proposition 13 "captured not a growing revolt against liberalism or a full-fledged embrace of conservatism, but a profound discontent with government itself. The debacle in Southeast Asia and the Watergate scandals had helped to shake the public's confidence in its elected officials, and public opinion in the 1970s seemed decidedly hostile toward the government."[54]

By the late 1970s, it was clear that many citizens and groups had lost confidence in government and viewed tax reform as a vehicle to express their discontent. While the focus was largely on state and local taxation, these citizens nonetheless constituted slack resources that could be mobilized by politicians seeking to win office. And while the advocates of tax reform were more diverse than is often recognized, it was also clear that the tax revolt of the period created an environment that was particularly hospitable to conservative politicians who could effectively argue that high taxes were emblematic of a government that had lost touch with the citizenry.

Growing Insecurity in the Wake of Stagflation

Arguably, the tax revolt in the states was only partially about the issue of taxation. The difficult economic environment of the 1970s created great insecurity for many Americans. Ironically, the conditions heightened the importance of social provision precisely as policy debates were questioning the efficacy of social policy and the mass-tax regime that had supported the expansion of the federal government's role in society. The next several decades would witness a reduction in savings rates, wage stagnation, an increase in levels of household debt, and a decline in the levels of support that employers provided to their employees. All of these trends found their origins in the pivotal decade of the 1970s. Let us consider them in turn, understanding that these trends would find their greatest political and economic manifestations in subsequent decades.

In 1960, the personal savings rate was 10.1 percent of disposable income. It increased to 13.5 percent by 1971 and remained relatively stable for the next few years. But as the economy deteriorated, the trend was reversed. Between 1975 and 2005, the savings rate fell steadily to a low of 3.1 percent. In response to the Great Recession (2008–2009), saving would increase to 8.8 percent of personal income (2012), but it would decline thereafter to 7.5 percent (2019), some 56 percent of what it had been in the early 1970s.[55] The decline in savings may well reflect the larger trajectory of wages, which also began to stagnate, in sharp contrast to the expectations of ongoing wage growth forged in the 1950s and 1960s. Between 1979 and 2018, workers in the 90th percentile realized a 37.6 percent cumulative increase in real wages. Yet, those in the 50th percentile experienced a 6.1 percent increase and those in the 10th percentile, a 1.6 percent increase, over this same four-decade period.[56] At a higher level of abstraction, one can see the long-term decline in labor's share of GDP. During the period 1950–1970, labor's share of GDP increased from 63.6 to 65.9 percent. Thereafter, it began a decades' long decline to 60.8 percent (1985), with some recovery to 64.6 in 2001, before collapsing to a new low of 58.8 percent in 2010 and recovering slightly in subsequent years (e.g., 59.7 percent in 2017).[57] There are multiple factors that may be responsible for this long-term trend. One part of the explanation may be the decline in unionization rates in an economy undergoing the transition from manufacturing to services. Union decline compromised the capacity of labor to secure higher levels of compensation. A second part of the explanation may be the growing costs of employment-based healthcare benefits that placed downward pressure on salary growth. A third factor may be offshoring or outsourcing of production and the rise in automation, all of which reduced the domestic demand for labor in what were previously higher wage manufacturing jobs. Similarly, growing reliance on imports from nations with lower wage rates suppressed wages in domestic industries, contributing to the trend.[58]

One can adjust to stagnant incomes in a variety of ways, including moving from one- to two-income households, working multiple jobs, or reducing levels of consumption. But the data suggests that households compensated by placing a greater reliance on debt. Household debt as a percentage of GDP increased steadily in the aftermath of World War II, and then stabilized in the range of

40–50 percent of GDP during the 1960s and 1970s, before ratcheting steadily upwards.[59] By 2008, the eve of the Great Recession, household debt had grown to exceed 99 percent of GDP. And while household debt was reduced in the aftermath of the recession, it only fell to approximately 76 percent of GDP (2019).[60] The assumption of higher debt levels was facilitated by financial deregulation and a host of innovations in credit markets; it was subsidized, with tax expenditures. Credit sustained higher levels of consumption than might otherwise have been possible, while helping fuel growth. With the retreat from active Keynesian policy, access to credit—and the growth in household debt—would become central to the growth model. As Monica Prasad has argued, Americans funded current consumption by incurring debt and drawing equity from their homes (what she calls "mortgage Keynesianism"). As Prasad notes, "there is an underlying demand for credit caused by the absence of sustaining welfare institutions in the United States. In the absence of welfare institutions common in Europe, credit is how Americans survive."[61]

As savings rates collapsed and indebtedness increased, private pensions became increasingly insecure. The federal government has long supported employment-based retirement benefits with tax expenditures (see Chapter 3). The federal government has played a central role in regulating private-sector pensions since the passage of the Employee Retirement Income Security Act (ERISA) of 1974. With ERISA, the federal government sought to reduce the risk associated with employment-based pensions by requiring, among other things, that employers meet prescribed fiduciary standards, minimum vesting standards, and funding standards. Pensions were also insured through a federal insurance program supervised by a newly created Pensions Benefit Guarantee Corporation. As James A. Wooten explains, rather than viewing pensions as simply instruments that private employers used to manage their employees under the conditions they set in labor contracts—the traditional position that supported more permissive regulation—reformers embraced "a worker-security conception of private pension plans." The passage of ERISA was informed by the belief that because "pension plans are tax-subsidized vehicles for providing retirement income to workers…the federal government should take a more assertive role in the private pension system."[62] Unsurprisingly, ERISA was met with the opposition of business and trade associations that viewed it as part of a broader regulatory expansion that intruded on corporate environmental and occupational safety and health practices and raised regulatory compliance costs.

The most important trend to begin in the 1970s was the decline of traditional defined benefit pensions and the growth of defined contribution pensions. Under defined benefit plans, some of which were secured through collective bargaining, companies guaranteed their workers a lifetime retirement annuity based on years of service and their salary history. In contrast, under defined contribution plans, workers are given an investment account that they control, funded by their own contributions and/or contributions from their employer. With the former, employees have a guaranteed level of support in retirement. Funds are professionally managed, and, under ERISA, employers must meet fiduciary standards, funding requirements, and purchase insurance through the Pensions Benefit Guarantee Corporation. In the latter, the level of support is contingent on the employee's contributions and investment decisions. According to Labor Department data, in 1975, the vast majority of active pension participants—some 70.8 percent—were enrolled in defined benefit plans. The share in defined benefit plans would fall to 61.4 percent by 1980 and by 1984, the majority would be in defined contribution plans. By the end of the 1990s, defined contribution plans would eclipse defined benefit plans, covering some 70 percent of active participants.[63] As Jacob S. Hacker has argued, the dominance of defined contribution pensions was part of the "great risk shift," in which citizens were forced to bear a larger part of the risks they encounter, including health care and the risk of not having a financially secure retirement.[64]

There are several explanations for the corporate decision to freeze or terminate their defined benefit plans. The costs of administering defined benefit plans were greater, given that firms were required to consider actuarial projections (retirement ages, mortality rates) when making funding decisions and they were responsible for making additional contributions to compensate for the performance of investments. The regulatory requirements of ERISA imposed additional costs that were not borne by defined contribution plans. The uncertain economic environment of the period created financial incentives for shedding traditional pensions. Moreover, as the economy shifted away from manufacturing and unionization rates declined, new service sector employers selected defined contribution plans, if they offered pensions at all.[65]

Taken as a whole, the changes in the 1970s that contributed to growing insecurity were profound. Keynesian economists who had a newfound confidence in their ability to fine-tune the economy were adrift in a sea of uncertainty, as their core assumptions were shaken by the stagflation of the decade. Citizens, who had enjoyed a period of robust growth in the 1950s and 1960s and the expectation that rising wages and consumption opportunities would extend into the future, found themselves in a moribund economy. High unemployment, high inflation, stagnant wages, depleted savings, growing indebtedness, and a deterioration of the employment-based welfare state that had emerged in the immediate postwar period created an environment that was ripe for change.

A Fiscal Rebalancing and the End of Deleveraging

The 1960s had witnessed growth in programmatic mandatory spending, as the increasing cost of Social Security was combined with the creation of Medicare and Medicaid. This trend would continue in the 1970s. The growth in social spending was, in part, a product of Congress's decision to liberalize eligibility requirements and benefits for numerous programs. But it was also facilitated by a decision to index eligibility and benefits to inflation. Eligibility for the food stamp program was indexed in 1971 and benefits were indexed to the "thrifty food plan." In 1972, Congress authorized automatic annual cost-of-living adjustments for Social Security benefits, effective 1975, putting an end to the established practice of erratic benefit increases. The next year, it extended indexing to Medicaid eligibility. The Social Security Act Amendments of 1972 also created a new Supplemental Security Income program, proposed by the Nixon administration, to federalize and consolidate means-tested cash assistance to the disabled and elderly. Benefits for this new program were indexed in 1974.[66]

The decision to index the largest entitlement programs occurred before the ramifications of high inflation were understood. Had Congress chosen another path, inflation would have eroded the real value of benefits and changed the trajectory of growth in mandatory spending. But in an environment of high inflation, indexing would ensure that rising prices would be transmitted into federal obligations. While programmatic mandatory spending would increase steadily over the course of the decade, domestic discretionary spending grew as well, driven in part by the ongoing funding of the Great Society/War on Poverty programs inherited from the Johnson administration. Total spending on these two categories of outlays constituted 71.7 percent of outlays (15.2 percent of GDP) by 1980, an inflation-adjusted increase of 195.4 percent over the course of a decade.[67]

The comparison with defense discretionary spending could not be more pronounced. During the Nixon and Ford presidencies, in particular, Congress rebuffed the administrations' requests for larger defense budgets, claiming the peace dividend to fund domestic commitments.[68] By the Carter presidency the peace dividend had been exhausted and there were growing concerns that the United States was increasingly at a strategic disadvantage with the Soviets. The next few years would bring increases in defense spending, with congressional appropriations exceeding the administration's requests but simultaneously ignoring Carter's efforts to hold the growth in social spending to a rate at or below that of defense. Thus, during the Carter presidency real defense spending grew by 6 percent, while domestic discretionary spending increased by some 20 percent.[69] Taken as a whole, the decade witnessed a significant reduction in defense both as a share of outlays and GDP. In 1970, defense spending accounted for 41.9 percent of outlays (7.8 percent GDP). It would fall to 22.8 percent of outlays (4.8 percent GDP) by 1980. When adjusted for inflation, 1980 outlays were 77.3 percent of what they had been in 1970. In sum, Congress had made the decision to rebalance national priorities, using the defense budget to finance the growing domestic welfare state.[70]

Congress could have decided to fund the escalating domestic commitments through revenue increases. But given the uncertain economic climate and the growing anti-tax sentiment, it relied on the peace dividend and secondarily on the issuance of new debt. Total receipts were superficially stable during the decade, claiming 18.4 percent of GDP in 1970 compared with 18.5 percent of GDP in 1980. But significant changes were occurring below the surface. Inflation translated into a growth in the revenues from the income tax. Households, regardless of income, watched the value of their personal and dependent exemptions shrink while inflation pushed them into higher marginal tax brackets. Many low-income households found themselves subject to an income tax for the first time.[71] Over the period 1970 to 1980, individual income tax increased from 46.9 percent of receipts (8.6 percent GDP) to 47.2 percent (8.7 percent GDP). The corporate income tax, in sharp contrast, fell from 17 percent of revenues (3.1 percent GDP) in 1970 to 12.5 percent (2.3 percent GDP) in 1980. Corporate tax expenditures proliferated as Democrats and Republicans advocated them a means of promoting growth in an environment in which traditional fiscal policy tools seemed ineffective. The most consequential change came in the growing importance of social insurance taxes. As a result of scheduled increases in the payroll tax, between 1970 and 1980, social insurance taxes increased from 23 percent of receipts (4.2 percent GDP) to 30.5 percent of receipts (5.7 percent GDP).[72] Taken together, inflation-driven bracket creep and the expansion of social insurance taxes fueled the anti-tax sentiment described earlier.

The disjunction between spending and revenues resulted in chronic deficits. The largest deficit was 4.1 percent of GDP (1976). But in six of the ten years of the period in question, deficits as a share of GDP exceeded the levels encountered during the peak of the Korean War (1.7 percent GDP) and were only exceeded by the immediate post-World War II deficit of 7 percent of GDP (1946). In the budget proposal for FY1981, submitted in a presidential election year, the Carter administration projected a deficit for the next year but attributed it to a faltering economy: "If, contrary to our assumptions, the economy were to perform strongly enough to keep the unemployment rate at its current level, the 1981 budget would be in surplus." The administration projected that deficits would decline steadily, becoming a surplus by 1982. But the proposed path to this surplus did not involve a significant departure from the spending priorities of the past several years. Rather, it relied on bracket creep to drive revenues to a level not witnessed since World War II. As the OMB explained, the revenue projections "reflect a rise in the average tax rate on personal income as inflation and real growth move taxpayers into higher tax brackets." The administration frankly admitted that it was "extremely concerned about the significant rise in tax burdens implied in these estimates" and proclaimed its intention of "reducing these burdens." But all would depend "on the future performance of the economy, especially progress in reducing inflation."[73] As noted in Chapter 5, the debt relative to the economy had fallen steadily in the immediate postwar decades, reaching a low of 23.3 percent of

GDP (1974). But given the economic conditions thereafter and the refusal of Congress to trim its domestic commitments or raise new revenues, the debt grew to 27.1 percent of GDP by 1977, declining to 25.5 percent of GDP by 1980.[74] The period of postwar deleveraging had been interrupted. Whether this would be a temporary aberration—a product of the unique economic disorder of the 1970s—or something more permanent, would be determined by subsequent policy decisions that were framed by the debates of the decade.

Conclusion

In the wake of Proposition 13, Milton Friedman drew a clear lesson in a 1978 *Newsweek* column: "To politicians around the country, the message from California should be clarion clear: The wave of taxpayer protest can carry politicians who learn to ride it to the highest offices in the land." A second lesson was evident to Friedman. To take advantage of nationwide tax revolt "will demand performance and not merely promises."[75] By the late 1970s, there was little to suggest that policymakers had discovered a policy mix that could respond to the problem of stagflation. In 1980, the year Carter ran for reelection, inflation was in the double digits, the unemployment rate peaked at 7.8 percent, and the nation was in the grips of another recession—the third in a decade.[76] Stagflation and the impasse of economic policy opened a window of opportunity for those intent on relitigating the policy and institutional changes of the New Deal and the Great Society. Moreover, there were clear signs that there was a sizable electorate that shared the critique of activist government and could be mobilized behind a tax-cutting agenda. With the election of a new Republican President, the policy arguments that had floated through the think tanks and been popularized in the past several years would find an expression in policy change.

Notes

1 James Tobin, "Growth as an Objective of Government Policy," *The American Economic Review,* 54, 3, Papers and Proceedings of the Seventy-Sixth Annual Meeting of the American Economic Association (1964), 1.
2 Frank E. Morris, "Opening Remarks," in *After the Phillips Curve: Persistence of High Inflation and High Unemployment* (Boston: Federal Reserve Bank of Boston, 1978), 8.
3 Arthur M. Okun, "Inflation: Its Mechanisms and Welfare Costs," *Brookings Papers on Economic Activity,* 1975, 2 (1975): 354.
4 Sidney Weintraub, *Keynes, Keynesians, and Monetarists* (Philadelphia: University of Pennsylvania Press, 1978), 43.
5 Arthur M. Okun, "The Great Stagflation Swamp," *The Brookings Bulletin,* 14, 3 (1977): 1.
6 See Leon N. Lindberg, "Models of the Inflation-Disinflation Process," in *The Politics of Inflation and Economic Stagnation,* ed. Leon N. Lindberg and Charles S. Maier (Washington, DC: The Brookings Institution, 1985), 25–50.

7 Richard N. Goodwin, "Awaiting the Copernican Question," *The New Yorker*, January 6, 1975, 38.
8 Judith Stein, *Pivotal Decade: How the United States Traded Factories for Finance in the Seventies* (New Haven: Yale University Press, 2010), 155.
9 Michael McGrath, "Beyond Distrust: When the Public Loses Faith in American Institutions," *National Civic Review*, 106, 2 (2017): 47.
10 Edward Foster, "Who Loses from Inflation?" *The Annals of the American Academy of Political and Social Science*, 456 (1981): 44.
11 Elmer B. Staats, "Inflation: Cancer on the American Body Politic," *The Annals of the American Academy of Political and Social Science*, 456 (1981): 124.
12 "Public Trust in Government: 1958–2017." Pew Research Center, December 14, 2017. Available at www.people-press.org/2017/12/14/public-trust-in-government-1958-2017/
13 For a more detailed discussion of this period, see Marc Allen Eisner, *The American Political Economy: Institutional Evolution of Market and State* (New York: Routledge, 2014), 104–22.
14 Paul W. McCracken, "Economic Policy in the Nixon Years," *Presidential Studies Quarterly*, 26, 1 (1996), 171.
15 Richard Nixon, "Statement about the Revenue Act of 1971," December 10, 1971. Available at www.presidency.ucsb.edu/node/240396
16 See W. Elliot Brownlee, *Federal Taxation in America: A History*, 3rd ed. (Cambridge: Cambridge University Press, 2016), 168.
17 Herbert Stein, *Presidential Economics: The Making of Economic Policy from Roosevelt to Clinton*, 3rd ed. (Washington, DC: American Enterprise Institute, 1994), 176–87. See Willard Z. Carr, Jr., Rex S. Heinke And Michael D. Ryan, "A Short Historical Perspective of Economic Controls in the United States: A Report Prepared for the Committee on Economic and Resources Controls," *The Business Lawyer*, 33, 1 (1977), 18–25.
18 John F. Witte, *The Politics and Development of the Federal Income Tax* (Madison: University of Wisconsin Press, 1985), 183–87.
19 Ibid., 198.
20 World Bank, Inflation, consumer prices for the United States [FPCPITOTLZGUSA], available at https://fred.stlouisfed.org/series/FPCPITOTLZGUSA, and US Bureau of Labor Statistics, Unemployment Rate [UNRATE], available at https://fred.stlouisfed.org/series/UNRATE
21 Stephen B. Reed, "One Hundred Years of Price Change: the Consumer Price Index and the American Inflation Experience," *Monthly Labor Review*, (April 2014): 25.
22 Okun, "The Great Stagflation Swamp," 1.
23 See "Highlights of the Tax Law Signed by President Carter," *New York Times*, November 9, 1978, D16.
24 Brownlee, *Federal Taxation in America*, 180.
25 Stein, *Pivotal Decade*, 193.
26 Jimmy Carter, "Address to the Nation on Energy and National Goals," July 15, 1979. Available at www.presidency.ucsb.edu/node/249458
27 Richard X. Chase, "The Failure of American Keynesianism," *Challenge*, 19, 1 (1976): 48.
28 Graham K. Wilson, "Why Is There No Corporatism in the United States," in *Patterns of Corporatist Policy-Making*, ed. Gerhard Lehmbruch and Philippe C. Schmitter (London: Sage, 1982), 219–36.

29 Sidney Weintraub and Henry C. Wallich, "A Tax-Based Incomes Policy," in Sidney Weintraub, *Keynes, Keynesians, and Monetarists* (Philadelphia: University of Pennsylvania Press, 1978), 260.
30 See Arthur M. Okun, "The Invisible Handshake and the Inflationary Process," *Challenge,* 22, 6 (1980): 5–12.
31 See Stein, *Pivotal Decade,* 250–252.
32 For an example of arguments for industrial policy, see Allan G. Gruchy, "Institutionalism, Planning, and the Current Crisis," *Journal of Economic Issues,* 11, 2 (1977): 431–48. See Otis L. Graham, Jr., *Losing Time: The Industrial Policy Debate* (Cambridge: Harvard University Press, 1992), and John Zysman, *Governments, Markets, and Growth: Financial Systems and the Politics of Industrial Change* (Ithaca, NY: Cornell University Press, 1983).
33 Milton Friedman, "The Role of Monetary Policy," *The American Economic Review,* 58, 1 (1968): 11.
34 Robert J. Gordon, "The History of the Phillips Curve: Consensus and Bifurcation," *Economica,* 78, 309 (2011): 16.
35 Thomas J. Sargent, *Rational Expectations and Inflation,* 3rd ed. (Princeton: Princeton University Press, 2013), 1.
36 Thomas J. Sargent and Neil Wallace, "'Rational' Expectations, the Optimal Monetary Instrument, and the Optimal Money Supply Rule," *Journal of Political Economy,* 83, 2 (1975): 241–54.
37 Bennett T. McCallum, "The Significance of Rational Expectations Theory," *Challenge,* 22, 6 (1980): 42.
38 Arthur B. Laffer, "Supply-Side Economics," *Financial Analysts Journal,* 37, 5 (1981): 32.
39 Ibid., 42.
40 See Jude Wanniski, *How the World Works: How Economies Fail—and Succeed* (New York Basic Books, 1978).
41 Martin Feldstein, "Supply Side Economics: Old Truths and New Claims," *The American Economic Review,* 76, 2 (1986): 27.
42 John L. Campbell, "Institutional Analysis and the Role of Ideas in Political Economy," in *The Rise of Neoliberalism and Institutional Analysis,* ed. John L. Campbell and Ove K. Pedersen (Princeton: Princeton University Press, 2001), 169.
43 Roger Starr, "The Way the World Works, by Jude Wanniski," *Commentary,* September 1, 1978. Available at www.commentarymagazine.com/articles/roger-starr-2/the-way-the-world-works-by-jude-wanniski/
44 James Tobin, "Stabilization Policy Ten Years After," *Brookings Papers on Economic Activity,* 1980, 1 (1980): 71.
45 Herbert Stein, "We Can Learn From The Past," *Challenge,* 26, 4 (1983): 29.
46 See David Vogel, "The Power of Business in America: A Re-Appraisal," *British Journal of Political Science,* 13, 1 (1983): 19–43.
47 See Milton Friedman and Rose Friedman, *Free to Choose: A Personal Statement* (New York: Harcourt Brace Javanovich, 1980). On Friedman's broader intellectual contributions, see William Ruger, *Milton Friedman* (New York: Bloomsbury, 2013).
48 See Brownlee, *Federal Taxation in America,* 177–80; Paul Craig Roberts, "My Time with Supply-Side Economics," *The Independent Review,* 7, 3 (2003): 393–97; Bill Peterson, "GOP Starts Push for Tax Cut," *Washington Post,* Sept. 21, 1978, available

at www.washingtonpost.com/archive/politics/1978/09/21/gop-starts-push-for-tax-cut-bill/3282e95e-2efb-4dd7-b9a0-b3a69d159674/, and Morton Kondracke and Fred Barnes, "The Kemp Era," *The Weekly Standard,* Oct. 12, 2015, available at www.washingtonexaminer.com/weekly-standard/the-kemp-era

49 See Witte, *The Politics and Development of the Federal Income Tax,* 218–19 and Edward Cowan, "Carlton Group Spurns Lobbying Limelight," *New York Times,* March 18, 1982, D1, available at www.nytimes.com/1982/03/18/business/carlton-group-spurns-lobbying-limelight.html

50 Milton Friedman, "The Limitations of Tax Limitation," *Policy Review,* 5 (1978): 11, 9.

51 Stein, *Presidential Economics,* 81.

52 Bruce Bartlett, "Starve the Beast": Origins and Development of a Budgetary Metaphor." *The Independent Review,* 12, 1 (2007), 9.

53 William Niskanen, "My Recent Contributions to Public Choice," *Southern Economic Journal,* 75, 1 (2008), 5.

54 Simon Hall, *American Patriotism, American Protest: Social Movements Since the Sixties* (Philadelphia: University of Pennsylvania Press, 2011), 113.

55 Federal Reserve Bank of St. Louis, Personal Savings Rate (PSAVERT). Available at https://fred.stlouisfed.org/series/PSAVERT#0

56 Sarah A. Donovan and David H. Bradley, *Real Wage Trends, 1979–2018,* CRS Report R45090 (Washington, DC: Congressional Research Service, 2019), 4–5. See Jay Shambaugh, Ryan Nunn, Patrick Liu, and Greg Nantz, *Thirteen Facts about Wage Growth* (Washington, DC: The Brookings Institute/Hamilton Project, 2017).

57 University of Groningen and University of California, Davis, Share of Labor Compensation in GDP at Current National Prices for United States [LABSHPUSA156NRUG]. Available from Federal Reserve Bank of St. Louis, https://fred.stlouisfed.org/series/LABSHPUSA156NRUG. See Michael D. Giandrea and Shawn A. Sprague, "Estimating the U.S. Labor Share," *Monthly Labor Review,* US Department of Labor, February 2017. Available at https://doi.org/10.21916/mlr.2017.7.

58 See Donovan and Bradley, *Real Wage Trends,* 21–25.

59 David O. Belm, "It's All about Debt," *Forbes,* March 19, 2009. Available at www.forbes.com/2009/03/19/household-debt-gdp-markets-beim.html#4bb389ce29a5

60 Federal Reserve Bank of St. Louis, Household Debt to GDP for United States (HDTGDPUSQ163N). Available at https://fred.stlouisfed.org/series/HDTGPDUSQ163N

61 Monica Prasad, *The Land of Too Much: American Abundance and the Paradox of Poverty* (Cambridge: Harvard University Press, 2012), 261.

62 James A. Wooten, *The Employee Retirement Income Security Act of 1974: A Political History* (Berkeley: University of California Press, 2004), 271.

63 Department of Labor, Employee Benefits Security Administration, *Private Pension Plan Bulletin Historical Tables and Graphs: 1975–2019* (Washington, DC: Department of Labor, 2021), Table E7.

64 See Jacob S. Hacker, *The Great Risk Shift* (Oxford: Oxford University Press, 2006).

65 Barbara A. Butrica, Howard M. Iams, Karen E. Smith, and Eric J. Toder, "The Disappearing Defined Benefit Pension and Its Potential Impact on the Retirement Incomes of Baby Boomers," *Social Security Bulletin,* 69, 3 (2009): 3.

66 Dennis S. Ippolito, *Deficits, Debt, and the New Politics of Tax Policy* (Cambridge: Cambridge University Press, 2012), 97–98.

67 Office of Management and Budget (OMB), *Budget of the United States Government, Fiscal Year 2023* (Washington, DC: Government Publishing Office, 2022), Historical Tables, Tables 8.2, 8.3, and 8.4.
68 Ippolito, *Deficits, Debt, and the New Politics of Tax Policy,* 92.
69 Ibid., 108.
70 OMB, *Budget of the United States Government, Fiscal Year 2023,* Historical Tables, Tables 8.2, 8.3, and 8.4.
71 Brownlee, *Federal Taxation in America*, 173.
72 OMB, *Budget of the United States Government, Fiscal Year 2023,* Historical Tables, Tables 2.2 and 2.3.
73 OMB, *Budget of the United States Government, Fiscal Year 1981* (Washington, DC: Government Printing Office, 1981), M3, 72.
74 OMB, *Budget of the United States Government, Fiscal Year 2023,* Historical Tables, Tables 1.3, 7.1.
75 Milton Friedman, "The Message from California," *Newsweek* June 19, 1978, 26.
76 World Bank, Inflation, consumer prices for the United States [FPCPITOTLZGUSA], available at https://fred.stlouisfed.org/series/FPCPITOTLZGUSA, and US Bureau of Labor Statistics, Civilian Unemployment Rate [UNRATE], available at https://fred.stlouisfed.org/series/UNRATE

7

THE GREAT REVERSAL

Growing Debt and the Quest for Fiscal Control

In 1980, Ronald Reagan won an overwhelming electoral victory in a nation weary of stagflation. In his first inaugural address, Reagan spoke of the "economic affliction of great proportions," the high inflation that "distorts our economic decisions, penalizes thrift, and crushes the struggling young and the fixed-income elderly alike." He decried the "idle industries" that "have cast workers into unemployment, human misery, and personal indignity." Public spending had outpaced taxation: "For decades we have piled deficit upon deficit, mortgaging our future and our children's future for the temporary convenience of the present." Reagan proclaimed, "It is time to reawaken this industrial giant, to get government back within its means, and to lighten our punitive tax burden."[1] On the campaign trail, Reagan had championed tax cuts. Because of the popularized versions of supply-side economics, they could be framed as offering a painless victory over stagflation, generating new revenues to move the nation to balanced budgets. As supply-side economics was translated into changes in tax policy, however, revenues declined. When combined with increased spending during the deep recession of 1981–1982 and an unprecedented peacetime defense buildup, the nation entered a period of growing indebtedness, which reversed much of the gains achieved in the immediate postwar decades. Unlike earlier episodes in US history, the post-1981 growth in debt was not a product of war or depression. It was a product of political choice. Remarkably, a new set of policy decisions during the Clinton administration would undo some of the damage, generating successive surpluses and a decline in the debt-to-GDP ratio. But this reversal would prove ephemeral.

A broad overview of the period addressed in this chapter is presented in Table 7.1. As the data shows, federal outlays claimed the same share of GDP

DOI: 10.4324/9781003395331-9

TABLE 7.1 Summary of Outlays, Receipts, Deficits/Surpluses, and Debt, 1980–2000 (Percentage of GDP)

Fiscal Year	*Outlays*	*Receipts*	*Surplus or Deficit (–)*	*Publicly Held Debt*
1980	21.2%	18.5%	–2.6%	25.5%
1985	22.2	17.2	–5.0	35.3
1990	21.2	17.5	–3.7	40.9
1995	20.0	17.9	–2.2	47.7
2000	17.7	20.0	2.3	33.7

Source: Office of Management and Budget, *Budget of the United States Government, Fiscal Year 2023* (Washington, DC: Government Publishing Office, 2022), Historical Tables, Tables 1.2, 7.1.

in 1990 as they had in 1980. For all of the claims that the so-called Reagan Revolution constituted a significant reduction in the size of the state, there is little empirical evidence in terms of outlays. Second, the greatest impact came in a reduction of revenues, largely the product of the deep tax cuts of the 1980s. The combination of relative stability in spending and a reduction in revenues had predictable consequences. By the 1990s, new budget controls enacted in response to the growing debt successfully reduced the levels of federal spending relative to GDP. Moreover, successive tax increases would raise revenues as a share of GDP to a level unwitnessed since World War II, resulting in budget surpluses and a reduction in the debt-to-GDP ratio. These changes would prove fleeting, however, as we will fully explore in Chapter 8.

The Reagan Releverage

Reagan's stunning victory in 1980—claiming 44 states and 489 electoral votes—carried over to Congress, where the Republicans assumed a majority in the Senate for the first time since 1955 and made appreciable gains in the House, where Republicans could form a working coalition with conservative Democrats. President Reagan presented the core features of his Economic Recovery Program in an address to Congress in February 1981. His four-point program focused on "reducing the growth in government spending and taxing, reforming and eliminating regulations which are unnecessary and underproductive or counterproductive, and encouraging a consistent monetary policy aimed at maintaining the value of the currency." Let us focus on the first two components. Reagan listed the kinds of programs that would need to be cut, eliminated, or restructured, along with the battle against "waste, fraud and abuse." While the President wanted spending cuts of $41.4 billion, he simultaneously called for new defense spending to counter Soviet investments that had outpaced those of the United States since 1970. On the issue of taxation, Reagan reiterated his campaign proposal for deep reductions in individual income tax rates. With respect to corporations, he called for an increase in depreciation allowances to create incentive for "the new investment which is needed to create millions of new jobs" and "make America competitive once again in the world market." The address ended with a question about his critics: "Have they an alternative which offers a greater chance of balancing the budget, reducing and eliminating inflation, stimulating the creation of jobs, and reducing the tax burden?"[2]

The Economic Recovery Tax Act and the Omnibus Budget Reconciliation Act of 1981

Reagan moved quickly to secure passage of the Economic Recovery Tax Act (ERTA) of 1981. The core of ERTA was the proposal developed by Representative Jack Kemp (R-NY) and Senator William V. Roth (R-DE) which called for a phased 30 percent reduction in individual marginal income tax rates and the indexing of tax brackets. Two of the core advocates of tax cuts in the 1970s, Paul Craig Roberts and Norman Ture, had been appointed to key positions in the Treasury (Assistant Secretary for Economic Policy and Undersecretary for Tax and Economic Affairs, respectively), creating a strong internal constituency for supply-side arguments. Congress, already predisposed to support tax cuts for business given the difficult economic conditions and subject to intense business lobbying, engaged in a complex bidding process that paired the Kemp–Roth plan with cuts in the corporate tax. In the end, a coalition of Republicans and conservative Democrats succeeded in passing the largest tax cut in US history.[3] ERTA had major implications for individual and corporate taxes. Let us consider them in turn.

Whereas Kemp–Roth had called for a 30 percent across-the-board reduction in marginal rates for individuals, ERTA provided a 23 percent cut in rates, to be phased in over a three-year period (5, 10, and 10 percent). The top marginal rate was cut immediately from 70 to 50 percent. A new exclusion of 10 percent for two-income married couples, an expansion of deductions for contributions in tax-deferred individual retirement accounts (IRAs) for all workers, a phased-in increase in the estate tax exemption, and a reduced rate on long-term capital gains further reduced individual taxes. The alternative minimum tax (AMT)—first introduced in 1969 to prevent high-income taxpayers from avoiding tax liability through the use of exclusions, deductions, and credits—was lowered to match the regular income tax. Most important, however, was the indexation of the personal exemption and tax brackets to the consumer price index beginning in 1985, thereby eliminating "bracket creep." Henceforth, Congress could not rely on inflation to generate automatic revenue increases but would have to vote to raise taxes, a politically hazardous endeavor in the anti-tax environment. The AMT, unlike the normal income tax, was not indexed, thereby allowing inflation to push a larger proportion of taxpayers into the alternative tax (and forcing Congress to periodically adjust the rate). The phasing of marginal rate cuts and the delay of indexing obscured the magnitude of the revenue losses, which would be largely deferred until 1984–1986.[4]

On the corporate side, the statutory corporate tax rate remained at 46 percent, where it had been placed by the Revenue Act of 1978. Nonfinancial firms that invest in fixed assets determine their tax liability by subtracting from gross sales the costs of inputs (e.g., wages, raw materials), interest payments, and capital costs. ERTA's greatest impact was on the calculation of capital costs. Prior to the passage of ERTA, corporations worked with a complex system of asset depreciation classes, using "straight line" depreciation over the life of the asset. Under inflationary conditions, it was argued, the depreciation schedule reduced the dollar value of plants, equipment, and commercial buildings when claimed, relative to when they were purchased. Inflation created disincentives to new investment. In the late 1970s, corporate lobbyists (the "Carleton Group") had proposed converting the depreciation rules to a new 10-5-3 formula, which would allow corporations to write off the costs of buildings in ten years, the costs of heavy equipment in five years, and light equipment and vehicles in three years (see Chapter 6). This proposal became the core of ERTA's new Accelerated Cost Recovery System (ACRS).[5] The Joint Committee on Taxation claimed that the new ACRS would "provide incentives for investment spending" and "contribute immediately to cash flow for the financing of such spending."[6]

Although there were disagreements within the administration as to whether tax cuts would generate the promised revenues, the Joint Committee on Taxation clearly made this argument in its overview of ERTA, claiming it "would improve incentives to work, produce, save, and invest, consistent with the goal of eliminating the Federal budget deficit by 1984." It also argued that tax cuts would restrain government growth. After reviewing the increase in federal spending over the 1970s, it claimed that growing government "intrusions" have produced "inefficiencies in the workings of the economy, misallocation of resources, uncertainty, and instability." Although the Committee did not employ the term "Starve the Beast," the basic argument resonated in the report: "The Congress believed that its program of tax reductions would increase the likelihood that Federal spending would be restrained over an extended period of time and would speed economic recovery by reducing governmental interference in the workings of the economy."[7]

Victory in taxation was combined with initial success in achieving sizeable spending cuts. Soon upon assuming office, the administration submitted formal revisions to the FY1981 budget and called for spending reductions of $48.6 billion, with additional cuts for FY1983–1984.[8] The Senate, now under Republican control, passed a reconciliation bill that represented the Reagan agenda. The use of reconciliation for this purpose marked a significant departure from the Congressional Budget Act of 1974, which created the expedited process to bring the first and second concurrent budget resolutions into alignment. When the Democratic leadership presented its version of the bill, Representatives Delbert Latta (R-OH) and Phil Gramm (D-TX) offered a reconciliation bill that was in keeping with the Reagan requests. Gramm–Latta passed as a substitute for the Democratic bill and became the foundation of the Omnibus Reconciliation Act (OBRA) of 1981, which cut a total of $45.1 billion for FY1982, for a total savings of $130.6 billion for FY1982–84.[9]

OBRA achieved its goals through several means. Some programs were terminated, including public service jobs programs created under the Comprehensive Employment and Training Act of 1973. In other programs, spending cuts were achieved through tightened eligibility requirements and restrictions on the time length of benefits. OBRA consolidated 57 categorical grants into nine block grants, which were reduced in size. Aid to Families with Dependent Children was hit particularly hard. OBRA cut the monthly deductions for work-related expenses and childcare, making it more difficult to qualify for AFDC. Eligibility was tightened to families with incomes below 150 percent of a state's standard of need and who had less than $1000 in assets. Ironically, it eliminated the $30-and-a-third income disregard after four months of employment (previously work was incentivized by allowing recipients to keep the first $30 they earned per month plus one-third of their remaining earnings). All told, within the next two years, more than 400,000 families lost their eligibility and another 300,000 weathered benefit reductions.[10] While OBRA focused on means-tested programs, it also made marginal changes to Social Security (it eliminated the minimum benefit for new beneficiaries, phased out benefits for college student survivors, capped disability payments) and Medicare (reduced payments for certain drugs, raised deductibles and coinsurance, cut reimbursement to hospitals).[11]

While the Reagan administration pressed for further reductions in domestic spending, Congress proved unwilling to replicate the deep cuts of OBRA 1981, particularly during a deep recession. The recession, which took hold in the summer of 1981 and extended until November 1982, drove unemployment to the highest level, thus far, in the postwar period, with dire implications for the poverty rate. As the administration sought to reshape the welfare state and build on OBRA's consolidation of categorical grants, Congress rebuffed the most significant proposals (e.g., the proposal for the federal government to assume full responsibility for Medicaid funding, whereas the states would assume responsibility for AFDC and food stamps).[12] And the goals of privatization or significant reform of the largest entitlement programs were never pursued in earnest. As Hugh Heclo notes: "if there ever was anything resembling a frontal assault on the American welfare state by something that might be called the 'Reagan Revolution,' that assault had essentially ended by 1982."[13] What didn't end was the commitment to expanded defense spending to close the "dollar gap" with the Soviet Union. In the 1970s, Congress had funded domestic spending by drawing down defense budgets. This practice would be truncated in the Reagan presidency. Force modernization, the goal of building a 600-ship naval fleet, the reversal of Carter's cancellation of the B-1 bomber, and the Strategic Defense Initiative had important fiscal consequences that will be addressed below. The combination of the revenue cuts, the continued growth of federal entitlements, and the defense buildup would have another fiscal consequence: deficits, and the need for further rounds of tax reform.

Tax Policy in the Wake of ERTA

The rapid growth of the deficit quickly elevated fiscal imbalances on the policy agenda. The 1981 deficit of $79 billion expanded to $208 billion by 1983, more than doubling as a share of the economy (2.5 percent versus 5.9 percent of GDP) and standing in real and nominal terms as the largest deficit since World War II demobilization.[14] The partial retreat from ERTA began almost immediately. In his 1982 State of the Union address, Reagan rebuffed calls for new taxes, rejecting efforts "to balance the budget on the backs of the American taxpayers." He pledged: "I will seek no tax increases this year, and I have no intention of retreating from our basic program of tax relief."[15] Yet, in February, the administration's budget proposal included some $44 billion in additional revenues over the next three years. Reagan's budget message noted "our emphasis thus far has been on reducing excessive tax rates and shrinking the Government's take from the paychecks of workers and the profits of business." While the President vowed to preserve the reductions in tax rates, additional receipts would come from another source: the correction of "unintended loopholes" and the elimination of "obsolete tax incentives." "In every case, these measures involve the collection of a tax that is owed now or that was intended by the Congress, or elimination of incentives that are no longer needed due to the sweeping reform of business taxation" achieved through ERTA.[16] The stage was set for tax reform.

The first revenue measure was Tax Equity and Fiscal Responsibility Act (TEFRA) of 1982, which passed Congress by narrow margins, reflecting the growing portion of the Republican caucus that refused to accept tax increases of any form. TEFRA made a few changes to the individual income tax (e.g., it raised the AMT and limited medical and casualty loss deductions) but did not delay or repeal the marginal rate reductions or scheduled indexing. TEFRA also raised some additional excise taxes (e.g., aviation, cigarettes, telephone), increased the tax rate and wage base for the unemployment tax, and extended the Medicare Part A payroll tax to federal workers. But its largest impact came in the corporate income tax. It modified the ACRS and eliminated or limited several other tax exemptions. In 1984, concerns over mounting fiscal imbalances led to the passage of the Deficit Reduction Act or DEFRA, that once again combined higher excise taxes (liquor, telephones) with restrictions on several individual and corporate tax expenditures. As with TEFRA, the changes in the Internal Revenue Code under DEFRA did not the scheduled reductions in marginal rates and indexation.[17]

As Reagan and Congress were struggling with the tension between revenue policy and the growing deficit, another crisis was mounting: Social Security. Concerns over the solvency of the trust fund had grown in the latter half of the 1970s, as annual trust program deficits had depleted trust fund reserves. Congress responded with piecemeal measures that allowed for the reallocation of payroll tax revenues from the DI Trust Fund to the OASI Trust Fund and authorized temporary inter-fund borrowing. After some highly politicized missteps by the administration, President Reagan gave a televised address to the nation on September 24, 1981 and announced his intention to create a bipartisan task force "to remove Social Security once and for all from politics" and "review all options and come up with a plan that assures the fiscal integrity" of the program so that "recipients will continue to receive their full benefits."[18] Under executive order, Reagan established the National Commission on Social Security Reform, placed under the direction of Alan Greenspan, former chairman of the Council of Economic Advisors. As the Commission's work commenced, the Social Security Board of Trustees informed Congress that insolvency was imminent, noting: "Without corrective legislation in the very near future, the Old-Age and Survivors Insurance Trust Fund will be unable to make benefit payments on time beginning no later than July 1983."[19]

The Commission completed its report in January 1983. Its recommendations included measures to broaden coverage of Social Security to federal civilian employees and non-profit organizations, accelerate scheduled increases in the payroll tax rate, and subject up to 50 percent of the benefits of high-income households to income taxation. It also called for delaying the cost-of-living adjustment and altering the formula for future increases. The Commission agreed that there was a need for a "fail-safe" mechanism (other than inter-fund borrowing) to prevent future crises and considered a range of possibilities, including borrowing from the general fund, permitting the trust fund to issue its own bonds for sale to the public, and automatic increases in revenues or reductions in benefits, but never arrived a consensus. Congress accepted the recommendations of the Commission and included a gradual increase in the age of eligibility for full benefits from 65 to 67 by 2027. Given the warning issued by the Trustees Report, Congress moved with incredible rapidity. By April 20, the Social Security Amendments of 1983 had been signed into law.[20]

Taken together, these three laws stood at tension with the promise of tax cuts that animated the 1980s campaign and found a full expression in the passage of ERTA. President Reagan and congressional Republicans fought hard to preserve the rate reductions and indexing, the two most consequential changes in the tax code. Reagan rarely if ever admitted to tax increases: the increases in the payroll tax authorized under the Social Security Act Amendments of 1983 were simply an acceleration of previously scheduled increases; the taxation of benefits among high-income households was cast as a benefit cut. Many of the other changes were relatively invisible (e.g., excise taxes) or worked within the intricacies of the Internal Revenue Code, restricting or eliminating the dense thicket of tax preferences that lowered tax liabilities (some of which, ironically, were products of ERTA). The efforts to raise revenues through this latter path, moreover, could be framed as reform, much as the administration had suggested in its FY1983 budget cited above. The support for tax expenditure reform would be combined with further rate reductions in the next round of tax policy changes.[21]

The Quest for Tax Reform

The Tax Reform Act (TRA) of 1986 marked the most significant changes in the tax code since the Eisenhower presidency. In sharp contrast with the ERTA, the TRA would aspire to simplify the code and lower rates without worsening the deficit. In the 1984 State of the Union address, Reagan assigned Treasury Secretary Donald T. Regan the responsibility of designing "a plan for action to simplify the entire tax code."[22] Following extensive deliberations in the Treasury, Reagan made the case for comprehensive tax reform in an address to the nation on May 28, 1985. He grounded the need for reform in terms of equity, arguing that we must

> radically change a system that still treats people's earnings, similar incomes, much differently regarding the tax that they pay; and, yes, radically change a system that still causes some to invest their money, not to make a better mousetrap but simply to avoid a tax trap.[23]

The next day, in an event in the White House, he described the tax code as "an outrage, one riddled through with special privileges and inequities that violates our most fundamental American values of justice and fair play." Through the elimination of various tax expenditures, reform could replace "the present steeply graded system of 14 different tax rates with a flatter, simpler, 3-step design" with sharply lower rates. A continuation of indexing, a doubling of the personal exemption, and the expansion of the Earned Income Tax Credit or EITC would ensure that "working families do not suffer under the burden of Federal taxation."[24]

While Congress embraced the concept of tax reform, its core element—the elimination of tax expenditures—would expose both chambers to intensive lobbying. Dan Rostenkowski (D-IL), chair of the House Ways and Means Committee, and Robert Packwood (R-OR), chair of the Senate Finance Committee limited the role of industry lobbyists by using closed sessions, rejecting recorded votes that would expose members to interest group pressures, and restricting debate once bills reached the floor, in essence using procedural strategies to create the kind of insulation that had been the hallmark of tax policymaking in the days of Wilbur Mills. They deployed the support of the Tax Reform Coalition, a loose collection of public interest lobbies and pro-reform businesses, for whom the benefits of the existing network of tax preferences were less valuable than a proposed rate reduction. There were obvious differences between the two chambers. For Rostenkowski and the Democratic House majority, the path to reform involved eliminating or curtailing key corporate tax preferences rather than focusing on those enjoyed by individuals and households; for Packwood and the Republican controlled Senate, the preference ordering was reversed. But the active intervention of the President in building and maintaining Republican support in the House and keeping reform on track by publicly anointing Packwood, normally sympathetic to business interests, as a leader in tax reform, bore fruit. The TRA was signed into law on October 22, 1986.[25] As the *New York Times* reported at the signing, the process of developing the Act "was a peculiarly American annealing. Few other measures have been shaped and reshaped by so many conflicts and by so much cooperation. Few have reflected so many political trade-offs by so many politicians with such different styles and viewpoints. No other legislation in years has survived so many narrow escapes."[26]

The TRA marked a significant change in federal taxation in several respects. As noted earlier, its key feature was a reduction in rates made possible through the broadening of the tax base via the elimination or reform of a host of expensive tax expenditures. Given the recent record of deficits, the bill was designed to be revenue neutral (a claim that was used to constrain the introduction of amendments in Congress). Corporations faced capped deductions, the elimination of the investment tax credit, reduced depreciation benefits, and a new AMT; provisions that allowed large commercial banks to deduct bad debts before the underlying loans were determined worthless were repealed. Even if businesses received an overall rate reduction (from a top rate of 48 percent to new top rate of 34 percent), the elimination or reduction of tax expenditures and the reduced value of those that remained took their toll. The net effect was to increase corporate tax liability by approximately $120 billion over the next five years (FY 1987–1991).[27]

Reflecting the constraint of revenue neutrality, the individual income tax was reduced by $120 billion. The TRA retained the most widely used individual deductions, but several tax expenditures were sacrificed in the name of reform: the mortgage interest deduction was now limited to first and second homes, the deduction of consumer interest and sales tax was repealed, and deduction for IRAs was retained, but only for those lacking pensions or married couples with an adjusted gross income of under $50,000. The long-term capital gains tax was raised to match the statutory marginal rates. The complex system of individual brackets (14 for individuals, 15 for families) was collapsed into two official brackets of 15 and 28 percent. In reality, the structure was somewhat more complicated insofar as a 33 percent rate "bubble" was applied to some higher income earners to recapture some of the savings they received through the application of the new 15 percent rate, creating a structure of 15, 28, 33 (i.e., 28 percent plus a 5 percent "rate adjustment") and 28 percent. But for the wealthiest taxpayers, the top marginal rate was almost cut in half.[28] The AMT was raised from 20 to 21 percent. Most impressive, the personal exemption and standard deduction for married couples were almost doubled and the EITC was expanded and indexed for inflation. As the Joint Committee on Taxation noted: "these provisions relieve approximately six million low-income individuals from income tax liability and ensure that no families below the poverty level will have Federal income tax liability."[29]

The importance of the TRA can be best viewed when placed in context. During the immediate postwar decades, the income tax was characterized, in part, by its progressivity. When one combines the individual, corporate, payroll and estate taxes and calculates the average tax by percentile of income groups, the average taxes were relatively flat between the 20th and 90th percentile, as Thomas Piketty and Emanuel Saez observe, rising sharply thereafter, particularly among the wealthiest households. By the 1980 election, the top individual rate remained high, at 70 percent. But by the conclusion of Reagan's two-term presidency, the top individual rate had been cut to 28 percent, with a top corporate rate of 34 percent. Certainly, reform had brought the elimination or reduction of tax expenditures that lowered the tax liability of top earners. But the rate cuts had more than offset the impact of reform for the wealthiest taxpayers. As Piketty and Saez observe, "From 1980 to 1990, tax rates at the top declined, while tax rates in the middle class stayed constant."[30]

The Reagan tax policy contributed to reductions in the individual and corporate income taxes as a source of revenues, as shown in Tables 7.2 and 7.3. Between 1980 and 1995, the individual income tax's contribution to revenues fell precipitously, reaching a low of 43.1 percent by 1994. The corporate income tax's contributions to overall revenues fell from 12.5 percent to a record low

TABLE 7.2 Percentage Composition of Federal Revenues by Source, 1980–2000

Fiscal Year	*Individual Income Tax*	*Corporate Income Tax*	*Social Insurance Tax*	*Excise Tax*	*Other*
1980	47.2%	12.5%	30.5%	4.7%	5.1%
1985	45.6	8.4	36.1	4.9	5.0
1990	45.2	9.1	36.8	3.4	5.4
1995	43.7	11.6	35.8	4.3	4.6
2000	49.6	10.2	32.2	3.4	4.5

Source: Office of Management and Budget, *Budget of the United States Government, Fiscal Year 2023* (Washington, DC: Government Publishing Office, 2022), Historical Tables, Table 2.2.

TABLE 7.3 Composition of Federal Revenues by Source, 1980–2000 (Percentage of GDP)

Fiscal Year	*Individual Income Tax*	*Corporate Income Tax*	*Social Insurance Tax*	*Excise Tax*	*Other*
1980	8.7%	2.3%	5.7%	0.9%	0.9%
1985	7.8	1.4	6.2	0.8	0.9
1990	7.9	1.6	6.4	0.6	1.0
1995	7.8	2.1	6.4	0.8	0.8
2000	9.9	2.0	6.5	0.7	0.9

Source: Office of Management and Budget, *Budget of the United States Government, Fiscal Year 2023* (Washington, DC: Government Publishing Office, 2022), Historical Tables, Table 2.3.

of 6.2 percent in 1982, as the provisions of ERTA were enacted. TEFRA and DEFRA 1984 removed some of the benefits that had been delivered via ERTA, raising the corporate share to 10.4 percent by 1988. But as the provisions of the TRA went into effect and corporations reorganized to become pass-through entities (e.g., partnerships) to take advantage of the lower individual rates, the corporate tax continued to decline as a share of revenues. Most striking was the growing importance of social insurance taxes as a share of overall revenues as the top rates for individuals and corporations declined.[31]

From the Laffer Curve to Gramm–Rudman–Hollings

If significant changes in the tax code would be one of the major policy legacies of the 1980s, a second would be the growing presence of the deficit and debt. The supply-side claim that cuts would generate new revenues and move the nation toward a balanced budget was severely challenged in the wake of ERTA. In 1981, the year ERTA was passed, federal receipts were 19.1 percent of GDP, the highest level since 1969. By 1984, receipts had fallen to a low of 16.9 percent of GDP. Receipts would not exceed 18 percent of GDP until 1996. Initially, the collapse of revenues was a product of the deep economic recession.[32] The reduction in receipts would have proven less consequential had it been combined with comparable cuts in federal spending. In 1981, ERTA was combined with deep cuts to domestic discretionary spending and some mandatory programs.[33] But Congress would never again accede to comparable cuts in domestic spending. Initially, the budgetary impacts of domestic spending cuts were partially offset by recession-related increases in means-tested programs. But the larger story was the unprecedented peacetime military expansion. Between 1980 and 1989, domestic discretionary spending fell from 24 percent of outlays (5.1 percent GDP) to 16.2 percent of outlays (3.3 percent GDP). Defense discretionary spending, in sharp contrast, increased from 22.8 percent of outlays (4.8 percent GDP) to a peak of 28.1 percent of outlays in 1987

(5.9 percent GDP), before receding to 26.6 percent of outlays in 1989 (5.5 percent GDP).[34] In inflation-adjusted dollars, the defense budget had grown by 47.6 percent. Domestic discretionary spending had fallen to 86 percent of what it had been when Reagan was elected.[35]

While Reagan had been successful in convincing Congress to reduce domestic spending through the tightening of eligibility requirements and cutting benefits for means-tested programs, mandatory programmatic spending continued to dominate federal spending and, as a result of the Social Security Act Amendments of 1983, the two largest program, Social Security and Medicare, were now on a firmer fiscal footing. By 1989, domestic discretionary and mandatory programmatic spending claimed a combined 58.6 percent of outlays (12.8 percent GDP).[36] As former Reagan OMB Director David Stockman noted, "the Reagan legacy" was not the "contraction" of the welfare state but its "consolidation." In Stockman's judgment, "consolidation, combined with the deep tax cuts" left "an untenable and unsustainable fiscal structure and financial burden." Critics charged that the deficits—the combined effect of tax cuts and defense spending—were strategically designed to limit the expansion of domestic spending. As Senator Daniel Patrick Moynihan (D-NY) observed in 1988, the Reagan administration "set about creating a fiscal crisis which they hoped would produce a political transformation." The record deficits and the bourgeoning debt were all that remained, the "protean and unnerving manifestations" of fiscal policy decisions.[37]

The combination of deep tax cuts and a failure to moderate overall spending had inevitable results. The deficit, which had been 2.5 percent of GDP in 1981, more than doubled by 1983, reaching 5.9 percent of GDP, a postwar record. Deficits would fall over the course of the next several years but would remain at levels well above those of the Carter presidency.[38] The successive deficits had obvious ramifications for the national debt. Between 1981 and 1988, the debt held by the public increased from 25.2 percent of GDP to 39.9 percent of GDP. In nominal terms, the debt more than doubled during the same period, growing from $789.4 billion to $2.05 trillion.[39]

Given the importance attached to budget deficits in 1980, the record requires some explication. During the campaign, Reagan had argued that budget deficits were of concern because they resulted in monetary expansion which had fueled inflation. As the economy recovered from the deep recession of 1981–1982, inflation failed to accelerate, rendering moot this justification for eliminating the deficit. In the end, the political difficulties of pursuing balanced budgets proved decisive. In the words of Herbert Stein, "the consequences of the surplus-deficit decision, although important, were general and deferred whereas the consequences of other budget decisions would be immediately felt by beneficiaries of expenditures or by taxpayers." While everyone seemed to agree that the growing deficits and debts were problematic, "hardly anyone was willing to give up anything he valued very much to reduce them."[40] This was particularly the case for the President. In 1982, Reagan endorsed a balanced budget amendment. But he cautioned that "all balanced budgets aren't created equal." He rejected seeking to balance the budget "by weaseling out of the first decent tax program since John Kennedy's tax cut nearly 20 years ago" or "by compromising defenses and placing our country's security in peril." Without providing details, the President called for a balanced budget "by bringing to heel a Federal establishment which has taken too much power from the States, too much liberty with the Constitution, and too much money from the people."[41] The balanced budget may have been attractive symbolically, but it was not sufficiently important to sacrifice the administration's policy priorities.

While the balanced budget amendment failed to receive sufficient support in the House, Congress would turn to procedural remedies to rein in spending. As Chapter 2 explained, efforts to control the deficits were enacted in 1985, with Gramm–Rudman–Hollings. Given the magnitude of the fiscal gap, legislatively prescribing declining annual budget deficits and a balanced budget by 1991 proved easier than achieving the reductions. Indeed, between 1985 and 1991, the debt held by the public increased from 35.3 to 44.1 percent of GDP.[42] By the 1990s, spending controls would need to be combined with new revenues through the partial reversal of the Reagan tax cuts, its most important legacy. Moreover, the new budgetary regime would impose rules that would place domestic discretionary spending and the defense budget at parity, thereby partially reversing the administration's second legacy, the defense buildup and larger rebalancing of federal priorities.

The Bush Interregnum

When Reagan signed the TRA, he framed it as "less a reform…than a revolution." As a result, "America will have the lowest marginal tax rates and the most modern tax code among major industrialized nations." After touting the benefits of the reforms he concluded with a warning:

> now that we've come this far, we cannot, and we will not, allow tax reform to be undone with tax rate hikes. We must restore certainty to our tax code and our economy. And I'll oppose with all my might any attempt to raise tax rates on the American people, and I hope that all here will join with me to make permanent the historic progress of tax reform.[43]

Whether the TRA would have the permanence that Reagan desired was unclear, given the large deficits that had been generated during his presidency and the Republican's loss of the Senate majority in the 1986 midterms. Without increases in revenues, any hope of deficit reduction would rest with Congress and the procedural changes it had invoked, albeit unsuccessfully, to reduce the magnitude of deficits.

As the 1988 Republican primaries approached, Vice President George H.W. Bush sought to strengthen his appeal to the Reagan coalition. In contrast to his chief contender, Senator Bob Dole (R-KS), Bush pledged that he would not raise taxes, thereby assuring voters that on fiscal policy, there were no disagreements between him and President Reagan. The "no new taxes" pledge provided some short-term political benefits. Bush's advisors argued that a balanced budget could be achieved by 1992 without new taxes, but all depended on a very stylized set of assumptions regarding the economy and the absence of significant domestic or international crises.[44] While Bush won an overwhelming victory in November, the core economic assumptions failed to hold. In 1989, Bush's first year as president, the deficit stood at $152.6 billion. But things deteriorated rapidly as a result of a mild recession, such that by 1990, the deficit had grown to $221 billion (3.71 percent of GDP), in nominal terms the largest deficit up to this point in the postwar period.[45] The debt, fueled by a steady stream of large deficits, had reached $32.4 trillion (40.9 percent of GDP).[46]

In a decision that alienated members of the Reagan coalition, Bush negotiated with the Democratically controlled Congress over a package of spending and revenue measures to reduce the deficit. Bush's decision to abandon his "no new taxes" pledge intensified intraparty conflicts within the Grand Old Party (GOP). House Republicans withdrew from the negotiations and the co-chairman of the National Republican Congressional Campaign Committee advised candidates in the mid-term elections to distance themselves from Bush's plan. While the administration favored increases in energy taxes which could be linked, at least rhetorically, to the ongoing conflict with Iraq, the final package included increases in marginal tax rates, reversing the broad cuts that candidate Bush had pledged to preserve. OBRA 1990 added a new marginal tax bracket of 31 percent, raised the AMT to 24 percent, and expanded the EITC, adding additional progressivity to the system. Democrats agreed to some domestic spending cuts over the next 5 years and imposed new PAYGO rules to constrain the growth of mandatory programs.[47] As W. Elliott Brownlee notes, for all its merits, the agreement "was a political disaster for Bush. He had alienated the Republicans who believed that tax cutting was their party's most popular policy instrument and most efficacious means of stimulating the economy and limiting the growth of government."[48] The combination of poor economic performance and the tax increases doomed Bush's reelection bid, leaving the Congress and the White House under unified Democratic control for the first time since the 1980.

Clinton, the Contract, and the Pursuit of Balanced Budgets

One might have predicted that Democratic control of the government would have set the stage for a return to the basic features of the postwar tax regime. On the campaign trail, Clinton had promised a stimulus program that would have included middle-class tax cuts, increased taxation of high-income households and corporations, and a new BTU tax to promote conservation. While the middle-class tax cut never occurred, Congress and the Clinton administration achieved the tax increases by employing the budget reconciliation process. OBRA 1993 added two new tax brackets, 36 and 39.6 percent and introduced graduated AMT rates of 26 and 28 percent and expanded the EITC. The corporate tax was expanded as well, supplementing the 34 percent rate with new brackets of 35 and 38 percent. OBRA 1993 also raised additional revenue for the two largest entitlement programs by eliminating the cap on Medicare taxes and increasing the proportion of Social Security benefits subject to taxation. The proposed BTU tax was replaced by a modest increase in the federal gasoline tax. When taken as a whole, the CBO estimated that some 80 percent of the net tax increases from OBRA 1993 would be paid by households with incomes of at least $200,000. As a result of the act, it projected that the effective tax rate on the top 1 percent of families would be at its highest level since 1979.[49]

OBRA 1993 had established the goal of reducing the deficit by 50 percent by FY1997 by extending discretionary caps and PAYGO procedures through FY1998 and, more importantly, raising new revenues.[50] While OBRA 1993 clearly did not mark a return to the pre-ERTA marginal rates, its passage was challenging. In the House, the bill passed by a narrow margin (218–216), attracting the opposition of all 175 Republicans and 41 Democrats. In the Senate, Republicans, unanimous in their opposition, were joined by six Democrats, forcing Vice President Al Gore to cast a tie-breaking vote. Republicans focused their attention on the tax increases rather than deficit reduction. Representative Dick Armey (R-TX) proclaimed that OBRA defined "the difference between Republicans and Democrats. Democrats believe that prosperity comes from bigger Government. Republicans know it comes from ordinary people acting on behalf of themselves and their families."[51] As Michael Meeropol observed, the "victory actually masked the important fact that the Reagan Revolution had succeeded in shackling even a reform-minded Democratic president supposedly working with a like-minded Democratic majority in Congress....Even though the tax increases were focused on very few Americans, those who had experienced dramatic increases in their incomes over the previous dozen years, they still barely won approval from that Democratic majority."[52]

The Contract, the Republican Coalition, and the Downward Ratchet

Following the 1994 midterm elections, the Republicans became the majority party in Congress. Running on the Contract with America—an agenda signed by 367 Republican House incumbents and candidates on the steps of the Capitol—the Republicans gained 54 seats in the House and 8 seats in the Senate, claiming unified control of Congress for the first time in four decades.

Newt Gingrich (R-GA), who would ascend to the speakership and become the face of the Republican Revolution, advocated tax cuts and balanced budgets. Let us focus on taxes, returning to the goal of balanced budgets below. Giving voice to the same Starve the Beast argument that had been articulated since the late 1970s, Gingrich found tax cuts to be the only means of fighting governmental expansion. As he explained in his book *To Renew America*: "I watched the Reagan, Bush, and Clinton administrations talk themselves into tax increases to 'fight the deficit,' and each time the liberals simply took the new revenues as an excuse for higher spending." By cutting government to the size it was in 1970, he argued, the median household could reduce its tax liability from 24 percent of its budget to 16 percent of its budget. "Imagine how much better off the average family would be if they could spend $4,000 more on their own children, their own education, their own savings."[53]

While taxation was only part of the Republican agenda, increasingly, it was the central component. For decades, conservatives had to manage a contentious and fractious coalition. This coalition, initially divided between traditionalists and classical liberals or libertarians, became more complicated as the Christian Right and neoconservatives joined the fray. Some traditionalists now distinguished themselves from the neoconservatives by describing themselves as paleoconservatives. As historian George H. Nash notes, "American conservatism did not speak with a single voice...There was a continuing gap between the traditionalist ethos of self-restraint, of limits on will, and the libertarian ethos of self-assertion, self-cultivation, and resistance to the State."[54] Early efforts to unify the conservative movement were in part intellectual. During the 1960s, under the moniker of fusionism, conservative intellectuals like Frank S. Meyer stressed the necessary connections between traditionalist and libertarian arguments. Traditional morality was meaningless without the liberty to choose, and liberty could degenerate into libertinism without the moorings of traditionalism.[55] But the existential threat of communism provided the cement that held the coalition together. By the 1980s, the mix of policies that were pursued by the Reagan administration—a combination of free-market economics supported by libertarians, social policies embraced by the traditionalists and the Religious Right, and a muscular foreign policy that responded to neoconservative demands—served a fusionist function as well.

The collapse of the Soviet Union in 1991 eliminated the unifying force of anti-communism. Nash explains, it "attenuated the fusionist imperative for American conservatives" and now, "many conservatives appeared to be searching for a new 'vital center'" and asking if the coalition had "grown too successful and too variegated to have a vital center any longer?"[56] In this context, the opposition to taxation could serve a fusionist function. Factions within the conservative coalition might have different preferences regarding a host of issues. Neoconservatives might emphasize military preparedness; libertarians might prefer a less adventurous foreign policy. Social conservatives might focus on defending traditional marriage or the rights of the unborn; many libertarians would emphasize individual liberty in the broadest of terms. But the commitment to low taxes would remain the central fusionist factor. In the words of Stephen Moore, former head of the Club for Growth, low taxes became "the central linchpin of conservatism," the one "unifying message."[57]

By the 1990s, the popular cry for tax cuts—so evident in the late 1970s and 1980s—had dissipated to some extent. Republicans, in turn, drew on an elite strategy. As Jacob S. Hacker and Paul Pierson explain, mass mobilization was replaced by

> the emergence of a much more institutionalized network of organizations, heavily funded by the most affluent members of American society, with a strong commitment to tax cuts....Well-funded organizations now play a key role in producing like-minded candidates—or at least candidates who face strong incentives to behave has if they are like-minded.[58]

As noted in Chapter 6, the conservative movement developed an increasingly sophisticated network of corporate- and foundation-funded think tanks and publications during the 1970s, reinforcing some of the divisions noted above and popularizing proposals on key policy issues. Chastened by the political defeats of the late 1960s and early 1970s, corporations also invested heavily in lobbying and political donations, a trend that has continued to this day. As part of the elite strategy, this organizational network became increasingly important in reinforcing the low tax regime.

Traditionally, corporations were pragmatic in their employment of lobbyists and campaign spending. They hired former Democratic and Republican lawmakers and often engaged in split giving as a means of maintaining access in a Democratically controlled Congress. But with the Republican victories in the 1994 and unified control of Congress, the opportunity structure changed and key congressional Republicans were intent on pursuing a new elite strategy to support for their agenda. The so-called K-Street Project was central to this effort. Organized by House Majority Whip Delay and Americans for Tax Reform's Grover Norquist, the initiative was designed to force lobbying firms to reinforce Republican goals through their campaign contributions and the placement of Republican loyalists in key positions in lobbying firms and trade associations. A failure to cooperate would block access to sites of policy-making.[59] This created, in the words of Thomas B. Edsall, "a working army" of lobbyists "committed to the party's entire leadership program, not just to the specific interests and concerns of their individual clients."[60]

The elite strategy had another important component: securing the public commitment of lawmakers to eschew any and all tax increases. At the forefront of this effort was Norquist's Americans for Tax Reform, founded in 1985, which worked in close coordination with corporate sponsors, trade associations, and conservative foundations. Norquist introduced the Taxpayer Protection Pledge, which committed signatories to oppose all tax increases, when Washington was engaged in debates over the TRA of 1986. The pledge helped assuage the fears of conservatives that TRA's elimination of tax expenditures would not be vitiated by subsequent rate increases. Thereafter, Michael J. Graetz and Ian Shapiro note, Americans for Tax Reform was devoted to "fingerprinting politicians" with the pledge and assuring that after elected officials and candidates signed the pledge, their names would be recorded in a public database. President George H.W. Bush, who signed and violated the pledge only to face electoral defeat, remained a salient symbol for politicians and helped assure that future tax increases would face the opposition of Republicans in Congress.[61]

The growing network of lobbyists and associations, when combined with the Taxpayer Protection Pledge, create powerful pressures for tax cuts and ongoing opposition to tax increases regardless of the justification. Cuts, when they occurred, would be insulated from erosion by the Taxpayer Protection Pledge and the willingness of the GOP to channel resources from the K-Street Project to loyalists. Absent support for tax increases among Republicans, the broad coalitions necessary for significant reforms would prove elusive and rate increases when they occurred, would fall into a fairly narrow range (e.g., the top rates of OBRA 1993 would never be exceeded in subsequent presidencies, regardless of party). All of this created a downward ratchet in revenues. It was consequential because it was combined with relative inattention to the growth in mandatory spending, driven by the aging of the population. The downward ratchet and the steady expansion of mandatory spending had an unavoidable effect—the growing problems of deficits and the debt.

The Path to Balanced Budgets

The first component of the Contract with America was the proposed Fiscal Responsibility Act, which included a balanced budget amendment. The constitutional amendment required that the budget be balanced annually unless waived by a three-fifths vote in each chamber or in the event of a declared military emergency. While it passed the House by overwhelming margins, it failed to achieve a two-thirds majority in the Senate.[62] With the balanced budget amendment derailed, attention turned to the budget process. Upon accepting the speakership, Newt Gingrich (R-GA) had reminded the House Republican Conference that the budget is "the transformational document for this system. When you change the budget, you've really changed government, and until you change the budget, you've just talked about changing government." Gingrich understood the vast powers granted Congress under Article I of the Constitution and focused on the role of appropriations: "we don't have to deauthorize [programs], we simply have to not pay for them.... if the spending doesn't originate in the House and Senate, it cannot be spent."[63]

TABLE 7.4 Composition of Outlays, Budget Enforcement Act Categories, 1980–2000 (Percentage of GDP)

Fiscal Year	*Total Outlays*	*Discretionary*		*Mandatory*	
		Defense	*Nondefense*	*Programmatic**	*Net Interest*
1980	21.2%	4.8%	5.1%	10.1%	1.9%
1981	21.6	5.0	4.8	10.5	2.2
1982	22.5	5.6	4.2	10.9	2.6
1983	22.9	5.9	4.1	11.3	2.5
1984	21.6	5.8	3.8	10.0	2.8
1985	22.2	5.9	3.8	10.2	3.0
1986	21.9	6.0	3.6	9.9	3.0
1987	21.1	5.9	3.4	9.7	2.9
1988	20.7	5.7	3.4	9.6	3.0
1989	20.6	5.5	3.3	9.5	3.0
1990	21.2	5.1	3.4	10.3	3.1
1991	21.7	5.2	3.5	10.4	3.2
1992	21.5	4.7	3.6	10.7	3.1
1993	20.8	4.3	3.7	10.5	2.9
1994	20.4	3.9	3.6	10.5	2.8
1995	20.0	3.6	3.6	10.4	3.1
1996	19.6	3.3	3.4	10.4	3.0
1997	18.9	3.2	3.3	10.2	2.9
1998	18.5	3.0	3.2	10.2	2.7
1999	18.0	2.9	3.1	9.9	2.4
2000	17.7	2.9	3.2	9.8	2.2

* Does not include undistributed offsetting receipts.

Source: Office of Management and Budget, *Budget of the United States Government, Fiscal Year 2023* (Washington, DC: Government Publishing Office, 2022), Historical Tables, Table 8.4.

But budgetary control would occur in an environment shaped by two factors: the growing presence of mandatory spending and the discretionary spending caps put into place as a result of the Budget Enforcement Act. As the data in Tables 7.4 and 7.5 reflect, programmatic mandatory spending was steadily growing as a share of outlays, becoming the majority of outlays from 1993 forward (as a result of economic growth, the claim on GDP declined somewhat over the period). When combined with net interest on the debt, some two-thirds of outlays now fell outside of the budget process. Reconciliation could be used to slow the growth of Medicare, and during the period efforts at cost saving focused on most margins of the program. The discretionary caps raised additional difficulties. During the Reagan years, defense spending had experienced an unprecedented peacetime growth rate, reflecting the President's commitment to reverse the downward trend of the post-Vietnam years.

TABLE 7.5 Composition of Outlays, Budget Enforcement Act Categories 1980–2000 (Percentage of Outlays)

Fiscal Year	*Discretionary*		*Mandatory*	
	Defense	*Nondefense*	*Programmatic★*	*Net Interest*
1980	22.8%	24.0%	47.7%	8.9%
1981	23.3	22.1	48.6	10.1
1982	24.9	18.8	48.4	11.4
1983	26.0	17.7	49.4	11.1
1984	26.8	17.8	46.2	13.0
1985	26.7	17.2	45.8	13.7
1986	27.6	16.6	45.3	13.7
1987	28.1	16.1	46.2	13.8
1988	27.3	16.3	46.3	14.3
1989	26.6	16.2	46.4	14.8
1990	24.0	16.0	48.3	14.7
1991	24.1	16.1	48.0	14.7
1992	21.9	16.7	49.8	14.4
1993	20.7	17.5	50.3	14.1
1994	19.3	17.7	51.7	13.9
1995	18.0	17.9	51.7	15.3
1996	17.0	17.1	52.8	15.4
1997	17.0	17.2	53.7	15.2
1998	16.4	17.1	54.9	14.6
1999	16.2	17.4	55.3	13.5
2000	16.5	17.9	55.6	12.5

★ Does not include undistributed offsetting receipts.

Source: Office of Management and Budget, *Budget of the United States Government, Fiscal Year 2023* (Washington, DC: Government Publishing Office, 2022), Historical Tables, Table 8.3.

Domestic discretionary spending had fallen simultaneously as a share of outlays. But under the spending caps, the two categories of discretionary spending would move toward parity in the mid-1990s, with domestic spending receiving more than defense by the end of the decade—a reflection of fiscal consequences of the end of the Cold War.

The budget resolution for FY1996 established the goal of a deficit reduction of $894 billion over seven years—combined with a $245 billion tax cut—to achieve a balanced budget by FY2002. Spending cuts of this magnitude, particularly when combined with tax reductions, would require a freeze on discretionary spending and proposed changes in Medicare, Medicaid, and other entitlement programs to limit their growth.[64] Much to the consternation of Democrats, President Clinton responded by proposing a ten-year timetable for a balanced budget, arguing that it should be achieved with fewer spending cuts and smaller, more targeted tax cuts for the middle class. While the House

GOP leadership was pleased by Clinton's embrace of the balanced budget goal, there were sharp disagreements on policy that plagued the budget process.[65] As George Hager and David S. Cloud reported, the distance between the two parties transcended levels of spending to "philosophical differences over the size of government and what it should do." Fiscal decisions and policy decisions were "inextricably intertwined," as appropriations bills embodied "bold legislative agendas" including "controversial overhauls of welfare and Medicare to get the savings the GOP needs to balance the budget."[66]

The next several months would prove to be nothing short of chaotic. The Republican majority attempted to force Clinton to accept its plan to balance the budget in seven years, tying it to an increase in the debt ceiling, only to meet with a veto. By October 1, 1995, only three regular appropriations bills had been enacted, forcing a reliance on continuing resolutions (CRs). When the CR was allowed to expire on November 13, Clinton vetoed the new CR, which would have extended budget authority through December 1, in response to increased Medicare premiums. After a five-day government shutdown that furloughed 800,000 federal employees, an agreement was reached to resume funding through December 15, albeit at reduced levels. During the interim, four regular appropriations bills were enacted and three were vetoed over policy differences. With the expiration of the CR, another government shutdown commenced, furloughing 280,000 workers. As public opinion turned against the Republicans and with Senate Majority Leader Robert Dole (R-KS) anxious to resolve the crisis as he prepared for a 1996 presidential bid, the government was reopened on January 26, 1996. The shutdowns, the series of some 14 CRs, and highly publicized battles over the budget had yielded little for the GOP other than some reductions in discretionary spending.[67]

The budgetary conflicts of 1995–1996 were exacerbated by battles over the welfare state. During the 1980s, the Reagan administration promoted reform in AFDC, focusing on greater devolution to the states and experimentation with "welfare-to-work" initiatives. In 1992, candidate Clinton had promised to "end welfare as we know it," and in 1994, he proposed reforms that would phase in work requirements for AFDC recipients and invest more heavily in job training. While the Clinton proposal never received consideration by Congress, following the 1994 midterm elections, the new Republican majority turned to welfare reform, which had been part of the Contract with America. The GOP proposal would eliminate AFDC in its entirety and replace it with Temporary Assistance for Needy Families (TANF), work requirements, and a five-year lifetime limit on cash assistance. While AFDC funding was permanently authorized, TANF would be funded through block grants to the states. States would have greater discretion in determining eligibility criteria and benefit levels and would receive financial incentives for moving a larger proportion of their caseload into the workplace and reducing out-of-wedlock births. The TANF proposal was incorporated in the budget reconciliation bill in 1995, which also included additional restrictions on Supplemental Security Income, provisions barring recent immigrants from receiving low-income federal social services for five years, and cuts in childcare, child nutrition, and food stamps.[68] Moreover, Congress sought to convert Medicaid into a block grant, giving states greater discretion over eligibility and benefits. It was promptly vetoed by Clinton. The proposal reemerged as a stand-alone welfare reform bill, which met with a second presidential veto in January 1996. The proposal was resurrected as part of the reconciliation process in 1996 with important modifications (e.g., the Medicaid provisions were dropped, additional funding was provided for childcare). Ultimately, the Personal Responsibility and Work Opportunity Reconciliation Act of 1996 was signed by Clinton, ending the nation's largest means-tested income support entitlement.[69]

The Return to Balanced Budgets

One of the unachieved goals of 1995 was to secure Clinton's agreement to balance the budget on an accelerated timetable. The deep cuts in Medicare and Medicaid and the proposed freeze on domestic discretionary spending that had been proposed at the time forestalled negotiations. Yet, by 1997, fiscal conditions had improved. Bolstered by new projections of revenues, the CBO reduced its deficit forecasts and set the stage for a budget agreement between Clinton and Congress to achieve a balanced budget by 2002. The administration and the GOP leadership entered closed-door negotiations surrounding the FY1998 budget, largely excluding the heads of the Democratic minority. The final deal combined spending reductions that were partially offset by tax cuts. With respect to spending, the agreement included significant entitlement savings ($115 billion from Medicare and $13.6 billion in Medicaid over five years) that were partially offset by restoration of some welfare benefits that were terminated under the 1996 welfare reforms, a new insurance program for children of low-income workers, and some increases in domestic discretionary spending. On the revenue side, the agreement included net tax cuts of $85 billion over five years, with a ten-year impact of some $250 billion. Because tax cuts would take effect before the spending cuts, the deficit was projected to increase in the near term with a surplus of $1.3 billion by FY2002.[70] As *Congressional Quarterly* reported, the deal "was evidence of how much Republicans have managed to change the political dynamic since they took over Congress—and how far they have dragged Clinton and his party."[71] The process resulted in two reconciliation bills: the Balanced Budget Act of 1997 and the Taxpayer Relief Act of 1997. Let us consider them in turn.

The Balanced Budget Act of 1997 made several changes in welfare policies. The most significant changes involved Medicare and a new insurance program for low-income children. As noted in Chapter 2, concerns that the fee-for-service structure of Medicare contributed to the escalation of costs led Congress in 1982 to authorize demonstration projects. The Balanced Budget Act formalized these experiments with a new Medicare Part C (Medicare+Choice) under which providers (e.g., health maintenance organizations or preferred-provider organizations) could provide Part A and B services and receive a capitation fee. It was anticipated that competition would result in greater efficiencies. The Act sought further cost savings by introducing the sustainable growth rate or SGR that would base annual increases in Medicare payments for physicians' services to growth in real GDP.[72] The efforts to control the growth in Medicare costs was combined with the creation of a new mandatory program, the State Children's Insurance Program or CHIP, under a new Title XXI of the Social Security Act. CHIP was designed to provide healthcare to uninsured children who were from families with incomes above the threshold for Medicaid. As with Medicaid, the federal government would provide funding to the states using a federal medical assistance formula that is based on average per capita income.[73] The Act also reduced Medicaid costs by granting states greater flexibility to place recipients in managed care programs, savings that were partially offset by restoring funding in public assistance benefits that had been restricted in the 1996 welfare reforms.[74]

The Taxpayer Relief Act of 1997, included several provisions that had been promoted in the Contract with America and included in the Balanced Budget Act of 1995, which had been successfully vetoed by Clinton. The largest item was the Child Tax Credit, which phased out at a relatively high Adjusted Gross Income ($110,000 for joint returns, $75,000 for single returns). The administration addressed the distributional issues by securing provisions that made the credit refundable for low-income families who did not have income tax liabilities. It also included a number of education tax credits (the Hope Scholarship and the Lifetime Learning credit), liberalized IRA participation, and authorized Roth IRAs, which permitted retirement investments in after-tax dollars in exchange for no income tax liability at the time of withdrawal. The Act reduced capital gains rates, including the exclusion of gains from the sale of a residence, and reduced the estate and gift tax. On the corporate side, the Act eliminated the AMT for small corporations and provided more favorable depreciation provisions for larger firms subject to the AMT. It also authorized the Welfare-to-Work Credit for companies that hired members of families that were long-term recipients of AFDC or TANF. The reduced revenue from the above provisions was partially offset by additional excise taxes.[75] Unlike the two landmark Reagan era tax bills, the Taxpayer Relief Act did not reduce marginal income tax rates. Unlike the TRA, it only added complexity to the already Byzantine tax code, adding 285 new sections and 824 amendments, some of which were retroactive, some effective immediately, others phased in over time.[76]

The Budget Enforcement Act (Title X of the Balanced Budget Act) extended the basic provisions that were originally established in the Budget Enforcement

Act of 1990, reauthorized in 1993, and had been scheduled to expire in 1998. It set spending caps for discretionary spending for 1998–2002. For FY1998–1999, discretionary spending was categorized as defense, nondefense, and violent crime reduction; for FY2000, the categories changed to discretionary and violent crime reduction, with a single discretionary cap thereafter. Moreover, it extended the PAYGO provisions for mandatory spending and revenue measures through FY2002, backed by sequestration, which would be enforced through FY2006. As in the past, several programs and activities were exempted from sequestration or covered by partial sequestration.[77] Over the five-year budget window, the Balanced Budget Act of 1997 was projected to reduce discretionary spending by some $90 billion and mandatory spending by $105 billion, largely through projected savings in reimbursements to healthcare providers.

Under the 1997 agreement, the budget was to be balanced by 2002. And yet, due to a robust economy, spending levels were lagging behind GDP growth while revenues exceeded projections. By 1998, the federal budget was in surplus for the first time since 1969, and would experience successive surpluses for the first time since the late 1940s (Ironically, the surplus would turn to deficit in 2002, the date that had been enshrined in the Republican budget plans). As one might expect, Gingrich, who resigned from the speakership in November 1998 and from Congress two months later, would claim credit for the fiscal turnaround. But a more plausible explanation would focus on the tax rate increases of 1990 and 1993, which Republicans strongly opposed, combined with growing incomes. During Clinton's two term presidency, tax receipts increased from 17 percent of GDP to 20 percent of GDP. At the same time, from when the new Republican majority assumed control of Congress in 1995 to 2000, federal outlays declined from 20 to 17.7 percent of GDP.[78] At the very least, the GOP of the 1990s shared a commitment to reigning in federal expenditures—a commitment that would wane as deficits turned to surpluses.

Conclusion

The two decades following the Reagan election were remarkable in multiple regards. First and most obviously, they reveal that policy matters. Largely as a result of the tax cuts of the 1980s which were not combined with commensurate reductions in spending, the publicly held debt nearly doubled between 1981 and 1993. But this trend was partially reversed. As a result of tax increases and new budgetary controls, the debt-to-GDP ratio would fall for the first time since the mid-1970s. While the new taxes introduced under OBRA 1990 and 1993 were an important part of the story, the staunch opposition of Republicans to any and all tax increases revealed a second lesson: politics matter. As low taxes became the unifying element in the Republican coalition, the trajectory of taxation would depend on whether Democrats could achieve and maintain a majority in Congress. As Chapter 8 will reveal, a return to unified Republican control would be translated into an escalation of the national debt, which would begin a trajectory toward levels comparable to what existed at the end of World War II.

A third lesson may be the most important. In a continuation of a long-term trend, mandatory spending would increasingly dominate federal spending. When Reagan was elected president, mandatory spending and net interest constituted 53.2 percent of outlays, a dramatic increase over the level a decade earlier, when they claimed 38.5 percent. By 2020, these categories of spending would account for 65.6 percent of outlays. Programmatic mandatory spending—the largest components being Social Security, Medicare, and Medicaid—would account for 55.6 percent of total outlays.[79] The PAYGO procedures put in place under OBRA 1990 and 1993 could not be used to control the growth of existing entitlement programs. While reconciliation could extract some savings out of Medicare, it could not be used to address Social Security under the Byrd rule. Certainly, Congress has the power to change the authorizing statutes covering mandatory program, but as part the budgetary process they are largely untouchable. One of the ramifications, clearly exhibited in the 1990s, would be the growing conflicts intrinsic to the annual budgeting over discretionary programs. Increasingly, the budgetary process would degenerate into a zero-sum context over a shrinking share of federal outlays.

Notes

1 Ronald Reagan, "Inaugural Address, January 20, 1981." Available at www.presidency.ucsb.edu/node/246336

2 Ronald Reagan, "Address Before a Joint Session of the Congress on the Program for Economic Recovery," February 18, 1981. Available at www.presidency.ucsb.edu/node/246567

3 For a detailed discussion of the congressional debates, see John F. Witte, *The Politics and Development of the Federal Income Tax* (Madison: University of Wisconsin Press, 1985), 221–35.

4 See Edward N. Delaney, "The Economic Recovery Tax Act of 1981," *American Bar Association Journal* 67, 10 (1981):1266–69.

5 See Alan J. Auerbach, "Corporate Taxation in the United States," *Brookings Papers on Economic Activity*, 1983, 2 (1983), 451– 505, and Don Fullerton and Yolanda Kodrzycki Henderson, "Long-Run Effects of the Accelerated Cost Recovery System," *The Review of Economics and Statistics*, 67, 3 (1985): 363–72.

6 Joint Committee on Taxation, *General Explanation of the Economic Recovery Tax Act of 1981 (H.R. 4242, 97th Congress; Public Law 97-34)* (Washington, DC: Government Printing Office, 1981), 19.

7 Ibid., 17.

8 See Office of Management and Budget (OMB), *Budget Revisions, Fiscal Year 1982* (March 1981) (Washington, DC: Government Printing Office, 1981), M-2.

9 Lance T. Leloup, "After the Blitz: Reagan and the U. S. Congressional Budget Process," *Legislative Studies Quarterly*, 7, 3 (1982), 321–39, and James P. Pfiffner, "The Carter-Reagan Transition: Hitting the Ground Running," *Presidential Studies Quarterly*, 13, 4 (1983), 629–31.
10 James T. Patterson, *America's Struggle Against Poverty, 1900–1985* (Cambridge: Harvard University Press, 1986), 221–23.
11 John Svahn, "Omnibus Reconciliation Act of 1981: Legislative History and Summary of OASDI and Medicare Provisions," *Social Security Bulletin*, 44, 10 (1981): 3–24.
12 See Richard S. Williamson, "A New Federalism: Proposals and Achievements of President Reagan's First Three Years," *Publius*, 16, 1 (1986): 11–28.
13 Hugh Heclo, "The Mixed Legacies of Ronald Reagan," *Presidential Studies Quarterly*, 38, 4 (2008), 559.
14 Office of Management and Budget (OMB), *Budget of the U.S. Government, Fiscal Year 2023* (Washington, DC: Government Publishing Office, 2022), Historical Tables, Tables 1.1 and 1.2.
15 Ronald Reagan, "Address Before a Joint Session of the Congress Reporting on the State of the Union," January 26, 1982. Available at www.presidency.ucsb.edu/node/245636
16 OMB, *Budget of the United States Government, Fiscal Year 1983* (Washington, DC: Government Printing Office, 1982), M-19.
17 Dennis S. Ippolito, *Deficits, Debt, and the New Politics of Taxation* (Cambridge: Cambridge University Press, 2012),121–29.
18 Ronald Reagan, "Address to the Nation on the Program for Economic Recovery," September 24, 1981. Available at www.presidency.ucsb.edu/node/247669
19 The Board of Trustees of the Federal Old-Age and Survivors Insurance and Disability Insurance Trust Funds, *1982 Annual Report, Federal Old-Age and Survivors Insurance and Disability Insurance Trust Funds* (Washington, DC: Government Printing Office, 1982), 2.
20 John A. Svahn and Mary Ross, "Social Security Amendments of 1983: Legislative History and Summary of Provisions," *Social Security Bulletin* 46, 7 (1983), 28–29.
21 See W. Elliot Brownlee, *Federal Taxation in America: A History* 3rd ed. (Cambridge: Cambridge University Press, 2016), 189–90.
22 Ronald Reagan, "Address Before a Joint Session of the Congress on the State of the Union," January 25, 1984. Available at www.presidency.ucsb.edu/node/261634.
23 Ronald Reagan, "Address to the Nation on Tax Reform," May 28, 1985. Available at www.presidency.ucsb.edu/node/259966.
24 Ronald Reagan, "Remarks on Tax Reform to Concerned Citizens," May 29, 1985. Available at www.presidency.ucsb.edu/node/259984.
25 See Brownlee, *Federal Taxation in America*, 197–209 and Eric M. Patashnik, *Reforms at Risk: What Happens After Major Policy Changes Are Enacted* (Princeton: Princeton University Press, 2008), 38–40. The classic study of the passage of the TRA is Alan Murry and Jeffrey Birnbaum, *Showdown and Gucci Gulch: Lawmakers, Lobbyists, and the Unlikely Triumph of Tax Reform* (New York: Random House, 1987).
26 David E. Rosenbaum, "The Tax Reform Act of 1986: How the Measure Came Together; a Tax Bill for the Textbooks." *New York Times* (October 23, 1986): D 16. Available at www.nytimes.com/1986/10/23/business/tax-reform-act-1986-measure-came-together-tax-bill-for-textbooks.html.

27 For an overview of the key provisions of TRA, see US Congress, Joint Committee on Taxation, *General Explanation of the Tax Reform Act of 1986* (H.R. 3838, 99th Congress; Public Law 99-514) (Washington, DC: Government Printing Office, 1986).
28 Alan J. Auerbach and Joel Slemrod, "The Economic Effects of the Tax Reform Act of 1986," *Journal of Economic Literature,* 37, 2 (1997): 595.
29 US Congress, Joint Committee on Taxation, *General Explanation of the Tax Reform Act of 1986*), 8.
30 Thomas Piketty and Emmanuel Saez, "How Progressive is the U.S. Federal Tax System? A Historical and International Perspective," *Journal of Economic Perspectives* 21,1 (2007): 13.
31 OMB, *Budget of the United States Government, Fiscal Year 2023,* Historical Tables, Table 2.2.
32 Ibid., Table 1.3.
33 Ippolito, *Deficits, Debt, and the New Politics of Taxation*, 144.
34 OMB, *Budget of the United States Government, Fiscal Year 2023,* Historical Tables, Tables 8.3 and 8.4.
35 Ibid., Table 8.2.
36 Ibid., Tables 8.3 and 8.4.
37 Quoted in Martin Tolchin, "Paradox of Reagan Budgets: Austere Talk vs. Record Debt," *New York Times,* February 16, 1988: A, 1. Available at www.nytimes.com/1988/02/16/us/paradox-of-reagan-budgets-austere-talk-vs-record-debt.html
38 OMB, *Budget of the United States Government, Fiscal Year 2023,* Historical Tables, Table 1.3.
39 Ibid., Table 7.1.
40 Herbert Stein, *Presidential Economics: The Making of Economic Policy from Roosevelt to Clinton,* 3rd ed. (Washington, DC: American Enterprise Institute, 1994), 292–93.
41 Ronald Reagan, "Remarks at a Rally Supporting the Proposed Constitutional Amendment for a Balanced Federal Budget, July 19, 1982." Available at www.presidency.ucsb.edu/node/245983
42 OMB, *Budget of the United States Government, Fiscal Year 2023,* Historical Tables, Table 7.1.
43 Ronald Reagan, "Remarks on Signing the Tax Reform Act of 1986," October 22, 1986. Available at www.presidency.ucsb.edu/node/254172
44 Timothy Naftali, *George H.W. Bush* (New York: Times Books, 2007), 54–55.
45 OMB, *Budget of the United States Government, Fiscal Year 2023,* Historical Tables, Table 1.2.
46 Ibid.
47 Jasmine Farrier, *Passing the Buck: Congress, the Budget, and Deficits* (Lexington: University of Kentucky Press, 2004), 137, 151.
48 Brownlee, *Federal Taxation in America,* 202.
49 Congressional Budget Office, *Economic and Budget Outlook: An Update* (Washington, DC: Congressional Budget Office, 1993), 31.
50 "The 1993 Reconciliation Act: How It Was Written," *CQ Weekly* (December 18, 1993): 5–21. Available at http://library.cqpress.com/cqmagazine/WR103403227.
51 Quoted in David E. Rosenbaum. "The Budget Struggle; House Passes Budget Plan, Backing Clinton by 218–216 after Hectic Maneuvering," *New York Times,* August 6, 1993, A1. Available at www.nytimes.com/1993/08/06/us/budget-struggle-house-passes-budget-plan-backing-clinton-218-216-after-hectic.html.

52 Michael Meeropol, *Surrender: How the Clinton Administration Completed the Reagan Revolution* (Ann Arbor: University of Michigan Press, 1998), 236.
53 Newt Gingrich, *To Renew America* (New York: HarperCollins, 1995), 89.
54 George H. Nash, *The Conservative Intellectual Movement in America Since 1945* (Wilmington, DE: Intercollegiate Studies Institute, 1996). 322.
55 See Frank S. Meyer, *In Defense of Freedom and Related Essays* (Indianapolis: Liberty Fund, 1996).
56 Nash, *The Conservative Intellectual Movement in America,* 339.
57 Quoted in Richard Meagher, "Death and Taxes: Issue Framing and Conservative Coalition Maintenance," *Political Science Quarterly,* 128, 3 (2013): 538.
58 Jacob S. Hacker and Paul Pierson, "Tax Politics and the Struggle over Activist Government," in *The Transformation of American Politics: Activist Government and the Rise of Conservatism*, ed. Paul Pierson and Theda Skocpol (Princeton: Princeton University Press, 2007), 267.
59 See Jacob S. Hacker and Paul Pierson, *The Republican Revolution and the Erosion of American Democracy* (New Haven: Yale University Press, 2005), 135–62.
60 Thomas B. Edsall, *Building Red America: The New Conservative Coalition and the Drive for Permanent Power* (New York: Basic Books, 2006), 46.
61 Michael J. Graetz and Ian Shapiro, *Death by a Thousand Cuts: The Fight over Taxing Inherited Wealth* (Princeton: Princeton University Press, 2005), 27. See Nicholas Confessore, "Breaking the Code," *New York Times*, January 16, 2005. Available at www.nytimes.com/2005/01/16/magazine/breaking-the-code.html
62 See David S. Cloud, "GOP's Balancing Act Gets Tricky As Budget Amendment Sinks," *CQ Weekly* (March 4, 1995): 671–76. Available at http://library.cqpress.com/cqmagazine/WR407313.
63 "Taking Speaker's Mantle, Gingrich Vows 'Profound Transformation'," *CQ Almanac 1994*, 50th ed. (Washington, DC: Congressional Quarterly, 1995). Available at http://library.cqpress.com/cqalmanac/cqal94-843-25141-1102119.
64 See Phillip Winters, *Budget for FY1996: Congressional Budget Resolutions,* CRS Report 94-744 E (Washington, DC: Congressional Research Service, 1995).
65 George Hager, "Clinton Shifts Tactics, Proposes Erasing Deficit in 10 Years," *CQ Weekly* (June 17, 1995): 1715-20. Available at http://library.cqpress.com/cqmagazine/WR408127.
66 George Hager and David S. Cloud. "Clinton and Congress Speeding Toward Collision Over Budget," *CQ Weekly* (September 2, 1995): 2611–13. Available at http://library.cqpress.com/cqmagazine/WR408756.
67 See Ippolito, *Why Budgets Matter*, 263–70.
68 Jeffrey L. Katz, "Clinton Vows to Veto Overhaul Measure," *CQ Weekly* (December 23, 1995): 3889–91, available at http://library.cqpress.com/cqmagazine/WR409695, and Jeffrey L. Katz, "WELFARE: Conference Report Highlights," *CQ Weekly* (December 23, 1995): 3890, available at http://library.cqpress.com/cqmagazine/WR409692.
69 See Gene Falk, *The Temporary Assistance for Needy Families (TANF) Block Grant: A Legislative History,* CRS Report R44668 (Washington, DC: Congressional Research Service, 2021).
70 Congressional Quarterly, "Pact Aims to Erase Deficit by 2002," In *CQ Almanac 1997*, 53rd ed. (Washington, DC: Congressional Quarterly, 1998), 2:18–23 Available at http://library.cqpress.com/cqalmanac/cqal97-0000181047.

71 George Hager, "Clinton, GOP Congress Strike Historic Budget Agreement." *CQ Weekly* (May 3, 1997): 993–97. Available at http://library.cqpress.com/cqmagazine/WR10519970503-18BUDGET001.

72 Jennifer O'Sullivan, Celinda Franco, Beth C. Fuchs, and Kathleen S. Swendiman, *Medicare Provisions in the Balanced Budget Act of 1997 (BBA 97, P.L. 105-33),* CRS Report 97-802 (Washington, DC: Congressional Research Service, 1997), 47-58, 21-22.

73 See Elicia J. Herz, Chris L. Peterson, and Evelyne P. Baumrucker, *State Children's Helath Insurance Program (CHIP) Legislative History,* CRS Report R40229 (Washington, DC: Congressional Research Service, 2009).

74 Ippolito, *Deficits, Debt, and the New Politics of Tax Policy,* 189–90, and Congressional Quarterly, "LEGISLATIVE OUTLOOK: SOCIAL POLICY," *CQ Weekly* (August 30, 1997): 2017–24, available at http://library.cqpress.com/cqmagazine/WR19970830-34SOCIALPOLICY001.

75 See David L. Brumbaugh, *The Taxpayer Relief Act of 1997: An Overview,* CRS Report 97-854 (Washington, DC: Congressional Research Service, 1997).

76 See Jonathan Weisman, "TAXES: Experts Calculate Rate of Pain From 'Taxpayer Relief Act'," *CQ Weekly* (December 20, 1997): 3120-22, available at http://library.cqpress.com/cqmagazine/WR19971220-50IRSFORM001.

77 See Robert Keith, *Budget Enforcement Act of 1997: Summary and Legislative History,* CRS Report 97-931 (Washington, DC: Congressional Research Service, 1997).

78 OMB, *Budget of the United States Government, Fiscal Year 2023,* Historical Tables, Table 1.2.

79 Ibid., Table 8.3.

8

BUDGETING IN HARD TIMES

Polarization, Gridlock, and Crisis

In 2000, thanks to the policies and procedures put into place during the 1990s reinforced by an extended period of economic growth, the budget was in surplus. The debt-to-GDP ratio had begun to decline for the first time since the early 1970s. The Cold War was over, the economy was expanding, and the stock market and homeownership rates were breaking new records. The fiscal imbalances of the Reagan years faded in relevance and projections of future surpluses created rare conditions for both presidential contenders. No one could have predicted the chaotic conditions and the rapid deterioration of the nation's finances that would mark the two-term presidencies of George W. Bush and Barack Obama, the subject of this chapter. A terrorist attack and two protracted wars stood as a stark reminder that the end of the Cold War did not guarantee international stability. The financial crisis and the Great Recession revealed that the "great moderation" of the Greenspan years was fragile. The costs of these events, when combined with deep tax cuts and escalating disorder in a budgetary process torn by political polarization proved that the fiscal victories of the late 1990s were tenuous, less the beginning of a new period of deleveraging than a temporary respite.

Before turning to the narrative, let us briefly review the fiscal record of the period. During the years covered by this chapter, outlays increased significantly relative to GDP while receipts moved in the opposite direction. Between 2000 and 2015, the debt held by the public more than doubled, from 33.7 to 72.5 percent of GDP, a level not witnessed since 1950 when the United States was still grappling with fiscal legacy of World War II (see Table 8.1). With respect to categories of spending, programmatic mandatory spending increased over the period, both as a share of GDP and outlays (see Tables 8.2 and 8.3). The spike

DOI: 10.4324/9781003395331-10

TABLE 8.1 Summary of Outlays, Receipts, Deficits/Surpluses, and Debt, 2000–2015 (Percentage of GDP)

Fiscal Year	*Outlays*	*Receipts*	*Surplus or Deficit (–)*	*Publicly Held Debt*
2000	17.7%	20.0%	2.3%	33.7%
2005	19.3	16.8	–2.5	35.8
2010	23.2	14.5	–8.7	60.6
2015	20.4	18.0	–2.4	72.5

Source: Office of Management and Budget, *Budget of the United States Government, Fiscal Year 2023* (Washington, DC: Government Publishing Office, 2022), Historical Tables, Tables 1.2, 7.1.

TABLE 8.2 Composition of Outlays, Budget Enforcement Act Categories, 2000–2016 (Percentage of GDP)

Fiscal Year	*Total Outlays*	*Discretionary*		*Mandatory*	
		Defense	*Nondefense*	*Programmatic**	*Net Interest*
2000	17.7%	2.9%	3.2%	9.8%	2.2%
2001	17.7	2.9	3.3	10.0	2.0
2002	18.6	3.2	3.6	10.7	1.6
2003	19.2	3.6	3.7	11.0	1.4
2004	19.1	3.8	3.7	10.8	1.3
2005	19.3	3.8	3.7	10.8	1.4
2006	19.5	3.8	3.6	10.9	1.7
2007	19.1	3.8	3.5	10.7	1.7
2008	20.2	4.1	3.5	11.4	1.7
2009	24.3	4.5	4.0	15.1	1.3
2010	23.2	4.6	4.4	13.4	1.3
2011	23.3	4.5	4.2	13.7	1.5
2012	21.9	4.2	3.8	13.2	1.4
2013	20.7	3.8	3.5	12.7	1.3
2014	20.2	3.4	3.4	12.6	1.3
2015	20.4	3.2	3.3	13.3	1.2
2016	20.8	3.2	3.2	13.6	1.3

* Does not include undistributed offsetting receipts.

Source: Office of Management and Budget, *Budget of the United States Government, Fiscal Year 2023* (Washington, DC: Government Publishing Office, 2022), Historical Tables, Table 8.4.

in mandatory spending to a peak of 15.1 percent of GDP and 62.1 percent of outlays in 2009 was a product of the financial crisis and the recession. But the drama of the financial collapse should not obscure the larger trend. In 2000, programmatic mandatory spending was 9.8 percent of GDP and 55.6 percent of outlays, numbers that would grow to 13.6 and 65.5 percent, respectively, by

TABLE 8.3 Composition of Outlays, Budget Enforcement Act Categories 2000–2016 (Percentage of Outlays)

Fiscal Year	*Discretionary*		*Mandatory*	
	Defense	*Nondefense*	*Programmatic**	*Net Interest*
2000	16.5%	17.9%	55.6%	12.5%
2001	16.4	18.4	56.6	11.1
2002	17.4	19.1	57.4	8.5
2003	18.7	19.4	57.3	7.1
2004	19.8	19.2	56.5	7.0
2005	20.0	19.2	56.0	7.4
2006	19.6	18.7	55.7	8.5
2007	20.1	18.1	56.2	8.7
2008	20.5	17.5	56.4	8.5
2009	18.7	16.5	62.1	5.3
2010	19.9	19.0	57.7	5.7
2011	19.4	18.0	58.7	6.4
2012	19.0	17.2	60.5	6.2
2013	18.1	16.7	61.5	6.4
2014	17.0	16.6	62.4	6.5
2015	15.8	15.9	65.3	6.0
2016	15.2	15.6	65.5	6.2

* Does not include undistributed offsetting receipts.

Source: Office of Management and Budget, *Budget of the United States Government, Fiscal Year 2023* (Washington, DC: Government Publishing Office, 2022), Historical Tables, Table 8.3.

2016. None of this should be surprising given that the aging of the baby boom generation. Net interest, fortunately, declined during the period, reflecting the broad demand for US debt which only intensified in the uncertain environment surrounding the financial crisis and the subsequent recession. This allowed discretionary spending to remain relatively stable as a share of gross domestic product (GDP), while falling as a share of overall outlays (from 34.4 to 30.8 percent).[1]

As noted in Table 8.1, revenues fell during the period as a share of GDP. But there were also important changes in the composition of revenues (see Tables 8.4 and 8.5). As a result of the Bush tax cuts, the individual income tax fell from 49.6 percent of revenues to a range of 43 – 43.4 percent of revenues in 2004–2006. During this same period, as much of the progressivity was stripped from the income tax, the share of revenues generated by social insurance or payroll taxes increased from 32.2 percent (2000) to a pre-recession peak of 40 percent (2003). As the Great Recession took hold, the individual income tax and the payroll tax approached parity, such that by 2010 they were generating 41.5 and 40 percent of revenues, respectively. This trend would

TABLE 8.4 Percentage Composition of Federal Revenues by Source, 2000–2015

Fiscal Year	*Individual Income Tax*	*Corporate Income Tax*	*Social Insurance Tax*	*Excise Tax*	*Other*
2000	49.6%	10.2%	32.2%	3.4%	4.5%
2005	43.1	12.9	36.9	3.4	3.8
2010	41.5	8.9	40.0	3.1	6.5
2015	47.4	10.6	32.8	3.0	6.2

Source: Office of Management and Budget, *Budget of the United States Government, Fiscal Year 2023* (Washington, DC: Government Publishing Office, 2022), Historical Tables, Table 2.2.

TABLE 8.5 Composition of Federal Revenues by Source, 2000–2015 (Percentage of GDP)

Fiscal Year	*Individual Income Tax*	*Corporate Income Tax*	*Social Insurance Tax*	*Excise Tax*	*Other*
2000	9.9%	2.0%	6.5%	0.7%	0.9%
2005	7.2	2.2	6.2	0.6	0.6
2010	6.0	1.3	5.8	0.4	0.9
2015	8.5	1.9	5.9	0.5	1.1

Source: Office of Management and Budget, *Budget of the United States Government, Fiscal Year 2023* (Washington, DC: Government Publishing Office, 2022), Historical Tables, Table 2.3.

be partially reversed once some of the Bush-era tax cuts for high-income households expired.[2]

The Budgetary Process in Disarray

Regular order in the budget process began to fray in the 1980s. As Congress adopted various procedural remedies to control deficits, budget resolutions lost much of their importance. Moreover, as mandatory spending claimed an ever-greater share of outlays, the pressures placed on discretionary spending raised the level of conflict intrinsic to the budgetary process. Everything was complicated by two factors. First, the growing problem of political polarization. While this trend was clear in the 1990s, during the post-2000 period, Congress experienced the highest levels of polarization since the end of Reconstruction. Parties became adept at exploiting budget reconciliation to translate narrow majorities into significant policy change. Minorities in the Senate became committed to using parliamentary maneuvers to block the majority. Second, disarray emerged from the extraordinary number of crises in the period which created incentives to work outside of the budget process. Let us consider these factors in turn.

Polarization versus Process

Legislating is an intrinsically difficult process, particularly when the issues at hand are complex or highly salient. Intraparty consensus can be difficult to build in the House, given the diversity of ideological and sectional constituencies. And legislating becomes ever more difficult given the supermajorities required to surmount the Senate filibuster and a presidential veto. Even under conditions of unified control, the majority frequently needs to rely on support from the minority to move important legislative initiatives and rarely enacts most of its top priorities. In the immediate postwar decades, coalition building was facilitated by the greater diversity of factions and a wide range of overlapping positions on key policies. Republicans could enlist the support of conservative Southern Democrats; Democrats could rely on moderate Eastern Republicans. But as a result of a long process of ideological sorting that many date to the passage of the Civil Rights Act of 1964 and the Voting Rights Act of 1965, the two parties became, increasingly, ideologically and geographically distinct.[3] Conservative Southern Democrats, most notably, gravitated to the Republican Party. The moderates who were once available for coalition-building declined in number. Simultaneously, majorities have been relatively thin compared with the early decades of the postwar period, accentuating intraparty differences. Given the greater ideological distance between parties, there are fewer centrists available for coalition building and efforts to attract their support can endanger intraparty consensus.[4]

During the past several decades, congressional leaders of both parties have adapted to the new polarized environment. Regular order, which used to be observed as the norm in the legislative process, has been supplanted by what Barbara Sinclair refers to as "unorthodox lawmaking."[5] Party leaders play a central role in shaping key legislative proposals, often bypassing the committee system, and then moving them rapidly through the legislative process. In the House, they have relied on their control of the Rules Committee to obtain closed or restricted rules to limit amendments from the floor. Of course, this assumes that the Speaker can overcome intraparty divisions, a precondition of bringing legislation to a vote. In recent years, successive Speakers have been unwilling to bring legislation to the floor unless there is majority support within their party caucus.[6] While the rules governing the legislative process in the House have allowed even narrow majorities to move legislation over the objections of the minority, the Senate is a much different institution. The majority leader may seek to limit the opportunities for amending legislation, but the threat or reality of a filibuster magnifies the power of the minority. As Sarah A. Binder and Frances E. Lee explain, "Given the Senate's supermajority procedures, increased intraparty homogeneity coupled with partisan conflict has rendered Senate obstruction rampant, with the minority party deploying the filibuster as a veto against the majority party's legislative agenda."[7] A chamber once renowned for its norms of collegiality has become rife with conflict, undermining the legislative productivity of Congress as a whole.

Unsurprisingly, polarization has found an expression in the budget process. The Budget Committees have become, largely, "instruments of the House and Senate Party leadership."[8] The majority is increasingly unwilling to engage in deliberation with the minority or to consider minority amendments, raising the incentives for obstructionism.[9] The reality of a unified minority party, when combined with the majority's difficulties in managing intraparty factions, may lead to the decision to never schedule a vote on budget resolutions. Assuming that the House passes appropriations bills, they frequently languish in the Senate. The majority leaders do not want to provide the minority with opportunities to introduce amendments that would embarrass the majority and resort to (or threaten) filibusters that would displace the consideration of other legislation. "The net effect of these tactics," Peter C. Hanson explains, "is to persuade the majority party to pull appropriations bills from the floor before a vote, or not to bring them to the floor at all." Congress may pass continuing resolutions (CRs) as a short-term expedient as the end of the fiscal year approaches, only to consolidate appropriations bills into omnibus spending bills that are passed without sustained debate. As Hanson notes

> limiting scrutiny is the goal. Leaders count on end-of-session pressures and the fear of a government shutdown to allow adoption of the package with minimal debate. In their view, it's the only way to push a budget through the gridlocked Senate floor.[10]

In the end, regular order is displaced by political necessity.

As explained in Chapter 7, the embrace of low taxes became the defining feature of the conservative coalition during the late 1980s and 1990s. The challenge of pursuing this goal in an age of polarization and razor-thin majorities has been met through the budget reconciliation process, which provides a means of negotiating the unique procedural features of the Senate. If the commitment to low taxes has become a constant, the embrace of fiscal restraint has proven highly variable, contingent on the party in control of the White House. In the 1990s, for example, President Clinton was successful in blocking tax cuts whereas the Grand Old Party (GOP) restrained domestic spending in the name of balanced budgets. This can be contrasted with the two-term presidency of George W. Bush (2001–2009), where the decisions to expand entitlement spending and fund two wars off-budget were combined with the repeated use of reconciliation to secure and extend tax cuts, despite the resulting deficit projections.[11] The Republican call for austerity would be renewed during the Obama presidency (2009–2017). The rise of the Tea Party and the GOP's Freedom Caucus led to ongoing battles to force fiscal restraint and to extend the Bush tax cuts, leading to brinksmanship surrounding the debt ceiling and the passage of appropriations. The only point of consistency was the ongoing Republican support for a low tax regime.

Budgeting under Conditions of Crisis

The period examined in this chapter was by any measure among the most turbulent of the postwar period. The decade began with a softening economy. As a result of what the Council of Economic Advisors (CEA) referred to as "a confluence of a series of unforeseen events" (e.g., the collapse of a speculative bubble in the tech-heavy NASDQ, rising interest rates and energy prices), the nation experienced a dramatic "deceleration of economic activity," bringing an end to a decade-long expansion. The slowing economy, when combined with large budget surpluses, was used to justify the passage of the largest tax cut since 1981. While there were hopes that the economy would return to expansion, these hopes were dashed on September 11, 2001. As the CEA noted: "The decline in consumer and business confidence following the terrorist attacks in September ... was sufficient to scuttle any possibility of avoiding a recession."[12] The National Bureau of Economic Research determines the dating of recessions, which requires, among other things, a decline in GDP for two quarters. While it is impossible to know how long the 2001 recession might have lasted absent the terrorist attacks—or whether it would have met the criteria for a recession—the Bureau determined that it lasted eight months, from March to November 2001. Unemployment, a lagging indicator, increased from 4.3 percent in March 2001 to a peak of 6.3 percent in June of 2003, before entering a decline to a low of 4.4 percent by the end of 2006.[13]

The fiscal consequences of the terrorist attacks were significant. On October 7, 2001, the US launched Operation Enduring Freedom against Al Qaeda and Taliban forces in Afghanistan, beginning what would become the longest military engagement in US history. On March 20, 2003, the United States expanded the conflict to Iraq, over claims that the regime had been developing weapons of mass destruction and harboring terrorists. While Operation Iraqi Freedom would not be as protracted as the 20-year war in Afghanistan, the continuing support for security and reconstruction and subsequent intervention against the Islamic State of Iraq and Syria would impose ongoing costs. Between September 11, 2001, and the end of FY2019, the costs of war-related activities would amount to some $1.6 trillion, an average expenditure of $4.2 billion per month.[14] These costs, first classified under the Global War on Terror and subsequently Overseas Contingency Operations, occurred separate from normal defense appropriations. As the Congressional Research Service noted: "At the outset of conflict, Congress has typically provided supplemental appropriations" and then "war funding was gradually incorporated into the annual base budgeting process." The funding for these conflicts has "broken this mold with the persistent use of a separate designation to pay for prolonged military operations."[15]

While the dual wars in Afghanistan and Iraq demanded high levels of spending, the decade was also marked by a number of natural disasters, particularly during the Bush presidency. The average annual number of major disaster declarations increased from 45.8 in the 1990s to 57.1 for the period 2000–2009. The most salient disasters occurred in 2005, as the hurricane season set a record both for the number of hurricanes and their severity. Three major storms—Katrina, Rita, and Wilma—left much of the Gulf Coast devastated. Most of the media attention focused on Hurricane Katrina, which forced the evacuation of 1.2 million people from metropolitan New Orleans, killed some 1,800 people, left 300,000 homes destroyed or uninhabitable, and imposed economic losses of between $125 and $150 billion. While the 2008 hurricane season was less severe, Gustav and Ike were both costly and deadly disasters. Over the 2005–2009 period, Congress responded to the hurricanes by passing eight emergency supplemental appropriations acts and providing additional resources through reconciliation and a CR. The total disaster spending during this four-year period was $121.7 billion.[16]

The fiscal impact of natural disasters paled in comparison with the economic disaster that ended the decade. Under normal circumstances, one would have expected 2008 to be a complicated year, given the impending presidential and congressional elections. But things would become far more chaotic as the collapse of the subprime mortgage market gave rise to a jarring financial crisis that quickly assumed global dimensions and left the nation in what would be known as the Great Recession. At the year's start, there was little sense of the cataclysmic events that would consume the upcoming months. The President's budget for FY2009 recognized that the economy was facing "significant headwinds." But the "current expectation [was] for ongoing growth" as problems in the housing market were resolved. Various forms of temporary assistance were provided in the Economic Stimulus Act of 2008, which delivered tax rebates to households and additional tax incentives for business, reducing revenues by $152 billion and $16 billion, respectively, in FY2008 and 2009. The Bush administration deemed this an adequate response and rejected "any costly 'bailout' … for individuals or institutions that had taken on excessive speculative risk," thereby "avoiding the longer-run costs from a perception of the Government bearing the cost of risky speculation or reckless financial decisions."[17]

But over the course of the next months, the economic crisis led to a wave of housing foreclosures and, by summer, many of the financial institutions that had been foundational to Wall Street were in ruin. The Dow Jones Industrial Average shed 18 percent of its value in a single week. Credit markets seized up and the turmoil spread into the broader economy. The unemployment rate increased from 5 to 7.3 percent, and with it, the demand for government assistance. The administration that cited the problem of moral hazard in its rejection of "costly bailouts" was forced to ask Congress to pass the Emergency Economic Stabilization Act of 2008 to authorize the purchase of some $700 billion in troubled assets from banks.[18] Barack Obama, elected President amid the crisis, worked quickly with Congress to craft the American Recovery and Reinvestment Act of 2009. At the time of passage, it was projected to add $787.2 billion to the debt over the next decade (the CBO would subsequently revise the cost estimate to $831 billion).[19] Of this sum, $575.3 billion would take the form of increased spending, with the remainder in tax cuts. Some of the spending provided support for extended unemployment, nutritional assistance, and construction projects; assistance was also provided to state and local governments that were struggling with revenue shortfalls. Economic stimulus, automatic stabilizers, and reduced revenues combined to create successive deficits in excess of $1 trillion, the largest of the postwar period.[20]

Thus, as the budget process became increasingly disorderly and often appeared to be a stage for larger partisan conflicts, policymakers were forced to respond to a sequence of crisis—some a product of choice, others exogenous shocks—that would carry important fiscal implications. Hoping to preserve the illusion of fiscal prudence, Congress often succumbed to the temptation to further depart from the established budget process (e.g., by funding extended wars through emergency supplemental appropriations). Presidents and Congress could accept projections of discretionary spending knowing full well that they did not incorporate major fiscal commitments that would be made off budget.

The Bush Releverage

The budget surplus in 2000 created unique conditions for an election year. As Adam Clymer observed in the *New York Times*:

> This is the first presidential election in memory when the candidates have a budget surplus to discuss, not a deficit, and their sharply contradictory approaches on how to use it are perhaps the biggest differences between Vice President Al Gore and Gov. George W. Bush of Texas.

Although both promoted tax cuts, the reductions proposed by candidate Bush were far larger than those of his opponent. And whereas Bush derided Gore's plans for additional spending, he claimed that he would pressure Congress to hold spending growth below inflation, thereby allowing him to assume larger projected surpluses that could be devoted to tax cuts.[21] As a result of the elections, the government was under unified Republican control for the first time since the Eisenhower presidency. Yet, control was fragile. Bush had won the presidency after a contested vote count in Florida.[22] In Congress, Republican majorities were thin, with a 221–212 margin in the House and an equally divided

Senate where control rested on the tie-breaking vote of Vice President Dick Cheney. By June of 2001, Senator Jim Jeffords (R-VT) renounced his membership in the GOP to caucus with the Democrats, resulting in a shift in party control of the chamber. The Republican Party would regain control in the 2002 midterms, expanding its majority in the House (229–204) and reclaiming control of the Senate (51–49). The growing ideological divide between the two parties and the narrow majorities forced an ongoing reliance on parliamentary maneuvers to secure or impede the passage of legislation.

President Bush's first budget, *A Blueprint for New Beginnings*, set out major policy initiatives, including paying down the federal debt and providing tax relief. The administration pledged to "accelerate" the trend of debt reduction "to record rates by retiring a historic $2 trillion in debt over the next 10 years," to a projected 7 percent of GDP. A greater reduction in the debt could not be achieved because "annual surpluses begin to outstrip the amount of maturing debt starting in 2007." Further reductions would force the Treasury to pay premiums to bondholders who relinquished their securities before maturity.[23] The second priority, providing tax relief, was framed in supply-side terms. "Reduced tax burdens give workers a greater incentive to work harder," the administration claimed, and "entrepreneurs a greater incentive to reinvest in their businesses and in turn, to hire more workers." While tax cuts would seem to stand at tension with debt reduction, they were deemed "fiscally responsible" insofar as they would account "for roughly one quarter of the projected 10-year budget surplus and only six percent of total projected tax receipts over this period." Given that projected surpluses would outstrip the debt that could be retired, the administration cited the advice of Federal Reserve Chairman Alan Greenspan that tax cuts could "pre-empt an accumulation of excess cash."[24]

Congress passed the budget resolution in May, with reconciliation instructions for a ten-year tax cut of some $1.35 trillion, less than the $1.6 trillion requested by the President. In less than a month, the Economic Growth and Tax Relief Reconciliation Act (EGTRRA) of 2001 had been signed into law.[25] Over the course of the next several months, congressional work on the appropriations bills proved contentious, reflecting the divided party control of Congress and, more importantly, September 11th and the subsequent anthrax attacks which derailed the consideration of these bills before the beginning of the fiscal year. Congress turned, instead, to the President's request for a $20 billion emergency supplemental appropriation to respond to 9/11, providing twice what the president requested. Following a series of CRs, Congress concluded its work on the appropriations bills, which were signed into law in December.[26]

The EGTRRA was the largest tax cut since the Economic Recovery Tax Act, passed two decades earlier. It phased in a reduction in individual tax rates (through 2010), with the top rate cut from 39.6 to 35 percent and the lowest bracket cut from 15 to 10 percent. It also phased in a reduction of the marriage penalty by doubling the standard deduction for married couples and temporarily increased the income threshold for the alternative minimum tax or AMT. In a nod to Senate moderates, it phased in a doubling of the Child Tax Credit, increased credits for childcare, credits and deductions for college education, and raised contribution limits to Individual Retirement Accounts. While the reduction in the lowest rate and the inclusion of more generous childcare credits were front-loaded thereby reducing the perceived distributional consequences of EGTRRA, there were several provisions targeted toward higher income earners. It included a repeal of the limit on itemized deductions for wealthier households and, most importantly, an increase of the estate tax exemption and ultimately, its repeal. These provisions, as the others, were phased in and, due to reconciliation, were scheduled to sunset after 2010.[27]

In 2002, the House budget resolution for FY2003 passed largely along party lines, but the Senate would prove problematic. Democrats had a one-vote majority and were internally divided between fiscal conservatives and liberals, who chafed under the reduced revenues from the tax cut and demanded more domestic social spending. Assuming that a budget resolution with the House would prove impossible, the Senate leadership never scheduled it for debate. The House passed a so-called deeming resolution so that it could develop spending bills under limits set in its resolution while the Senate proceeded under its own set of limits. Conflict was passed to appropriations, a series of CRs, and ultimately the next Congress.[28] While the normal budget process fell into disorder, Congress provided an emergency supplemental appropriation to fund the war on terror and the new Department of Homeland Security while exempting them from spending controls. By the end of the fiscal year, PAYGO provisions were allowed to expire and by December, Congress had passed, and Bush signed an act setting the balances on the PAYGO scorecard to zero, thereby ending sequestration.[29] The decision to jettison PAYGO was important for what it represented. As CBO Director Peter R. Orszag observed: "any set of rules tends to become less effective (or perhaps not effective at all) when the underlying objective no longer has support among policymakers."[30]

The Republicans prevailed in the 2002 midterms. While the margins were slim, the GOP opened the 108 Congress with unified control of government. After passing the Consolidated Appropriations Resolution to replace the CRs secured in the waning days of 2002, Congress passed a budget resolution for FY2004 which contained reconciliation instructions for another significant tax cut, the Jobs and Growth Tax Relief Reconciliation Act (JGTRRA) of 2003. It accelerated key provisions of the 2001 Act, including the rate cuts, the marriage penalty relief, and a Child Tax Credit expansion. In keeping with the 2001 Act, it provided additional benefits for higher income households. Top individual income tax rate on dividends and capital gains were reduced, while providing sizable increases in corporate depreciation allowances. Although there were some progressive elements to the two tax cuts, when combined with changes in top marginal rates, the repeal of the personal exemption phaseout, and the reduced dividend and capital gains tax rates, they lavished the greatest benefits on top income earners. Those in the 95–99th percentile enjoyed a 2.8 percent increase in after-tax income, whereas those in the top 1 percent witnessed an increase of 5.6 percent.[31] As for the fiscal effects, the Treasury concluded that EGTRRA reduced revenues an average of 3.6 percent over the four years following passage, whereas JGTRRA cut revenues by a more modest 2.5 percent over the next four years.[32] In previous wars, military mobilization had been financed, in part, through higher taxes. But during the Bush presidency, the dual wars were combined with tax cuts, thereby necessitating a higher reliance on debt. As W. Elliott Brownlee notes, the nation witnessed "heavier reliance on borrowing than in any time since World War II, heavier reliance on borrowing from abroad than at any time since the 1790s, and greater pressure on domestic discretionary spending than during the previous three presidential administrations."[33]

While Congress was cutting taxes, it was growing more expansive in spending. It passed two supplemental appropriation acts to deliver $166 billion for operations in Iraq. Of greater enduring consequence, Congress passed the Medicare Prescription Drug, Improvement, and Modernization Act of 2003, which constituted the largest expansion of the welfare state since the Johnson administration. It created a new prescription drug benefit (Medicare Part D) and a new Medicare Advantage Program to replace the existing Medicare Part C program (Medicare+Choice). Congressional efforts to cut reimbursement rates in the 1990s had led to a decline in the number of plans, leaving some beneficiaries involuntarily disenrolled. Congress anticipated that Medicare Advantage would fare better, particularly when combined with higher payments, thereby partially obviating the goal of cost containment.[34] While the Act included some cost-saving provisions and increased premiums for high income beneficiaries, the CBO projected that the changes in Medicare Part C would cost $14.2 billion and the new drug benefit would cost $409.8 billion over the next decade.[35] Disputes almost scuttled the Medicare reforms, pitting fiscal conservatives who objected to the creation of a new Part D against defenders of the program who believed the new Part C would destroy the fee-for-service program that was popular among senior citizens and their advocates.[36] As in earlier years, the regular appropriations process languished, forcing a series of CRs. Drawing on the example of the spring, Congress moved once again to pass the Consolidated Appropriations Act of 2004, which included the remainder of the appropriations.[37]

The Failed Quest for Deficit Control and Entitlement Reform

By 2004, the deficit had become increasingly salient to fiscal conservatives in the Senate. Between FY2001 and 2003, a surplus of $128.2 billion (1.2 percent

GDP) had turned into a deficit of $377.6 billion (3.3 percent GDP).[38] The Bush administration projected a deficit of $521 billion for FY2004, and the tax cuts and Medicare expansion of the previous year would only elevate the likelihood of greater deficits over time. Moderate Republicans in the Senate demanded a return to PAYGO provisions. Following the lead of the Bush administration, the Republican leadership in the House would consent to PAYGO only if it contained a five-year exemption for tax cuts advanced under reconciliation. With the realization that the so-called Gang of Moderates would reject this version of PAYGO, the Senate leadership once again failed to bring the resolution to the floor, forcing the two chambers to function under deeming resolutions. By the beginning of FY2005, only one appropriations act had been signed into law, forcing, once again, reliance on a series of CRs and the passage of a consolidated appropriations act in 2005.[39]

President Bush devoted part of his 2004 State of the Union—the last before his successful reelection campaign—to the goal of reducing the deficit by one-half over the next five years, largely by holding discretionary spending growth to less than 4 percent annually.[40] His FY2005 budget called for a 3.9 percent increase in discretionary spending, but it represented a 7.1 percent increase for defense, a 9.1 percent increase for homeland security, and 0.5 percent increase for the remainder of domestic discretionary spending.[41] In subsequent years, the president's budget would request even sharper limits on domestic discretionary spending, while emphasizing the need for expanded defense and homeland security spending. While deficit hawks may have welcomed the renewed focus on deficits, its effects were limited. Deficit control could not entail tax increases. The congressional budget resolution for FY2006, for example, included reconciliation instructions to reduce mandatory spending by $35 billion and to cut revenues by $70 billion. The Deficit Reduction Act of 2005 would meet the first goal through cuts in Medicare, Medicaid, student loans and agricultural subsidies, whereas the Tax Increase Prevention and Reconciliation Act of 2005 would extend some of the earlier tax cuts.[42] Moreover, the goal would not entail a return to regular order or the elimination of spending outside the budget process. By the beginning of FY2006, only two appropriations bills had been signed into law, forcing government by CR. The remaining bills were enacted on December 30, three months into the new fiscal year. In addition to its normal appropriations, Congress passed, at the administration's request, emergency supplemental appropriations. The first, the Emergency Supplemental Appropriations Act for Defense, the Global War on Terror, and Tsunami Relief provided $82 billion, whereas two supplemental appropriations provided $62.3 billion in FY2005 to respond to Hurricane Katrina.[43] The reliance on supplemental appropriations was of particular concern. The administration could announce its deficit reduction plans only to circumvent them by requesting tens of billions of dollars in off-budget spending. Congress, in turn, could comply with the President's requests while avoiding the difficult decisions that would need to be made if spending occurred within the budget process. The goal of controlling the deficit was compromised as Congress succumbed to the temptation to spend outside of the budget process and avoid tradeoffs.[44]

Entitlement reform was also on the Bush agenda. In 2000, candidate Bush had announced that partial privatization of Social Security would be a top priority. He proposed the creation of private accounts that would be funded with a portion of the payroll tax or with the budget surplus. The creation of private accounts with superior rates of return, it was argued, would help future beneficiaries build additional retirement savings before the trust fund became insolvent, which was projected, at that time, for 2038. In May 2001, Bush appointed a 16-member Commission to Strengthen Social Security and charged it with delivering recommendations by the fall. The prospects of reform were complicated by the tax cut—the administration's top priority—the recession, and new wartime spending, which devoured the surplus. Moreover, when the committee report supported partial privatization (albeit without endorsing a specific model), it noted the inevitability of benefit cuts and tax increases. Absent an impending crisis in the near term, there was little prospect of Republicans addressing the "third rail" of American politics during an election year. Entitlement reform would be deferred.[45]

With Bush's successful 2004 reelection, expectations were high that the President would return to his plan for partial privatization. But even if the GOP majority supported the broad goal of reform, there were deep divisions in the ranks over potential benefit cuts and the financing of new accounts. Congress was waiting for the President to lay out the specifics of his program. The leaders of the two chambers had reserved H.R. 1 and S.1 for reform legislation. While Bush devoted part of his second inaugural address to make the case for reform, the plan was short on details. By April 2005, the administration's proposal began to take shape. The two key elements were (1) private accounts for workers younger than 55 years old funded through a carve out from the payroll tax and (2) progressive indexing, which would change the formula for the calculation of benefits for higher income workers, thereby helping to eliminate part of the system's 75-year deficit.[46] By the fall, separate bills had been introduced in the House and the Senate with different funding mechanisms. The House bill would have funded accounts through general revenues whereas the Senate bill would have drawn on surpluses from the Social Security system. But the House Ways and Means Committee and the Senate Finance Committee did not schedule hearings. Intraparty disputes on several complex issues made it unlikely that any bill would pass absent support from the Democratic minority. It was unified in its opposition, raising the likelihood of a filibuster. Partial privatization and progressive indexing died a quiet death as the 2006 midterm year approached.[47]

In 2006, budgetary disorder continued. The House and Senate failed to resolve differences between their versions of the budget resolution, a product of intraparty rifts between fiscal conservatives and appropriators seeking to circumvent discretionary spending controls. Both chambers relied on deeming resolutions and only passed two of the regular appropriations bills (Defense and Homeland Security) before the start of the fiscal year, forcing a reliance on CRs and pushing the conflicts into the next Congress. Another point of continuity: Congress worked outside of the budget process, acceding to the president's requests for emergency supplemental appropriations to cover the ongoing costs of defense, the war on terror and hurricane recovery.[48]

The Return of Divided Government

In 2006, Democrats successfully framed the midterm election as a referendum on an unpopular war, the mishandling of Katrina, and fiscal irresponsibility. For the first time since the 1994 midterms, Democrats would exercise unified control of the Congress. The change in party control did not bring order to the budget process. While there was agreement on a budget resolution, appropriations bills languished, forcing a series of short-term CRs and a consolidated appropriations act, signed into law more than three months into the fiscal year.[49] But the Democratic Congress began to exercise the power of the purse in ways that would have been previously unimaginable. When the Bush administration submitted a request for supplemental appropriations for FY2007, most of which was to be devoted to the dual wars, Congress complied but required the President to report by July 1, whether Iraq had met specific security and political benchmarks; failure to issue a positive report would trigger automatic troops withdrawal, to be completed in 180 days (a positive report would simply delay redeployment until October 1). Bush vetoed the bill calling the deadline "arbitrary," decrying congressional attempts to "micromanage the commanders in the field" and "embolden our enemies."[50] He threatened to veto any subsequent bill that would impose similar conditions. Congress ultimately provided the supplemental appropriation but made future assistance contingent on progress toward a set of congressional benchmarks. Reflecting the change in party control, the bill included some unrequested domestic spending and some policy riders to circumvent the normal legislative process, the most notable of which provided additional funding for the Children's Health Insurance Program and the first increase in the minimum wage in more than a decade.[51]

By 2008, divided government was combined with a financial crisis and a rapidly deteriorating economy. The President's budget for FY2009 requested $2.931 trillion in outlays and projected a deficit of $407 billion for FY2008. The deficit had been projected at $162 billion a year earlier, but the weakening economy and the passage in January of a stimulus bill had significant consequences for spending and revenues.[52] Nonetheless, the administration seemed optimistic about the future, projecting that the deficits would turn to surpluses by 2012.

The House and Senate passed their budget resolutions and then arrived at a compromise of $2.94 trillion, above the amount requested by the President.[53] But with the collapse of the much of the financial sector in the summer of 2008, the crisis rendered any projections of future deficits or surpluses irrelevant. The new president, Barack Obama, would inherit a deep recession that would force sequential trillion-dollar deficits, the largest since World War II.

The Bush Record in Brief

In 2001, the surpluses and projections of future surpluses created an opportunity for the newly inaugurated President Bush to announce his priorities of tax cuts and debt retirement. But the tax cuts—when combined with the costs of the war on terror, the dual wars in Afghanistan and Iraq, the expansion of Medicare, and a sequence of natural disasters—quickly reversed the fiscal trajectory of the late 1990s. Policy choices and exogenous shocks coalesced to consume the surpluses that served as a premise for the Bush agenda. The administration's overtures toward fiscal responsibility in budget policy stood at odds with practices that exhibited little concern for the predictable costs of the wars that should have been incorporated into the Defense Department's base budget. Emergency supplementals could simultaneously reduce the estimates of the deficit and allow the administration to increase its discretionary authority over the funding for the war. The reliance on emergency supplementals was combined with various gimmicks to claim savings that would never materialize (e.g., Medicare cost reductions from the Sustainable Growth Rate or SGR formula were included in projections, even though Congress routinely suspended scheduled reductions in reimbursement). On the revenue side, the fiscal impact of the tax cuts was obscured by baseline assumptions and the numerous sunsets and extenders. Once again, revenue estimates were inflated through various expedients (e.g., incorporating projections of inflation-driven revenue increases from the Alternative Minimum Tax, even though it would subsequently work with Congress to suspend those increases).[54]

While the budgets of the period obscured the de facto fiscal policy, the empirical record is clear. Given that FY2008 was unusual given the unfolding of the financial crisis and deep recession, the most relevant comparisons are between FY2000 and FY2007. In 2000, discretionary spending constituted 6.1 percent of GDP (34.4 percent of total outlays). Of this sum, defense claimed 2.9 percent of GDP (16.5 percent of outlays) whereas non-defense discretionary spending accounted for 3.2 percent of GDP (17.9 percent of outlays). By 2007, discretionary spending had increased to 7.3 percent of GDP (38.2 percent of outlays); defense spending had grown to 3.8 percent of GDP (20.1 percent of outlays) and non-defense discretionary spending had grown to 3.5 percent of GDP (18.1 percent of outlays). In 2000, programmatic mandatory spending equaled 9.8 percent of GDP (55.6 percent of total outlays). By 2007, it had increased to 10.7 percent of GDP (56.2 percent of outlays). The only category that declined was the one least dependent on the Bush administration's policies: net interest. In 2000, interest on the debt claimed 2.2 percent of GDP (12.5 percent of outlays). By 2007, it had fallen to 1.7 percent of GDP (8.7 percent of outlays).[55]

What of the debt? The lower priority attached by the Bush administration and most congressional Republicans to the deficit and debt redemption marked a departure from the position struck by the GOP in the 1990s. Tax cuts had always been prized by the GOP. But the combination of successive tax cuts, increases in spending, and the expansion of Medicare raised concerns among the marginalized deficit hawks that the party had lost its moorings. Perhaps the shift was explained by a simple political calculus. Public opinion polling revealed that the deficit had lost the resonance that it had in the 1990s.[56] The National Association of Manufacturers, the US Chamber of Commerce, and the Business Roundtable—advocates of balanced budgets in the 1990s—were increasingly tolerant of deficits, particularly if they were accompanied by low interest rates and business tax cuts.[57] Moreover, there was little evidence that Republican legislators were rewarded for the surpluses of the late 1990s; most of the credit went to Clinton. In Congress, fiscal watchdogs do not garner the same support as legislators who expand popular spending programs. In this context, Bush's first Treasury Secretary Paul O'Neill provides a revealing vignette. When he raised concerns over the growth of long-term debt and the potential for a fiscal crisis with Vice-President Cheney, he was simply told that "Reagan proved deficits don't matter." Cheney continued: "We won the midterms. This is our due."[58] The Bush administration had proposed a combination broad-based tax cuts and debt reduction. The tax cuts were a primary fiscal legacy of the Bush presidency and the Republican Congress, but they could only be achieved through greater debt. By FY2007, the debt had grown to $5 trillion (35.2 percent GDP) and the next year, a deficit of 3.1 percent of GDP would drive the debt to $5.8 billion, or 39.4 percent of GDP, the highest debt-to-GDP ratio since 1998.[59]

The Great Recession and the Battle over Austerity

The chaotic economic conditions and the war in Iraq framed the 2008 elections. Senator Barack Obama (D-IL) was elected president and Democrats had a net gain of 21 seats in the House and eight seats in the Senate, allowing for unified control for the first time in 14 years. But this control would be exercised under difficult economic conditions and extreme levels of polarization. The recession was the deepest of the postwar period. Unemployment, which had reached a low of 4.4 percent in the spring of 2007, spiked to 10 percent by the fall of 2009.[60] As one might expect, federal revenues fell dramatically given the depth of the recession, from 17.1 percent of GDP in 2008 to 14.5 percent (2009 and 2010).[61] The collapse of revenues when combined with automatic stabilizers and the crisis-related stimulus packages produced a 2009 deficit of $1.4 trillion

(9.8 percent GDP), the largest since 1945, followed by three more years of deficits above $1 trillion.[62]

The response to the financial collapse, as noted earlier, began under Bush with the passage of the Economic Stimulus Act and the Emergency Economic Stabilization Act. The Obama administration worked closely with congressional Democrats to achieve passage of the $787 billion American Recovery and Reinvestment Act of 2009, a bill that attracted no Republican support in the House and three GOP votes in the Senate. In addition, Congress moved quickly to pass two of the more consequential statutes of the postwar period. The Dodd–Frank Wall Street Reform and Consumer Protection Act of 2010 made several reforms to the financial system in the wake of the recent crisis. The Patient Protection and Affordable Care Act (ACA) of 2010 marked the most significant reform in healthcare since the passage of the Social Security Amendments of 1965. It expanded health insurance coverage by imposing a personal mandate with income-based subsidies, extended Medicaid eligibility to 133 percent of the federal poverty line with full federal funding for the initial years, required insurance companies to provide coverage for young adults on their parents' policies, and banned discrimination based on pre-existing conditions.

The Tea Party and the Politics of Austerity

The dislocations of the Great Recession, the growth of the deficit and debt, and the expansion of the government's role in healthcare provision contributed to the rise of the Tea Party and its ascension would bring new calls for austerity. The Tea Party was, in part, a grassroots movement, a populist and libertarian reaction to the economic collapse and expansion of public spending. But, as Theda Skocpol and Vanessa Williamson note, the economic crisis also created an opening for a "panoply of national funders and ultra-free-market advocacy groups" that used the grassroots efforts to promote "their long-term goal of remaking the Republican Party, pushing it towards the hard right on matters of taxation, public spending, and government regulation," often buoyed by the conservative media.[63] The Tea Party and its institutional advocates were united behind a coalition of Republican congressional candidates demanding fiscal austerity. The first signs of trouble for Democrats emerged when the special election to fill the seat left vacant by the death of Senator Ted Kennedy (D-MA) brought the victory of Scott Brown, a Republican, thus ending the Democrats' filibuster-proof majority. During the next months of 2010, Republicans ran on a platform (The Pledge to America) that made several promises, including the extension of Bush-era tax cuts and a reduction of expenditures to 2008 levels, a feat that would require $100 billion in spending cuts in an economy mired in recession. In the 2010 midterm elections, the GOP added 63 seats in the House to gain control of the lower chamber and further deplete the Democrat's Senate majority.

President Obama had tried to preempt the critique of rising deficits before the midterm elections. On June 9, 2009, he submitted a legislative proposal for the Statutory Pay-As-You-Go Act. In his message to Congress, he noted that the current deficits were a product of the recession but also of "years of failing to pay for new policies—including large tax cuts that disproportionately benefited the affluent." The lack of "fiscal discipline contributed to transforming surpluses projected at the beginning of this decade into trillions of dollars in deficits."[64] Congressional Republicans strongly opposed the proposed legislation, despite the Tea Party's call for fiscal restraint.[65] Congress ultimately passed the Statutory Pay-As-You Go Act of 2010, with significant revisions, in combination with an increase in the debt ceiling. As with the earlier PAYGO mechanism, the new act focused on the budgetary consequences of revenue and mandatory spending, requiring that they not increase the deficit. Under the Act, the OMB would record costs and savings on two rolling PAYGO scorecards (5 and 10 year). In cases where there was a violation of the PAYGO requirements, the president would issue an across-the-board sequestration order in non-exempt programs. Unlike the earlier PAYGO program in effect during the 1990s, the new act carried no expiration date.[66]

The new PAYGO process—like the old one—had distinct limitations. At the broadest level, it did not carry implications for discretionary spending, or for existing revenue and mandatory spending programs; these could be addressed via the normal congressional budget process and reconciliation instructions. Second, Congress exempted from the PAYGO scorecards any costs designated as emergencies, the cost of legislation on "current policy" in four areas (Medicare physician payments, the estate and gift tax, the AMT, and middle-class tax cuts passed in 2001 and 2003), and any potential savings from a provision of the ACA that sought to create an insurance system for long-term care. Moreover, should sequestration be required, the Act exempted Social Security, railroad retirement benefits, federal employee and disability programs, veterans' programs, much of the social safety net, as well as refundable income tax credits and net interest. Medicare sequestration was limited to 4 percent. In practice, Congress would further blunt the impact of PAYGO by placing exclusionary provisions within legislation, a common means of extending or passing new tax cuts without triggering sequestration.[67]

In February 2010, Obama turned to create a special commission to address long-term fiscal issues that seemed to be beyond the reach of a broken budget process. Under Executive Order 13531, he established the National Commission on Fiscal Responsibility. The 18-members bipartisan commission, co-chaired by retired Senator Alan Simpson (R-WY) and former Clinton Chief of Staff Erskine Bowles, was given the task of developing a plan that would "balance the budget, excluding interest payments on the debt, by 2015" and "stabilize the debt-to-GDP ratio at an acceptable level once the economy recovers."[68] Its final report recommended mandatory caps for discretionary spending combined with entitlement reforms that would slow the growth of the costs of Medicare and Social Security (e.g., by raising the retirement age, changing the formula for cost-of-living adjustments, and increasing taxation of benefits). The tax reforms involved eliminating some tax expenditures and reducing marginal rates to 12, 22, and 28 percent. With federal outlays capped at 21 percent of GDP, the Commission projected that the deficit would fall to 2.3 percent of GDP by 2015, with a balanced budget thereafter.[69]

The Commission's work came under heavy criticism. Economist Paul Krugman objected to the recommendation to cap revenues at 21 percent of GDP, asking "why is a commission charged with finding every possible route to a balanced budget setting an upper (but not lower) limit on revenue?" He concluded: "as so often happens in modern Washington, a process meant to deal with real problems has been hijacked on behalf of an ideological agenda" that included the "same old tax cuts for the rich and erosion of the social safety net."[70] On the Right, the Heritage Foundation concluded that the target of 21 percent of GDP would require "the highest tax level in American history." The correct solution was to cut spending which "is driving long-term deficits," and then limit it "to the amount Washington has historically taxed—18 percent of GDP."[71] Under the executive order, the Commission's report required the approval of 14 of its 18 members. Alas, the final report failed to generate the needed support: seven members voted against the recommendations, including all three House Republicans, a group which included Rep. Paul Ryan (R-WI), ranking Republican member of the Budget Committee. With no budget resolution in place for 2011 and no appropriations bills passed by the beginning of the fiscal year, the federal government would be relying on CRs for funding.

The Budget Control Act of 2011

In 2011, the new House Republican majority made several rule changes that would prove consequential. It imposed a new CUTGO (or Cut-As-You-Go) rule, which applied to the net effects of new mandatory spending, but excluded the consideration of changes in revenues, allowing it to pursue additional tax cuts without considering the impact on deficits. Freshman Republicans who had run on a pledge of austerity found convenient opportunities for maximizing their influence. Each CR provided a chance to extract spending cuts; limitation amendments on appropriations proliferated, preventing agencies from using funds for specific policy-related activities. It repealed the Gephardt rule under which the budget resolution would automatically generate a joint resolution, deemed to have been passed by the House, authorizing an increase in the debt ceiling.[72] The repeal of the rule would set the stage for a significant conflict and the passage of the Budget Control Act.

In 2011, the debt ceiling, which stood at $14.3 trillion, and would soon prove insufficient absent legislative action. Treasury Secretary Timothy F. Geithner sought to prevent the use of the debt ceiling for political leverage, warning Congress in January that "even a very short-term or limited default would have catastrophic economic consequences that would last for decades."[73] But by May 16, Geithner was forced to announce that the Treasury had reached the statutory limit and declared a suspension in the issuance of debt. Nonetheless, by taking "extraordinary measures" the government could avoid default until August 2, 2011.[74] Over the course of the spring and summer, negotiations between the Obama administration and the Republican controlled House were conflict ridden, as Speaker John Boehner (R-OH) had little room for compromise given the intraparty divisions. A simple bill "to implement the President's request to increase the statutory limit on the public debt" to $16.7 trillion was defeated. In July, the House moved to pass the Tea Party-backed Cut, Cap, and Balance Act of 2011, which would have raised the debt ceiling in exchange for $111 billion cuts in domestic discretionary spending, caps on future spending to be enforced through mandatory sequestration, and passage of a balanced budget amendment to be transmitted to the states.[75] As Geithner would later recall: "Republican leaders knew the limit had to be raised to avoid a global financial meltdown. But they also recognized its value as a hostage." Given the role of Treasury debt in global financial markets, default "would have created an economic Armageddon."[76]

Finally, in the last week of July, both chambers simultaneously considered and passed the Budget Control Act (BCA), which was signed into law on August 2, 2011, the date the government was projected to go into default. It met the impending crisis, by raising the debt ceiling by $400 billion immediately and another $500 billion automatically if Congress failed to pass a joint resolution of disapproval. The increases in the debt ceiling were dependent on the enactment of spending cuts of $917 billion over the next decade. The BCA also authorized a subsequent increase in the debt ceiling of between $1.2 and $1.5 trillion. If Congress passed a balanced budget amendment and submitted it to the states for ratification, the debt ceiling would be raised by $1.5 trillion. Alternatively, if a newly created Joint Committee on Deficit Reduction successfully reported a bill recommending between $1.2 trillion and $1.5 trillion of additional cuts for FY2012–2021, the debt ceiling would be raised to match the sum. The Committee bill would be considered under expedited procedures, subject to a vote without amendments and limited debate (thus avoiding a potential filibuster). If it failed to generate or Congress failed to pass the deficit reduction plan, the BCA authorized an additional increase of $1.2 trillion in the debt ceiling. However, this would trigger the imposition of statutory limits on discretionary spending (divided equally between defense and non-defense spending) that would be reduced annually over the next decade (FY2012–2021). A failure to adhere to the statutory limits would be met with across-the-board sequestration. As in the past, several programs were exempted from sequestration. It was expected that this catastrophic trigger mechanism would create powerful incentives for Congress to develop a deficit reduction plan that reflected the larger priorities of the BCA's sponsors.[77]

Although Congress avoided "economic Armageddon," the conflicts of the past several months took a toll. In July, Standard & Poor's had warned that a failure to resolve the dispute over fiscal policy could force it to downgrade the credit rating on US debt. Even though Congress had narrowly avoided default with the last-minute passage of the BCA, S&P announced its decision to downgrade long-term debt from AAA to AA+ and simultaneously issued a "negative outlook" with respect to the United States reclaiming its AAA rating in the short term. S&P explained that it "reflects our opinion that the fiscal consolidation plan that Congress and the administration recently agreed to falls short of what, in our view, would be necessary to stabilize the government's medium-term debt dynamics." The stock market reacted by hemorrhaging 6.7 percent of its value. And while the other credit rating agencies—Fitch and Moody's Investor Services—refused to follow suit, the downgrade raised concerns. The *Wall Street Journal* warned that the downgrade "could serve as a psychological haymaker for an American economic recovery that can't find much traction, and could do more damage to investors' increasingly lack of faith in a political system that is struggling to reach consensus even on everyday policy matters."[78]

Although congressional Republicans had risked much to extract a major legislative concession, it was largely symbolic. The mandated balanced budget amendment failed to muster the necessary two-thirds vote in the House. The Joint Committee reached a stalemate and, by late November it announced that it would not be able to meet the deadline. By January of 2012, the Obama administration requested an increase in the debt ceiling, thereby initiating the mechanism presented in the BCA. But with the failure of the Joint Committee, a new fear emerged: the so-called fiscal cliff. Several Bush-era tax cuts secured via reconciliation were scheduled to expire at the end of the year along with some of the tax provisions introduced under the American Recovery and Reinvestment Act, while new taxes were to be imposed under the provisions of the ACA. Moreover, extended unemployment benefits and a temporary override of scheduled reductions in physician payments under Medicare were scheduled to expire. Combined with sequestration, the scheduled changes in policy could reduce the budget deficit. But would austerity push the nation back into recession?

Austerity Avoidance under the Budget Control Act

Congress and the Obama administration battled over the fiscal cliff in a presidential election year. Mitt Romney, former governor of Massachusetts and Budget Committee Chairman Paul Ryan were the Republican standard bearers. The Republican platform called for "immediate reductions in federal spending, as a down payment on the much larger task of long-range fiscal control."

Any progress toward fiscal control, however, would not be made through tax increases. The platform called for extending the Bush tax cuts, reducing marginal rates by 20 percent across-the-board while retaining revenue neutrality though the reform of tax expenditures, eliminating the taxes on interest, dividends, and capital gains for lower- and middle-income households, and the elimination of the AMT and the "death tax." To prevent future expansion of taxation, it proposed a constitutional amendment requiring a supermajority for tax increases, combined with a spending cap to restrain spending to the historical average percentage of GDP.[79] During the summer, Senate Democrats passed their proposal along party lines to end the Bush tax cuts for those earning over $250,000 while preserving domestic discretionary spending. The GOP-controlled House passed its proposal seeking to maintain the Bush tax cuts and reduce domestic discretionary spending. The two sides were at an impasse.

Following Obama's reelection, with modest Democratic gains in the House and Senate, the two parties were no less gridlocked than before the election. But with the fiscal cliff rapidly approaching, Congress came to an agreement. The American Taxpayer Relief Act of 2012, enacted January 3, 2013, postponed sequestration from January to March, cutting the spending reductions by $24 billion. While it allowed the Bush era rate changes to expire as scheduled for Americans earning more than $450,000, it made permanent the lower rates for low- and moderate-income households. The marginal rate on long-term capital gains, which had been reduced in 2003, was allowed to expire, as scheduled. The limitations of personal exemptions and itemized deductions for high-income households which had been reduced and then repealed under Bush were reinstated. The Act also expanded the EITC and the Child Tax Credit, both of which were important for low- and moderate-income families. The Act provided concessions to Republicans. The income exemption for the alternative minimum tax was not indexed for inflation, pushing a larger number of households into the AMT and forcing Congress to pass periodic "patches." The Act indexed the AMT exemption to inflation, thereby eliminating another vestige of bracket creep. More important, it made significant changes to the estate tax. Prior to 2001, the federal estate tax had provided a $1 million exemption and a top rate of 55 percent. The EGTRRA of 2001 had included a ten-year phaseout of the estate tax. But Congress had reinstated the estate tax in 2010, albeit with a $5 million exemption and a top rate of 35 percent. These provisions, which were scheduled to expire in 2012, would have returned the estate tax to pre-Bush levels. Instead, the $5 million exemption was retained and indexed for inflation, with a top rate of 40 percent.[80]

By the beginning of 2013, the federal government had reached, once again, the debt ceiling, forcing the Treasury to rely on extraordinary measures. Hoping to avoid a replay of 2011, Congress responded in a novel way: it suspended the debt ceiling for three months with the No Budget, No Pay Act of 2013. It permitted the Treasury to issue new debt during this period and then the debt ceiling would "reset" to reflect the new level of debt ($16.4 trillion plus borrowing during the suspension period). But with the reinstatement of the debt ceiling, the Treasury was once again forced to adopt extraordinary measures. By October 1, the failure of Congress to pass any of its appropriations bills for the new fiscal year or pass a CR, forced a partial government shutdown. In this case, the CR approved by the House would have prohibited funding of the ACA or delayed its implementation. Partisan battles over healthcare cascaded into battles over the budget.[81] In a decision that echoed the earlier debt crisis, Fitch Ratings placed the US credit rating on negative watch, citing "repeated brinksmanship over raising the debt ceiling."[82]

The federal government reopened after Congress passed a CR to provide funding through January 15, 2014, and simultaneously suspended the debt ceiling through February 7. Negotiations between Representative Paul Ryan and Senator Patty Murray (D-WA), chairs of the respective budget committees culminated in the Bipartisan Budget Act of 2013, a two-year budget agreement. Given that Congress had not produced a traditional budget resolution since 2009, there was some hope that a biennial agreement could bring greater coherence to a broken budget process. The scheduled reductions in spending limits under the BCA was a default that no one wanted to endure.[83] Without action, automatic cuts would have dug deeply into the Pentagon's budget and the funding for education, transportation, and social services. The Act once again softened the provisions of the BCA, raising the defense and domestic discretionary spending caps for FY2014–15, while extending the sequestration to FY2023. The cuts were partially offset by increased contribution requirements for civil service pensions, reductions in Medicare provider payments, and increased taxes on airline tickets.[84]

Despite the passage of the Bipartisan Budget Act of 2013, the federal government continued to grind against the debt ceiling. When the debt ceiling was reinstated in February, the Treasury was forced to use extraordinary measures which would do little more than prolong the crisis for a month. Once again, Congress suspended the debt ceiling until March 16, 2015, without conditions. By allowing the vote, House Speaker John Boehner (R-OH) signaled that he was bringing an end to "a three-year Tea Party-inspired era of budget showdowns that had raised the threat of default and government shutdowns, rattled economic confidence and brought serious scrutiny from other nations." The reaction of the Tea Party was predictable. As the co-founder of the Tea Party Patriots noted, the bill was a "complete capitulation" that demonstrated that Boehner had "lost the ability to lead the House … It is time for him to go."[85] The remainder of the year was characterized by disorder. Congress failed to pass any of its appropriations bills by the start of the new fiscal year, forcing a 16-day partial government shutdown; Homeland Security were funded through CR. A CR was passed on October 16 to end the government shutdown on the eve of the midterm elections. By December, Congress had passed the so called

"CRomnibus," a cross between a short-term CR for Homeland Security and an omnibus spending bill that would fund the rest of the government through September 2015. Although the CRomnibus contained 11 of the appropriations bills, it excluded the Department of Homeland Security—a Republican ploy to force Obama to revise his executive orders on immigration.[86] Ultimately, when the CR was about to expire, Congress passed an extension and then funded Homeland Security without extracting the concessions.

The 2014 Midterms brought significant gains for the Republicans. In the House, they added 13 seats, creating the largest GOP majority since the Hoover presidency. In the Senate, the Republicans added nine seats and claimed a majority. With the new Republican majority seated, 2015 would prove fitful. Yet, there was one moment of bipartisanship: the passage of the Medicare Access and CHIP reauthorization Act of 2015. The Act eliminated the Sustainable Growth Rate or SGR. Fear that the SGR would constrain the supply of services for Medicare beneficiaries, Congress had been forced to pass so-called doc fix bills on a perennial basis. The SGR was replaced with a combination of automatic increases and incentives for more efficient care. The Act simultaneously provided funding for the Children's Health Insurance Program and community health centers. Speaker Boehner and his staff entered into secret negotiations with Democratic Minority Leader Pelosi (D-CA) and her staff, extending discussions to interest group representatives, Medicare administrators, and key members of the House and Senate rather than engaging the normal process of committee hearings, which would have been contentious in the hyper partisan environment.[87] President Obama celebrated the work of Boehner and Pelosi at the signing celebration and "thank[ed] everybody for showing that Republicans and Democrats can come together and put aside partisanship for something important."[88] The spirit of bipartisanship would prove short-lived.

Once the debt ceiling was reinstated, the Treasury again employed extraordinary measures to avoid default. After four years of battling with the Tea Party and its successor, the House Freedom Caucus, John Boehner resigned from the speakership and Congress in October, passing the mantle to Paul Ryan. Beforehand, Boehner negotiated the Bipartisan Budget Act of 2015, hoping to forestall future efforts to leverage the debt ceiling. The Act followed the pattern established earlier. Once again, the discretionary spending caps set by the BCA were raised and sequestration was extended to FY2025. The Act suspended the debt limit through March 15, 2017, thereby minimizing the extent to which it could be used to spark additional crises in the coming years.[89] After passing a series of three short-term CRs to prevent a government shutdown, in December, Congress finally passed the Consolidated Appropriations Act, which authorized $1.15 trillion to fund the government through the end of the fiscal year. The quick approach of the winter recess, the Republican desire to avoid more disorder and the threat of government shutdowns in a presidential election year, and Speaker Ryan's success in controlling the Freedom Caucus were undoubtedly critical. But as the *New York Times* reported, "the agreement also showed just how easily a fractious legislature can seem functional again when there is an agreement to spend more money, adding at least $2 trillion in debt over the next 20 years."[90]

Things would once again degenerate into disorder in 2016. When President Obama submitted his final budget request for FY2017, the House and Senate refused to schedule hearings with the OMB Director.[91] House Republicans could not even build a consensus on a budget resolution. The Freedom Caucus, which had been sidelined by the recent Bipartisan Budget Act, refused to consent to the $1.07 trillion figures negotiated by Boehner. For the second time since the passage of the Congressional Budget Act, the House considered appropriations bills without a budget resolution, forcing the Appropriations Committee to use the figures in the Bipartisan Budget Act as the default. Successive appropriations bills went down for defeat, largely as a result of poison pill amendments, forcing Speaker Ryan to resort to structured rules to limit amendments from the floor. As the end of the fiscal year arrived without a budget and members of Congress anxious to campaign on the eve of the 2016 elections, Congress turned to a CR to fund government through December 9 and prevent a shutdown. Following the election of Donald Trump as president and the return of Republican majorities in the House and the Senate, Congress funded the government through April, deferring other budgetary action until after the inauguration.[92]

Conclusion

The partisan battles of the 1990s were difficult, but Clinton and Congress had achieved what few thought possible: budget surpluses and a decline in the debt-to-GDP ratio. The Bush and Obama presidencies, in contrast, would witness a series of crises and policy decisions that undermined revenues and drove higher levels of spending. In a matter of 16 years, the debt held by the public had more than doubled, from 31.5 to 76.2 percent of GDP.[93] While the years covered in this chapter were particularly turbulent, crises were not unique to this period. In the past, the fiscal consequences of crisis had been moderated. The pattern of leveraging and deleveraging that had occurred in the past no longer appeared to be in the opportunity set. Trends in polarization had now fully compromised the ability of Congress to execute its basic duties. It repeatedly failed to pass budget resolutions, and even if it did, the resort to emergency supplemental spending stripped them of their importance. Efforts to address the fiscal gap through the BCA may have borne a superficial resemblance to earlier procedural remedies. But the commitment to a low tax regime when combined with an unwillingness to abide by the spending cuts legislated by Congress made budgetary control impossible.[94] As hard as it might have been to imagine, events in the next several years would only intensify the disorder and drive the debt to levels that were projected to surpass the historical precedent of World War II. We turn to this episode in Chapter 9.

Notes

1 Office of Management and Budget (OMB), *Budget of the United States Government, Fiscal Year 2023* (Washington, DC: Government Publishing Office, 2022), Historical Tables, Tables 7.1, 8.3, and 8.4.
2 Ibid., Tables 2.2 and 2.3.
3 See Nolan McCarty, "The Policy Effects of Political Polarization," in *The Transformation of American Politics: Activist Government and the Rise of Conservatism*, Paul Pierson, Theda Skocpol eds. (Princeton: Princeton University Press, 2007), 223–55.
4 See Frances E. Lee, "The Challenges of Measuring Party Unity in a Polarized Era: The 115th Congress," in *Dynamics of American Democracy: Partisan Polarization, Political Competition and Government Performance*, ed. Eric M. Patashnik and Wendy J. Schiller (Lawrence: University Press of Kansas, 2021), 87–111, and James M. Curry and Frances E. Lee, *The Limits of Party: Congress and Lawmaking in a Polarized Era* (Chicago: University of Chicago Press, 2020).
5 See Barbara Sinclair, *Unorthodox Lawmaking: New Legislative Processes in the U.S. Congress,* 5th ed. (Washington, DC: CQ Press, 2016).
6 Lee, "The Challenges of Measuring Party Unity in a Polarized Era," 101.
7 Sarah A. Binder and Frances E. Lee, "Making Deals in Congress," in *Political Negotiation: A Handbook,* ed. Jane Mansbridge and Cathie Jo Martin (Washington, DC: Brookings Institution Press, 2016), 113.
8 Allen Schick, *The Federal Budget: Politics, Policy, Process*, 2nd ed (Washington, DC: Brookings Institution Press, 2007)*, 132.*
9 Joseph Bafumi, "The Senate Budget Committee: The Impact of Polarization on Institutional Design," *PS: Political Science and Politics*, 45, 1 (2012): 161–67.
10 Peter C. Hanson, "Ending the Omnibus: Restoring Regular Order in Congressional Appropriations," in *Is Congress Broken? The Virtues and Defects of Partisanship, Polarization, and Gridlock,* ed. William F. Connelly and John J. Pitney (Washington, DC: Brookings Institution Press, 2017), 179–80, 175.
11 Lance T. LeLoup, *Parties, Rules, and the Evolution of Congressional Budgeting* (Columbia: The Ohio State University Press, 2005), 181–200.
12 Council of Economic Advisors, *Economic Report of the President* (Washington, DC: Government Printing Office, 2002), 42.
13 Bureau of Labor Statistics, Unemployment Rate [UNRATE]. Available at FRED, Federal Reserve Bank of St. Louis; https://fred.stlouisfed.org/series/UNRATE
14 See Department of Defense, *FY2019 Quarter 4, Cost of War Update as of September 30, 2019* (Washington, DC: Department of Defense, 2019), 2–3.
15 Christopher T. Mann, *U.S. War Costs, Casualties, and Personnel Levels Since 9/11,* CRS In Focus IF1182 (Washington, DC Congressional Research Service, 2019), 2.
16 Bruce R. Lindsay and Jared C. Nagel, *Federal Disaster Assistance After Hurricanes Katrina, Rita, Wilma, Gustav, and Ike,* CRS Report R43139 (Washington, DC Congressional Research Service, 2019), 70, 2–3, 13.

17 OMB, *Budget of the United States Government, Fiscal Year 2009* (Washington, DC: Government Printing Office, 2008), 11–12.

18 See Marc Allen Eisner, *The American Political Economy: Institutional Evolution of Market and State,* 2nd ed. (New York: Routledge, 2014), 188–215, and Bureau of Labor Statistics, Unemployment Rate [UNRATE], available at https://fred.stlouisfed.org/series/UNRATE

19 Clinton T. Brass, Jennifer E. Lake, Carol Hardy Vincent, Karen Spar, and Pamela J. Jackson, *American Recovery and Reinvestment Act of 2009 (P.L. 111-5): Summary and Legislative History*, CRS Report R40537 (Washington, DC: Congressional Research Service, 2009), and Congressional Budget Office (CBO), *Estimated Impact of the American Recovery and Reinvestment Act on Employment and Economic Output from October 2011 through December 2011,* Pub, No 4435 (Washington, DC: CBO, 2012).

20 OMB, *Budget of the United States Government, Fiscal Year 2023*, Historical Tables, Table 1.1.

21 Adam Clymer, "Surplus a Gulf Between Candidates," *New York Times,* April 30, 2000, 30. Available at https://archive.nytimes.com/www.nytimes.com/library/politics/camp/043000wh-gop-bush.html.

22 *Bush v. Gore*, 531 US 98 (2000).

23 OMB, *A Blueprint for New Beginnings: A Responsible Budget for America's Priorities* (Washington, DC: Government Printing Office, 2001), 29.

24 Ibid., 35–36.

25 Lori Nitschke and Wendy Boudreau, "Provisions of the Tax Law," *CQ Weekly* (June 9, 2001): 1390–94. Available at http://library.cqpress.com/cqmagazine/weeklyreport107-000000264491

26 Philip D. Winters, *The Budget for Fiscal Year 2002*, CRS Report RL31566 (Washington, DC: Congressional Research Service, 2002), 1, 7–9.

27 W. Elliot Brownlee, *Federal Taxation in America: A History*, 3rd ed. (Cambridge: Cambridge University Press, 2016), 251–52, Hacker and Pierson, "Tax Politics and the Struggle over Activist Government," 271.

28 David Nather, "Will Absence of a Budget Plan Weaken the Democratic Message?" *CQ Weekly* (April 13, 2002): 954–55, available at http://library.cqpress.com/cqmagazine/weeklyreport107-000000413865, and "2002 Legislative Summary: Fiscal 2003 Budget Resolution," *CQ Weekly* (December 7, 2002): 3188, available at http://library.cqpress.com/cqmagazine/weeklyreport107-000000555202.

29 Bill Heniff Jr., *Congressional Budget Actions in 2002*, CRS Issue Brief IB10096 (Washington, DC: Congressional Research Service, 2002).

30 Peter R. Orszag, "Issues in Restating a Statutory Pay-As-You-Go Requirement," Statement of Peter R. Orszag, Director, before the Committee on the Budget, U.S. House of Representatives, July 25, 2007 (Washington, DC: Congressional Budget Office, 2007), 6.

31 Thomas L. Hungerford, *The Bush Tax Cuts and the Economy*, CRS Report R41393 (Washington, DC: Congressional Research Service, 2010), 11.

32 Jerry Tempalski, Revenue Effects of Major Tax Bills: Office of Tax Analysis Working Paper 81 (Washington, DC: Department of the Treasury, 2006), 17.

33 Brownlee, *Federal Taxation in America,* 265–66.

34 See Thomas G. McGuire, Joseph P. Newhouse, and Anna D. Sinaiko, "An Economic History of Medicare Part C." *The Milbank Quarterly,* 89, 2 (2011): 293–332.

35 See Jennifer O'Sullivan, Hinda Chaikind, Sibyl Tilson, Jennifer L. Boulanger, and Paulette C. Morgan, *Overview of the Medicare Prescription Drug, Improvement, and*

Modernization Act of 2003, CRS Report RL31966 (Washington, DC: Congressional Research Service, 2004).

36 Mary Agnes Carey, "Medicare Deal Goes to Wire in Late-Night House Vote," *CQ Weekly* (November 22, 2003): 2879–83. Available at http://library.cqpress.com/cqmagazine/weeklyreport108-000000919850.

37 Bill Heniff Jr., *Congressional Budget Actions in 2003*, CRS Report RL31754 (Washington, DC: Congressional Research Service, 2004), 1, 22, 26–27, and Jill Barshay, "For Bush, Tax Cut Package Is Next Must-Win Battle," *CQ Weekly* (April 26, 2003): 974–79, available at http://library.cqpress.com/cqmagazine/weeklyreport108-000000674493.

38 OMB, *Budget of the United States Government, Fiscal Year 2023*, Historical Tables, Tables 1.1 and 1.2.

39 OMB, *Budget of the United States Government, Fiscal Year 2005* (Washington, DC: Government Printing Office, 2004), 42; "2004 Legislative Summary: Fiscal 2005 Budget Resolution," *CQ Weekly* (December 4, 2004): 2850, available at http://library.cqpress.com/cqmagazine/weeklyreport108-000001444256; and Bill Heniff Jr., *Congressional Budget Actions in 2004*, CRS Report RL32246 (Washington DC: Congressional Research Service, 2004),1, 11–13.

40 George W. Bush, "Address Before a Joint Session of the Congress on the State of the Union," January 20, 2004. Available at www.presidency.ucsb.edu/node/211969

41 OMB, *Budget of the United States Government, Fiscal Year 2005*, 38.

42 See Steven T. Dennis, "Details of Budget Reconciliation Law," *CQ Weekly* (April 17, 2006): 1036–42. Available at http://library.cqpress.com/cqmagazine/weeklyreport109-000002147368.

43 See Bill Heniff Jr., *Congressional Budget Actions in 2005*, CRS Report RL32791 (Washington, DC: Congressional Research Service, 2006). For a legislative history of the two reconciliation bills, see Robert Keith, *Budget Reconciliation Legislation in 2005–2006 Under the FY2006 Budget Resolution*, CRS Report RL 33132 (Washington, DC: Congressional Research Service, 2007).

44 John Cranford, "Political Economy: The Defense Deceit," *CQ Weekly* (January 30, 2006): 262. Available at http://library.cqpress.com/cqmagazine/weeklyreport109-000002040609.

45 Samuel Goldreich, "Bush Names Social Security Panel as Politically Palatable Options for Overhaul Begin to Narrow," *CQ Weekly* (May 5, 2001): 1021, available at http://library.cqpress.com/cqmagazine/weeklyreport107-000000247178, and David Nather, and Anjetta McQueen, "Social Security Overhaul Panel's Report Lands With a Thud," *CQ Weekly* (December 15, 2001): 2982–83, available at http://library.cqpress.com/cqmagazine/weeklyreport107-000000356328.

46 Adriel Bettelheim and Alex Wayne, "Dependable Bush Supporters Hang Back on Social Security," *CQ Weekly* (January 17, 2005): 112–14, available at http://library.cqpress.com/cqmagazine/weeklyreport109-000001489730, and Alex Wayne, "Bush Takes New Tack on Social Security," *CQ Weekly* (May 2, 2005): 1147, available at http://library.cqpress.com/cqmagazine/weeklyreport109-000001650632.

47 See Curry and Lee, *The Limits of Party*, 67–68, Alex Wayne, "Fall Agenda: Social Security Overhaul," *CQ Weekly* (September 5, 2005): 2319, available at http://library.cqpress.com/cqmagazine/weeklyreport109-000001843141, and Alex Wayne, "2005 Legislative Summary: Social Security Overhaul," *CQ Weekly* (January 2, 2006): 50, available at http://library.cqpress.com/cqmagazine/weeklyreport109-000002022076.

48 See Bill Heniff Jr., *Congressional Budget Actions in 2006*, CRS Report RL33291 (Washington, DC: Congressional Research Service, 2006), and Steven T. Dennis, "2006 Legislative Summary: Budget Resolution," *CQ Weekly* (December 18, 2006): 3338, available at http://library.cqpress.com/cqmagazine/weeklyreport109-000002418325.

49 See Bill Heniff Jr., *Congressional Budget Actions in 2007*, CRS Report RL34015 (Washington, DC: Congressional Research Service, 2007) and Sandy Streeter, *Continuing Resolutions: FY2008 Actions and Brief Overview of Recent Practices*, CRS Report RL30343 (Washington, DC: Congressional Research Service, 2008).

50 George W. Bush, "Veto Message on H.R. 1591: Message from the President of the United States Transmitting Notification of the Veto of H.R. 1591, the US Troop Readiness, Veterans Care, Katrina Recovery, and Iraq Accountability Appropriations Act of 2007," 110th Congress, 1st Session, House Document 110–31 (Washington, DC: Government Printing Office, 2007), 1.

51 See Stephen Daggett, Amy Belasco, Pat Towell, Susan B. Epstein, Connie Veillette, Curt Tarnoff, Rhoda Margesson, and Bart Elias, *FY2007 Supplemental Appropriations for Defense, Foreign Affairs, and Other Purposes*, CRS Report RL33900 (Washington, D..C: Congressional Research Service, 2007) and Carl Hulse, "Congress Passes War Funds Bill, Ending Impasse," *New York Times*, May 25, 2007, A1, available at www.nytimes.com/2007/05/25/washington/25cong.html.

52 OMB, *Budget of the United States Government, Fiscal Year 2009* (Washington, DC: Government Printing Office, 2008), 11–12, 139.

53 D. Andrew Austin, *The Budget for Fiscal Year 2009*, CRS Report RL34419 (Washington, DC: Congressional Research Service, 2008), 9.

54 Irene Rubin, "Budgeting During the Bush Administration," *Public Budgeting and Finance*, 29, 3 (2009): 3–4.

55 OMB, *Budget of the United States Government, Fiscal Year 2023,* Historical Tables, Tables 8.3 and 8.4.

56 Tom Rosentiel and Carroll Doherty, "Do Deficits Mater Anymore: Apparently Not to the Public," Pew Research Center, March 14, 2006. Available at www.pewresearch.org/2006/03/14/do-deficits-matter-anymore-apparently-not-to-the-public/.

57 Alan K. Ota, "Business Newly Tolerant of 'Manageable' Deficit," *CQ Weekly* (January 17, 2004): 162–64. Available at http://library.cqpress.com/cqmagazine/weeklyreport108-000000969537.

58 Ron Suskind, *The Price of Loyalty: George W. Bush, the White House, and the Education of Paul O'Neill* (New York: Simon & Schuster, 2004), 291.

59 OMB, *Budget of the United States Government, Fiscal Year 2023,* Historical Tables, Table 1.2.

60 See Marc Allen Eisner, *The American Political Economy: Institutional Evolution of Market and State,* 2nd ed. (New York: Routledge, 2014), 188–215, and Bureau of Labor Statistics, Unemployment Rate [UNRATE], available at https://fred.stlouisfed.org/series/UNRATE.

61 OMB, *Budget of the United States Government, Fiscal Year 2023*, Historical Tables, Table 1.2.

62 OMB, *Budget of the United States Government, Fiscal Year 2023*, Historical Tables, Tables 1.1 and 1.2.

63 Theda Skocpol and Vanessa Williamson, *The Tea Party and the Remaking of Republican Conservatism* (New York: Oxford University Press, 2012), 12.

64 Barack Obama, "Message to the Congress on Proposed Pay-As-You-Go Legislation, June 9, 2009," *Public Papers of the Presidents of the United States: Barack Obama* (Washington, DC: Government Printing Office, 2010), Book 1, 801.
65 Sheryl Gay Stolbert, "Obama Aims to Revive 'Pay as You Go,'" *New York Times*, June 9, 2009. Available at www.nytimes.com/2009/06/10/us/politics/10obama.html.
66 This discussion draws on Robert Keith, *The Statutory Pay-As-You-Go Act of 2012: Summary and Legislative History*, CRS Report R41157 (Washington, DC: Congressional Research Service, 2010).
67 See Bill Heniff Jr., "Memorandum: Budgetary Effects Excluded from the Statutory Pay-As-You-Go (Stat-PAYGO) Scorecards" (Washington, DC: Congressional Research Service, 2017).
68 Executive Order 13531 (2010), sec. 4.
69 Eisner, *The American Political Economy*, 212.
70 Paul Krugman, "The Hijacked Commission," *New York Times*, November 12, 2010, A31. Available at www.nytimes.com/2010/11/12/opinion/12krugman.html.
71 Brian Riedl, "Fiscal Commission Report: Too Much Taxes, Not Enough Spending Cuts" Heritage Foundation, Web Memo 3071, December 3, 2000, 1. Available at http://thf_media.s3.amazonaws.com/2010/pdf/wm3071.pdf.
72 Donald R. Wolfensberger, *Changing Cultures in Congress: From Fair Play to Power Plays* (New York: Columbia University Press, 2018), 71, 74.
73 Quoted in John Cranford, "Taking the Federal Debt Ceiling to Its Limit." *CQ Weekly*, January 24, 2011, 200.
74 This discussion draws on D. Andrew Austin, *The Debt Limit Since 2011*, CRS Report R43389 (Washington, DC: Congressional Research Service, 2019), 7–8, and D. Andrew Austin, Dawn Nuschler, and Clinton T. Brass, *Reaching the Debt Limit: Background and Potential Effects on Government Operations*, CRS Report R41633 (Washington, DC: Congressional Research Service, 2015), 6.
75 See H.R. 2560 Bill Summary and Status—112th Congress (2011–2012) THOMAS (Library of Congress). Available at www.congress.gov/bill/112th-congress/house-bill/2560.
76 Timothy F. Geithner, *Stress Test: Reflections on Financial Crises* (New York: Crown Publishers, 2014), 464, 465.
77 See "Highlights of the Budget Control Act." *CQ Weekly* (August 8, 2011): 1761–62, Bill Heniff Jr., Elizabeth Rybicki, and Shannon M. Mahan, *The Budget Control Act of 2011*, CRS Report R41965 (Washington, DC: Congressional Research Service, 2011), and Mindy R. Levit and Marc Labonte, *The Budget Control Act of 2011: The Effects on Spending and the Budget Deficit When the Automatic Spending Cuts Are Implemented,* CRS Report R42506 (Washington, DC: Congressional Research Service, 2012).
78 Damian Paletta and Matt Phillips, "S&P Strips U.S. of Top Credit Rating." *Wall Street Journal,* August 6, 2011. Available at www.wsj.com/articles/SB10001424053111903366504576491421339802788.
79 Republican National Committee, *We Believe in America: 2012 Republican Platform*, August 27, 2012. Available at www.presidency.ucsb.edu/node/302338
80 Eisner, *The American Political Economy*, 212–13, Curry and Lee, *The Limits of Party*, 116–17, Mindy R. Levit, Margot L. Crandall-Hollick, Jim Hahn, Jim Monke, Janemarie Mulvey, and Julie M. Wittaker, *The "Fiscal Cliff" and the American Tax*

Relief Act of 2012, CRS Report R42884 (Washington, DC: Congressional Research Service, 2013), 1–8; Jim Gravelle, *The "Fiscal Cliff": Macroeconomic Consequences of Tax Increases and Spending Cuts*, CRS Report R42700 (Washington, DC: Congressional Research Service, 2013), 2–6, and Grant A. Driessen and Megan S. Lynch, *The Budget Control Act: Frequently Asked Questions*, CRS Report R44874 (Washington, DC: Congressional Research Service, 2018), 5.

81 C. Stephen Redhead, Edward C, Lie, Jessica Tollestrup, and Clinton T. Brass, *Affordable Care Act (ACA) and the Appropriations Process: FAQs Regarding Potential Legislative Changes and Effects of a Government Shutdown*, CRS Report R43246 (Washington, DC: Congressional Research Service, 2013), 1.

82 Neil Irwin, "Fitch Puts U.S. Government Credit on 'Ratings Watch Negative'," *Washington Post*, October 15, 2013. Available at www.washingtonpost.com/news/wonk/wp/2013/10/15/read-fitch-puts-u-s-government-credit-on-ratings-watch-negative/

83 Jill Lawrence, "Profiles in Negotiation: The Murray-Ryan Budget Deal," Brookings Center for Effective Public Management, February 2015, 4. Available at www.brookings.edu/research/profiles-in-negotiation-the-murray-ryan-budget-deal/.

84 Megan S. Lynch, *Provisions in the Bipartisan Budget Act of 2013 as an Alternative to a Traditional Budget Resolution*, CRS Report R43535 (Washington, DC: Congressional Research Service, 2014).

85 Jonathan Weisman and Ashly Parker, "House Approves Higher Debt Limit Without Conditions," *New York Times*, February 12, 2014, A1. Available at www.nytimes.com/2014/02/12/us/politics/boehner-to-bring-debt-ceiling-to-vote-without-policy-attachments.html.

86 Rebecca Shabad, "What Is the 'Cromnibus?'" *The Hill*, December 3, 2014. Available at https://thehill.com/policy/finance/225783-what-is-the-cromnibus

87 Adriel Bettelheim and Melissa Attias, "Doc Fix: Fond Farewell to a Regular Ritual," *CQ Weekly* (April 20, 2015): 12, available at http://library.cqpress.com/cqmagazine/weeklyreport114-000004665454. On the secretive process employed to develop the legislation, see Curry and Lee, *The Limits of Party*, 145–48.

88 Barack Obama, "Remarks on Congressional Passage of the Medicare Access and CHIP Reauthorization Act of 2015, April 21, 2015." Available at www.presidency.ucsb.edu/node/310469

89 Grant Driessen, "Bipartisan Budget Act of 2015: Adjustments to the Budget Control Act of 2011," CRS Insight IN10389 (Washington, DC: Congressional Research Service, 2015).

90 David M. Herszenhorn, "Avoiding Rancor, Congress Passes a Fiscal Package," *New York Times*, December 19, 2015, A1. Available at www.nytimes.com/2015/12/19/us/congress-spending-bill.html.

91 Molly E. Reynolds, "The Office of Management and Budget and the Congressional Budget Process: The View from Capitol Hill," in *Executive Policymaking: The Role of the OMB in the Presidency*, ed. Meena Bose and Andrew Rudalevige (Washington, DC: Brookings Institution Press, 2020), 48.

92 Grant A. Driessen and Megan S. Lynch, *Congress and the Budget: 2016 Actions and Events*, CRS Report R44347 (Washington, DC: Congressional Research Service, 2016) and Mark Harkins, "Unusual Appropriations," Government Affairs Institute,

Georgetown University, May 20, 2016, available at https://gai.georgetown.edu/unusual-appropriations/.

93 OMB, *Budget of the United States Government, Fiscal Year 2023,* Historical Tables, Table 7.1.

94 See Roy T. Meyers, "The Implosion of the Federal Budget Process: Triggers, Commissions, Cliffs, Sequesters, Debt Ceilings, and Shutdown," *Public Budgeting and Finance*, 34, 4 (2014): 1–23.

9

POPULISM AND PANDEMIC

The Road to Record Debt

After concerted efforts to reduce deficits and the debt in the 1990s, tax cuts, crisis, and political dysfunction combined to more than double the debt-to-GDP ratio over the two-term presidencies of George W. Bush and Barack Obama. Few could have imagined that the fiscal situation would deteriorate at an even more rapid pace in the next several years. Polarization, which had become so potent a force during the past two decades, seemed to tear the political institutions and much of the nation into warring camps during the presidency of Donald Trump. Republicans had narrow majorities in the House and Senate in 2017, and thus they returned to the Bush-era playbook and relied on reconciliation to push through a new round of tax cuts. At the same time, there was little hope for a bipartisan process to control discretionary spending and little sustained efforts to reform mandatory programs. As with the financial crisis of 2007 and the subsequent recession, the situation was exacerbated by a crisis. This time, the crisis took the form of a global pandemic that would claim the lives of hundreds of thousands of Americans in 2020. The passage of successive relief packages would drive the debt to over 100 percent of GDP, a figure that had not been witnessed since the nation demobilized from World War II. While the pandemic subsided during the early years of the presidency of Joseph Biden, by the spring of 2022 the death toll exceeded 1 million. The call for new social welfare and infrastructural spending, only partially tempered by a spike in inflation, gave rise to projections of record debt.

Making American Great Again

In January 2017, Donald Trump was inaugurated president and the 115th Congress convened, with Republican majorities in both chambers. As a

DOI: 10.4324/9781003395331-11

candidate, Trump had issued a populist appeal, running as a political outsider with claims that he alone had the experience and the skills to "put American first" through dramatic changes in trade, immigration, tax, and fiscal policies.[1] On the campaign trail, he made casual and unrealistic claims about the debt, suggesting that he could retire the debt in its entirety "over a period of eight years."[2] The Republican Party did not share Trump's optimism even if its aspirations proved only marginally more realistic. Its 2016 platform promised to "accelerate the repayment of the trillions we now owe in order to reaffirm our principles of responsible and limited government, and remove the burdens we are placing on future generations." To this end, it once again proposed a constitutional amendment requiring a balanced budget. The proposal would impose a spending cap based on "the appropriate historical average percentage of our nation's gross domestic product," and would require a super-majority for tax increases.[3] On January 3, 2017, Representative Bob Goodlatte (R-VA) introduced the amendment, which would have required a three-fifths majority in each chamber to increase the debt limit or allow for outlays in excess of receipts. As with the previous effort to secure a balanced budget amendment, this proposal failed to attract the required two-thirds majority in the House.[4]

Tax Cuts versus the Debt

President Trump's first budget (FY2018), entitled *A New Foundation for American Greatness*, proclaimed a goal that was less ambitious than that which had been touted on the campaign trail. It promised to balance the budget and generate surpluses by 2027 while reducing the debt held by the public from 77 to 66 percent of GDP. "Under this plan, the debt will continue to fall both in nominal dollars and as a share of GDP beyond that point, putting us on a path to repay the debt in full within a few decades." The means of achieving this reduction included proposed spending cuts of $3.6 trillion over the next decade. The largest savings would come from the proposed repeal of the Affordable Care Act (ACA) and the enactment of reforms that would emphasize competition and an expanded reliance on Health Savings Accounts ($250 billion over ten years), reforms in Medicaid and the Children's Health Insurance Program via a transition toward block grants ($616 billion over ten years), and unspecified welfare reforms ($272 billion over ten years). Additional savings would come from cuts in foreign assistance, and an annual 2 percent reduction in nondefense discretionary spending (the "2-penny plan"). This would be accompanied by increases in defense discretionary spending ($469 billion over ten years). As with the first budget presented by George W. Bush some 16 years earlier, the Trump budget aspired to use tax cuts to stimulate growth while simultaneously reducing the debt. It was asserted that changes in fiscal, economic, and regulatory policy would stimulate higher rates of growth, thereby reducing the deficit by $5.6 trillion when compared with the current fiscal path.[5]

Given the narrow majorities in the House (241-194) and the Senate (52-48), the budget reconciliation process was, once again, the chosen vehicle for policy change. As noted in the last chapter, Congress had failed to pass a budget resolution during the previous year, thereby providing the Republican majority the opportunity to pass a "shell" resolution for FY2017 to engage the reconciliation process to pursue policy changes that would not have survived a Democratic filibuster. The resolution was deployed to achieve "significant savings" through a partial repeal of the ACA via the passage of the American Health Care Act. The proposed American Health Care Act would have eliminated the individual and employer mandate, cut Medicaid, and removed other key components of the ACA. In the past, the Republican-controlled House had voted more than 50 times to repeal Obamacare. Now that Republicans had unified control, the vote to repeal and replace the ACA was not simply a symbolic refutation of President Obama. The American Health Care Act narrowly passed the House after extended negotiations between Speaker Ryan and the White House and key revisions made to mollify members of the Freedom Caucus. But intraparty divisions within the Senate were more difficult to manage, given the slim Republican majority. Ultimately, opposition from moderates prevented its passage.[6]

Although a replacement for the ACA would never materialize, the Trump administration and the Republican Congress succeeded, once again, in achieving significant changes in tax policy through reconciliation. A shell budget resolution for FY2018 included reconciliation instructions for the House Ways and Means and the Senate Finance Committee to report legislation that would increase the deficit by $1.5 trillion over the ten-year budget window, with instructions for significant changes in taxation. Unsurprisingly, the tax cut was framed in supply-side terms. Steve Forbes, Larry Kudlow, Artur Laffer, and Stephen Moore, key economic advisors to candidate Trump, argued that the tax cuts would reduce the deficit and debt by promoting higher growth rates. After reviewing Congressional Budget Office (CBO) projections, they argued that austerity—a mix of new taxes and reduced spending—could not provide a path to fiscal balance. However, tax cuts that would generate "growth on a sustainable 3 percent to 4 percent growth trajectory can cut the debt as a share of GDP almost in half by 2030." The increases in GDP would be akin to "adding another Michigan, Ohio and Pennsylvania to the U.S. economic output."[7] Even if many would question the value of supply-side arguments given the empirical record of the post-1981 period, the political reality was clear. In the absence of significant legislative achievements thus far, success in cutting taxes was deemed essential. In the words of Senator Lindsey Graham (R SC), "I think all of us realize that if we fail on taxes, that's the end of the Republican Party's governing majority in 2018."[8]

The Tax Cuts and Jobs Act of 2017 made several significant revisions to the tax code. With respect to individual income taxes, it retained the several brackets but, with the exception of the 10 percent bracket, made cuts in each of the rates. Under the previous law, a top rate of 39.6 percent was applied to taxable income over $480,050 (married, joint filers). Under the 2017 changes, it was cut to 37 percent and would apply to incomes over $600,000 (married, joint filers). The standard deduction, which would have been $13,000 for 2018 (married, joint filers) was increased significantly to $24,000. The Child Tax Credit was doubled. While rates were reduced, new limits were placed on several itemized deductions, most notably for state and local taxes and mortgage interest, two of the largest tax expenditures. The federal estate and gift exemption—a target of conservative tax reformers—was doubled from $5 million to $10 million, per decedent. Pass-through entities (e.g., sole proprietorships, partnerships, and S corporations) that are not subject to the corporate income tax benefitted both from the lower marginal rates and more generous deductions that reduced the effective tax. Given the use of the reconciliation process, the changes in the individual income tax were scheduled to expire at the end of 2025. The change in the corporate income tax were equally profound. Under the Act, the graduated rate structure that was in place, with a top rate of 35 percent, was replaced by a flat rate of 21 percent and the corporate alternative minimum tax was repealed. Unlike the changes in the individual income tax, the new 21 percent flat rate was made permanent (largely on the claim that impacts outside the budget window would be offset by the sunsets on the individual tax rate). In an effort to further erode the Obama administration's Affordable Care Act, the penalty for noncompliance was reduced to $0, effective 2019.[9]

The distributional effects of the tax cut were evaluated by the Joint Committee on Taxation. Reduction in tax liability was projected to be the greatest in the early years, reflecting the sunsets applied to individual rates. For top households with income of $1 million and over, the average tax rate fell from 32.5 to 30.2 percent in 2019. For this income category, the reduction in federal taxes ranged from $36.8 billion (2019) to a projected $8.5 billion (2027). At the same time, the tax liability for incomes below $75,000 actually increased over the pre-Trump tax structure.[10] The Tax Policy Center, a joint effort of the Urban Institute and the Brookings Institution, estimated that the individual income tax provisions would raise the income of households in the lowest quintile by 0.3 percent, whereas it would provide a 2.2 percent increase in after-tax income for the top quintile and a 3.4 percent increase for households in the 95th to 99th percentile. The top 1 percent of households would realize after-tax income gains of 2.2 percent. If tax provisions expired as scheduled, the impacts would be even more skewed, such that by 2027, taxpayers in the top 5 percent would receive all of the benefits, with 83 percent of the total benefit going to the top 1 percent of households—an outcome that few would associate with populism.[11]

But there were other concerns, primarily with respect to the fiscal impact of the tax cut. Many advocates of the Tax Cuts and Jobs Act claimed that it would spur economic growth, reducing the impact on revenues. But a Brookings

Institution comparison of projected revenues under the laws in place prior to the passage of the tax cuts and actual revenues for 2018 revealed that the impacts departed significantly from these expectations. Total revenues declined from a projected 18.1 percent of GDP to 16.4 percent of GDP. Total income tax revenues declined from 8.9 to 8.3 percent of GDP, whereas corporate tax revenues fell from 1.7 to 1 percent of GDP.[12] The CBO found similar results but anticipated that the impact on revenues would be short-lived, given that nearly all of the income tax provisions were scheduled to sunset after the 2025 tax year. Yet, even under the assumption that tax cuts would expire on schedule, the deficit projections were of some concern given the trajectory in spending. In 2018, the CBO projected that deficits would average $1.2 trillion per year over the 2019–2028 period, a total of some $12.4 trillion and would increase the publicly held debt to 96.2 percent of GDP, "higher as a percentage of GDP than at any point since just after World War II—and heading still higher."[13]

Budget Disorder and Presidential Unilateralism

While the Trump administration had achieved a legislative victory in taxation, the larger goal of reducing expenditures remained difficult given the disorder in the budgetary process. The Bipartisan Budget Act of 2015, as noted in Chapter 8, had suspended the debt ceiling through March 15, 2017. The next day, the debt limit was reset at $19.89 trillion, and the Treasury was once again forced to undertake extraordinary measures, which Treasury Secretary Steve Mnuchin indicated would be exhausted by September 29.[14] The debt limit was suspended once again, as a result of a continuing resolution (CR), through December 8, 2017. At that time, the debt limit was set at $20.46 trillion, and the Treasury was once again forced to adopt extraordinary measures. Ultimately, the debt ceiling would be suspended once again as a result of the Bipartisan Budget Act of 2018, which extended suspension to March 1, 2019.[15] The path to this outcome was a difficult one. As noted above, Congress had employed the budget reconciliation process to attempt significant policy changes in health and tax policies, forcing a reliance on CRs. When the last of these resolutions expired on January 19, the government shut down and federal workers were furloughed until a new CR was passed on January 22, 2018. In addition to the suspension of the debt ceiling, the Bipartisan Budget Act of 2018 raised the caps for discretionary spending for FY2018 and 2019 and extended the mandatory spending sequester through FY2027.[16] Once again, Congress had found a means of avoiding the constraints it had placed on itself.

By October 1, 2018, only five appropriations bills had been enacted, in part reflecting the demands of a midterm election year. Before Congress turned to campaigning, it covered the funding gap with a CR, which was scheduled to expire on December 7. That November, the Republicans added two seats to their Senate majority, but Democrats took control of the House, gaining 40 seats and ending the period of unified Republican control. Congress managed to pass a second CR, which would extend funding to December 21, 2018. However, when the House would not accede to President Trump's demand for $5.7 billion in appropriations for the construction of a wall on the US–Mexico border, a government shutdown commenced that lasted a record 34 full days. Congress and the president were at an impasse. The House, now under Democratic control, was willing to pass a CR but not fund a border wall; President Trump threatened to veto such a bill and the Republican-controlled Senate refused to schedule a vote on any bill that the president could not support. President Trump ultimately retreated from his position and signed a CR on January 25, 2019. On February 18, 2019, Trump circumvented the budgetary process and ended negotiations with a Democratic House opposed to his immigration policy. He declared a national emergency and ordered that the boarder wall be constructed with $6 billion already appropriated to the Department of Defense. In a rare act of bipartisanship, the House and Senate passed a resolution to overturn Trump's emergency declaration. Trump's veto of the resolution was sustained.[17]

The decision to reprogram funds from the Department of Defense to fund construction of a wall without congressional appropriations was a striking case of presidential unilateralism, but it was neither the first nor the last. While Congress grants the executive some discretion in the apportioning of appropriated funds, committee approval is often mandated before funds can be transferred or reprogrammed for other uses. During the summer of 2018, the administration circumvented congressional will when it provided additional resources for Immigration and Customs Enforcement and the Unaccompanied Alien program, transferring hundreds of millions of dollars from other Homeland Security programs. Congress, under unified Republican control, did not mount a response. But a year later, President Trump pressured the president of Ukraine to investigate Joseph Biden—the probable Democratic nominee for the 2020 election—and directed appointees at the OMB to place a hold on funding from the State Department, the United States Agency for International Development, and Department of Defense. This latter act of unilateralism engendered a response in the form of an impeachment by the House (President Trump was acquitted in the Senate).[18]

The crisis environment of early 2019 subsided, at least in part, allowing Congress to return to the pattern of sequestration avoidance established in the past several years. The Bipartisan Budget Act of 2019, enacted in August, once again raised the discretionary spending limits for FY2020 and 2021, continuing a pattern that began with the Ryan-Murray pact of 2013. The combined increase of $322 billion was the largest authorized by any of the series of Bipartisan Budget Acts. The mandatory sequestration, which was scheduled to end in 2021 under the Budget Control Act, was extended through FY2029, once again exempting the bulk of government spending. Since March 2019, the Treasury had once again been employing extraordinary measures to avoid breaching the debt ceiling. Once again, Congress suspended the debt ceiling, this time until August 1, 2021, at which time it would reset to reflect new debt incurred during the suspension.[19]

The fiscal record of the first three years of the Trump administration bore little resemblance to what had been promised in the 2016 election or envisioned in successive budget messages. Between 2017 and 2019, total outlays increased from $3.98 trillion (20.6 percent GDP) to $4.45 trillion (21 percent GDP). Although receipts increased in current dollars, from $3.32 trillion to $3.46 trillion, they declined from 17.2 to 16.3 percent of GDP. Deficits, in turn, increased from $628 billion (3.5 GDP) to $892 billion (4.6 percent GDP).[20] The FY2021 budget, submitted in February of 2020, communicated Trump's frustration with the largest deficits since the Great Recession and the projections of future deficits exceeding the $1 trillion mark under conditions of economic growth. While "the President has laid out a vision to drive down deficits and debt through spending restraint in every Budget he has submitted to Congress," the administration proclaimed, "the Congress continues to reject any efforts to restrain spending." While the budget focused attention on spending control through the reduction of waste, fraud, and abuse (e.g., elimination of duplicative programs, ending improper payments and end-of-year spending), it did not engage the largest source of spending growth: mandatory programmatic outlays.[21] Moreover, it did not address the primary driver of the growing fiscal imbalances: the drop in federal receipts following the passage of the tax cuts of 2017.

The Pandemic

In the FY2020 budget, the Trump administration noted that the current debt trajectory was on course to "surpass a percent of GDP not seen since 1947." It warned: "Even with high levels of economic growth, excessive deficits continue to threaten the Nation's progress, and any unforeseen shocks to the economy could make deficits unsustainable."[22] The past two decades had witnessed a number of "unforeseen shocks" that had significant budgetary implications. This time, the shock took the form of a global pandemic. The first case of the novel coronavirus, COVID-19, in the United States was confirmed on January 21, 2020. The next two months would witness the declaration of a public health emergency followed by the declaration of a national emergency. To prevent a surge of new cases that would overwhelm hospitals already overridden by COVID-19 patients, the Trump administration urged Americans to stay home and "slow the spread." Several states issued their own stay at home orders, creating a patchwork of policies that effectively shuttered much of the nation's economy. The unemployment rate, which was 3.5 percent at the beginning of 2020, spiked to 14.8 percent in April, surpassing the peaks of the Great

Recession (10 percent) and the deep recession of 1981–1982 (10.8 percent). While the unemployment rate fell to 6.8 percent by the end of the year, by that time, the number of Americans infected by COVID-19 had exceeded 20 million, with over 346,000 dead.[23]

The pandemic demanded a significant bipartisan policy response, including a series of relief packages that made the American Recovery and Reinvestment Act of 2009 look anemic. The Coronavirus Preparedness and Response Supplemental Appropriations Act, signed into law March 6, provided additional funding for the Public Health and Social Services Emergency Fund in the Department of Health and Human Services (HHS) for the development and purchase of vaccines, therapeutics, and medical supplies, and for the Center for Disease Control to support additional surveillance, laboratories, and infection control. The Act also delivered additional funding to the Food and Drug Administration and the National Institutes of Health. On March 18, the Families First Coronavirus Response Act was signed into law. It provided additional funding for nutritional assistance programs, mandated expanded family medical leave and paid sick leave for COVID-19 patients, extended unemployment compensation, and provided free testing for certain categories of the population (e.g., military, the uninsured, veterans). The Coronavirus Aid, Relief, and Economic Security Act (CARES Act), the centerpiece of the relief efforts, was signed into law on March 27. It authorized one-time cash payments of $1,200 to individuals. It created the Paycheck Protection Program, which provided loans to small businesses, sole proprietors, and independent contractors and smaller nonprofit and veterans organizations to cover payroll costs; loans were forgiven if borrowers maintained their employees without more than a 25 percent reduction in compensation. In addition, it enhanced unemployment compensation payments; provided additional funding for Medicare, Medicaid, and public health more generally; provided additional assistance for distressed sectors of the economy; and channeled COVID-19 relief funding to the states. The Paycheck Protection Program and Health Care Enhancement Act was signed into law on April 24, to provide supplemental appropriations for the Paycheck Protection Program and HHS to fund healthcare providers and testing. When combined, the COVID relief legislation passed in the spring of 2020 authorized $2.33 trillion of emergency spending. Because some of the measures affected mandatory spending in future years, the CBO estimated the five-year cost to be $2.44 trillion.[24]

In the wake of the original wave of COVID legislation, the House passed the Health and Economic Recovery Omnibus Emergency Solutions or HEROES Act that would have appropriated an additional $2.2 trillion to extend key features of the earlier CARES Act and a new round of $1,200 stimulus checks. The bill died in the Senate, as the Republican majority raised concerns about the growing deficit and debt. Given the turmoil of the COVID pandemic and the upcoming presidential and congressional elections, little progress had been made on passing appropriations bills before the start of the fiscal year. After a series of CRs and protracted negotiations in the fall involving the two chambers and the White House, the Consolidated Appropriations Act of 2021 was signed into law on December 27. It combined the 12 appropriations bills and provided additional stimulus, including more targeted $600 stimulus checks, a more modest increase in unemployment payments than had been provided under the CARES Act, and additional funding for the Paycheck Protection Program. The CBO scored the COVID-19-related outlays of the Act as adding some $867 billion to the deficit over the 2021–2030 period. In each case, the statutes explicitly stated that the budgetary effects would not be entered on the PAYGO scorecards under the Statutory Pay-As-You-Go Act, thereby preventing future sequestration.[25]

In the 2020 presidential campaign, Democratic candidate Joseph Biden had promised to reverse many of the policies embraced by the Trump administration, including the tax cuts for wealthy households and corporations. He had also pledged to secure a large COVID-19 relief package. In November, Biden was elected president. While the Democratic majority was depleted in the House, Democrats picked up three seats in the Senate, a number sufficient to assume control of the chamber with the tie-breaking vote of Vice President Kamala Harris. The months following the election were dominated by contentious political struggles, as President Trump refused to concede the election and made unsubstantiated claims of widespread electoral fraud that were echoed by many Republicans in Congress. The drama culminated on January 6, 2021. Following a rally organized by Trump and his supporters, thousands engaged in an assault on the Capitol in an attempt to prevent the congressional certification of the election results. The House quickly moved to impeach the president a second time, this time for inciting insurrection (the subsequent trial, held after Trump left office, would result in another acquittal). As this drama played out, newly inaugurated President Biden had to attend to a larger crisis. With extended unemployment insurance scheduled to expire in March, the administration turned to additional relief. The spending package, initially slated at $1.9 trillion, would become the first order of business. Given the deep polarization in Congress and the narrow majority in the Senate, the administration decided to turn to the budget reconciliation process to pass the American Rescue Plan Act of 2021. As Congress debated the relief package, the nation reached two milestones that would have been unimaginable a year earlier: COVID-19 deaths exceeded one-half million, and the federal debt held by the public surpassed 100 percent of GDP.

Among wealthy nations, the United States had seemed well-positioned to manage a healthcare crisis like the pandemic. But persistent underfunding of public health—much of it a product of sequestration or the diversion of funds to forestall scheduled reductions in Medicare physicians' fees or other health-related programs—left the nation more vulnerable than many had anticipated.[26]

By August of 2020, the United States, with some 4 percent of the world population, had weathered 23 percent of the world's deaths. The health impacts fell disproportionately on minority populations (e.g., the hospitalization rate for Black Americans was five times higher than White Americans; the death rate was twice as high, with similar discrepancies among the Latino population). Underinvestment in public health translated into higher levels of comorbidity, which translated into higher levels of hospitalization and fatalities. In the words of one study, "COVID-19 wove many of America's best-known problems—health disparities, the uninsured, and a fraying social safety net—into a single, horrible, tapestry."[27] And performance was compromised by muddled messaging and the politicization of nonpharmaceutical interventions and, later, vaccinations. While the emergency legislation of 2020–2021 was impressive in its scope, it was also largely reactive, much as had been past responses to health crises. A question that would occur among public health experts was whether Washington would respond to the COVID-19 pandemic by investing in a more robust set of social and healthcare policies.

The aggregate fiscal impact of the pandemic was striking. In 2020, revenues remained steady at $3.42 trillion (16.3 percent GDP). Spending, however, reached a postwar record of $6.55 trillion (or 31.3 percent GDP). By way of comparison, outlays during the Great Recession peaked at 24.3 percent of GDP in 2009. The 2020 deficit reached a new record of $3.13 trillion (or 15 percent GDP). Once again, by way of comparison, the 2009 deficit was 9.8 percent of GDP.[28] One should not be surprised by these numbers given that the pandemic would be the largest public health crisis in over a century. When combined, the downward ratchet in taxation, the growth in government spending, the escalating disorder in the budgetary process, and the response to the pandemic set the stage for a more than a tripling of the federal debt in some two decades, which now stood at 100.3 percent of GDP—the highest level since 1946—and was projected to grow rapidly over the course of the next several years.[29]

A Crisis Is a Terrible Thing to Waste

In the immediate aftermath of the financial collapse, Rahm Emmanuel, Obama's chief of staff, famously remarked "You never want a serious crisis to go to waste." The financial crisis, in Emmanuel's judgment, created a window of opportunity to extend reform to the healthcare system. Although the origins of the quote are in dispute, it appears that the core lesson was not lost on then Vice President Biden.[30] On May 28, 2021, the Biden administration released its budget requests for FY2022, calling for what would be the largest expansion of the welfare state since the Great Society era as a means of addressing the weaknesses exhibited by COVID-19. Building on the American Recovery Plan Act, the budget requested historic increases in nondefense discretionary spending. The proposed American Jobs Plan was designed to address the reduction in public investment since the 1960s, calling for significant spending on physical infrastructure and what was framed as the infrastructure of the "care economy" (e.g., home- and community-based care for the elderly and disabled). The proposed American Families Plan, in contrast, focused on social spending, including two years of universal prekindergarten education for children and two years of community college education, paid family and medical leave, and an extension of key tax provisions in the American Rescue Plan targeting low- and middle-income families (e.g., expanded Child Tax Credit, Earned Income Tax Credit, Dependent Care Tax Credit, and health insurance tax credits to reduce premiums under the Affordable Care Act). All told, the administration requested $6.01 trillion in spending, some 25.6 percent of GDP. With revenues projected at $4.17 trillion (17.8 percent GDP), the budget, if enacted, would create a deficit of 7.8 percent of GDP, raising the debt held by the public to 111.8 percent of GDP. By the end of the ten-year budget window, the debt was projected to reach 117 percent of GDP.[31]

Although the budget projected that the debt would rise to unprecedented levels in the next decade, there was no indication that this was a concern. "Over the past several decades," the budget noted, "interest rates have fallen, even as debt has risen." The reduction in interest rates has been a global phenomenon, which had the felicitous effect of reducing the burden of debt repayment. "Given these structural dynamics, the level of interest payments, rather than the size of the debt, is the most relevant benchmark for whether the debt is burdening the economy." The kinds of investments that were prioritized in the budget would contribute, it was argued, to future productivity growth. Given that the federal government had "the fiscal space to make critical investments to expand the productive capacity of the economy…failing to make investments now that support growth and shared prosperity would leave future generations worse off."[32]

The fiscal impact of the proposed budget would depend, ultimately, on the administration's success in raising additional revenues. The American Jobs Plan included several revenue provisions addressing corporate taxation. The administration proposed increasing the domestic corporate tax rate to 28 percent, imposing a minimum 15 percent tax, and reducing the tax incentives for profit sharing and offshoring of production. It also proposed eliminating a host of corporate tax expenditures that subsidized fossil fuel while strengthening tax expenditures to incentivize clean energy. The American Families Plan included provisions for the individual income tax. The administration proposed returning the highest marginal rate for top income earners to 39.6 percent, reforming the taxation of capital income and the carried interest preference, and providing more funding for the Internal Revenue Service and additional reforms to strengthen tax collections. At the same time, the extent to which the Biden proposals could sharply change the revenue picture was limited by the commitment that taxes would not be raised on those making under $400,000 per year, a decision that would retain and potentially make permanent some of the rate cuts achieved in 2017.[33]

There was, admittedly, uncertainty about future interest rates. Interest rates had been low for the past two decades for reasons discussed in Chapter 4, and in 2021, as the nation was recovering from the worst phase of the pandemic. While forecasts of interest rates during the ten-year budget window remained below historical averages, critics of the Biden proposals—including former Clinton Treasury Secretary Lawrence H. Summers—would argue that trillions of dollars of additional deficit spending could unleash higher levels of inflation, which would carry implications for interest rates.[34] At the same time, some Progressives drew on Modern Monetary Theory to counter these concerns. As noted in Chapter 4, Modern Monetary Theory rests on the claim that because the United States spends and borrows money that it creates, it is in a unique position. Debt issued by the Treasury could be purchased by the Federal Reserve, which could create new monetary reserves for this purpose. But, in the words of one critic, Modern Monetary Theory served as "the progressive counterpoint to supply-side economics," both of which were "carefully crafted to provide elected officials seemingly plausible economic grounds to support their preferred policy options" with no recognition of the trade-offs involved.[35]

The Biden proposals were bold. But were they achievable given the narrow Democratic margins in the House and an evenly split Senate? Progressive and moderate Democrats were divided over the level of proposed spending and the strategy of framing social spending as infrastructure for the "care economy." Finding revenues to cover the proposed spending would be a sticking point for Republicans who were unwilling to continence a repeal of what they had secured with the Tax Cut and Jobs Act, which remained the most significant legislative achievement of the Trump presidency. The controversy over taxation carried over into the Democratic caucus, where progressives were intent on raising individual and corporate income tax rates and, more importantly, imposing a wealth surtax and addressing some of the provisions in the tax code that allowed high income households to avoid taxation. The wealthiest households do not draw most of their income through wages, but from their holdings of equities, real estate, and other assets that are sheltered from taxes that fell on labor. Real tax reform, progressives argued, would target the special treatment of dividends, inherited wealth, income from pass-through entities, and the carried interest loophole, which allowed private equity managers to pay a lower capital gains tax on the fees they received from their clients. Moderates, fearful of the political backlash against what would be framed as "soak the rich" policies, were far more supportive of raising revenue through more modest increases in marginal tax rates for top earners and corporations. The intraparty divisions were most consequential in the Senate, which was equally divided between Democrats and Republicans.[36]

Biden's American Jobs Plan proposed some $2.3 billion in new infrastructure spending. In the Congress, counterproposals flourished, and the administration responded first, by reducing the requested level of spending, and then by turning to an infrastructure bill that was being developed by a bipartisan group of 20 senators. While the bill envisioned some $900 billion in spending, it provided a means for the President to exhibit his commitment to bipartisan compromise, a theme he had emphasized in the campaign. The negotiations were fitful, as Republicans rebuffed any proposed changes in the tax code that would reverse the 2017 tax cuts. Even a proposal to provide the Internal Revenue Service with additional funding to achieve higher levels of compliance with the current tax laws proved to be a nonstarter. Instead, Republicans hoped to draw on $210 billion of unspent COVID-19 funds and other assorted revenue measures, a decision that limited the size of the final package while undermining the claims that the bill would not contribute to the deficit. The final package was significant: according to the CBO scoring, it authorized $782.5 billion in spending over the next ten years while contributing a projected $256 billion to the debt.[37] The final bill, the Infrastructure Investment and Jobs Act, passed in the Senate 60-29, with strong bipartisan support. And yet, its future was unclear as it moved to the House.

As Senate moderates had been working on the infrastructure bill, Democratic leadership was developing reconciliation instructions for an ambitious spending bill (the Build Back Better Act) of some $3.5 trillion. Unlike the Infrastructure Investment and Jobs Act, which was devoted to traditional infrastructure, the reconciliation bill contained many of the key "social infrastructure" and climate change measures proposed in the President's budget and a reversal of some of the 2017 rate cuts for upper income households and corporations. To complicate things, moderates in the House refused to vote for the reconciliation bill until it received a scoring from the CBO and then, only after a vote on the Infrastructure Investment and Jobs Act. Members of the Progressive Caucus, in turn, threatened to make their support for the infrastructure bill contingent on the passage of the reconciliation bill in the Senate. The decision to link the two bills carried intrinsic risks. While necessary to assuage the fears of progressives who saw their social agenda at stake, the linkage threatened to undermine Republican support. While infrastructural spending had a long history of bipartisan support, many House Republicans were wary that their support for the bill would facilitate a significant expansion of social spending and further Biden's broader agenda (a point emphasized repeatedly by the former president, who urged the Republican caucus to vote against the bill). Ultimately, Speaker Nancy Pelosi (D-CA) relented at the urging of the President and called a vote on the infrastructure bill, along with a rule to schedule consideration of the Build Back Better Act once it received a CBO scoring. It passed the House 228-206 and was signed into law on November 15, 2021.[38]

But questions remained about how much could be achieved through reconciliation. In an evenly divided Senate and unified Republican opposition, any Democratic defection could doom the Build Back Better Act. All attention would turn to two moderate Senate Democrats, Joe Manchin (D-WV) and Krysten Sinema (D-AZ), who questioned whether they could accept the various revenue measures and a spending bill of $3.5 trillion given the uncertain economic environment. Manchin signaled that he could not support a bill in excess of $1.5 trillion, forcing the White House to offer a revised framework with a top line figure of $2 trillion. The concessions frustrated progressives and could only be achieved by jettisoning some parts of the Act (e.g., free community college), rendering others less generous (e.g., family leave), and making funding for other components temporary (e.g., pre-K education, the expanded Child Tax Credit). In the end, the version of the Build Back Better Act passed the House on November 19, 2021 received no Republican votes. It called for $2.2 trillion in new spending, a number that Manchin would ultimately reject given its departure from the Biden framework and the expectation that the costs would only escalate as temporary programs like the expanded Child Tax Credit were extended, thereby contributing to the debt. Equally important, Manchin joined Summers and expressed his concern over the acceleration of inflation in the wake of the pandemic.[39] By mid-December, Manchin announced that he could not support the bill and it appeared that further negotiations had reached an impasse.

The Debt Ceiling versus Build Back Better

While the Biden administration and the Democratic leadership in the House and Senate considered different tactical options for moving the administration's agenda, there were growing concerns about another crisis on the horizon: the debt ceiling. Although the Budget Control Act of 2011 established a series of discretionary spending caps and a sequestration process, since 2013, Congress had passed a series of Bipartisan Budget Acts, on each occasion raising the caps, extending sequestration, and temporarily suspending the debt limit. Most recently, the Bipartisan Budget Act of 2019 suspended the debt limit through July 31, 2021, at which time it was reset at $28.4 trillion to accommodate borrowing during the suspension period. As in the past, following the reset on the debt ceiling, the Treasury was forced to engage in extraordinary measures. Because the discretionary caps set in 2011 were scheduled to expire at the end of FY 2021, it was no longer possible to pass another Bipartisan Budget Act and suspend the debt ceiling.[40] In a letter to congressional leaders, Treasury Secretary Janet L. Yellen noted that the Treasury's cash balances and extraordinary measures would "be exhausted" in October (greater precision was impossible given the uncertainty regarding COVID-19). She warned: "delay that calls into question the federal government's ability to meet all its obligations" could cause "irreparable damage" to the economy and the world's financial system. Given that the nation was "still suffering from the effects of the ongoing global pandemic, it would be particularly irresponsible to put the full faith and credit of the United States at risk."[41]

Minority Leader Mitch McConnell (R-KY) vowed that Democrats would get no support from Senate Republicans in raising the debt ceiling. He argued that if the Democrats had been willing to use reconciliation to pass an additional $1.9 trillion in pandemic relief and were currently in the process of resorting to reconciliation to pass the Build Back Better Act, they could use this same instrument to raise the debt ceiling on their own. "If they want 50 lock-step Democratic votes to spend trillions and trillions more," he warned in an August floor speech, "they can find 50 Democratic votes to finance it. If they don't want Republicans' input, they don't need our help."[42] Efforts in September to use a stop-gap spending bill to enact a debt-ceiling suspension through the 2022 midterms was filibustered by Senate Republicans. For Democrats, it was unclear that a reconciliation bill could pass in time to avoid a debt crisis nor was it clear that the Senate parliamentarian would permit reconciliation to be used for this purpose. Ultimately, McConnell offered to provide the votes necessary to invoke closure on a debt-ceiling bill, as long as Democrats agreed to raise the debt by a specific dollar amount rather than suspending the ceiling. In the end, 11 Republicans voted to invoke closure and then forced the Democratic majority to increase the debt ceiling by $480 billion on a strict party-line vote. Donald Trump attacked McConnell for extending the Democrats a "lifeline... they were in a big bind; they were unable to do anything...He had the weapon and was able to use it. It's a shame."[43]

The $480 billion increase in the debt limit was only enough to move the crisis to mid-December (because some of the COVID-19 relief money had yet to be dispersed and remained in Treasury accounts, it was difficult to predict when the Treasury's resources would be exhausted). In October, McConnell warned President Biden that the minority would not assist the Democrats in subsequent efforts to raise the debt ceiling, particularly since they could use the reconciliation process. But McConnell and Senate Majority Leader Charles E. Schumer (D-NY) arrived at a compromise that paired a bill that would delay sequestration and related cuts in Medicare with a onetime change in Senate rules. Under the agreement, the Democratic majority would be able to raise the debt limit without having to secure the Republican votes to overcome the filibuster. With an eye to the 2022 midterms, McConnell remarked: "Every single Senate Democrat will have to put their name to the gigantic amount of debt they're prepared to pile on the American people." Having negotiated a complicated procedural thicket, Congress passed a $2.5 trillion debt limit increase on December 15—raising the debt limit to some $31.4 trillion—which was signed into law the next day.[44]

In the past decade, Congress had exhibited rare bipartisanship in support for debt ceiling suspension. Now that Senate Republicans were no longer in the majority and Democrats were moving an ambitious policy agenda, cooperation was endangered. In words reminiscent of the 2011 debt crisis, Minority Leader McConnell proclaimed: "Democrats keep boasting about how wild and revolutionary their partisan vision is! So our friends across the aisle should not expect traditional bipartisan borrowing to finance their nontraditional reckless taxing and spending spree."[45] Would the Republicans leverage the debt ceiling and the threat of default, once again, to force concessions from the opposition? There was a distinct chance that Congress would reach the beginning of the new fiscal year without having raised the debt ceiling and with none of the annual appropriations bills passed into law.

Inflation and the Pivot to the Center

The pandemic seemed to recede by 2022, and the prior year had witnessed robust growth of 5.8 percent and record levels of job creation that brought the unemployment rate down from 6.4 to 3.8 percent.[46] Economic conditions appeared far more favorable than anyone would have imagined a year earlier. But a sudden surge in inflation created new complications, making the earlier warnings expressed by Summers, Manchin, and others appear prescient. The explanations for the spike in prices had several components. Pent up demand from the peak of the pandemic combined with high levels of fiscal stimulus to create demand-side pressures. The impacts were exacerbated by supply-chain problems. Companies across the global economy had depleted their inventories during the pandemic and a lack of labor, equipment, and key components like microchips translated into lengthy delays in meeting the high levels of demand. During the pandemic, dramatic decline in the demand for gasoline had led to plummeting oil prices and refineries cut back on production. Subsequently, rising levels of demand translated into surging prices at the pump. Things would become ever more complex in February, when Russia invaded Ukraine. The next several months would witness waves of international sanctions against Russia and emergency supplementals to provide security and humanitarian support to Ukraine. Given Russia's oil exports, there was little question that the conflict would contribute to global inflation. As the United States was experiencing the highest nominal gas prices on record and the highest inflation rates in four decades, the Federal Reserve began to raise interest rates to slow down the economy. Whether the Fed would be able to moderate inflation without inducing a recession (a "soft landing") remained an open question. Some analysts began discussing the potential of stagflation, harkening back to the conditions of the 1970s. In this chaotic environment, the stock market shed much of its value and public opinion turned sharply against the Biden administration.[47]

President Biden's FY2023 budget message clearly acknowledged the changing economic conditions the nation was facing. "America was not immune to the worldwide inflation that has followed the pandemic—leaving too many families struggling to keep up with their bills." All of this was worsened by the conflict in Ukraine. In what many analysts interpreted as a pivot to the center, the broad social initiatives unveiled the previous year were scaled back (or eliminated) and paired with requests for higher levels of defense spending. From a practical perspective, the administration could no longer rely on an assumption of low net interest expenditures and the fiscal space it created to frame expansive new spending programs. Reiterating a theme that had been presented during the State of the Union Address, Biden noted that the budget reflected "a bipartisan unity agenda—areas where we can all come together to make progress." The President claimed his proposed budget "fights inflation and helps families deal with rising costs by growing our economy, making more goods in America, and lowering the costs families face." He committed to keeping the nation on "a sound fiscal course" by offsetting spending via tax increases on wealthy households and corporations, thereby keeping the nation "on track to reducing the deficit this year to less than half of what it was before I took office."[48]

The kinds of reforms that were linked to "lowering the costs for American families"—cutting the costs of prescription drugs, healthcare premiums, childcare, long-term care, housing, and college—may have had broad popular support, but could they survive a polarized Congress with narrow majorities?[49] And even if they did, would they have any effects on the immediate problem of inflation? The proposed tax reforms, which included raising the top marginal rate in the individual income tax to 39.6 percent, increasing the corporate tax to 28 percent, and a new 20 percent minimum tax on billionaires, would need to be pursued through reconciliation, a problematic task given the impending mid-term elections. Even if Congress proved capable of passing the President's budget in its entirety—an unlikely scenario—the goal of reducing the deficit to less than half the level of 2020 seemed modest, given that 2020 had the highest level of spending and the largest deficit of the postwar period.

Regardless of its merits, the President's budget would need to overcome the ongoing dysfunction of Congress and the budgetary process. As the OMB completed its work on the budget, for example, it could not compare proposed spending levels with those of FY2022 for a simple reason: Congress had not passed its omnibus spending bill until March—halfway into the fiscal year—forcing the administration to rely on figures from FY2021.[50] The prior year's reconciliation bill that was supposed to provide a vehicle for tax reforms and the Build Back Better Act remained stalled in the Senate. While Congress had until the end of the fiscal year to move the package of spending and tax reforms, there was little reason to believe that progress would be forthcoming given the growing specter of inflation. Despite the unified Democratic control of the House and the Senate, by the summer bicameral negotiations had failed to generate a budget resolution and an agreement on topline numbers or the balance between defense and nondefense discretionary spending. As in the past, the House pushed forward with a "deeming resolution," deferring to the House Appropriation Committee to make these decisions and allocate budgetary authority to the subcommittees. As in the past, the disorderly process would result, quite predictably, in government by CR and the passage of omnibus spending bills well into the next fiscal year.[51]

And then there were the midterm elections just over the horizon. Historically, the party of the sitting president suffers large losses in the midterm elections. During the postwar period, the losses in the midterms during the first presidential term of office had averaged one seat in the Senate and 23 in the House of Representatives (the losses during the midterm of a second presidential term have been even more brutal). Losses of this magnitude would be sufficient to shift control of the two chambers to the Republican Party, ending any hope of Biden achieving his larger social and environmental agenda or reversing the Tax Cuts and Jobs Act. As inflation reached the highest levels in four decades, gasoline and food prices stressed family budgets, and the Federal Reserve imposed higher interest rates, there was little reason to anticipate that the Democratic Party could buck historical trends. Perhaps a good crisis would go to waste.[52]

In the waning days of summer 2022, a dramatically scaled back version of the Build Back Better Act reemerged as the Inflation Reduction Act of 2022, a product of behind-the-scenes negotiations between Senator Manchin, Senate Majority Leader Schumer (and belatedly, Senator Sinema). The social policy components of the Build Back Better Act were largely abandoned as were most of the significant tax provisions. What remained was a bill that would raise an estimated $737 billion via a new 15 percent minimum tax on corporations, a 1 percent excise tax on stock buybacks, additional IRS enforcement, and savings from a provision authorizing Medicare to negotiate prices on prescription drug prices (beginning in 2026). On the spending side, it provided support for energy security and climate change ($369 billion) largely through incentives to businesses and households, a three-year extension on ACA subsidies ($64 billion) provided under the American Rescue Plan, funding for drought resiliency in the West ($4 billion), and additional funding for IRS modernization and enforcement ($80 billion). Reflecting Manchin's concerns over excessive spending in an inflationary environment and the debt, spending was limited to a fraction of the $2.2 trillion Build Back Better Act passed by the House; $300 billion was reserved for deficit reduction. The Inflation Reduction Act passed both chambers on a straight party-line vote, marking a surprising end to what had been an extended and largely unsuccessful effort to enact the Biden administration's broader policy agenda via reconciliation.[53]

A week after the Inflation Reduction Act was signed into law, President Biden announced an executive action to cancel student loan debt of $10,000 for individuals with incomes of less than $125,000 ($250,000 for married couples). Recipients of Pell Grants—made available to students from low-income households—would receive $20,000 in loan cancellation. During the pandemic, a pause had been placed on student loan payments. Biden announced that the loan forbearance would be extended for a final time, with payments commencing in 2023. He simultaneously announced that monthly undergraduate student loan payments for current and future borrowers would be capped at 5 percent, one-half of the rate most borrowers were currently paying.[54] While Progressives had pressed for a higher level of loan forgiveness—in some cases, complete cancellation of all student debt—they welcomed the change in policy. But the costs of the executive action stood at tension with the Inflation Reduction Act. The Penn Wharton Budget Model estimated that the ten-year cost of debt cancellation would cost between $469 and $519 billion, the extension of loan forbearance would cost an additional $16 billion, and changes in monthly payments would impose an additional $70 billion, for a total cost in excess of $600 billion—more than twice the deficit reduction promised under the Inflation Reduction Act.[55] The potential impact on inflation raised additional concerns. Jason Furman, former chair of the Council of Economic Advisors under President Obama, warned: "Pouring roughly half a trillion dollars of gasoline on the inflationary fire that is already burning is reckless."[56]

As the end of the 2022 fiscal year approached, a familiar pattern reasserted itself. Congress had failed to pass a budget resolution. The House had managed to move appropriations bills under a deeming resolution, but they languished in the Senate. There was little appetite for a government shutdown as members were anxious to escape the Capitol and campaign in the midterm elections. Congress would pass a CR to keep the government open into the new fiscal year. But even the passage of a CR would be complicated by the political battles of the past several months. Senator Manchin, who had been instrumental in the passage of the Inflation Reduction Act, had extracted a promise to move provisions to reform energy permitting—a boon to fossil fuel states like West Virginia but also critical, he argued, to expedite the kinds of changes to the electrical grid that would be necessary to enact some of the climate provisions in the Act. Perhaps the CR could provide a vehicle for permitting reform? Progressives objected to the inclusion of provisions that supported the fossil fuel industry; many Senate Republicans, who supported the industry, nonetheless felt blindsided by Manchin's support for the reconciliation bill and opposed attaching provisions to the CR. Ultimately, the permitting provisions would be discarded. The CR to provide funding until December 6 was combined with $12.4 billion in security assistance for Ukraine and another $18.8 billion for domestic disaster recovery. While it would be passed by a bipartisan majority in the Senate, in the House, it passed over the nay votes of all but ten members of the Republican caucus. As members of Congress left Washington for the campaign trail, the Treasury announced that the gross national debt exceeded a record $31 trillion, raising new concerns about the fiscal implications in an environment of high inflation and interest rates.[57]

Conclusion

Joseph Biden had the distinction of being both the oldest individual ever elected to serve as President of the United States and the occupant of the White House with the longest history of public service. When Biden was sworn into the US Senate in 1973, the debt held by the public was 25.2 percent of GDP, less than a quarter of what it had been at the beginning of the postwar period. By 2008, his last full year in the Senate, the debt stood at 39.4 percent of GDP, and it would almost double to 76.2 percent of GDP eight years later, when he completed his time as Vice President. By the time Biden was inaugurated as the 46th President of the United States, the debt had exceeded 100 percent of GDP and was projected to soon surpass the record levels of debt incurred during World War II.[58] A political career that spanned half a century had witnessed wars, economic and financial crises, and a global pandemic, all of which carried significant implications for the levels of national indebtedness. But the nation had encountered crises in the past, and debts incurred under these conditions were normally followed by periods of deleveraging. What made this period different?

First, the changing composition of spending. During the decades separating Biden's first days in the Senate and his assumption of the presidency, mandatory spending had increased from 39.9 percent (7.2 percent GDP) to over 70 percent of outlays (21.8 percent GDP); discretionary spending had fallen from some 53 percent (9.6 percent GDP) to some 23 percent of outlays (7.7 percent of GDP). The uncontrollable portion of federal spending had grown dramatically, forcing policymakers to make far more difficult choices.[59] Second, federal revenues had fallen from 17.1 to 16.3 percent of GDP.[60] The Republican Party's commitment to tax cuts and the maintenance of a low tax regime had increased the gap between expenditures and revenues. Third, the growing polarization in American politics had undermined the capacity of Congress to build broad bipartisan coalitions behind policy change and magnified the importance of intraparty divisions. It had increased the incentives for bypassing regular order and engaging in unorthodox lawmaking. The Congressional Budget Act of 1974, passed when Biden was a freshman Senator from the state of Delaware, seemed to have lost most of its relevance. Biden may have run for office in 2020 touting his support for bipartisan solutions and celebrating his ability to forge compromises, but for many observers of American politics, these claims seemed to rest on a nostalgic vision of politics formed in another era.

Notes

1 See Nicholas F. Jacobs and Sidney M. Milkis, "Our "Undivided Support": Donald Trump, the Republican Party, and Executive-Centered Partisanship," in *Dynamics of American Democracy: Partisan Polarization, Political Competition and Government*, ed. Eric M. Patashnik, Wendy J. Schiller (Lawrence: University Press of Kansas, 2021), 291–322.

2 Quoted in Bob Woodward and Robert Costa, "In a revealing interview, Trump predicts a 'massive recession' but intends to eliminate the national debt in 8 years," *Washington Post*, April 2, 2016. Available at www.washingtonpost.com/politics/in-turmoil-or-triumph-donald-trump-stands-alone/2016/04/02/8c0619b6-f8d6-11e5-a3ce-f06b5ba21f33_story.html?utm_term=.d6b42cbf9b8c

3 Republican Platform 2016, available at www.presidency.ucsb.edu/node/318311

4 James V. Saturno and Megan S, Lynch, *A Balanced Budget Constitutional Amendment: Background and Congressional Options*, CRS Report R41907 (Washington, DC: Congressional Research Service, 2019), 20.

5 Office of Management and Budget (OMB), *A New Foundation for American Greatness: Budget of the U.S. Government, Fiscal Year 2018* (Washington, DC: Government Publishing Office, 2017), 9, 13, 26–27.

6 Grant A. Driessen and Megan S. Lynch, *Budget Actions in 2017*, CRS Report R44799 (Washington, DC: Congressional Research Service, 2017), 7.

7 Steve Forbes, Larry Kudlow, Artur Laffer, and Stephen Moore, "GOP, Deliver Trump's Tax Reform to the American People by Christmas," *The Hill*, October 18, 2017. Available at https://thehill.com/opinion/finance/356105-gop-give-the-american-people-trumps-tax-cut-gift-by-christmas

8 Quoted in "Few Big Wins in First Half of Congress Spells Trouble for the GOP." *CQ Magazine*, December 4, 2017. Available at http://library.cqpress.com/cqweekly/weeklyreport115-000005226305

9 See Molly F. Sherlock and Donald J. Marples, *The 2017 Tax Revision (P.L. 115-97): Comparison to 2017 Tax Law*, CRS Report R45092 (Washington, DC: Congressional Research Service, 2018). On the decision to make the corporate tax changes permanent and the potential conflicts with the Byrd Rule, see George K. Yin, "How the Byrd Rule Might Have Killed the 2017 Tax Bill…and Why It Didn't," *ABA Tax Times*, 37, 4 (2018). Available at www.americanbar.org/groups/taxation/publications/abataxtimes_home/18aug/18aug-pp-yin-how-the-byrd-rule-might-have-killed-the-2017-tax-bill/

10 See "Distributional Effects of the Conference Agreement for H.R. 1, the 'Tax Cut and Jobs Act'." Joint Committee on Taxation, JCX-68-17, December 18, 2017. Available at www.jct.gov/publications.html?func=download&id=5054&chk=5054&no_html=1

11 William G. Gale, Hilary Gelfond, Aaron Krupkin, Mark J. Mazur, and Eirc Toder, *Effects of the Tax Cuts and Jobs Act: A Preliminary Analysis* (Washington, DC: Tax Policy Center, 2018), 13.

12 William G. Gale, "Did the 2017 Tax Cut—the Tax Cuts and Jobs Act—Pay for Itself?" Brookings Institution, February 14, 2020. Available at www.brookings.edu/policy2020/votervital/did-the-2017-tax-cut-the-tax-cuts-and-jobs-act-pay-for-itself/

13 CBO, *The Budget and Economic Outlook: 2018-2028* (Washington, DC: CBO, 2018), 79.

14 Driessen and Lynch, *Budget Actions in 2017*, 14.

15 D. Andrew Austin, *The Debt Limit Since 2011*, CRS Report R43389 (Washington, DC: Congressional Research Service, 2019), 26–28.

16 Grant A. Driessen, *The Federal Budget: Overview and Issues for FY2019 and Beyond*, CRS Report R45202 (Washington, DC: Congressional Research Service, 2018), 13.

17 James V. Satumo, *Federal Funding Gaps: A Brief Overview*, CRS Report RS20348 (Washington, DC: Congressional Research Service, 2019), 8; Jordain Carney, "Shutdown Ends without Funding for Trump's Border Wall," *The Hill*, January 25, 2019, available at https://thehill.com/homenews/senate/427041-senate-votes-to-reopen-government-after-trump-agrees-to-end-shutdown; and Jennifer K. Elsea, Jay B. Sykes, and Edward C. Liu, "Can the Department of Defense Build the Border Wall?" CRS Legal Sidebar LSB10242 (Washington, DC: Congressional Research Service, 2019).

18 Eloise Pasachoff, "The President's Budget Powers in the Trump Era," in *Executive Policymaking: The Role of the OMB in the Presidency*, ed. Meena Bose and Andrew Rudalevige (Washington, DC: Brookings Institution Press, 2020), 77–81.

19 Grant Driessen and Megan S. Lynch, "The Bipartisan Budget Act of 2019: Changes to the BCA and Debt Limit," CRS Insight IN11148 (Washington, DC: Congressional Research Service, 2019).

20 OMB, *Budget of the U.S. Government, Fiscal Year 2023* (Washington, DC: Government Publishing Office, 2022), Historical Tables, Table 1.3.

21 OMB, *A Budget for America's Future: Budget of the U.S. Government, Fiscal Year 2021* (Washington DC: Government Publishing Office, 2020), 7, 14.

22 OMB, *A Budget for a Better America: Budget of the U.S. Government, Fiscal Year 2020* (Washington, DC: U.S. Government Publishing Office, 2019), 5.

23 See *American Journal of Managed Care*, "A Timeline of COVID-19 Developments in 2020," January 1, 2021, available at www.ajmc.com/view/a-timeline-of-covid19-developments-in-2020; US Bureau of Labor Statistics, Unemployment Rate [UNRATE], available at https://fred.stlouisfed.org/series/UNRATE

24 See Kavya Sekar, Agata Bodie, Bruce R. Lindsay, Sarah A. Lister, Karen E. Lynch, Emily M. Morgenstern, and Sara M. Tharakan, *Coronavirus Preparedness and Response Supplemental Appropriations Act, 2020 (P.L. 116-123): First Coronavirus Supplemental*, CRS Report R46285 (Washington, DC: Congressional Research Service, 2020); Molly F. Sherlock, Jane G. Gravelle, Katelin P. Isaacs, Sean Lowry, and Julie M. Whittaker, *CARES Act Assistance for Employers and Employees—The Paycheck Protection Program, Employee Retention Tax Credit, and Unemployment Insurance Benefits: Overview*, CRS In Focus IN11324 (Washington, DC: Congressional Research Service, 2020); and William L. Painter, *Tallying Federal Funding for COVID-19: In Brief*, CRS Report R46449 (Washington, DC: Congressional Research Service, 2020).

25 CBO, Summary Estimate for Division M Through FF, H.R. 133, Consolidated Appropriations Act, 2021, Public Law 116-260, Enacted on December 27, 2020 (Washington, DC: Congressional Budget Office, 2021).

26 See Nason Maani and Sandro Galea, "COVID-19 and Underinvestment in the Public Health Infrastructure of the United States," *The Milbank Quarterly*, 98, 2 (2020): 250–59.

27 Phillip M. Singer, Charley E. Willison, N'dea Moore-Petinak and Scott L. Greer, "Anatomy of A Failure: Covid-19 in the United States," in *Coronavirus Politics: The Comparative Politics and Policy of COVID-19*, ed. Scott L. Greer, Elizabeth J. King, Elize Massard da Fonseca, and André Peralta- Santos (Ann Arbor: University of Michigan Press, 2021), 478, 482, and 485.

28 OMB *Budget of the U.S. Government, Fiscal Year 2023*, Historical Tables, Table 1.3.

29 Ibid., Table 7.1.

30 See Jack Rosenthal, "On Language: A Terrible Thing to Waste," *New York Times Magazine*, July 31, 2009. Available at www.nytimes.com/2009/08/02/magazine/02FOB-onlanguage-t.html
31 OMB, *Budget of the U.S. Government for Fiscal Year 2022* (Washington, DC: Government Publishing Office, 2021), 37.
32 Ibid., 26.
33 See Department of Treasury, *General Explanations of the Administration's Fiscal Year 2022 Revenue Proposals* (Washington, DC: Department of the Treasury, 2021).
34 Jim Tankersley, "As They Planned Big Spending, Biden's Advisers Kept a Close Watch on Inflation," *New York Times*, April 14, 2021, A20.
35 Eric M. Leeper, *Modern Monetary Theory: The End of Policy Norms as We Know Them?* (Washington, DC: Progressive Policy Institute, 2021), 2.
36 For a good review of the debates within the Democratic caucus, see Jonathan Weisman and Jim Tankersley, "Plan to Tax Rich Aims at Incomes, Not Big Fortunes," *New York Times*, September 14, 2021, A1.
37 CBO, "Senate Amendment 2137 to H.R.3684, the Infrastructure Investment and Jobs Act, as Proposed on August 1, 2021," August 9, 2021. Available at www.cbo.gov/system/files/2021-08/hr3684_infrastructure.pdf
38 "Anatomy of a Vote: Timeline of GOP votes for infrastructure bill," *CQ Magazine* November 15, 2021), available at http://library.cqpress.com/cqmagazine/weeklyreport117-000006390457, and Jonathan Weisman, Emily Cochrane, and Catie Edmondson, "House Passes $1 Trillion Infrastructure Bill, Putting Social Policy Bill on Hold," *New York Times*, November 15, 2021, available at www.nytimes.com/2021/11/05/us/politics/house-infrastructure-reconciliation.html
39 "Fall Legislative Preview: Reconciliation," *CQ Magazine*, September 13, 2021, available at http://library.cqpress.com/cqmagazine/weeklyreport117-000006335311 and Erica L. Green, Coral Davenport, Margot Sanger-Katz, Luke Broadwater, Madeleine Ngo, and Alan Rappeport, "What's in the $2.2 Trillion Social Policy and Climate Bill," *New York Times*, November 21, 2021, available at www.nytimes.com/article/build-back-better-explained.html
40 D. Andrew Austin, *The Debt Limit in 2021,* CRS Insight IN11702 (Washington, DC, Congressional Research Service, 2021).
41 Treasury Secretary Janet L. Yellen, "Debt Limit Letter to Congress," September 8, 2021. Available at https://home.treasury.gov/system/files/136/Debt-Limit-Letter-to-Congress_20210908_FINAL-Pelosi.pdf
42 Quoted in "Fall Legislative Preview: Debt ceiling." *CQ Magazine*, September 13, 2021. Available at http://library.cqpress.com/cqmagazine/weeklyreport117-000006333258
43 "Anatomy of a vote: A deal on the debt limit extends the fight," *CQ Magazine*, October 18, 2021. Available at http://library.cqpress.com/cqmagazine/weeklyreport117-000006365174
44 D. Andrew Austin, The Debt Limit in 2021, CRS Insight IN11702 (Washington, DC: Congressional Research Service, 2021), and "Medicare cuts scare helps put debt limit bill on fast track," *CQ Magazine*, December 13, 2021. Available at http://library.cqpress.com/cqmagazine/weeklyreport117-000006414197
45 Quoted in Aris Folley, "Schumer Points to Debt Incurred under Trump to Highlight Need for Bipartisan Action," *The Hill*, September 13, 2021. Available at

https://thehill.com/policy/finance/budget/572061-schumer-points-to-debt-incurred-under-trump-to-highlight-need-for
46 US Bureau of Economic Analysis, Real Gross Domestic Product [A191RO1Q156NBEA], available at https://fred.stlouisfed.org/series/A191RO1Q156NBEA, and US Bureau of Labor Statistics, Unemployment Rate [UNRATE], available at https://fred.stlouisfed.org/series/UNRATE
47 See Alan Rappeport, "Yellen Defends Stimulus Aid As Prices Continue to Rise," *New York Times*, June 8, 2022, B1.
48 OMB, *Budget of the U.S. Government for Fiscal Year 2023* (Washington, DC: Government Publishing Office, 2022), 1, 2.
49 Ibid., 13.
50 Ibid., 14.
51 Paul M. Krawzak, "House Sets $1.6 Trillion Cap for Fiscal 2023 Appropriations," *Rollcall*, June 8, 2022. Available at https://rollcall.com/2022/06/08/house-sets-1-6-trillion-cap-for-fiscal-2023-appropriations/
52 See Charlie Cook, "A History Democrats are Doomed to Repeat? Overreach on a Coronavirus Package Could be a Ticket to Political Oblivion," *National Journal*, January 29, 2021. Available at www.nationaljournal.com/s/712293/a-history-democrats-are-doomed-to-repeat/
53 See "Summary: Inflation Reduction Act of 2022," August 11, 2022, available at www.democrats.senate.gov/imo/media/doc/inflation_reduction_act_one_page_summary.pdf, and "What's In the Inflation Reduction Act?," Committee for a Responsible Federal Budget, July 28, 2022, available at www.crfb.org/blogs/whats-inflation-reduction-act
54 Alexandra Hegji, "The Administration's Newly Announced Student Load Debt Cancellation Policy, CRS Insight IN11997 (Washington, DC: Congressional Research Service, 2022).
55 "The Biden Student Loan Forgiveness Plan: Budgetary Costs and Distributional Impact." Available at https://budgetmodel.wharton.upenn.edu/issues/2022/8/26/biden-student-loan-forgiveness. For a discussion of competing cost estimates, see Katie Rogers and Jim Tankersley, "Cost of Erasing Students' Debt Will Be Steep," *New York Times*, September 27, 2022, A1.
56 Quoted in Jim Tankersley, "Economists Split on Plan to Drop Debt," *New York Times*, August 30, 2022, B1.
57 Marianna Sotomayor and Jacob Bogage, "Biden Signs Bill to Fund Government, Hours Before Deadline," *Washington Post*, September 30, 2022, available at www.washingtonpost.com/politics/2022/09/30/house-set-ok-bill-averting-government-shutdown-with-hours-spare/, and Alan Rappeport and Jim Tankersley, "U.S. Debt Surpasses $31 Trillion," *New York Times*, October 5, 2022, B1.
58 OMB, *Budget of the U.S. Government, Fiscal Year 2023*, Historical Tables, 7.1.
59 Ibid., Tables 8.3, 8.4.
60 Ibid., Table 1.3.

10

CONCLUSION

The Politics of Paper Shackles

This book began with a brief vignette drawn from 2000. A combination of decisions about taxation and spending, fortuitous economic conditions, and the end of the Cold War allowed for the generation of successive surpluses and the first reduction in the debt-to-GDP ratio since the mid-1970s. Based on Congressional Budget Office projections of future surpluses, policymakers could contemplate the elimination of the national debt, something that had not occurred since the presidency of Andrew Jackson. Ultimately, the projections were negated by policy decisions (tax cuts, entitlement expansion, protracted wars), extraordinary shocks (September 11, the financial crisis, the pandemic), and the growing dysfunction of a Congress torn by polarization into competing camps that exhibited an incapacity to complete the basic functions intrinsic to budgeting. Two decades after Fed Chairman Alan Greenspan contemplated the ramifications of surpluses as far as the eyes could see, the nation was going to generate deficits as far as the eyes could see.

It would be convenient to attribute the reversal of fortunes to the vagaries of post-2000 politics. From the rise of the Tea Party to the 2021 insurrection at the Capitol, these have been unique times. But it is the argument of the previous chapters that political disorder has been embedded in, and exacerbated by, a larger fiscal story. To recap, for most of US history, periods of high indebtedness were followed by extended periods of deleveraging. In the aftermath of World War II, this pattern exhibited itself once again. The retention of the mass-tax regime forged in the war, when combined with small departures from balanced budgets and steady growth allowed the nation to reduce the debt from 106.1 to 23.2 percent of GDP in less than three decades.[1] Remarkably, this deleveraging occurred as Congress engaged in unprecedented infrastructure spending, funded two wars, and expanded social provision in ways that

DOI: 10.4324/9781003395331-12

transformed the role of the state in the economy and society more generally. But the stagflation of the 1970s created a window of opportunity to relitigate key features of the postwar policy mix, with a particular focus on taxation. Supply-side arguments prevailed, and by the 1980s, they found an expression in the deepest tax cuts in US history. The new revenue constraint would be reinforced by the growing centrality of a low tax regime to the conservative coalition. Given the diversity of factions in this coalition, taxation proved to be the one unifying point of agreement.

The revenue constraint was combined with long-term changes in the composition of federal outlays. Mandatory outlays, driven by programmatic expansion and an aging population, steadily grew until they came to dominate federal spending. In 1965, the year Congress passed the Social Security Act Amendments creating Medicare and Medicaid, programmatic mandatory spending accounted for less than one-third of outlays. By 1993, it had grown to claim a majority of outlays and by 2019, the eve of the COVID-19 pandemic, it claimed almost two-thirds of spending. The remarkable growth in mandatory spending placed downward pressure on discretionary spending, and the budget process fell into disorder. As polarization found a growing manifestation in Congress and eroded regular order, budgeting became far more conflictive. Rules that might have allowed Congress to exert some control over the public credit—the kinds of changes that were implemented in in the 1990s—were no longer in the political opportunity set, at least if they included new taxes.

The Budget Control Act of 2011 was the most significant effort since the 1990s to reimpose rules with spending caps backed with mandatory sequestration. But as Chapters 8 and 9 revealed, the caps and timetables established by the Act were ephemeral. Congress proved adept at raising the caps on a biennial basis, extending sequestration into the future, and moving expenditures off budget. The revenue constraint, worsened by the extension of Bush-era tax cuts and the tax cuts of 2017, created enormous barriers to exercising control over the deficit. As noted in Chapter 1, on the eve of the COVID-19 pandemic, the gap between outlays (21 percent of GDP) and revenues (16.3 percent of GDP) was so great that a balanced budget would require a 73 percent cut in discretionary spending, an impossibility without eliminating much of what government does.[2] Even the stabilization of the debt-to-GDP ratio would require debilitating cuts to key programs. One should not be surprised that Congress repeatedly circumvented the rules that it designed for itself, leaving fiscal reform to some hypothetical future.

During the early 1990s, interest on the debt claimed some 3 percent of GDP, exceeding 15 percent of outlays in several years. But the United States benefitted from relatively low interest rates in the post-2000 period. A reduction in interest payments partially cushioned the pressure that mandatory programs were placing on discretionary spending. In 2019, net interest claimed 1.8 percent of GDP or 8.4 percent of outlays.[3] As noted in the last chapter, the Biden administration's FY2022 budget requests deflected concerns over the projected deficit, in part, by citing the low interest environment that created "fiscal space" for more expansionary spending and investment. Indeed, it argued that to shun such investments would be irresponsible given the role they could play in increasing productivity and repairing the frayed social safety net that had been temporarily backstopped during the pandemic.

Yet, the low interest rate environment is not permanent, particularly as global inflation began to take hold in the wake of the pandemic. The Congressional Budget Office (CBO) projects that net interest will continue to grow as a share of GDP, reaching 2.1 percent by 2025 and doubling to 4.2 percent by 2039. By 2049, it projects that interest on the debt will claim 6.5 percent of GDP—some 22.2 percent of federal outlays—eclipsing Social Security (6.3 percent of GDP) and Medicare (5.8 percent of GDP). The growth continues through the CBO's 30-year projections, reaching a high of 7.2 percent of GDP by 2052. At that point, it would claim 23.8 percent of federal outlays.[4] When combined with programmatic mandatory spending, the growth in interest payments would leave little space for discretionary spending. Future elected officials would face some difficult decisions about whether to impose significant new taxes, eliminate key government programs, or accept the ongoing growth of the debt and defer reform, once again, to a future generation of decisionmakers.

The long-term ramifications of the debt were explored earlier in this volume. To the extent that today's outlays improve the lives of future generations, the decision to incur debt may be justified. To the extent that Congress incurs debt to reduce today's tax liabilities or to lock in political coalitions, the justification is less clear. If ongoing growth in public debt raises the costs in capital markets, it may impede private investment. Combined, we may be consigning our descendants to higher levels of taxation in a slow growth economy. Of course, there are more dramatic scenarios, including raising the potential for a future fiscal crisis. While each is the subject of lively debates given the special status of the dollar and the robust demand for Treasuries, one impact of debt is clear: it places limits on the extent to which democratic institutions can translate broadly shared national commitments into public policies. The perpetual underfunding of key programs carries costs. So does the decision to ignore the needs and aspirations of the citizenry. It can erode support for government and democratic processes. Debt can serve as paper shackles that limit what government can achieve. Are there ways to break the paper shackles or, at the very least, loosen their grip?

The fiscal story of the past half century has involved constraints in taxation, the growth of mandatory programs, and political polarization. While a variety of crises in the post-2000 decades have played an important role, crises have not been exclusive to this period. Yet, the difficulties of mitigating the fiscal impact of these crises have reflected the factors noted above. The remainder of this chapter briefly explores the potential for change in taxation and mandatory programs. Although there are no direct solutions for polarization, there may be procedural reforms that could provide partial remedies for a broken budgetary process that has limited the ability of Congress to execute its Article I duties. But along each of these dimensions, contemporary politics places limits on the extent of reform.

Taxation and the Revenue Constraint

Changes in tax policy have been proposed as a response to the growing debt, albeit usually under the guise of the counterintuitive claim that the correct response is further tax cuts. As noted in the last chapter, this was one of the ways that President Trump's economic advisors framed the 2017 tax cut. They argued that there was no way to get out of the current levels of debt without dramatically increasing the economic growth rate; tax cuts were framed as the cornerstone of a pro-growth policy. Variations on this theme have circulated since the economic debates of the 1970s, when some supply-side advocates made bold claims that tax cuts would incentivize investment and work effort, expand the economy, and generate new revenues—a painless remedy to stagflation and deficits, free of trade-offs. Certainly, increasing the rate of GDP growth could reduce the debt-to-GDP ratio but only if the debt grew at a pace that was less than the rate of economic growth. These claims were tested in the 1980s, the 2000s, and again in the aftermath of the 2017 tax cuts. In each case, the impact of tax cuts on economic growth was minimal. In each case, revenues declined relative to GDP, precisely as one might expect. In each case, tax cuts were followed by increases in the debt-to-GDP ratio, the opposite of what had been promised.

In fact, the single most important response to the debt is also the most commonsensical: to raise taxes. One of the persistent claims of this book is that one of the key factors in shaping long-term fiscal problems and budgetary politics has been the revenue constraint, a product of the history of tax cuts in the decades following the 1980 election and the persistent Republican opposition to any and all tax increases. Indeed, the only period when the fiscal trajectory was changed—albeit briefly—was in aftermath of the tax increases of the 1990s. While spending restraint was an important part of the story of the period, the decision to raise the top marginal tax rate allowed receipts to increase from 17 percent of GDP in 1993 to 20 percent of GDP in 2000. Had receipts been at a comparable level in the years following the recovery from the Great Recession and prior to the pandemic—without any changes in levels of spending—the deficit would have been relatively trivial, ranging from a low of 0.2 percent GDP to 1 percent GDP (instead, deficits were in the range of 2.8 to 4.6 percent GDP, with the highest deficits occurring in the two years following the implementation of the 2017 tax cuts).[5] Although a return to the tax rates of the 1990s would not balance the budget, they would more than stabilize the size of the debt relative to the economy.

Part of the revenue shortfall could be resolved with the passage of time. Key provisions of the Tax Cuts and Jobs Act of 2017 are scheduled to expire at the end of 2025, reflecting the fact that they were secured through the reconciliation process. But the political opposition to tax increases remains significant in the Republican Party and the Grand Old Party (GOP) has been successful in framing the larger debate about taxation. President Biden, who joined fellow Democrats in portraying the 2017 cuts as a giveaway to the wealthy, pledged to return the top marginal rate to 39.6 percent, but simultaneously promised that individuals making under $400,000 per year would not have their taxes raised. Indeed, Treasury Secretary Janet L. Yellen committed to work with Congress to make the tax cuts permanent for households below this threshold. And while the President pledged to raise the corporate rate from 21 to 28 percent, it was short of the 35 percent in effect prior to the 2017 Act.[6] Ultimately, intraparty divisions in the Senate prevented the tax increases proposed by President Biden.

The opposition to tax increases of any form by the majority of Republicans suggests that, absent unified Democratic control and a filibuster-proof majority in the Senate, any changes that are enacted will have to occur through reconciliation, thus limiting their permanence and rendering them vulnerable to the next change in partisan control. The reconciliation process provides a poor vehicle for comprehensive tax reform. Impacts are limited to the budget window and the compressed timetable of the budget process does not provide an opportunity for addressing the complexities of the tax code. The last significant tax reform occurred in 1986, when Congress passed the Tax Reform Act. As noted in Chapter 7, Congress was able to cut rates and maintain revenue neutrality by eliminating or reducing the generosity of major tax expenditures. But this was difficult and protracted work that required bipartisan support. In the current fiscal conditions, the elimination of some key tax expenditures could provide a path to raising revenues. Tax expenditures in 2021 were worth some $1.8 trillion or 8.2 percent of GDP, more than one-half of total federal revenues (16.3 percent of GDP) and greater than the revenues generated by the individual income tax (7.7 percent of GDP).[7] Some tax expenditures, like the Home Mortgage Interest Deduction, provide their greatest benefits to the top quintile of the income distribution.[8] While tax expenditures are not created equal—some, like the Earned Income Tax Credit and the Child Tax Credit deliver benefits to the lower quintiles—there is room for a careful consideration of whether the tax system should be used to subsidize the incomes of wealthier households while pushing the costs of fiscal reform on to future generations.

Comprehensive tax reform has been an elusive goal in recent decades given the levels of polarization in Congress and the recourse to the reconciliation process to translate slim partisan majorities into significant changes in the tax code. Moreover, as of this writing 84 percent of the Republicans in the House and 88 percent in the Senate (including the Republican caucus leaders in each chamber) have signed the Americans for Tax Reform "Taxpayer Protection Pledge." In doing so, they have committed to "oppose any and all efforts to increase the marginal income tax rates" and "oppose any net reduction or elimination of deductions and credits, unless matched dollar for dollar by further reducing tax rates."[9] To the extent that they abide by this pledge, comprehensive reform—or any reform at all—would appear to be difficult to achieve. Nonetheless, to the extent that debt is another word for deferred taxation, the Taxpayer Protection Pledge may be simply a commitment to raise taxes on future generations.

Reforming Mandatory Spending

Lifting the revenue constraint is critical. But much of the disorder in the budgetary process has also emanated from the growth of programmatic mandatory spending and the consequent pressure it has placed on discretionary spending. In 2020, Social Security and Disability Insurance costs equaled $1.09 trillion (5.2 percent of GDP). The CBO projects that the costs will grow to 6 percent of GDP by 2033, reaching 6.4 percent of GDP by 2052. The major healthcare programs cost $1.45 trillion in 2020 (5.7 percent of GDP), the largest component of which was Medicare ($917 billion, or 3.1 percent of GDP). While Medicare costs were elevated by the COVID-19 pandemic, by 2033, the CBO projects that Medicare will claim 4.5 percent of GDP. Reflecting the combination of demographics and cost escalation, by 2052, Medicare will grow to reach 5.9 percent of GDP. The two largest mandatory programs will claim 13.1 percent of GDP, almost 41 percent of outlays.[10] The literature on entitlement reform is vast and a detailed discussion is well beyond the scope of this chapter. But a few comments are in order.

Reforming Social Security

The trust funds that support Social Security are projected to go insolvent in the near term. Given that neither are authorized to draw on general revenues, insolvency would translate into a reduced level of support for beneficiaries. In the past, projections of insolvency have provided a window of opportunity for advocates of reform. For example, in response to concerns over looming trust fund insolvency, Congress passed the Social Security Act Amendments of 1983, accelerating scheduled increases in the payroll tax and imposing some benefit reductions. The large surpluses that accumulated in the Old-Age, Survivors and Disability Insurance (OASDI) trust funds in the past several decades were a product of political choice, not of happenstance. They reflected a prudent decision to generate surpluses that could pre-fund the retirement of the baby boom generation. Depletion of these surpluses was fully expected. One might draw an analogy with patterns of household savings in anticipation of retirement: the dissaving at the time of retirement would not be considered an indicator of crisis. Indeed, it is precisely the point. One might argue that the focus on insolvency should not divert attention from whether Congress will act to prefund the retirements of subsequent generations.[11]

In the next few decades, the large bipartisan majorities that supported the 1983 reforms had withered and the GOP's commitment to a low tax regime became solidified. Instead of advocating tax increases to cover the trust fund depletion, some conservative think tanks advocated full or partial privatization, the latter of which would involve a partial diversion of a portion of the payroll tax into private accounts combined with additional tax incentives for supplemental retirement savings. These accounts, it was argued, could provide future beneficiaries with the opportunity to realize market rates of return, thereby compensating for the reduced levels of support from Social Security. The Bush proposal for partial privatization, as noted in Chapter 8, never gained traction in the Republican Congress, wary of the threat of a Democratic filibuster and the electoral consequences. The next time Republicans claimed unified control of the presidency and Congress, there was scant support for reform, despite the mounting concerns over long-term insolvency. Undoubtedly, this reflected a calculation of the political costs of that would accompany any attempts to fundamentally reform the popular program.

Is trust fund insolvency a crisis? The Social Security Act of 1935 was premised on the assumption that payroll tax revenues, which began in 1937, would accumulate in the Old Age Reserve Account (subsequently converted to a trust fund) prior to the commencement of benefits, which was scheduled for 1942. These and subsequent surpluses would be used to purchase government debt and compound interest of reserve holdings would be sufficient to cover most programmatic costs without significant increases in the payroll tax. The complicated structure reflected the larger effort to frame old-age pensions as social insurance thereby distinguishing it from public assistance or welfare. The former would rely on earmarked revenues and would be in actuarial balance whereas the latter would be funded through general revenues. By 1939, Congress decided to accelerate the payment of benefits (to 1940) and suspend scheduled increases in the payroll tax, thereby converting Social Security to a pay-as-you-go system. As the coverage of Social Security expanded in the postwar decades and benefit levels were successively increased, trust fund balances became a source of concern even though the trust fund no longer served the originally intended purpose.[12]

To some extent, concerns over trust fund insolvency are simply an artifact of original program design. The initial decisions to fund what would become the nation's largest social welfare commitment through an earmarked payroll tax rather than general revenues and to use a trust fund to manage surplus revenues raised questions that were unique to Social Security (and to a lesser extent, Medicare). Discussions regarding other priorities—the annual expenditures for defense, education, or environmental protection—are not framed by projections of 75-year actuarial balances in the related trust funds because such trust funds do not exist. Because they are covered by the general fund of the Treasury, a question regarding their "solvency" would be a category error. Ideally, levels of spending of these and other commitments would reflect political decisions regarding the relative importance of the underlying policy goals.[13]

The issue of trust fund insolvency could be taken off the table if policymakers admitted that the original financial structure created under the Social Security Act is no longer relevant and simply authorized the use of general revenues to supplement the payroll tax. In so doing, the OASDI trust funds would serve a role comparable to Medicare's Supplementary Medical Insurance (SMI) trust fund that covers Medicare Part B and Part D. As explained in Chapter 2, on an annual basis, premiums are set to cover the percentage of costs mandated by a statutory formula, thereby determining the draw on general revenues. As a result, the SMI trust fund serves what is largely an accounting function. The SMI trust fund, unlike the OASDI trust funds, cannot become insolvent. As with Medicare Part B and Part D, Congress could determine what share of Social Security should be funded via the payroll tax and what portion should be funded via general revenues, and the payroll tax rate could be adjusted accordingly. Alternatively, it could simply fund these programs through general revenues.

One might object that the combination of the payroll tax and the general fund as sources of financing would transform the nature of Social Security. Recalling the discussion above, it would transform this social insurance programs into a public assistance program. Historically, the stable support for Social Security has rested on the broad perception that because potential beneficiaries made "contributions," there was a contractual bond between individual citizens and the government that was fundamentally different than what existed in public assistance.[14] Would the reliance on general revenues undermine this stability? In reality, the segregation of trust fund assets and the general fund is already somewhat tenuous. As explained in Chapter 4, although there are reasons to distinguish between different components of the gross debt, in the end, intragovernmental debt is debt owed by the Treasury to the trust funds. When the expenditures for Social Security exceed revenues, the Treasury redeems the bonds it issued. As trust fund balances are depleted, the federal government will have to fund redemptions through tax increases, the diversion of spending from other programs, or the issuance of debt to the public. Given the strong opposition to tax increases and the declining share of outlays devoted to discretionary programs, public borrowing is the default response. In short, the general fund is already supporting program expenditures as intragovernmental debt is being converted into publicly held debt.

Absent authorization to draw on the general fund, increases in the payroll tax or raising/eliminating the earnings cap could provide new revenues for Social Security. Whether any reforms that would require new taxation would be feasible in the current political environment remains questionable. But none of this addresses the trajectory of growth. The literature on Social Security reform is immense and beyond the scope of this chapter.[15] Let us consider two reforms that could limit the growth of future benefits. As is commonly noted, life expectancies for Americans who reached the age of 65 have increased significantly during the postwar period, providing some justification for raising the full retirement age. Indeed, this argument was key when Congress passed the 1983 amendments. Yet, life expectancy varies systematically based on income, race, and gender.[16] Raising the retirement age to 70, for example, would require lifelong taxation of income while denying benefits to a large proportion of African American males who would expire before reaching this age.[17] Any efforts to reduce the cost of benefits by raising the retirement age would reinforce existing economic and racial disparities, preventing those who face the greatest income insecurity from receiving any benefits at all.

One might also seek to reform the provision of benefits and address inequities through changing the calculation of cost-of-living adjustments, which are currently based on the CPI-W, to an alternative measure of inflation (e.g., the Chained CPI-U). While the changes would be subtle at first, they would have the greatest negative impact on low-income recipients.[18] To avoid this outcome, some analysts have proposed progressive indexing. Under progressive indexing, the current trajectory of growth for low-income recipients would be preserved while the growth of benefits for higher income recipients would be reduced. This could be achieved by changing the methodology for determining the average indexed monthly earnings for higher income earners and/or by changing the primary insurance amounts for different increments of income.[19]

Progressive indexing would alter the trajectory of growth, but it could carry high political costs. While the benefits of low-income workers would be preserved, the future benefits of higher-income workers would be reduced. By severing the perceived connections between lifetime "contributions" and lifetime benefits, the reforms could erode the status of Social Security as universal social insurance and transform it into a form of welfare that is, at least implicitly, means-tested. This change could eliminate the features of the policy that historically insulated Social Security from the political opposition that has confronted means-tested policies. Thus, while many reformers appreciate the policy justification for progressive indexing, they have been reluctant to make it the cornerstone of reform. In the words of Jason Furman, former Chair of the Council of Economic Advisors: "Any reform that makes Social Security more progressive must balance the benefits of a more progressive system against the risk of undermining the broad-based political support that helps sustain the nation's most effective anti-poverty program."[20]

Thus, while one can identify any number of reform proposals that could alter the trajectory of growth in the costs of Social Security, the political barriers are significant. Republicans may object to proposals that include an expansion of the payroll tax or a heavier reliance on the general fund, a decision that could create pressures for increases in the income tax. Democrats may be rightfully wary of the political implications of efforts to promote greater progressivity. Even implicit means testing could erode the support for Social Security as social insurance. Given the contentious political environment characterized by high levels of polarization and narrow partisan majorities, a broad bipartisan reform coalition may be difficult to build. In the end, the political costs of reform may exceed the benefits.

Reforming Medicare

What of the large and growing portion of mandatory spending devoted to healthcare? Building on the precedent set in the Social Security Act of 1935, the Social Security Act Amendments of 1965 replicated the dual tracks of social insurance and public assistance in healthcare. Medicare hospital insurance was funded via payroll taxes and layered on top of the Social Security system. Medicaid, the means-tested program providing healthcare to the low-income population, was to be funded through general revenues.[21] Yet, the separation was somewhat artificial for two reasons. First, Medicare Part B (inpatient services) was to be supported by a combination of premiums and general revenues. The same structure would be replicated for Medicare Part D (prescription drugs). Second, a large proportion of Medicare recipients—and the costliest part of the Medicare population—are "dual eligible." They receive Medicare by virtue of their age and Medicaid by virtue of their income.[22]

Medicare, in sharp contrast with Social Security, has been in a protracted process of reform almost since its inception. As detailed in earlier chapters, Congress and successive presidential administrations have adopted various changes in Medicare in the hope of achieving cost containment and these efforts have touched on most margins of the services and provider reimbursement. The cost containment strategies have focused on fees for hospital inpatient services, outpatient services, and physician payments. Much of the savings in spending have been secured through reductions or freezes in the annual payment updates to hospitals and physicians. In the 1990s, efforts to extract savings through greater competition led to the creation of Part C Medicare+Choice plans. But as scheduled cuts in reimbursement led some providers to abandon their Part C plans and strand recipients, Congress rebranded Part C as Medicare Advantage and provided higher levels of reimbursement to incentivize plan expansions. These actions and the passage of so-called "doc-fix" legislation to suspend or delay scheduled reductions in compensation, vitiated efforts at cost-controls. The Patient Protection and Affordable Care Act (2010) and the Medicare Access and CHIPS Authorization Act (2015) made numerous changes to increase efficiency and promote cost controls without disincentivizing participation by healthcare providers, who are under no obligation to accept Medicare recipients.[23]

Despite the ongoing reform efforts, the growth in Medicare spending has been unrelenting, driven by demographics, the growing complexity of medical services, and the medical inflation rate. Between 1980 and 2019—the eve of the COVID-19 pandemic—Medicare spending increased from 1.1 percent of GDP to 3 percent of GDP; Medicaid, which is increasingly intertwined with Medicare, grew from 0.5 percent of GDP to 1.9 percent of GDP during the same period.[24] The story of Medicare reflects, in many ways, the larger story of healthcare expenditures in the United States. Between 1980 and 2019, healthcare expenditures increased from 8.8 percent of GDP to 17.6 percent of GDP.[25] This stands in sharp contrast with the average healthcare expenditures for other OECD countries. In 2019, the average for the OECD was 8.8 percent of GDP, one-half of the level of spending in the United States. And while the United States spent more than any other OECD country, its health outcomes were inferior among multiple dimensions.[26]

The failure of decades of Medicare reform to find a solution to the growth of costs when combined with the larger story of healthcare expenditures in the United States suggest that comprehensive reform may provide the only path to controlling this core entitlement. There has been no shortage of models of reform over the past several decades. At one extreme, more market conforming models could make more extensive use of health savings accounts to disincentivize overuse of medical services and convert Medicare and Medicaid to vouchers, to force higher levels of competition among providers. At the other extreme, one could replace the existing private–public patchwork with one of the models prevalent in the OECD, including the social insurance model (or the Bismarck model prevalent in Germany, Belgium, Japan, and Switzerland) or a single-payer national health service (the Beveridge Model, prevalent in the United Kingdom, Spain, and New Zealand).[27] Each model has intrinsic strengths, weaknesses, and trade-offs, but the voluminous data on the performance of competing systems could inform policy debates.

Yet, there are extraordinary hurdles to overcome. The problem of polarization has proven to be an obstacle to reform in the past, as exhibited by successive efforts to impede and repeal the Affordable Care Act. But in sharp contrast with Social Security, reform may be thwarted by the heavy industry expenditures to shape health policy. Given the importance of public policy in undergirding the profitability of the healthcare sector, it should be no surprise that some of these profits are recirculated into politics. Consider industry expenditures on lobbying. In 2019, the health sector invested $607.3 million in lobbying. The COVID-19 pandemic may have marked a significant blow to the industry, but with healthcare reform gaining salience and Congress passing large relief bills, lobbying expenditures increased to $630.5 million in 2020 and $675.8 million the next year. During the 2020 electoral cycle, the industry invested another $49 million in campaign contributions, split almost equally between Democrats and Republicans.[28] As long as elected official benefit from the continuation of the status quo, the long-term budgetary consequences are deferred to the future. Once again, politics impedes the formation of broad bipartisan reform coalitions necessary for comprehensive healthcare reform.

Procedural Reforms

Processes can play essential roles in the formation of public policy. Properly structured, they can contain the scope of conflict and prevent parties from defecting from agreements. The need to defer to rules or the decisions imposed by an external body—be it a specially constituted committee or the Office of Management and Budget—can insulate elected officials from the ire of lobbyists, interest groups, and constituents. The Social Security Act Amendments of 1983, for example, might have been impossible absent the decision to delegate authority to the Greenspan Commission and the warnings of impending insolvency issued by the Trustees. Although presidents and Congress may have disagreed on their broader political agendas in the 1990s, they agreed on the importance of deficit reduction. Democrats may have preferred the expansion of social spending; Republicans may have hoped for a return to the tax rates that had been enacted in the 1980s. But the processes imposed through the Budget Enforcement Act—discretionary spending caps and PAYGO backed with sequestration—limited the scope of conflict and allowed for the achievement of goals that seemed elusive a decade earlier. In both cases, parties agreed on the importance of the broader goal, be it extending the solvency of Social Security or controlling the deficit.[29]

Although the Social Security Act Amendments and the Budget Enforcement Act are examples of success, the past few decades offer important counter examples. The processes put in place in the 1990s were abandoned during the Bush presidency. The combination of deep tax cuts, the relaxation of budgeting rules, and a willingness to fund significant commitments off-budget generated predictable results that were only made worse by the series of crises that punctuated the period. During the Obama presidency, the resort to commissions (the Bowles-Simpson Commission of 2010, the "Super Committee" of 2011) ended in failure. The new budgetary regime put into place under the Budget Control Act was routinely circumvented as Congress raised discretionary caps and extended sequestration. Perhaps the deficit and debt had lost some of their salience? Perhaps the growing levels of polarization had foreclosed the kinds of broad agreements on process that existed in the 1990s? Perhaps in a world of narrow partisan majorities, the majority party, be it Democratic or Republican, could not risk fiscal measures that would increase the chances of losing seats and potentially the control of Congress?

As detailed in the past two chapters, the budget process has fallen into a state of disorder, raising the question of whether new processes could generate different results. No Congress can place unbreakable constraints on future congresses, and there are no rules that Congress can impose that it cannot subsequently rescind, circumvent, or ignore. Before we begin a brief overview of some of the procedural changes that could be incorporated into a new budgetary regime, it is useful to consider a perennial solution that appears to be no solution at all: a balanced budget amendment.

A Balanced Budget Amendment

The promotion of a balanced budget amendment has become one of the staples of American politics in the past several decades. In Chapter 4, we briefly reviewed the argument offered by James M. Buchanan and Richard E. Wagner. They asserted that there are powerful incentives to engage in deficit spending and the assumption of debt in a democratic system. Following their argument, the precursor of the growth in deficit spending was the abandonment of the traditional fiscal constitution, something they ascribe to the transition to Keynesianism. Once the traditional fiscal constitution was discarded, the political incentives found their full expression. Elected officials were rewarded politically for deficit spending and deferring costs to future-period taxpayers. The imposition of a balanced budget amendment as a constitutional rule, they argued, would force policymakers to be fiscally prudent and less responsive to mobilized constituencies.[30] One can question whether this account is compatible with the empirical record, given the significant reduction in the debt-to-GDP ratio that occurred in the immediate postwar decades, when the support for Keynesianism was at its apogee. The growth in deficits and the debt is of more recent vintage, more clearly a product of the dismantling of the World War II mass-tax regime than the abandonment of a fiscal constitution. But many have found the basic argument persuasive.

The balanced budget amendment was promoted by the Republican-controlled Senate in 1982, the year after the passage of the Economic Recovery Tax Act. It was one of the demands of the Republican Congress under the Contract with America. It was embraced by the Tea Party and reemerged during the debates surrounding the Budget Control Act of 2011. It once again rose to prominence in the Republican Party platform of 2016. There were two common features in its recent incarnations. First, advocates of the balanced budget amendment simultaneously promoted tax cuts and an expansion or maintenance of defense spending. Given this connection, one might conclude that the balanced budget was attractive because it could drive domestic policy retrenchment and give the calls for tax cuts a patina of fiscal responsibility. Second, it never received the two-thirds majority vote from each chamber of Congress, as required under Article V of the Constitution. Members of Congress may have understood the practical implications that the only path to a balanced budget would be disabling cuts in key programs. They may have understood that while there is public opinion support for an amendment, the support would rapidly dissipate once the programmatic consequences became clear.[31]

Critics of a balanced budget amendment have noted that such a rule would not provide the fiscal space for deficit spending when justified by downturns in the business cycle, wars, natural disasters, or public health crises like the COVID-19 pandemic. Moreover, there are questions as to the implications for the balance of power between the branches, the enforceability of such an amendment, the intrinsic uncertainty of revenue and spending projections on an annual basis, and the incentives it could create to simply use alternative mechanisms for federal spending (e.g., loan guarantees, tax expenditures, or activities by government-sponsored enterprises).[32] But certainly, a rule could be crafted to meet some of these contingencies. Under current conditions, however, the problem with even a modified amendment is a practical one. As the numbers reviewed earlier in this chapter suggest, a balanced budget is currently unachievable without dramatic increases in levels of taxation, equally dramatic reductions in levels of spending, or some combination of the two. Until a balanced budget is technically achievable, the promotion of a balanced budget amendment offers no solution.

From Symbol to Process

There have been any number of recommendations for improving federal budgeting. Some focus on the accounting treatment of expenditures. The budget employs cash accounting, recognizing revenues when they are received and payments when they are made; the impact is considered over the ten-year budget window. This method of accounting may be sufficient for most purposes, but there have been proposals to make greater use of accrual accounting, particularly with respect to long-term liabilities, which have become a growing part of the fiscal picture. Under accrual accounting, future liabilities would be discounted to present value at the time the obligation was made rather than deferring the costs until the date that transfers occurred. Accrual accounting is currently used for some financial obligations like direct loans or loan guarantees but could be used more extensively.[33] There have been recommendations, moreover, that Congress could use capital budgeting for assets like buildings and infrastructure (a practice that is common in state and local governments, which maintain separate operating and capital budgets, charging debt service on capital investments to the operating budget). Costs could be spread across the useful life of the asset rather than the current practice of recognizing the full cost in the year it is incurred. It is commonly argued that the failure to adopt a capital budget forces long-term investments to compete with annual operating expenses, which may favor the latter as discretionary outlays shrink as a share of the fiscal pie.[34]

Another simple change would involve the treatment of emergency spending. As noted in the past two chapters, Congress and presidents have routinely circumvented procedures designed to impose budgetary control by passing emergency supplemental appropriations. Indeed, the wars in Afghanistan and Iraq were largely funded off-budget. The budget process could be amended to take into account the costs of various contingencies and emergencies. As F. Stevens Redburn argues, "Based on a long-term average of annual emergency spending—largely provided through ad hoc appropriations—annual budgets might include an amount estimated to be sufficient to address emergencies including unexpected military actions, terrorist attacks, economic shocks, and natural disasters." As a result, "budgets would not understate spending and deficits, the amounts would be available when needed, and the mischief and lack of fiscal discipline that accompanies urgent action to appropriate spending authority after the event would disappear."[35] Alternatively, Congress could make the decision to run perennial surpluses so that funds would be available as needed to cover various contingencies, although this option seems foreclosed under current circumstances. While each of the proposals carries costs and benefits, let us turn to broader considerations of process changes.

Biennial Budgeting

One part of a solution to the disorder in the budget process could be a movement to biennial budgeting with two-year budget resolutions, appropriations, and authorizations. Hypothetically, a two-year budget cycle could have several benefits. It could conserve on congressional and executive branch resources by eliminating the repetition that is intrinsic to an annual budget cycle. In the best case, Congress could replace the current focus on incremental annual adjustments to something akin to longer-term planning. In the off years, Congress could focus its resources on authorization to establish policy and oversight to monitor performance, activities that arguably receive less attention given the demands that the annual budgeting place on limited congressional resources. Agencies at the federal, state, and local levels, in turn, would have greater stability in their budgets, allowing them to adopt a longer-term time horizon when developing and managing their programs. If paired with provisions for automatic continuing resolutions, biennial budgeting could provide a partial remedy to the current disorder.

Critics of biennial budgeting find the case unpersuasive on several grounds. From a technical perspective, the formulation of an annual budget relies on projections of expenditures and revenues some 18 months in advance. Biennial budgeting would force a reliance on much longer projections, which could translate into the over-funding of some programs and the underfunding of others. It would invariably force Congress to pass supplemental appropriations, which would occur off-budget and obviate the supposed efficiency gains. From a political perspective, one might argue that the failure of the current budget process is not the problem but rather a symptom of the unwillingness of members of Congress to reach bipartisan compromise. In the current political environment, biennial budgeting could raise the incentives for obstructionism, thereby increasing the likelihood of conflict over budget resolutions and appropriations bills. Finally, the annual appropriations process is one of the means by which Congress exercises its Article I powers and holds the executive accountable. The decision to engage in biennial budgeting would necessarily require granting agencies and the president greater latitude in the use of funds, further ceding congressional power to the executive.[36]

Countering Fiscal Fragmentation

Fiscal decision-making occurs under conditions of extreme institutional fragmentation. The budget process focuses primarily on discretionary spending. Mandatory programs are controlled by the authorizing committees. Tax expenditures and revenue policy more generally fall to the House Ways and Means and Senate Finance Committees. Under the current procedures, the funds available for discretionary spending are largely a function of decisions made outside of the budgetary process. One response to this fragmentation has been the incentives it has created to designate new programs as mandatory or seek to make policy through tax expenditures, parts of the fiscal system that are insulated from the pressure of the annual appropriations process. As Alice Rivlin, former director of the CBO and the OMB noted: "Under the current process, a dwindling portion of the budget (discretionary spending) is subject to annual scrutiny and increasingly complex rules, while major mandatory programs and the tax code operate on automatic pilot." She concluded: "Congress must bring the retirement programs and tax expenditures into a process of periodic review and decision, so that you can actually control the major drivers of the budget, the deficit, and the debt."[37]

Rivlin embraced the proposal to move to a biennial budget for the reasons suggested earlier and argued that it would simultaneously give Congress the space to review mandatory spending and tax expenditures on a five- or six-year cycle. A more ambitious proposal has been made for "portfolio budgeting." The federal government uses discretionary spending, mandatory spending, tax expenditures, and regulations to address common goals. The annual budgetary process, which focuses on incremental adjustments to discretionary programs, and the larger fragmentation of the policy system impede the systematic consideration of the compatibility, effectiveness, or coherence of the mix of policy instruments. Under the proposal, the executive budget would identify major policy objectives. Assuming a biennial budget process, off years could be devoted to the portfolio of spending, tax, and regulatory policies related to a given objective, to evaluate the collective impact and the benefits and costs of budget alternatives. Ultimately, portfolio budgeting could be institutionalized in the congressional budget process, with Congress using the budget resolution to identify the selected policy goals that would be subject to evaluation, perhaps under the direction of strengthened House and Senate budget committees. Ideally, the process would provide a means of countering the institutional fragmentation that characterizes fiscal policymaking and allow for a goal-focused approach to decision-making.[38]

The proposal for a more comprehensive evaluation of public policy makes great sense from a technical perspective. But the barriers are once again significant. Congress may well view the priority placed on the executive branch to identify policies best subjected to portfolio budgeting to be tantamount to an elevation of the president in setting the national policy agenda. Moreover, the committee system is well entrenched, and any efforts to engage in portfolio budgeting would require a significant reconfiguration of the committee system to combine authorization and appropriations and move tax expenditures from the tax committees to those that have the substantive expertise in particular policies. But committee reform would diminish the importance of key committees and stand at tension with legislators' incentives.[39] Moreover, one could expect significant opposition from Republicans, who have made the maintenance of a low tax regime central to their political agenda. In 2017, for example, the Republican-controlled House Budget Committee objected to portfolio budgeting because it would require

> the portfolios' inclusion of both spending and tax provisions...This would increase the temptation to treat tax provisions as identical to spending, so that eliminating a tax "expenditure"—a revenue increase—would be viewed as a spending reduction to offset higher spending elsewhere in the portfolio. This would be an out-and-out "tax and spend" result.

In short, the aversion to tax increase would treat any effort to reduce tax expenditures as tantamount to an increase in taxation.[40]

Conclusion

The fiscal health of the nation is significant both for what it represents and the challenges that it creates for the future. Although it embodies an array of political commitments, there is no assurance that the commitments are compatible. The postwar era witnessed profound changes in the role of the state in society and the extent of social provision. Key social programs inherited from the New Deal were expanded and supplemented with new policies, and within a matter of decades, the expenditures for these broadly popular programs became the single greatest drivers of federal spending. Never had a larger proportion of the population found greater protection from the vicissitudes of the business cycle and the life cycle. While the preservation of the mass-tax system forged in World War II would prove essential in funding these commitments, it would prove short-lived. In the post-1980 period, the decision to constrain revenues—also broadly popular—took hold, opening a growing fiscal gap.

The determination of "who gets what, when, and how"—the classic definition of politics offered by Harold Laswell in 1936—is assigned to political institutions.[41] It finds its financial expression in the budget. When political institutions can no longer provide a context in which reasoned and transparent deliberation over policy commitments results in a sober assessment of tradeoffs and the need for broad compromises, it finds a manifestation in persistent deficits and growth in the debt. In the end, the deterioration of the nation's fiscal health is not a technically insoluble problem. It is a political problem. Short-term political incentives and commitments militate against the search for long-term solutions. Difficult decisions over the compatibility of commitments—the commitment to social provision and the maintenance of a low tax regime—are deferred to the future, along with the costs that emanate from political failure.

Notes

1 Office of Management and Budget (OMB), *Budget of the United States Government, Fiscal Year 2023*(Washington, DC: U.S. Government Publishing Office, 2022), Historical Tables, Table 7.1.
2 Ibid., Tables 1.3, 8.4.
3 Ibid., Tables 8.3, 8.4.
4 CBO data available at www.cbo.gov/system/files/2022-07/57971-Data.xlsx
5 OMB, *Budget of the United States Government, Fiscal Year 2023, Historical Tables*, Table 1.3.
6 Jim Tankersley, "Tax Changes Under Trump Are Not All Going Away," *New York Times*, January 3, 2021: B1.
7 CBO, *The Budget and Economic Outlook: 2021 to 2031* (Washington, DC: CBO, 2021), 19, 2.
8 Joint Committee on Taxation, *Estimates of Federal Tax Expenditures for Fiscal Years 2020-2024* (JCX-23-20), November 5, 2020, 42.
9 Americans for Tax Reform, "Federal Taxpayer Protection Pledge." Available at www.atr.org/sites/default/files/assets/2020PledgeFederal.pdf
10 CBO data. Available at www.cbo.gov/system/files/2022-07/57971-Data.xlsx
11 See Neil H. Buchanan, "Social Security Is Fair to All Generations: Demystifying the Trust Fund, Solvency, and the Promise to Younger Americans," *Cornell Journal of Law and Public Policy*, 27, 2 (2017): 237–300.
12 See Julian E. Zelizer, "'Where Is the Money Coming From?' The Reconstruction of Social Security Finance," in *Governing America: The Revival of Political History* (Princeton: Princeton University Press, 2012), 153–67.
13 See Buchanan, "Social Security Is Fair to All Generations."

14 Theda Skocpol and G. John Ikenberry, "The Road to Social Security," in *Social Policy in the United States: Future Possibilities in Historical Perspective*, ed. Theda Skocpol (Princeton: Princeton University Press, 1995), 182.

15 For a review of a wide variety of reform options and their fiscal consequences, see CBO, *Social Security Policy Options, 2015* (Washington, DC: CBO, 2015).

16 See Raj Chetty, Michael Stepner, Sarah Abraham, Shelby Lin, Benjamin Scuderi, Nicholas Turner, Augustin Bergeron, and David Cutler, "The Association Between Income and Life Expectancy in the United States, 2001–2014." *JAMA*, 315, 16 (2016): 1750–66.

17 Elizabeth Arias and Jiaquan Xu, "United States Life Tables, 2017," *National Vital Statistics Reports*, 68, 7 (2019): 3, 4.

18 Government Accountability Office, *Cost-of-Living Adjustments for Older Americans* (GAO-19-218R) (Washington, DC: Government Accountability Office, 2019), 3, 4.

19 As explained in Chapter 2, the calculation of benefit level involves calculating the average indexed monthly earnings or AIME, which involves adjusting the current value of 30 years of income to reflect the growth in average wages, and then determining the Primary Insurance Amount (or PIA) by applying different PIA factors to successive increments of income, which are indexed, once again, to reflect growth in average wages. Under various progressive indexing proposals, high-income earners who had reached the taxable maximum for 35 years or were among the top 50 percent of earners would have initial benefits determined through the application of the CPI-W rather than the average wage index, whereas lower-income retirees would have initial benefits calculated as they are under current law. This could be combined with other reforms, including changing the PIA factors from their current values (90 percent, 32 percent, and 15 percent) to some other set of values (e.g., 90 percent, 32 percent, 21 percent, and 10 percent), which could once again preserve the benefits of lower-income beneficiaries while reducing the benefits for higher earners. See CBO, *Social Security Policy Options*, 53–61.

20 Jason Furman, *An Analysis of Using 'Progressive Price Indexing' to Set Social Security Benefits* (Washington, DC: Center on Budget and Policy Priorities, 2005), 8.

21 See Rosemary Stevens and Robert Stevens, "Medicaid: Anatomy of a Dilemma." *Law and Contemporary Problems*, 35, 2 (1970): 354–56.

22 James S. Powers and Laura M. Keohane, "Dual Eligibles: Challenges for Medicare and Medicaid Coordination," in *Value Driven Healthcare and Geriatric Medicine: Implications for Today's Changing Health System*, ed. James S. Powers (Cham, Switzerland: Springer, 2018), 129–30.

23 For an overview of Medicare and past reform efforts, see Patricia A. Davis, Cliff Binder, Jim Hahn, Suzanne M. Kirchhoff, Paulette C. Morgan, Marco A. Villagrana, and Phoenix Voorhies, *Medicare Primer*, CRS Report R40425 (Washington, DC: Congressional Research Service, 2020).

24 OMB, *Budget of the United States Government, Fiscal Year 2023, Historical Tables*, Table 8.4.

25 Department of Health and Human Services, Center for Medicare & Medicaid Services, National Health Expenditure Accounts, NHE20 Summary. Available at www.cms.gov/files/zip/nhe-summary-including-share-gdp-cy-1960-2020.zip

26 OECD, *Health at a Glance 2021: OECD Indicators* (Paris: OECD Publishing, 2021), 189.

27 For a brief description of competing models, see Mimi Chung, "Healthcare Reform: Learning from Other Major Health Care Systems," *Princeton Public Health Review*, December 2, 2017. Available at https://pphr.princeton.edu/2017/12/02/unhealthy-health-care-a-cursory-overview-of-major-health-care-systems/

28 www.opensecrets.org/federal-lobbying/sectors/summary?cycle=2017&id=H, and www.opensecrets.org/political-action-committees-pacs/industry-breakdown/2020

29 See the discussion of the role of process in Paul L. Posner, "Budget Process Reform: Waiting for Godot," *Public Administration Review*, 69, 2 (2009): 421–22.

30 See James M. Buchanan and Richard E. Wagner, *Democracy in Deficit: The Political Legacy of Lord Keynes*, in *The Collected Works of James M. Buchanan*, vol. 8 (Indianapolis: Liberty Fund, 2000).

31 See James V. Saturno and Megan S. Lynch, *A Balanced Budget Constitutional Amendment: Background and Congressional Options*, CRS Report R41907 (Washington, DC: Congressional Research Service, 2019) and Andrew Crosby and Allyson L. Holbrook, "Public Support for a Balanced Budget Amendment to the U.S. Constitution: Trends and Predictors," *Public Budgeting & Finance*, 39, 2 (2019): 44–67.

32 This discussion draws on Saturno and Lynch, *A Balanced Budget Constitutional Amendment.*

33 See CBO, *Cash and Accrual Measures in Federal Budgeting* (Washington, DC: CBO, 2018).

34 See Allen Schick, *The Federal Budget: Politics, Policy, Process*, 3rd ed. (Washington, DC: Brookings Institution, 2007), 49–50.

35 F. Stevens Redburn, "Practical Imagination: A Possible Future for Federal Budgeting," *Public Budgeting and Finance*, 35, 4 (2015): 11.

36 See the discussion of the various proposals, arguments for and against biennial budgeting in James V. Saturno, *Biennial Budgeting: Issues, Options, and Congressional Actions*, CRS Report R44732 (Washington, DC: Congressional Research Service, 2017).

37 Alice M. Rivlin, "Rescuing the Budget Process," *Public Budgeting & Finance*, 32, 3 (2012): 55.

38 See Steve Redburn and Paul Posner, "Portfolio Budgeting: How a New Approach to the Budget Could Yield Better Decisions," Economic Studies at Brookings, Discussion Paper 1 (Washington, DC: Brookings Institution, 2015).

39 Roy T. Meyers, "Is the U.S. Congress an Insurmountable Obstacle to Any 'Far-Sighted Conception of Budgeting'?," *Public Budgeting and Finance*, 37, 4 (2017): 21.

40 House of Representatives, Concurrent Resolution on the Budget—Fiscal Year 2018, Report of the Committee on the Budget, House of Representatives, to accompany H. Con. Res. 71 (Report 115-240). July 21, 2017, 292.

41 Harold D. Lasswell, *Politics: Who Gets What, When, How* (New York: Whittlesey House, 1936).

INDEX

Note: Endnotes are indicated by the page number followed by "n" and the note number e.g., 262n19 refers to note 262 on page 19.